Essential Elements in Early Intervention

Visual Impairment and Multiple Disabilities

Deborah Chen

Editor

Foreword by Marci J. Hanson

Printed in the United States of America
2006 reprinting

Library of Congress Cataloging-in-Publication Data
Essential elements in early intervention : visual impairment and
    multiple disabilities / Deborah Chen, editor.
        p.   cm.
    Includes bibliographical references and index.
    ISBN 978-0-89128-305-8 (alk. paper)
    1. Visually handicapped children.   2. Handicapped children.
    3. Handicapped children—Development.   4. Infants—Development.
    I. Chen, Deborah.
    HV1596.2.E77   1999
    362.4'18'083—dc21   99-41221
                                                             CIP

Earlier versions of Chapters 4, 5, 7, 9, and 10 in this volume appeared in *Effective Practices in Early Intervention: Infants Whose Multiple Disabilities Include Both Vision and Hearing Loss,* the project manual of "The Model Demonstration Early Intervention Network Serving Infants Who Are Deaf-Blind and Their Families," a project of the California State University, Northridge, funded by the U.S. Department of Education Grant No. H025D30002.

The mission of the American Foundation for the Blind (AFB) is to enable persons who are blind or visually impaired to achieve equality of access and opportunity that will ensure freedom of choice in their lives.

Acknowledgments

This publication represents the combined efforts of all the contributors. It has been a special honor to collaborate with friends and colleagues who serve families and young children with disabilities. I appreciate their generosity in sharing their professional expertise, their many years of experience, and the time required to complete each contribution on top of their already busy schedules. Special thanks go to Barbara L. Porter, for her fine illustrations, and to the teams at AFB Press and Chernow Editorial Services for their patience, good ideas, and skills. I also express my appreciation to the many families and infants who have taught me so much. Most important, I want to thank Philip and Winnie Chen, for giving me a great start in life and a good education, and Andrew Gach, for his support, humor, and love.

Deborah Chen

About the Authors

EDITOR

Deborah Chen, Ph.D., is professor, Department of Special Education, at California State University, Northridge, where she teaches in the areas of early childhood special education and severe disabilities. Her extensive background in early intervention services as a service provider, program administrator, in-service and preservice instructor, and researcher includes the administration of several federally funded grant projects related to professional development in early intervention/ early childhood special education and program development for infants with multiple disabilities/sensory impairments, as well as work with families from diverse cultural and linguistic backgrounds. Her research and publications have focused on early communication in infants with multiple disabilities and sensory impairments, infant-caregiver interactions, and effective practices for working with families from diverse cultures. In collaboration with Dr. Downing, she has recently received a federally funded project to identify and develop strategies and materials for enhancing tactile communication methods with children who are deaf-blind.

CONTRIBUTORS

Carolina Abdala, Ph.D., is scientist, House Ear Institute, Los Angeles; part-time assistant professor, Department of Communicative Disorders and Sciences, California State University, Northridge, and assistant professor of pediatrics, Department of Neonatology, School of Medicine,

University of Southern California. Dr. Abdala's research and publications focus on the development, maturation, and physiology of the human auditory system, neonatal hearing screening, and use of otoacoustic emissions for testing infants and young children. Her current research, funded by the National Institutes of Health, Deafness, and other Communicative Disorders, involves studying the function and development of the human cochlea.

Jamie Dote-Kwan, Ph.D., is associate dean for student services, Charter School of Education, California State University, Los Angeles. Dr. Dote-Kwan was professor and coordinator of the teacher training program in visual impairments and blindness at California State University, Los Angeles. She began her career as a teacher of young children with visual impairments. Her current research and publications focus on caregiver–child interactions and early home environments of young children with visual impairments and specific intervention strategies for working with children whose multiple disabilities include visual impairment. Her federally funded projects have been related to identifying cultural influences on caregiver interactions with their infants with visual impairment, preparing personnel in the field of visual impairment and severe disabilities, and establishing a braille transcription center for the California State Universities.

June Downing, Ph.D., is professor, Department of Special Education, California State University, Northridge, where she teaches in the areas of moderate, severe, and multiple disabilities. Dr. Downing has been a paraprofessional, teacher, work experience coordinator, project director and national consultant for programs serving students who are visual impaired or deaf-blind. Her extensive research and publication areas include supporting the communicative skills of students with severe disabilities, adapting curriculum for the unique learning needs of individual students, developing skills of paraprofessionals, and preparing teachers for the inclusive education of children with severe and multiple disabilities. She had directed several federally funded projects related to preparing teachers to educate students with severe and multiple disabilities or deaf-blindness.

Deborah Orel-Bixler, Ph.D., O.D., is residency director and assistant clinical professor, School of Optometry, University of California at Berkeley. Her primary research interests and publications involve pediatric optometry, vision screening and assessment techniques for infants, children and individuals with multiple disabilities, visual evoked potentials, and photoscreening.

Pamela Haag Schachter, M.S. Ed., was formerly project coordinator of the Early Intervention Network Model Demonstration Project for Infants who are Deaf-Blind and their Families, California State University, Northridge, and an educational specialist, California Deaf-Blind Services, El Toro, California. Recently, she has been technical assistance and training coordinator of the Northwest New Jersey Regional Early Intervention Collaborative in Randolph, New Jersey.

Irene L. Topor, Ph.D., low vision specialist, Arizona State Schools for the Deaf and Blind, is a certified low vision therapist and adjunct associate professor at the University of Arizona, Tucson. Her publications focus on visual assessment and instruction of young children with multiple disabilities and working with their families. She has conducted research on delayed visual maturation. Dr. Topor has extensive experience as a teacher of students with visual impairments (all ages and abilities), consultant, and instructor to many programs across the country serving young children with visual impairments and multiple disabilities.

Contents

Foreword

The early years of development have become a primary focus in the news media. This emphasis has resulted from recent findings in neuroscience, advances in brain imaging techniques, and attention from political newsmakers. This recent research has confirmed what has long been acknowledged by developmentalists, namely that rapid growth occurs in the early months and years of a child's life, and that development in the early years is crucial for subsequent development. For children with sensory impairments, these early years are particularly crucial. Developmental research with these youngsters had documented the increased risks resulting from sensory loss and also the secondary effects associated with this sensory deprivation. Research also has shown that early diagnosis and intervention supports can produce more positive developmental outcomes for these children. It is to this purpose that this text is devoted.

Interventions in the early years may necessitate techniques and procedures that differ from those applied with older children. For instance, early intervention requires the coordination of health, educational, and social services. Interventions also must center on the young child within the context of that child's family. Thus, the skills and knowledge base demanded for professionals working with young children must include professional training in working with families and coordinating services, as well as techniques in assessment and developmental enrichment for young children.

One of the primary strengths of this text is the breadth and interweaving of these many important intervention facets. Chapters are devoted to specialized assessment techniques, supporting early caregiver-child interaction and early communication, and specific interventions for enhancing the development of children with visual and hearing impairments. This information is gleaned from multiple sources, including the authors' academic training and experience, as well as data from focus groups conducted through a federally funded education demonstration project.

The presentation of these topics in one text makes it an ideal resource for early intervention service providers, diagnosticians, and service program administrators. The breadth of focus lends support to its use as a resource in university level personnel preparation programs, as well. Given the interdisciplinary focus of the topics and the range of information presented, it is appropriate to training programs in education, physical and occupational therapy, speech and language pathology, audiology, and psychology.

Early support for young children with multiple and sensory impairments is essential. This text is a comprehensive resource for professionals who provide this support.

Marci J. Hanson, Ph.D.
Professor and Coordinator
Early Childhood Special Education
San Francisco State University

Introduction

The first three years of life is the most critical period in every child's development. Recognition of its significance has resulted in federal legislation that mandates early intervention services for infants who have disabilities and for their families. The primary purpose of early intervention services is to support families in enhancing their infants' development and to ensure optimal outcomes for these children. When infants are diagnosed with visual impairments and additional disabilities, early intervention services are even more critical in promoting optimal developmental outcomes for them.

In this book, a wide variety of terms are used, and some definitions are in order (for this reason a glossary also appears at the back of this volume). The term *early intervention* refers to the comprehensive system of multidisciplinary services from the fields of education, medicine, mental health, and social welfare that are provided to infants who have disabilities and to their families. The term *infant* is used broadly to encompass the early childhood period from birth to 36 months. *Early interventionist* refers to a primary service provider who works with an infant and family to promote the infant's development. *Caregiver* is defined as a parent or other adult who is responsible for and participates in the daily care of an infant. *Family* is used as a more inclusive term than caregiver and includes parents, siblings, grandparents, and other people who share the infant's home or who are involved in the infant's life. *Caregiving environment* encompasses both social and physical characteristics—the people who are involved in caring for the infant; their feelings and responses; the care they provide; and the availability of food, shelter, other physical resources, and equipment.

As is explained in Chapter 1, early interventionists come from a variety of disciplines and backgrounds, and early intervention services vary from one geographic area to the next. The content of this publication is designed to be particularly helpful to early interventionists who work with infants who have multiple disabilities that include sensory losses. It is anticipated that the readers of this book may have backgrounds in early childhood special education, visual impairment, hearing loss, or severe disabilities, but the topics covered should also benefit service providers with backgrounds in child development and those from specialized disciplines (occupational therapy, physical therapy, speech and language therapy, and orientation and mobility) who provide early intervention services directly to infants and families or who provide consultation to early intervention programs.

BACKGROUND

This book is derived from The Model Demonstration Early Intervention Network Serving Infants Who Are Deaf-Blind and Their Families, a project of California State University, Northridge, funded by the U.S. Department of Education from October 1, 1993, to February 28, 1997. The project focused on building the capacity of early intervention programs to serve infants who have both visual and hearing impairments. Sixteen early intervention programs in California that serve infants with a variety of disabilities and their families participated in various components of the project. Nine of these programs were involved in major components in all three years of the project. These programs served infants with visual impairments, infants with hearing losses, infants with severe and multiple disabilities, or infants with a range of disabilities. All nine programs served one or more infants who had both visual impairments and hearing losses, and four served many infants with visual impairments and additional disabilities.

The project conducted family-professional focus groups and program self-reviews to identify the primary needs of the programs and to examine effective practices. This process revealed a common need for in-service training opportunities and materials on the following topics: developing communication in infants with severe and multiple disabilities; understanding clinical vision and audiological assessments; conducting functional vision assessments; identifying hearing loss in infants with multiple disabilities; promoting the functional use of vision, hearing, and communication throughout the daily routine; promoting the use of transdisciplinary teams in implementing intervention strategies; and providing appropriate instruction when children make the transition to preschool. In general, family members also wanted materials that would help service providers work with their infants more effectively.

The project addressed the identified training needs through a series of workshops, on-site consultations, and the development of videos. The resulting manual, *Effective Practices in Early Intervention* (Chen, 1997) documented the training topics, effective practices, and key strategies that were identified and developed during the project. Five chapters from the project manual have been reorganized and expanded to be included in this book: "Clinical Vision Assessments for Infants" by Deborah Orel-Bixler, Ph.D., OD.; "Functional Vision Assessments and Interventions" by Irene Topor, Ph.D.; "Pediatric Audiology: Evaluating Infants" by Caroline Abdala, Ph.D.; "Beginning Communication with Infants" by Deborah Chen, Ph.D.; and "Critical Transitions: Educating Young Children in a Typical Preschool" by June Downing, Ph.D. This material has been supplemented by a large amount of additional information in the present volume to meet the needs of early interventionists who are working with a diverse population of young children.

SCOPE

It is beyond the scope of a single publication to address every major topic related to early intervention services with infants who have multiple disabilities and with their families. The specific topics chosen for this book reflect the focus of the original project, The Model Demonstration Early Intervention Network Serving Infants Who Are Deaf-Blind and Their Families, on infants who had both vision and hearing losses, as well as other disabilities. The chapters also respond to the needs identified by the project for additional training and materials in these areas. The intent of this book is to provide early interventionists with relevant research, specific information, and key strategies to support young children with severe and multiple disabilities in early social interactions and for helping caregivers to enhance their infants' development. This book discusses topics that are particularly significant for promoting the early development of infants with visual impairments and other disabilities. The goal is to provide information that will assist service providers in helping the infants to gain access to sensory information and to participate in social interactions and everyday activities. In addition, this book seeks to fill a gap by addressing the inquiries of service providers regarding available research and effective intervention practices with families and infants whose multiple disabilities include visual impairments.

OVERVIEW

The book presents 10 chapters to build the knowledge and skills of early interventionists working with families and their infants whose multiple disabilities include visual impairment. Although the sequence of chapters is intended to provide a cohesive approach to early intervention practice, each chapter may be used separately, and an early interventionist may choose to refer to selected chapters to obtain specific information.

Part I, Principles of Early Intervention, provides the legal background of early intervention and focuses on the underlying principles of working with both infants and their families. The additional needs of infants who have other disabilities besides vision and hearing loss are outlined in this section as well, to inform the planning and implementation of all assessments and interventions discussed throughout this book.

Chapter 1: Early Intervention: Purpose and Principles summarizes recent research on the early development of the brain that supports the need for early intervention, current federal requirements for and the characteristics of early intervention services; the competencies, role, and responsibilities of early interventionists; and approaches that guide early intervention practices: the family-centered philosophy and the transactional model of development (Sameroff & Chandler, 1975).

Chapter 2: Interactions Between Infants and Caregivers: The Context for Early Intervention identifies key developmental needs in the early years, discusses the importance of caregivers' interactions with infants on infants' early development, suggests the possible influences of visual impairment and other disabilities, provides evidence of the effectiveness of interactions between caregivers and infants as a context for early intervention, links the development of infants and the caregiving environment to the transactional model, discusses the difference between contingent and noncontingent stimulation, and suggests effective strategies to promote infants' interactions with the caregiving environment.

Chapter 3: Meeting the Intervention Needs of Infants identifies various prenatal conditions that contribute to multiple disabilities among infants, links these conditions to disabilities that commonly accompany visual impairment, discusses critical considerations regarding these disabilities to guide the planning and implementing of interventions, describes the learning needs of infants and the early intervention environment in relation to the transactional model, and discusses the range of team models and the importance of collaboration among disciplines in early intervention services.

Part II, Assessment: The Foundation of Intervention, provides the basic information that early interventionists need to understand clinical assessments of sensory losses and to participate in functional assessments.

Chapter 4: Clinical Vision Assessments for Infants provides information on the incidence of visual impairment with other disabilities, describes the process of a clinical vision examination, discusses the types of clinical tests used with infants, defines relevant terms, and presents sample assessment reports. This chapter is intended to assist service providers in understanding the purpose of different vision tests so they will be able to answer questions that parents may have, obtain information about the infant's visual status from an ophthalmologist or optometrist, and interpret assessment reports.

Chapter 5: Functional Vision Assessments and Early Interventions presents a framework for conducting a functional vision assessment, differentiates between procedures for vision screening and a functional vision assessment, includes sample forms with explanations of their use and purpose, discusses the types of visual impairments that commonly occur with additional disabilities, and provides selected adaptations and interventions to promote infants' use of functional vision within the context of infants' interactions with caregivers and everyday routines. Because infants are usually diagnosed as having visual impairments before they receive early intervention services to address these particular needs, information on conducting functional vision assessments and promoting functional vision is provided after the previous chapter on clinical vision tests.

Chapter 6: Understanding Hearing Loss: Implications for Early Intervention identifies the need for infants with multiple disabilities and visual impairments to receive audiological evaluations, presents an overview of the auditory system, discusses different types of hearing loss, presents a process for gathering information about an infant's hearing status with sample forms, indicates how various types of disabilities may influence an infant's response to sound, and provides adaptations to promote an infant's listening skills within the context of interactions with caregivers and everyday routines. Although recommended practice dictates that all newborns with risk factors receive clinical hearing tests, such tests may not be performed. Even when hearing loss has been identified, some infants with multiple disabilities may not receive any follow-up care to address this need. The majority of early interventionists (except for those trained in the field of deafness and hearing impairment) have limited knowledge about hearing loss and audiological tests. Many infants with multiple disabilities receive audiological evaluations only through the persistence of their families and service providers. Knowledge of the types and effects of hearing loss and ways to observe an infant's use of hearing will assist an early interventionist in documenting concerns about the infant's hearing. For these reasons, this chapter on the hearing system, functional hearing screening, and related interventions is followed by the chapter on audiological tests.

Chapter 7: Pediatric Audiology: Evaluating Infants provides information on hearing loss, describes an audiogram, discusses the types of audiological tests used with infants, defines relevant terms, and provides sample audiological reports. This chapter is intended to help service providers understand the purpose of different tests so they will be able to answer questions that parents may have, obtain information about an infant's hearing status from an audiologist, and interpret audiological reports.

Part III, Developing Learning Strategies, builds on the basic information presented in the first two parts to discuss how to plan and implement specific interventions that meet the needs of each infant.

Chapter 8: Developing Meaningful Interventions presents a framework for gathering information from families, for identifying intervention priorities, and for infusing objectives within the daily routine. The chapter provides specific strategies for promoting infants' communication and use of sensory information and suggests specific intervention strategies through vignettes of three infants who represent a variety of multiple disabilities and visual impairments.

Chapter 9: Beginning Communication with Infants discusses the importance of interventions that focus on early communication, identifies the ways to interpret early communication behaviors, and provides strategies for promoting the development of communication in infants who have multiple disabilities. This chapter follows the chapters on vision tests, audiological evaluation, and strategies for enhancing available vision and hearing because an infant's sensory status will influence his or her development of communication and determine whether alternative methods of communication may be needed.

Chapter 10: Critical Transitions: Educating Young Children in a Typical Preschool discusses the benefits of inclusive education; identifies the roles of service providers in supporting young children in inclusive settings; presents strategies for supporting the participation of preschoolers with multiple disabilities in preschool environments; discusses the need for service providers to understand adaptations for children who have visual impairments and hearing losses, motor disabilities, or significant developmental disabilities so they can address the individual learning style of each child with a visual impairment and another disability. This chapter is included in this book to stress the importance of supporting the children's transition from early intervention services to preschool programs.

The content of this book assumes that the reader has a basic knowledge of the typical and atypical development of infants and of general early intervention practices. It offers the reader a synthesis of relevant research and current recommended practices. In so doing, it gives the reader a basis for planning and implementing effective interventions with infants who have visual impairments and additional disabilities and for collaborating with families and other service providers in promoting the early development of infants with multiple disabilities.

REFERENCES

Chen, D. (1997). *Effective practices in early intervention: Infants whose multiple disabilities include both vision and hearing loss.* Northridge: California State University, Northridge, Department of Special Education. ERIC Document Reproduction Service No. ED 406 795.

Sameroff, A. J., & Chandler, M. J. (1985). Reproductive risk and the continuum of caregiving causality. In F. D. Horowitz (Ed.), *Review of child development research* (Vol. 4, pp. 187–244). Chicago: University of Chicago Press.

PART I

Principles of Early Intervention

Environmental influences can have a profound impact on a child's development. Because an infant's world consists primarily of his or her family and other people who may be caregivers, effective early intervention cannot focus on the child alone but also needs to include the family. The chapters that follow explore the importance of early learning experiences in the life of a child who is visually impaired and has additional disabilities, as well as the essential considerations involved in early intervention services.

1

Early Intervention: Purpose and Principles

Deborah Chen

The primary purpose of early intervention is to enhance the development of infants, particularly by working with and supporting caregivers and families. Working together, early interventionists and families identify, develop, and provide early and appropriate learning experiences that will promote the infants' learning and development. The need to provide early intervention services during infancy is supported by developmental research and theory. Studies with nondisabled infants have documented the incredible abilities of infants as young as a few days old to process sensory information and to learn (Stone, Smith, & Murphy, 1973). The seminal works of several theorists (Hunt, 1961; Piaget, 1936/1952; Sameroff & Chandler, 1975) have described the significance of early experiences on later development and have influenced current perspectives on early intervention.

When an infant is visually impaired and has additional disabilities, he or she has to develop specific ways to assess sensory information and to interact with the environment. Learning how to obtain and interpret information and becoming motivated to explore surroundings and undertake activities are essential for development in many areas, such as cognitive and linguistic development. Caregivers play a crucial role in promoting an infant's progress in many ways. However, on the most basic level, they may need to learn how to interact with a baby with disabilities. Many infants demonstrate subtle or unusual behaviors that are difficult to interpret. They may be passive, fussy, or difficult to engage, and caregivers, who may be in the process of making emotional adjustments to the reality of having a child with disabilities, may feel ineffective in their interactions with these infants. Along with visual impairments, these infants may have hearing losses, severe physical disabilities, developmental delays, or other conditions that also influence their early experiences. Infants with disabilities, as well as their families, need early intervention services to foster the social aspects of the caregiving environment (interactions with caregivers, siblings, and other people) as well as the nonsocial aspects (toys, materials, and equipment) and to prevent negative effects that may occur because of their disabilities (Hanson & Lynch, 1995). Without specific assistance, infants who are visually impaired and have additional disabilities are likely to have restricted experiences and are unlikely to achieve their developmental potential.

THE EFFECTS OF EARLY EXPERIENCE ON BRAIN DEVELOPMENT

Recent publicity about children's development during the first three years of life underscores the significance of early experiences. In 1997, a special edition of *Newsweek* (Bagley, 1997) and a special report in *Time* (Nash, 1997) highlighted current research on brain development and the importance of learning during the early childhood years. These issues were discussed later that year at the White House Conference on Early Childhood Development and Learning (National Parent Teacher Association, 1997). The five key findings of this research are the following:

> First, the brain development that takes place before age one is more rapid and extensive than we previously realized. . . . Second, brain development is much more vulnerable to environmental influence than we ever suspected. . . . Third, the influence of early environment on brain development is long lasting. . . . Fourth, the environment affects not only the number of brain cells and number of

connections among them, but also the way these connections are "wired." . . . And fifth, we have new scientific evidence for the negative impact of early stress on brain function. (Carnegie Corporation of New York, 1994, pp. 7–8)

Reports of improvements in the visual functioning of infants with visual impairments during early childhood have been associated with the ongoing development of neural connections in infants' brains (Farel & Hooper, 1995; Harel, Holtzman, & Feinsod, 1985; Hart, 1984) and emphasize the importance of early intervention. During the first three years, brain development involves a continual process of organization and reorganization of neural connections, or synapses. Up to 15,000 connections are generated to each of 100 billion cells of an infant's brain. The formation of synapses increases rapidly in response to the sensory environment that an infant experiences (Illig, 1998; Nash, 1997). By 8 months, an infant's brain may have as many as 1,000 trillion synapses (Huttenlocher, 1994, cited in Hawley, 1998). The number of synapses in a 2 year old surpasses the number in an adult. After these first years, connections are pruned until puberty, when there are about 500 trillion synapses.

Researchers have found that children with limited play skills and who were rarely touched had brains that were 20 percent to 30 percent smaller than normal (Nash, 1997). Similar studies with rats have indicated that early experiences affect the process of neural connections and contribute to an increase or decrease of up to 25 percent in the final number of synapses (Turner & Greenough, 1985, cited in Hawley, 1998). Other studies have shown that rats who were reared in enriched environments demonstrated more dendritic branching (receptors in neural connections) than did rats who were reared in typical social or isolated environments (Greenough, Volkmar, & Jurasks, 1973; Rosenzweig, Krech, Bennett, & Diamond, 1968). These studies also found that rats who were raised in enriched environments with toys developed better problem-solving behaviors than did rats who were reared in sterile cages. Studies with chimpanzees and cats have also revealed the influence of the environment, sensory deprivation, and reduced sensory experiences on the development of the brain, visual functioning, and other behaviors (Held, 1965; Riesen, 1950; Wiesel, 1982; Wiesel & Hubel, 1963). Current research on the influence of environmental experiences on a young child's brain, along with older studies of animals, provides empirical evidence that infants who have disabilities need early intervention that supports responsive caregiving environments.

THE TRANSACTIONAL MODEL AS A CONCEPTUAL FRAMEWORK FOR EARLY INTERVENTION

The significance of the caregiving environment is a fundamental belief of the *transactional model of development.* According to this framework, a child's developmental outcome is a consequence of the dynamic and reciprocal interactions between the child and the environment (Sameroff & Chandler, 1975). Therefore, it is likely that an infant who is visually impaired and has additional disabilities and who is reared in a poor caregiving environment will demonstrate a less positive outcome than an infant who has similar learning needs and is fortunate enough to be reared in an optimal caregiving environment.

An optimal environment is responsive to an infant's needs and interests and provides loving care. Furthermore, according to the transactional model, the adaptation of the environment to promote the infant's interaction and participation will have a positive influence on the infant's learning and development. For example, without early intervention assistance, it may be difficult for the caregiver of a totally blind infant with spastic cerebral palsy to determine the infant's focus of attention, to cuddle the baby, to feed him or her, and to provide basic care. At the same time, this infant cannot respond to the caregiver by meeting the caregiver's gaze or by molding easily to the caregiver's body when held. In this situation, the infant's responses do not reinforce the caregiver's interactions, and vice versa. Thus begins a cycle of unfulfilled expectations and unsatisfying interactions between the caregiver and the infant. In contrast, with early intervention support, a physical therapist or occupational therapist will help the caregiver learn how to position and handle the infant; feed, bathe, and diaper the baby; and support the infant's motor and adaptive development.

The early interventionist (typically a teacher certified in the area of visual impairments or a qualified early childhood special educator) will assist the caregiver in identifying, interpreting, and responding to the infant's signals; in helping the infant gain access to information through nonvisual means; in implementing physical or occupational therapy techniques; and in promoting the infant's overall development and participation in the family. In this way, the transactional model of development provides an essential conceptual framework for planning and implementing early intervention services.

FAMILY-CENTERED PHILOSOPHY

Theories of early childhood development, federal legislation, and common sense also support a family-centered approach to early intervention. Families are composed of the most significant people in infants' lives, and babies usually spend most of their time in the care of their families. It is through interactions with caregivers and families that infants develop emotional ties, become social beings, and discover that their actions have meaning. Thus, a primary focus of early intervention services should be to support interactions between caregivers and infants and caregiving environments to promote infants' optimal development (Hanson & Lynch, 1995). (This principle is explored in more detail in Chapter 2.) In addition, parents have the legal right to make decisions about their infants and children's intervention programs. These rights, along with a family-centered philosophy, enable families to decide whether they want early intervention services for their infants, and if they do, how, when, and in what ways they want to participate. It is therefore essential for early interventionists to listen carefully to families' concerns about their infants and to respond by providing strategies that meet these concerns. In this way, early intervention services support families in caring for their infants.

Research has demonstrated that infants show more progress when families are involved in their early intervention programs (Shonkoff & Hauser-Cram, 1987; Shonkoff, Hauser-Cram, Krauss, & Upshur, 1992). Interventions that are implemented by service providers only for a short time each week cannot be effective without follow-through at home. For example, in a clinic, a physical therapist may work on handling and positioning an infant with a visual impairment and low muscle to increase stability and tone. However, the family will need to use these techniques consistently at home to promote the child's motor development. Similarly, a teacher who is certified in the field of deafness and hearing impairments may use signs with an infant who has both a visual impairment and a hearing loss, but the family will need to use these signs as well to support the infant's development of communication.

No studies have documented the intensity of early intervention services provided to infants with visual impairments and their families. A study of infants with Down syndrome (mean age of 11 months) before the implementation of P.L. 99-457 (Shonkoff et al., 1992) revealed a weekly average of 1.7 hours of early intervention services. This finding was replicated by a more recent study of older infants (mean age of 22.5 months) who had established risk conditions or developmental delays or were at a substantial risk for developmental delays (Kochanek & Buka, 1998). However, older infants and mothers of a higher socioeconomic status received more weekly services than did younger infants and mothers with lower levels of education and income.

Anecdotal reports, experience in the field, and related research on infants with visual impairments and their families (Behl, White, & Escobar, 1993) have indicated that a weekly home visit of approximately one hour is a common practice. The findings that an early interventionist is present with an infant and his or her family for less than two hours a week and for a limited period of the infant's development reinforce the notion that intervention strategies should focus on assisting the caregivers and families who are the primary influences on infants' development.

FEDERAL LEGISLATION

Landmark federal mandates have significantly influenced the state of early intervention services in the United States. In 1975, P.L. 94-142, the Education for All Handicapped Children Act, mandated free and appropriate public education to all children with disabilities (aged 3–21). Although this law did not require services for infants and toddlers, it established the Preschool Incentive Grant to encourage states to provide services to 3–5 five year olds with disabilities.

In 1986, however, amendments to the Education for All Handicapped Children Act under P.L. 99-457 expanded preschool services to all 3–5 year olds with disabilities and, under Part H, mandated early intervention services for infants with disabilities and those who are at risk for developmental delays. The primary intent of Part H was

> to enhance the development of handicapped infants and toddlers and to minimize their potential for developmental delays . . . to enhance the capacity of families to meet the special needs of their infants and toddlers with handicaps. . . . To provide assistance to States to develop and implement a statewide, comprehensive, coordinated, multidisciplinary, interagency program of early intervention services for infants and toddlers and their families, . . . and to enhance its capacity to provide quality early intervention services and expand and improve existing early intervention services being provided to handicapped infants, toddlers, and their families. (Sec. 671)

Furthermore, P.L. 99-457 requires that each eligible infant or toddler and the family receive

> (1) a multidisciplinary assessment of unique needs and the identification of services appropriate to meet such needs, and

> (2) a written individualized family service plan developed by a multidisciplinary team, including the parent or guardian. (Sec. 677)

In 1990, the Education for All Handicapped Children Act was reauthorized under P.L. 101-476 and renamed the Individuals with Disabilities Education Act (IDEA). In 1997, IDEA amendments under P.L. 105-17 specified that services are to be delivered to infants from birth through 36 months under Part C. These amendments became law in July 1998. Thus, federal law requires that eligible infants receive comprehensive, multidisciplinary evaluations and that Individualized Family Service Plans (IFSPs) are developed for eligible infants and their families.

Eligibility

IDEA identifies three criteria for eligibility for early intervention services:

- a developmental delay in one or more of the following areas: physical development; adaptive behavior; and cognitive, communication, and social-emotional development
- an established risk or a diagnosed condition that has a high probability of resulting in delay, including Down syndrome, cerebral palsy, visual impairment, and multiple disabilities
- a biological or environmental risk, such as medical or home conditions that may significantly compromise a child's health and development if early intervention is not provided (Fraas, 1986).

However, the federal government has allowed each state to define *developmental delay* and to decide whether to serve infants who demonstrate a "biological or environmental risk." Given the large number of infants who demonstrate risk conditions, many states have elected not to include this population in their early intervention system (Howard, Williams, Port, & Lepper, 1997).

Assessment Practices

Federal legislation requires that each infant with a disability and his or her family receive

- a multidisciplinary assessment of the infant's strengths and needs and identification of appropriate services to meet these needs
- if the family agrees, a family-directed assessment of the family's concerns, resources, and priorities and identification of appropriate supports needed to promote the family's ability to meet the child's developmental needs
- a written IFSP developed by a multidisciplinary team, including the family.

Current best practices in assessment require information about the infant to be gathered from multiple sources (caregivers, as well as past and present service providers) on a number of occasions and using multiple measures (such as both criterion-referenced and norm-referenced tests, interviews, and observations); furthermore, assessment instruments and procedures should be appropriate for the individual infant's culture, disability, interests, and abilities (DEC Task Force, 1993; Meisels & Fenichel, 1996). The assessment process should identify the infant's optimal way of functioning within the context of interactions with a trusted caregiver (Greenspan & Meisels, 1996).

It is beyond the scope of this book to discuss the complexity of assessment in early intervention or to discuss adaptations to available instruments for infants' visual impairments and other disabilities. Given the heterogeneity of infants whose multiple disabilities include visual impairments, there cannot be a single norm-referenced test for this population. However, a number of curriculum-based and criterion-referenced tools that are linked to curricula are used widely in early intervention programs (Bricker, 1993; Furuno et al., 1985). Other tools and procedures have been described elsewhere (Bradley-Johnson, 1994; Chen & Dote-Kwan, 1998; Chen, Friedman, & Calvello, 1990; Rossetti, 1990). When appropriate, selected chapters identify assessment strategies that focus on interviews with caregivers and observations of infants in daily activities and structured situations.

The IFSP

When an infant is found to be eligible for early intervention services, an IFSP must be developed. This IFSP document must include

1. the infant's current levels of physical (fine and gross motor, vision, hearing, and health), cognitive, communication, social or emotional, and adaptive (or self-help) development
2. if the family agrees, information on the family's concerns, priorities, and resources related to promoting the infant's development
3. the main outcomes expected for the child, criteria for accomplishment, timelines, and procedures for measuring progress
4. the specific early intervention services that will be provided and the frequency, intensity, and methods of delivering them
5. the natural environments (such as the home, a child care center, or community settings with nondisabled peers) in which early intervention services will be provided and, if applicable, justification for services that will not be provided in the natural environment
6. the initiation dates and duration of services

7. the name of the service coordinator who is qualified to implement and coordinate the IFSP

8. steps to be taken to support the child's and family's transition from Part C services.

The IFSP is important both as a process and as a document for providing appropriate and coordinated services to an infant and his or her family. The process facilitates a family's collaboration with service providers, the sharing of information among service providers from various disciplines, early intervention outcomes that are valued by the family, and the coordination of services from different service providers and agencies.

Early Intervention Services

IDEA identifies a variety of services that may be provided through early intervention when appropriate. To meet the individual needs of an infant, the IFSP may include

1. audiological services
2. coordination of services
3. family training, counseling, and home visits
4. health services that are necessary for the infant to benefit from other early intervention services
5. medical services for diagnosis and evaluation
6. nursing services
7. nutritional services
8. occupational therapy
9. physical therapy
10. social work services
11. psychological services
12. special education services
13. speech and language therapy
14. transportation to enable the infant and family to receive early intervention services
15. vision services
16. assistive technology devices
17. respite care
18. other family support services.

Depending on their needs, infants with visual impairments and their families could receive many or all of these services. The number and variety of possible services and service providers highlight the need for a coordinated approach to serving these infants and their families.

WHO ARE EARLY INTERVENTIONISTS?

Early interventionist is a generic term that refers to a primary service provider who is working with an infant (birth through 36 months) who has a disability and with the infant's family. Service providers who work with infants who have visual impairments and additional disabilities come from a variety of disciplines and backgrounds, including child development, special education (the fields of early childhood special education, visual impairments, deafness and hearing loss, and severe and multiple disabilities), occupational or physical therapy, orientation and mobility, and speech and language therapy.

The role of these professionals in early intervention services with infants who have multiple disabilities vary from state to state and from one geographic area to another. In some areas, the primary early interventionist for an infant who has a visual impairment with additional disabilities is a teacher who is certified in the field of visual impairment. In others, the primary early interventionist may be a teacher certified in the field of severe disabilities or early childhood special education or a service provider who has no specific training or background (Hanson & Lovett, 1992). If an infant who is visually impaired also has a hearing loss, the primary early interventionist may be a teacher who is certified to work with infants who are deaf and hard of hearing. In many areas, a teacher who is certified in the field of visual impairments provides consultation to the primary early interventionist who is serving an infant with multiple disabilities or specific intervention strategies to encourage the baby's development of compensatory skills or use of functional vision (Chen & Dote-Kwan, 1998).

Many individuals who serve infants with disabilities and their families are not called early interventionists and would not identify themselves as such. Teachers who provide itinerant services to a number of children of different ages with various disabilities do not consider themselves early interventionists. Similarly, respite care workers, bus drivers, audiologists, ophthalmologists, nurses, and physical therapists would identify themselves by their professions, not as early interventionists.

Professional Competencies

The implementation of IDEA requires specific competencies for service providers who work with infants and their families. Professional organizations have attempted to determine the unique competencies that service providers need in early intervention (Hanson & Lynch, 1995). Basic areas of competence include knowledge of typical and atypical early development; knowledge and skills in working with families; the ability to conduct assessments and develop and implement IFSPs; and effective interaction skills with infants, families, and team members (Hanson & Brekken, 1991).

It is likely that most teachers who are certified in the field of visual impairments received minimal training specific to working with infants and their families and are even less likely to have been introduced to the needs of infants with severe and multiple disabilities (Erin, 1986; Erin, Daugherty, Dignan, & Pearson, 1990; Huebner & Paige-Strumwasser, 1987; Seitz, 1994; SKI-HI Institute, 1994). Furthermore, early interventionists who serve infants with visual impairments, particularly those with additional disabilities, are likely to lack training and experience in the specific learning needs of this population (Behl et al., 1993; Morgan, 1994). In general, early interventionists who work with infants with visual impairments and those with additional disabilities would benefit from in-service training opportunities, exposure to relevant intervention strategies, and appropriate written materials (Morgan, 1994; SKI-HI Institute, 1994; Watkins; 1989), such as those included in this book.

TEAM MODELS IN EARLY INTERVENTION SERVICES

IDEA mandates a multidisciplinary service system and multidisciplinary assessments for eligible infants. However, the early intervention literature describes three models for teaming: multidisciplinary, interdisciplinary, and transdisciplinary (McCollum & Hughes, 1988; Woodruff & McGonigel, 1988). The multidisciplinary model is used frequently for conducting assessments (McCollum & Hughes, 1988) and is based on a medical model. Each service provider (including an early childhood educator, teacher certified in the field of visual impairments, occupational therapist, psychologist, and speech and language therapist) conducts his or her own assessment of the infant and develops and implements the resulting interventions. Information from the perspective of each discipline is shared mainly through access to written reports.

The interdisciplinary model, which is commonly used in implementing interventions, is a more coordinated approach to early intervention services (McCollum & Hughes, 1988). Although service providers still conduct individual assessments and provide discipline-specific interventions, they make a concerted effort to share the results of their assessments and to develop interventions collaboratively. For example, in this model, the early childhood educator, teacher certified in the field of visual impairments, occupational therapist, and speech and language therapist collaborate on interventions to promote the infant's communication and play.

The transdisciplinary model is a true team approach. Families are active participants, and interventions are integrated within the family's routine. Service providers work together to conduct assessments, to share their expertise in developing interventions, and to move beyond their own discipline-specific objectives for the infant by implementing interventions that promote overall development. For example, in this model, the infant's parents identify the infant's strengths and interests and their concerns and priorities for the infant; the early childhood educator shares developmentally appropriate (for the infant's age and interests) play strategies; the teacher who is certified in the field of visual impairments provides strategies to enhance the infant's functional vision or development of compensatory skills, the occupational therapist shares strategies for motivating the infant to handle and manipulate objects and to feed himself or herself (adaptive skills), and the speech and language therapist shares strategies for promoting the infant's communication. Service providers and family members learn from each other and use shared strategies in their interactions with the infant. For instance, during snack time, the early childhood special educator uses appropriate strategies to assist the infant to locate a cracker on the tray of the high chair (a functional vision skill), pick it up, and eat it (an adaptive skill) and to request more to eat or drink (a communication skill). The transdisciplinary model is used less frequently than the other two models (McCollum & Hughes, 1988). The issue of team approaches is discussed further in Chapter 3, "Meeting the Intervention Needs of

Infants." The transdisciplinary approach is an effective model for infusing the infant's objectives within the daily routine and for providing consistent intervention support across activities, people, and settings. A format for integrating objectives throughout the daily routine is presented in Chapter 8, "Developing Meaningful Interventions."

SETTINGS FOR EARLY INTERVENTION

In current practice, early intervention services are provided in a child's home and in a variety of community settings, such as day care centers, community play groups, center-based programs for young children with disabilities, Early Head Start programs, and specialized clinics for vision and hearing tests, speech and language services, or occupational and physical therapy. Research has revealed that early intervention services are most frequently provided through home visits or in center-based programs (Kochanek & Buka, 1998; Shonkoff et al., 1992). Younger infants (less than 18 months) are more likely to receive home visits than are older infants. Kochanek and Buka (1998) found that when infants had college-educated mothers and service providers, services were more likely to be provided in community-based, inclusive settings (child care centers, libraries, churches, and hospitals). Field observations, program reports, and research have indicated that infants with visual impairments and additional disabilities receive services in a variety of environments, including the home and center-based and community settings (Behl et al., 1993; Chen, 1996; Friedman, 1989; Klein, Van Hasselt, Trefelner, Sandstrom, & Brandt-Snyder, 1988).

In 1998, new language in IDEA, Part C, strengthened the requirement that early intervention services should be provided "in natural environments to the maximum extent appropriate." Furthermore, the IFSP should describe these natural environments or provide a justification for why services cannot be provided in natural environments, which have been defined as environments in which children would naturally be if they did not have disabilities. The language and intent of the law have been interpreted to mean settings that would exist if there were no children with disabilities. Many states interpret the strengthened requirement as mandating the provision of services in homes and day care centers and other community settings that serve infants without disabilities, and this interpretation has been confirmed by the U.S. Department of Education (Ingel & Stettner-Eaton, 1998). Considerable controversy exists, however, over whether this mandate limits the ability of infants and their families to receive specialized services from a variety of service providers, a service delivery combination that may be available only in a center-based program, or whether it would deny the rights of the family to choose their own options. Many believe that center-based programs have certain unique benefits for some infants and families and that the most appropriate services for a child need to be selected from a continuum of options. (More information about this issue appears in Chen, 1999.) Therefore, it is crucial that early interventionists collaborate with families to identify and provide optimal caregiving and learning environments for infants with visual impairments and additional disabilities.

CONCLUSION

In the past decade, federal legislation has provided an impetus for the development and implementation of standards for professional qualifications and early intervention practices. The roles and responsibilities of early interventionists vary according to their particular program philosophy, team model, and where services are provided to infants and families. Current philosophies guide efforts in early intervention toward a collaborative approach with families and across professional disciplines. Recent research has emphasized the importance of starting early with infants who have disabilities and the role of the family and the influence of the caregiving environment on early development. Early intervention services for infants with disabilities and their families is still a developing professional field. Attaining and maintaining effective early intervention practices is an ongoing process by which service providers learn to work more effectively with infants who have disabilities and their families. The encouragement, promotion, and support of this process are the main purposes of this book. In the chapters that follow, information for formulating effective early intervention is offered.

REFERENCES

Bagley, S. (1997, Spring–Summer). How to build a baby's brain. In "Your child: From birth to three," *Newsweek* [Special Issue].

Behl, D., White, K. R., & Escobar, C. M. (1993). New Orleans early intervention study of children with visual impairments. *Early Education and Development, 4,* 256–273.

Bradley-Johnson, S. (1994). *Psychoeducational assessment of students who are visually impaired or blind. Infancy through high school* (2nd ed.). Austin, TX: PRO-ED.

Bricker, D. (Ed.). (1993). *Assessment, evaluation, and programming systems for infants and children, Vol. 1: AEPS measurement for birth to three years.* Baltimore, MD: Paul H. Brookes.

Carnegie Corporation of New York. (1994). *Starting points. Meeting the needs of our youngest children.* New York: Author.

Chen, D. (1996). Parent-infant communication: Early intervention for very young children with visual impairment or hearing loss. *Infants and Young Children, 9*(2), 1–12.

Chen, D. (1999). Center-based programs for infants with visual impairments: "Natural" or "unnatural" learning environments? *Journal of Visual Impairment & Blindness, 93,* 390–392.

Chen, D., & Dote-Kwan, J. (1998). Early intervention services for young children who have visual impairments with other disabilities and their families. In S. Z. Sacks & R. K. Silberman (Eds.), *Educating students who have visual impairments with other disabilities* (pp. 303–338). Baltimore, MD: Paul H. Brookes.

Chen, D., Friedman, C. T., & Calvello, G. (1990). *Parents and visually impaired infants.* Louisville, KY: American Printing House for the Blind.

DEC Task Force on Recommended Practices. (1993). *DEC recommended practices: Indicators of quality programs for infants and young children with special needs and their families.* Reston, VA: Council for Exceptional Children.

Erin, J., Daugherty, W., Dignan, K., & Pearson, N. (1990). Teachers of visually handicapped students with multiple disabilities: Perceptions of adequacy. *Journal of Visual Impairment & Blindness, 84,* 16–20.

Erin, J. N. (1986). Teachers of the visually handicapped: How can they best serve children with profound handicaps? *Education of the Visually Handicapped, 18,* 15–25.

Farel, R. B., & Hooper, C. R. (1995). Biological limits to behavioral recovery following injury to the central nervous system: Implications for early intervention. *Infants and Young Children, 8,* 1–7.

Fraas, C. J. (1986). *Summary of the Education of the Handicapped Act Amendments of 1986, P. L. 99-457.* Washington, DC: Library of Congress Research Service.

Friedman, C. T. (1988). Integrating infants. *Exceptional Parent, 19,* 52–57.

Furono, S., Inatsuka, T. T., O'Reilly, K. A., Hosaka, C. M., Zeisloft-Falbey, B., & Allman, T. (1985). *Hawaii Early Learning Profile (HELP) activity guide.* Palo Alto, CA: VORT Corp.

Greenough, W. T., Volkmar, R. R., & Jurasks, J. M. (1973). Effects of rearing complexity on dendritic branching in frontolateral and temporal cortex of the rat. *Experimental Neurology, 41,* 371–378.

Greenspan, S., & Meisels, S. (1996). Toward a new vision of development assessment of infants and young children. In S. J. Meisels & E. Fenichel (Eds.), *New visions for the developmental assessment of infants and young children* (pp. 11–26). Washington, DC: Zero to Three/National Center for Infants, Toddlers, and Families.

Hanson, M. J., & Brekken, L. (1991). Early intervention personnel model and standards: An interdisciplinary field-developed approach. *Infants and Young Children, 4*(1), 54–61.

Hanson, M. J., & Lovett, D. (1992). Personnel preparation for early interventionists: A cross-disciplinary study. *Journal of Early Intervention, 16,* 123–135.

Hanson, M. J., & Lynch, E. W. (1995). *Early intervention: Implementing child and family services for infants and toddlers who are at risk or disabled* (2nd ed.). Austin, TX: PRO-ED.

Harel, S., Holtzman, M., & Feinsod, M. (1985). The late visual bloomer. In S. Harel & N. J. Anastasiow (Eds.), *The at-risk infant: Psycho/socio/medical aspects* (pp. 359–362). Baltimore: MD: Paul H. Brookes.

Hart, V. (1984). Research as a basis for assessment and curriculum development for visually impaired infants. *Journal of Visual Impairment & Blindness, 78,* 314–318.

Hawley, T. (1998). *Starting smart: How early experiences affect brain development.* Chicago: Ounce of Prevention Fund; Washington, DC: Zero to Three.

Held, R. (1972). Plasticity in sensory motor systems. In *The nature and nurture of behavior: Developmental Psychobiology. Readings from Scientific American* (pp. 73–80). San Francisco: W. H. Freeman.

Howard, V. F., Williams, B. F., Port, P. D., & Lepper, C. (1997). *Very young children with special needs. A formative approach for the 21st century.* Upper Saddle River, NJ: Prentice Hall.

Huebner, K. M., & Paige-Strumwasser, K. (1987). State certification of teachers of blind and visually impaired students: A report of a national study. *Journal of Visual Impairment & Blindness, 81,* 244–250.

Hunt, J. M. (1961). *Intelligence and experience.* New York: Ronald Press.

Huttenlocher, P. R. (1994). Synaptogenesis, synapse elimination, and neural plasticity in human cerebral cortex. In C. A. Nelson (Ed.), Threats to optimal development: Integrating biological, psychological, and social risk factors. *The Minnesota Symposia in Child Psychology, 27,* 35–54.

Illig, D. C. (1998). *Birth to kindergarten: The importance of the early years.* (California Research Bureau, California State Library No. CRB-98-001). Sacramento: California State Library.

Ingel, R., & Stettner-Eaton, B. (1998, December). *Embracing paradigm shifts in service delivery to infants/toddlers and their families.* Paper presented at the Annual International Division for Early Childhood Conference on Children with Special Needs and their Families, Chicago.

Klein, B., Van Hasselt, V. B., Trefelner, M., Sandstrom, D. J., & Brandt-Snyder, P. (1988). The parent and toddler training project for visually impaired and blind multihandicapped children. *Journal of Visual Impairment & Blindness, 82,* 59–62.

Kochanek, T. T., & Buka, S. L. (1998). Patterns of early intervention service utilization: Child, maternal, and provider factors. *Journal of Early Intervention, 21,* 217–231.

McCollum, J. A., & Hughes, M. (1988). Staffing patterns and team models in infancy programs. In J. B. Jordan, J. J. Gallagher, P. L. Hutinger, & M. B. Karnes (Eds.), *Early childhood special education: Birth to three* (pp. 129–146). Reston, VA: Council for Exceptional Children.

Meisels, S. J., & Fenichel, E. (1996). *New visions for the developmental assessment of infants and young children.* Washington, DC: Zero to Three/National Center for Infants, Toddlers, and Families.

Morgan, E. (1994). *Resources for family-centered intervention for infants, toddlers, and preschoolers who are visually impaired: VIISA Project* (2nd ed.,Vol. 1–2). Logan, UT: Hope.

Nash, J. M. (1997, February 3). Fertile minds. *Time, 149,* 48–56.

National Parent Teacher Association. (1997). *White House Conference on Early Childhood Development and Learning: What new research on the brain tells us about our youngest children* [On-line]. Available: http://www.pta.org/programs/wh_ecc.htm

Piaget, J. (1952). *The origins of intelligence in children* (M. Cook, Trans.). New York: International Universities Press. (Original French ed., 1936).

Riesen, A. H. (1972). Arrested vision. In *The nature and nurture of behavior: Developmental Psychobiology. Readings from Scientific American* (pp. 62–65). San Francisco: W. H. Freeman.

Rosenzweig, M. R., Krech, D., Bennett, E. L., & Diamond, M. C. (1968). Modifying brain chemistry and anatomy by enrichment or impoverishment of experience. In G. Newton & S. Levine (Eds.), *Early experience and behavior* (pp. 258–298). Springfield, IL: Charles C Thomas.

Rossetti, L. M. (1990). *Infant-toddler assessment. An interdisciplinary approach.* Austin, TX: PRO-ED.

Sameroff, A. J., & Chandler, M. J. (1975). Reproductive risk and the continuum of caretaking causality. In F. D. Horowitz (Ed.). *Review of child development research* (Vol. 4, pp. 187–244). Chicago: University of Chicago Press.

Seitz, J. A. (1994). Seeing through the isolation: A study of first-year teachers of the visually impaired. *Journal of Visual Impairment & Blindness, 88,* 299–309.

SKI-HI Institute. (1994). *Project VIISA (Vision impaired In-service in America): A model inservice training program for early intervention/ early childhood professionals serving infants, toddlers, and preschoolers who are blind and visually impaired. Introduction to the instructor's manuals for both VIISA courses.* Logan, UT: Author.

Shonkoff, J., & Hauser-Cram, P. (1987). Early intervention for disabled infants and their families: A quantitative analysis. *Pediatrics, 80,* 650–658.

Shonkoff, J., Hauser-Cram, P., Kauss, M., & Upshur, C. (1992). *Development of infants with disabilities and their families.* (Society for Research in Child Development Monograph No. 230). Chicago: University of Chicago Press.

Stone, J. L., Smith, H. T., & Murphy, L. B. (Eds.). (1973). *The competent infant.* New York: Basic Books.

Turner, A. M., & Greenough, W. T. (1985). Differential rearing effects on rat visual cortex synapses: I. Synapse and neural density and synapses per neuron. *Brain Research, 329,* 195–203.

Watkins, S. (1989). *The INSITE Model: A model of home intervention for infant, toddler, and preschool aged multihandicapped sensory impaired children* (Vol. 1–2). Logan, UT: Hope.

Wiesel, T. N. (1982). The postnatal development of the visual cortex and the influence of environment (Nobel Lecture 1981). *Bioscience Reports, 2,* 351–377.

Wiesel, T. N., & Hubel, D. H. (1963). Effects of visual deprivation on morphology and physiology of cells in the cat's lateral geniculate body. *Journal of Neurophysiology, 26,* 978–993.

Woodruff, G., & McGonigel, M. (1988). Early intervention team approaches: The transdisciplinary team. In J. B. Jordan, J. J. Gallagher, P. L. Hutinger, & M. B. Karnes (Eds.), *Early childhood special education: Birth to three* (pp. 163–181). Reston, VA: Council for Exceptional Children.

2

Interactions Between Infants and Caregivers: The Context for Early Intervention

Deborah Chen

Early interventionists enter the lives and homes of families when infants with visual impairments and additional disabilities are perhaps only a few days, weeks, or months old. In this short period, families have been told about their infants' disabilities, have received a variety of referrals, and have begun an unfamiliar path to early intervention services. Think about the parents of a baby who is visually impaired navigating the medical system—having multiple appointments with a pediatrician, neurologist, and ophthalmologist and then being referred to the early intervention system. Imagine their feelings as the members of the early intervention team conduct multiple assessments, develop plans, and implement interventions with their baby. Consider their experiences as an occupational therapist, infant development specialist, and teacher who is certified in visual impairments "work with" their infant.

How should early interventionists begin their work with infants and families? Federal legislation requires that early intervention services meet a family's concerns, support the family's efforts and ability to promote the infant's development, and enhance the family's confidence in caring for their infant. Thus, as noted in Chapter 1, the focus of early intervention should be on the infant, the caregivers, and the family because it is within this context that an infant interacts, learns, and develops.

This chapter examines relevant research as a basis for developing meaningful interventions for infants who have severe and multiple disabilities and for their families. First, the chapter discusses the key developmental needs of an infant and the transactional model of development as a conceptual framework for guiding early intervention practice. Next, it reviews the literature on interactions between infants and caregivers, including contingency experiences and their relationship to these interactions. Finally, the chapter discusses implications of this research for intervention practices with infants who have visual impairments and additional disabilities and provides suggestions for strategies that support these interactions and promote contingent learning experiences for infants who have multiple disabilities.

KEY DEVELOPMENTAL NEEDS OF THE INFANT IN THE CAREGIVING PROCESS

In the first few months, newborns are learning to regulate stimulation by responding selectively to social interactions. The primary role of early interventionists at this time is to assist caregivers in supporting infants' efforts to regulate themselves, interpreting infants' cues, engaging infants' attention, and responding to infants' behavior (Vanden-Berg & Hanson, 1993). Caregivers of infants with multiple disabilities may need help from early interventionists to identify when the infants seem alert and available for interaction and when they are drowsy or fussy and need to be left alone. Through careful and systematic observations, caregivers will learn to recognize their infants' early signals and how to respond accordingly. Caregivers' responsiveness to infants' cues are vital. It is through consistent and responsive caregiving that infants develop a sense of trust and security (Erikson, 1963) and attachment to their primary caregivers (Ainsworth, 1969; Greenspan & Greenspan, 1985).

Later in the first year, if the infants' medical conditions are stable, interventions may focus on opportunities for the communication, play, and social skills within the context of everyday activities. Caregivers may need assistance in helping their infants to differentiate them from other adults. For example, an infant who is visually impaired may learn to recognize a primary caregiver by a special scent, particular greeting, or typical way that the caregiver holds him or her (Lueck, Chen, & Kekelis, 1997). Daily caregiving routines, such as diapering, feeding, and bathing, provide natural and consistent opportunities for infants to cooperate with familiar activities, to anticipate what will happen next, to participate actively in these everyday events, to attend to their caregivers and environment, and to develop communication.

During the second year, interventions may expand to encourage the infants' more active participation in family routines and simple daily activities like eating with their fingers (Teplin, 1995). When appropriate, activities may involve opportunities for increased mobility, play, and social interaction with other children. For typical children, the period of toddlerhood during the second year is a time for developing a sense of self and control through increased abilities, such as walking, feeding themselves, talking, and playing with toys. In this period, some toddlers with visual impairments and additional disabilities may demonstrate limited motor skills, may not be ambulatory, and may not be talking. However, early interventionists can assist caregivers in providing alternative means to support the toddlers' communication (such as using object cues or signs) and other ways for developing a sense of self (for example, by making choices between foods). When children are 30 months old, early interventionists have the legal responsibility to plan with the families for the infants' transition to a preschool program. It is evident from this summary of the early years that caregivers and other family members play a critical role in an infant's development.

SIGNIFICANCE OF CAREGIVER RESPONSIVENESS

The report of the Carnegie Task Force on Meeting the Needs of Young Children (Carnegie Corporation, 1994) identified dependable caregiving as a key influence on the development of all young children. These findings underscore the need for early intervention to support caregivers' interactions with their infants and to provide early experiences that promote learning and development. Similarly, the California Infant Mental Health Work Group (1996) stressed that early intervention programs should support interactions between caregivers and infants, assist caregivers to interpret infants' cues, and develop caregiving strategies to meet the specialized needs of infants who have difficulty processing sensory information. A number of studies have also emphasized the importance of facilitating the relationship between infants and caregivers as a focus of early intervention (Aydlett, 1993; Bromwich, 1981; Hadadian, 1996; Mahoney, Boyce, Fewell, Spiker, & Wheeden, 1998). (See the section on implications of research for early intervention services to infants with disabilities and their families at the end of this chapter.)

Previous developmental research has found that a supportive, responsive, and stable caregiving environment is crucial for an infant's emotional well-being (Goldberg, 1977; Sameroff, 1982). A caregiver's responsiveness appears to build an infant's anticipation that his or her behavior has some effect. This realization encourages the infant's efforts to interact and motivation to learn. Developmental psychologists (Watson, 1972, 1979; Watson & Ramey, 1972) suggested that the significance of interactions between an infant and a caregiver lies in an infant's sensitivity to contingency experiences (experiences that are dependent, or contingent, on the infant's behavior), that is, the infant's ability to perceive that his or her behavior elicits a response from the caregiver. (Contingency experiences are discussed in more detail later in this chapter.) Research with typical infants indicates that a caregiver's responsiveness to an infant's signals is associated with the infant's security of attachment; learning; and early social, communicative, and cognitive development (Ainsworth, Blehar, Waters, & Wall, 1978; Blehar, Leiberman, & Ainsworth, 1977; Field, 1978; J. Lewis & Goldberg, 1969; Londerville & Main, 1981). Given these findings, it seems that early intervention services should support a responsive caregiving environment as a primary influence for enhancing an infant's developmental outcome.

THE TRANSACTIONAL MODEL OF DEVELOPMENT

A focus on the interaction of caregivers and infants in early intervention is also supported by the transactional model of development. This conceptual framework views an infant's developmental outcome as a consequence of the reciprocal interactions between the infant and the caregiving environment (Sameroff, 1987; Sameroff & Chandler, 1975) (see Chapter 1). Not only does the environment affect the infant, but the infant influences the caregiving environment in many ways. First, how the family responds affects the caregiving environment. Families vary in their reactions, and their feelings change over time, as do the needs and interests of the baby. Second, the infant's diagnosis and medical needs influence the environment. An infant may require prolonged and frequent hospitalizations that interrupt the natural interactions and activities with his or her caregivers, and the home may need to be filled with life-sustaining equipment. Third, the family structure, roles, responsibilities, and values influence the caregiving environment by determining who takes care of the baby, when, and how. Thus, the caregiving environment is influenced by the complexity of the family's characteristics, the infant's characteristics, and the ongoing interaction between them.

When the characteristics and expectations of the caregiving situation match the infant's needs and abilities, there is a goodness of fit, and the infant is likely to have an optimal developmental outcome (Thomas & Chess, 1977). However, when there is a poor fit between the infant's needs and the environment, the infant is likely to have a suboptimal outcome. For example, for a 12 month old who is blind and has cerebral palsy, the caregiving environment needs to be adapted to accommodate the infant's vision loss and motor disability. The infant's learning and development will be supported if the infant is given accessible information through his or her available senses, specific positioning and handling techniques to facilitate normal tone and other motor needs, and adaptive equipment and activity modifications to support participation in activities. Accordingly, the caregiver's interactions and caregiving routines with the baby should be modified to fit not only the infant's needs but also the family's situation. On the other hand, if compensatory strategies are not used to give the infant access to information and positioning and handling techniques are not implemented, then it is likely that the infant's motor development and other developmental areas will be affected negatively.

For a 12 month old with cortical visual impairment, seizures, and other medical needs, the caregiver needs to provide the necessary medications, identify when the infant is alert and available for interaction, interpret the infant's visual attention, structure the environment to encourage the infant's functional use of vision, and assist the infant to touch and handle objects to develop visual recognition. As a final example, consider an 18 month old who has both a visual impairment and hearing loss and is an active and ambulatory child who loves to climb on furniture and delights in jumping on the bed. The caregiver needs not only to adapt interactions to meet the child's sensory needs, but to provide frequent and consistent opportunities for the child to engage in physical activities. Accordingly, caregivers' interactions with and caregiving routines for these infants need to be modified for both the infant's needs and the family's situation and practices. The conceptual framework of the transactional model highlights the significance of caregivers' responsiveness on infants' early development, the need to identify features of the caregiving environment that support the infants' interactions, and the importance of understanding how the infants' characteristics interact with the caregiving environment.

CAREGIVERS' INTERACTIONS WITH INFANTS WHO HAVE DISABILITIES

An infant's congenital disability affects both the caregiver's responsiveness and the infant's ability to respond to the caregiver and, consequently, influences the nature of the interactions between the caregiver and the infant. Infants who have multiple disabilities may require prolonged or frequent hospitalizations and medical care that interfere with the development of early emotional ties with their caregivers and families. In addition, even when their health is stable, these infants may not demonstrate typical behaviors that elicit their caregivers' attention, such as looking, vocalizing, or responding positively to the caregivers' interactions. Studies have found that caregivers' interactions with infants who are at risk or have disabilities are of a different quality from those with healthy and nondisabled infants. Furthermore, caregivers appear to have difficulty maintaining contingent responsiveness (that is, responding to the infants' signals) when the infants have disabilities. However, research has also revealed the positive effect of interventions that focus on supporting caregivers' interactions with their infants who have a variety of disabilities. These findings highlight the need for early intervention to promote interactions within the context of the home that are mutually satisfying for both caregivers and infants.

Given the dearth of research on caregivers' interactions with infants who are visually impaired and have additional disabilities, information must be derived from related populations. The commonality among infants who are visually impaired and have additional disabilities is visual impairment. Hearing loss, physical disabilities, and developmental delays are the most frequent disabilities that accompany visual impairments that are diagnosed in the first two years. Furthermore, many of these infants were born prematurely. This section reviews the related literature on caregivers' interaction with these populations of infants to identify the influences of visual impairments and additional disabilities on early interactions.

Caregivers' Interactions with Infants Who Are Blind or Visually Impaired

There have been only a few studies of caregivers' interactions with infants who are visually impaired, and it is difficult to generalize their findings to the larger population of other infants with visual impairments. First, visual impairment is a low-incidence disability, so studies tend to involve a small number of children. Second, infants who are visually impaired vary in the type and severity of their vision loss. The majority of infants who are legally blind or visually impaired have some degree of functional vision, so one needs to differentiate between infants with some functional vision and infants who are blind. Third, the samples of infants in different studies vary on many factors, including the infants' etiology, intervention histories, additional disabilities, and other individual differences and the families' socioeconomic status, culture, and other characteristics. Fourth, each researcher had a particular focus and a different method of analyzing the characteristics of interactions. Even given these limitations, however, it is known that severe visual impairment affects an infant's interaction with caregivers.

Blindness severely restricts an infant's repertoire of facial expressions and other nonvocal means of communication and thus the infant's ability to engage a caregiver's attention. The absence of gaze and eye contact complicates the caregiver's ability to monitor and respond to the infant's attention. An infant who is visually impaired may not respond to a caregiver's interactions in a way that the caregiver expects. For example, he or she may seem to ignore the caregiver's vocalization. When a blind infant is quiet and still, it is likely that the infant is alert and listening (Burlingham, 1974; Rowland, 1983). Research has also indicated that the lack of eye contact and visual attention in an infant who is visually impaired results in decreased visual attention (Rogers & Pulchalski, 1984) and vocal responsiveness from the caregiver (Rowland, 1983). These findings emphasize the need to support caregivers in identifying and interpreting their infants' signals (Fraiberg, 1974). Such strategies have had positive influences on caregiver-infant interactions. For instance, Urwin (1983) observed that mothers of two totally blind infants and one infant with low vision observed their infants' faces carefully and used vocal intonation to mirror their facial expressions and body movements. These mothers also developed elaborate play routines using touching, tickling, and other body movements; engaged in prolonged vocal imitation sequences; responded to their infants' vocalizations; and prompted their infants to respond. Another study found that a mother's responsiveness to an infant's initiations (such as the request for an object or assistance), expansion of the infant's communicative behaviors, and use of pacing and pauses to engage the infant in conversational turns was related to the infant's developmental progress (Dote-Kwan, 1995).

In general, infants with visual impairments have been characterized as fussier and less socially responsive than sighted infants in play situations with their mothers (Rogers & Puchalski, 1984). To counteract their infants' passivity, parents have used tickling games and other body play as reliable ways to elicit smiles (Fraiberg, 1977). By the end of their first year, blind infants have been found to participate actively in physical-tactile and vocal imitation routines (Als, Tronick, & Brazelton, 1980; Fraiberg, 1977; Urwin, 1983). Furthermore, Urwin (1983) reported that the first words of the infants with visual impairments in her study emerged during affective, familiar play routines.

Infants with Visual Impairments and Additional Disabilities

There have been even fewer studies on caregivers' interactions with infants who have visual impairments and additional disabilities. One study of seven such infants and their mothers found that these infants had severely restricted signals and that their mothers' interpretations of and responses to these behaviors were limited (Baird, Mayfield, & Baker, 1997). A study of three infants who were blind and had significant developmental delays and delays in language development reported that the mothers' responses to the infants' vocalizations were inconsistent and that these infants were more likely to smile than to vocalize in response to their mothers' maternal vocalizations (Rowland, 1983). Rowland suggested that early interventionists should assist caregivers in responding consistently to infants' vocalizations, given that vocal behavior indicates blind children's attention to the environment. Another study found that the parents of five blind or visually impaired infants (two of whom had significant developmental delays) frequently imitated their infants' vocalizations and used other sounds, movement, and familiar rough-and-tumble games to engage their infants' attention and participation in interactions (Chen, 1996). Research and practice have confirmed that familiar exchanges and play routines provide predictable social interactions that promote early communication in infants with visual impairments and those with additional disabilities (Chen, 1996; Chen, Friedman, & Calvello, 1990; Chen, Haney, Klein, & Alsop, 1998; Fraiberg, 1977; Rowland, 1983, 1984; Rogow, 1983; Urwin, 1983). Strategies for developing and expanding turn-taking routines are described in Chapter 9, "Beginning Communication with Infants."

Infants Who Are Deaf-Blind

There is even less research on infants who are deaf-blind, given the lower incidence of this disability compared to visual impairment alone. Furthermore, as is discussed in Chapter 3, infants who are called deaf-blind vary greatly in the type and severity of their visual impairments and hearing loss and in the nature of their additional disabilities. However, the literature indicates that the combination of vision and hearing loss results in significant difficulties in social and communication development; caregivers and infants who are deaf-blind display fewer mutually enjoyable interactions, and the infants use fewer initiation and interactive behaviors, more self-stimulatory behaviors, fewer "readable" signals, and fewer preverbal communication behaviors (Chen & Haney, 1995; Freeman, 1985; Hyvarinen, 1988, McGinnes & Treffrey, 1982; Michael & Paul, 1991; Walker, 1982; Walker & Kershman, 1981). Recent research found that interventions that emphasize caregivers' interactions with their infants whose multiple disabilities include both vision and hearing loss can increase the caregivers' sensitivity to the infants' signals and use of tactile, auditory, visual, and olfactory cues, as appropriate, during caregiving routines (Chen et al., 1998).

Deaf Infants

Research with deaf infants has focused on the differences in the communication styles of hearing and deaf mothers. Hearing mothers have been found to be directive and noncontingent in interactions with their deaf infants (Power, Wood, Wood, & MacDougall, 1990; Spencer, Bodner-Johnson, & Gutfreund, 1992; Wedell-Monnig & Lumley, 1980), whereas deaf mothers have been found to demonstrate contingent responsiveness to their deaf infants (Maestas y Moores, 1980; Spencer et al., 1992) and to use specific strategies to engage their infants, such as moving their hands within the infants' visual field so the infants can see both the mothers' signs and the referent objects and signing on the infants' bodies (Harris et al., 1987; Maestas y Moores, 1980). Hearing parents of deaf infants in a total communication program demonstrated similar adaptive strategies for their infants' hearing loss, as well as the use of action-based exchange routines and other visual means to engage their infants in early interactions (Chen, 1996). Another study of a total communication program that emphasized responsiveness to infants' communication found that the parents of infants with severe to profound hearing loss who participated in the program were more positive with and less controlling of their infants than were parents who did not participate in the program (Greenberg, Calderon, & Kusche, 1984). These studies suggest that early intervention programs can assist hearing parents of deaf infants to provide appropriate and responsive communication.

Infants Who Have Physical Disabilities

Supporting the quality of interactions between caregivers and infants has been found to promote the positive social-emotional development of children with physical disabilities (Wasserman, Lennon, Allen, & Shilansky, 1987). Whereas Kogan, Tyler, and Turner (1974) and Wasserman, Allen, and Soloman (1985) characterized mothers of infants with physical disabilities as more controlling and directive than mothers of nondisabled infants, Blasco, Hrncir, and Blasco (1990) found no difference in the quality and appropriateness of the interactions of mothers of infants with cerebral palsy and those of mothers of nondisabled infants. In fact, maternal behaviors that appear to be controlling and directive, such as holding an infant's hands to help the infant catch a ball, may be adaptive and meet the needs of the infant who has physical disabilities.

Infants Who Are Developmentally Disabled

Research with mothers and their infants with Down syndrome has revealed that mothers' high level of directive behavior is associated with infants' low levels of initiation and responsive behavior (Crawley & Spiker, 1983; Mahoney, Finger, & Powell, 1985). Infants who have mild to severe developmental disabilities tend to initiate fewer interactions and to be less responsive than their nondisabled peers (Buckhalt, Rutherford, & Goldberg, 1978; Mahoney, 1983; Richards, 1986; Stevenson, Leavitt, & Silverberg, 1985). In addition, their mothers have been found to be less responsive and more directive (Mahoney, 1988; Tannock, 1988). Some mothers in these studies, however, developed specific strategies that enabled them to participate with their infants in mutually satisfying, contingent interactions. These strategies included increased attention to their infants' cues and signals, waiting longer for their infants' responses, and adapting the environment to create opportunities for their infants to initiate interactions.

Infants Who Are Premature

Infants who are born too early and small are at a high risk for visual impairments and additional disabilities. Although research has focused on premature infants without disabilities, findings have demonstrated that prematurity can have a significant influence on the quality of infants' early interactions. Observations of mothers and their premature infants have indicated that compared to full-term infants, premature infants spend less time attending to caregivers, vocalizing, smiling, or interacting face to face (Brown & Bakeman, 1980). On the other hand, interactions that are less attentive, quieter, and involve less smiling avoid overstimulating premature infants may actually be helpful to the infants' early development. Interventions that support high-quality interactions between premature infants and their caregivers have been found to contribute to their cognitive development (Resnick, Armstrong, & Carter, 1988).

The Importance of Contingency Experiences

As was noted earlier, developmental research (Watson, 1972, 1979; Watson & Ramey, 1972) has suggested that contingency experiences, in which an infant's behavior elicits a response from the environment, encourages the infant's development; moreover, interactions with caregivers are the earliest and most significant contingency experiences for all infants. Through these early interactions, infants learn that their behavior can elicit a response from their caregivers. For example, when infants fuss and caregivers respond by picking them up, the infants learn that their behavior has an effect on the caregivers' response. Being picked up was contingent on the infants' behavior—fussing. *Contingent responsivity* is defined as caregivers' behavior that is closely related to the infants' signals in time and function. It is related to the caregivers' ability to identify, interpret, and respond to the infants' cues. Contingency experiences help infants realize that they can control aspects of the social and physical environment (M. Lewis, 1978). In contrast, consistent exposure to noncontingent experiences—experiences that occur independent of an infant's behavior—are likely to decrease an infant's motivation, ability to learn, initiation, and responsive behaviors (Fincham & Cain, 1986; Seligman, 1975).

Contingency experiences provide infants with stimulation that is dependent on their behavior, so *contingent stimulation* is another term for contingency experiences. Contingent stimulation refers to sensory stimulation that immediately follows and is dependent on a particular behavior of infants (Seligman, 1975). For example, infants experience social contingent stimulation when they look toward their caregivers and the caregivers consistently respond by greeting the baby. Similarly, infants experience nonsocial contingent stimulation when they bat at a toy and the toy moves and plays music. The contingent relationship between infants' behavior and the stimulation is the significant component of the experience (Watson, 1979), resulting in an increase in the infants' sense of control over the social and nonsocial aspects of the environment. In addition to the positive emotional consequences for both infants and caregivers, caregivers' responsive interactions increase the infants' contingency experiences.

Contingent Stimulation of Nondisabled Infants

Studies with young infants have demonstrated the power of nonsocial contingency experiences. Watson (1972, 1979) found that 2 month olds smiled and cooed when they activated a mobile by moving their heads or kicking their feet, but that they did not show the same positive reactions when the mobile was activated independent of their movements. In another study, two groups of two-month-old infants experienced either a mobile activated by their head movements on a pressure-sensitive pillow or the movement of a mobile independent of their head movements during a session in their homes (Watson & Ramey, 1972). The frequency of head movements increased above baseline levels in the contingent stimulation group, indicating that these babies learned how to activate the mobile. Six weeks later, both groups of infants were observed in a laboratory setting in which a mobile was activated by head movements. The infants who had experienced contingent stimulation in their homes learned how to control the new mobile, whereas infants who had been subjected to noncontingent stimulation did not. Not only does contingent stimulation promote infants' learning, but noncontingent stimulation interferes with the infants' learning of contingent relationships. Similarly, in a study with infants aged 10 to 24 weeks, one group received stimulation (a 3-second presentation of a colored slide with sounds of children singing) contingent on a motor response (pulling a string attached to the wrist), and the other group received equal amounts of the same stimulation independent of their actions. Those who received contingent stimulation learned to pull the string to activate the slide, demonstrated interest for an average of 17 minutes, smiled more, and were more alert and less fussy than infants who received noncontingent stimulation and were interested in the display for about 8 minutes (M. Lewis, Sullivan, & Brooks-Gunn, 1985).

Newborns have also demonstrated the ability to perceive the cause-and-effect relationship between their sucking behavior and the sound of singing voices. Stimulation was activated contingent on sucks of a short or much longer duration. Butterfield and Siperstein (1972) found that these 2 day olds learned to increase or decrease the duration of individual sucks to hear the singing. In a similar study (DeCasper & Carstens, 1981), one group of newborns learned that they could activate the sound of a woman singing while they sucked and that the singing stopped when they paused. Another group heard the woman singing independent of their various sucking patterns. Both groups received the same amount and timing of stimulation. In a second session 18 hours later, the infants experienced the opposite condition so that those who had received contingent stimulation now received noncontingent stimulation and vice versa. Infants who received contingent stimulation in the first session demonstrated the previous pattern of sucking in the second session. However, when they discovered that this behavior was not effective, they became upset. Those who received noncontingent stimulation in the first session did not perceive the relationship between their sucking patterns and the singing in the contingent stimulation condition. These studies demonstrated that babies can detect and remember whether stimulation is dependent or independent of their actions. Research has also revealed that previous noncontingent stimulation experiences inhibit infants' ability to learn even when contingent stimulation becomes available (Maier & Seligman, 1976).

Contingent Stimulation of Infants Who Are Disabled

The majority of contingent stimulation interventions with infants with severe disabilities have involved the activation of battery-operated toys or other stimuli as a consequence of the infants' motor behavior on a switch (Hanson & Hanline, 1985; Sullivan & Lewis, 1990, 1993). These infants learned how to activate a switch to produce stimuli and, in turn, attended to the stimuli. In a study of six infants with severe and profound disabilities, multicolored lights were presented above their cribs contingent on their turning their heads toward their midlines. These infants learned to elicit the visual stimuli with sufficient time and initial physical prompting (Dunst, Cushing, & Vance, 1985). Another study reported that infants who had multiple disabilities in addition to visual impairments fixated longer on a light display that occurred after they attended to it visually than on a display that provided noncontingent visual stimulation (Utley, Duncan, Strain, & Scanlon, 1983).

Other research with children who had severe cognitive and multiple disabilities (aged 6–50 months, with mental ages of 2–5 months) found that they learned to initiate arm or leg movements to produce auditory, visual, or tactile stimuli. These children learned to differentiate between reinforced and nonreinforced motor responses after 13 intervention sessions, whereas children with less severe disabilities learned this differentiation immediately. There is some evidence that variety is an important factor in children with disabilities maintaining their interest in and continuing to activate switches. Observations indicate that infants both with and without disabilities become bored with the frequent repetition of a single toy after 4 to 6 minutes (Sullivan & Lewis, 1993).

The Little Room has been effective in eliciting manual exploration in infants who are visually impaired and have additional disabilities because it provides contingency experiences. This equipment was designed to promote the development of spatial relations, object permanence, and cause and effect in infants who are blind (Nielsen, 1992a,b). The Little Room is a plexiglass structure with objects attached to the top and the sides that is placed over an infant. In it, infants who are visually impaired and developmentally disabled have demonstrated attention to their vocalizations and tactile exploration of objects. They handled different types of objects, such as rattles and rubber pads, and seemed to compare objects that were moderately different in tactile qualities, such as spoons and keys. Infants have been observed to vocalize, repeat vocalizations, and handle objects in a sequential way. The Little Room seems to encourage the repetition of actions because the objects are in consistent positions. Many teachers have introduced the Little Room to infants who are visually impaired, especially those with multiple disabilities. However, care should be taken to limit the time an infant spends in the Little Room, to monitor the activities of the infant while in it, and to identify the characteristics of the Little Room environment that motivate an infant to engage in vocalization and tactile exploration. Otherwise, infants may be in the Little Room for extended periods without supervision and thus may have fewer opportunities for social learning experiences (Dote-Kwan & Chen, 1995).

Another program, the Contingency Intervention Project (Brinker & Lewis, 1982), found that the responses of infants with mild, moderate, and profound retardation and multiple disabilities increased when stimulation (visual or auditory stimulation by mothers' faces, voices, or music) was contingent on the infants moving their arms or legs. A number of studies have reported that contingent stimulation experiences through interactions with caregivers and toys facilitate the attention, interaction, and communication of infants who have disabilities (Dunst et al., 1985; Field, 1978; Holdgrafer & Dunst, 1986). These findings demonstrate the influence of contingent learning experiences on infants' learning and development.

IMPLICATIONS FOR INTERVENTION

Interventions Focused on Interactions Between Caregivers and Infants

The research that has been discussed thus far in this chapter has significant implications for the types of interventions practitioners use with infants who are visually impaired and have other disabilities. Given the evidence that underscores the significance of responsive caregiving in the early development of typical infants and infants with disabilities, several early intervention programs have focused on interactions between caregivers and infants (Aydlett, 1993; Badger, Edwards, & Burns, 1981; Bromwich, 1981; Clark & Seifer, 1983, 1985; Mahoney & Powell, 1984; Mahoney, Robinson, & Powell, 1992), with successful outcomes. Caregivers of infants who are at a high risk or are developmentally delayed have developed mutually enjoyable interactions by interpreting their infant's signals and modifying their own interactive behaviors to match their infants' abilities (Bromwich, 1981; Field, 1978, 1979, 1982; McCollum, 1984; McCollum & Stayton, 1985).

Early intervention programs with infants who are visually impaired, including those with additional disabilities, have also emphasized such interactions (Chen et al., 1990, 1998; Fraiberg, 1974; Klein, Van Hasselt, Trefelner, Sandstrom, & Brandt-Snyder, 1988). A program with infants with severe and profound disabilities developed interventions to promote caregiver responsiveness, for example, by helping caregivers to identify and respond to infants' cries and other signals (Calhoun & Rose, 1988; Calhoun, Rose, & Prendergast, 1991). Therefore, interactions between caregivers and infants are an appropriate context for promoting the development of infants with visual impairments and additional disabilities.

Contingency Experiences and Intervention Practices

Although studies have found that both infants with disabilities and those without disabilities can perceive relationships between their behavior and contingency experiences (Brinker & Lewis, 1982; Dunst et al., 1985; Spence, 1991; Sullivan & Lewis, 1990), these learning opportunities are more difficult to provide for those infants whose disabilities influence their interactive behaviors. Many infants who are premature, visually impaired, or medically fragile may undergo lengthy hospital stays and other medical interventions that disrupt typical experiences (Glass, 1993; Lueck et al., 1997). Infants with severe and multiple disabilities have frequent experiences, such as medical interventions for their survival and health, over which they have no control and that may be painful or otherwise unpleasant.

Furthermore, many infants with visual impairments and additional disabilities have restricted access to environmental cues by which to understand an activity and limited means by which they can make their needs and preferences known to their caregivers. For instance, they may live in an unpredictable world where people and objects suddenly appear and disappear. They may be picked up, fed, placed in a crib, picked up, undressed, bathed, dressed, and left alone, without any opportunity to indicate their preferences, make choices, or participate in any way. Moreover, the behaviors of these infants may be subtle or difficult to interpret. As a result of the diagnoses of the infants' disabilities and the infants' lack of typical responses, their caregivers may be less responsive to the infants when their attempts to engage them continue to be unsuccessful. Hence, the infants receive few contingent responses to their behavior and do not learn that they can control the social environment. Consequently, they become more passive and disinterested in the world.

At the same time, early intervention programs may implement noncontingent or passive sensory stimulation activities with these infants. Noncontingent stimulation refers to sensory stimulation that is independent of an infant's behavior. For example, the music and movement of a musical mobile that is activated by winding it up or turning an "on" switch is not contingent on an infant's attention or actions. Unfortunately, many early intervention programs use repetitive presentations of noncontingent and artificial stimulation in activities with infants who have severe and multiple disabilities. These activities may include shaking a rattle to the side of an infant's head to encourage the baby to locate the source of sound, shaking a tinsel pom-pom or moving a flashlight in front of the infant to encourage visual attention and tracking, or manipulating the infant's hands to spread paint on paper to encourage the infant to play with finger paints (Chen & Haney, 1995). As studies with newborns and nondisabled infants have shown, an emphasis on noncontingent sensory stimulation is likely to decrease, rather than increase, infants' motivation and ability to learn. In effect, consistent and prolonged experiences with noncontingent stimulation are likely to increase passivity in infants with disabilities and decrease their active participation in learning opportunities (Dunst & Lesko, 1988).

Infants whose severe and multiple disabilities include visual impairment usually require interventions that encourage them to use their available senses and participate in everyday activities. The purpose of these interventions is to provide access to sensory information that the infants need to stimulate their curiosity and motivate them to interact and to develop concepts, communication, play, movement, and other developmental skills. The ultimate goal of these sensory stimulation activities is to enable the infants to become more active participants in their families and related communities. With this goal in mind, early interventionists should evaluate whether activities provide noncontingent or contingent stimulation and will contribute to a meaningful outcome for the infants.

Sensory Stimulation: Vision, Hearing, and Touch

Sensory stimulation is defined as an arousal of one or more of the senses. The previous section on contingency stimulation emphasized the importance of providing opportunities for infants who have multiple disabilities to elicit sensory stimulation through their actions. It is equally important for early interventionists to observe how an infant responds to familiar sensory stimulation to determine whether he or she is developing an understanding of what is heard, seen, or touched, as appropriate for his or her abilities. For example, does an infant with low vision recognize his or her mother's face? How does a blind infant react to his or her father's voice? How does an infant respond when he or she touches the parent's face? Sidebar 2.1 presents a hierarchy of responses to visual, auditory, or tactile stimulation that is a synthesis of several sources (Barraga, 1976; Hall & Bailey, 1989; Northern & Downs 1991). This hierarchy provides a framework that early interventionists can use to evaluate the infant's learning and development. In many cases, careful observations of an infant's responses to everyday stimuli (such as caregivers, family members, activities, foods, and toys) will reveal when the infant is attending to some types of stimuli and may be recognizing others. These observations may also provide information on the types of sensory stimulation that are most meaningful and accessible to an infant.

In general, sensory stimulation should be provided by using real, preferred, and meaningful stimuli (people, sounds, objects, toys, and other familiar objects) within natural contexts; by encouraging the infant to look, listen, and touch, when appropriate; by reducing sensory "noise" (visual clutter and background sounds) to allow the infant to attend to critical features; by following the infant's interests; and by adding words or cues to actions, when appropriate. Interventions that are focused on stimulating infants with multiple disabilities to use their available senses should occur in natural activities that are both developmentally and individually appropriate for them (Chen, 1996; Chen & Dote-Kwan, 1998; Dote-Kwan & Chen, 1995; Ferrell & Muir, 1996). Most important, sensory stimulation should be presented consistently as a consequence of a specific behavior of the infant in an effort to contribute to the infant's motivation to explore and interact with the environment.

Hand-Over-Hand Guidance

Because of their limited behavioral repertoire, infants who have multiple and severe disabilities are subjected to noncontingent experiences when they are physically manipulated through activities without any regard for their preferences or abilities. For example, "hand-over-hand" guidance (the placement of an adult's hand over an infant's) is used frequently in programs. It involves an adult communicating with an infant or showing him or her an object or how to do something, by guiding his or her hands (Freeman, 1985; McGinnes & Treffery, 1982) through an action, such as pressing a switch, taking off a shoe, or picking up a

Sidebar 2.1 HIERARCHY OF RESPONSES TO VISUAL, AUDITORY, OR TACTILE STIMULI

Awareness/reflexive reaction   At this level, an infant's responses to stimuli involve changes in body movement, such as the startle response (extending the arms and legs and then bringing them close to the body in response to a sudden noise or movement), blinking the eyes at the rapid approach of a visual stimuli to the face, slowing or accelerating respiration, tensing the body, and increasing or decreasing activity. These behaviors may occur at the brainstem level; they indicate reflexive responses or an awareness of stimuli but are not indicators of learning.

Attention/Alerting   These responses indicate that the infant is attending to the stimuli. Behaviors include smiling, frowning or fussing, moving the body toward or away from the source of stimulation, reaching for or grasping the stimulus, changing the quality of vocalization, and moving the fingers to explore the stimulus. If artificial visual stimuli (pom-poms, tinsel, or colored lights) or auditory stimuli (bells, horns, or drums) are needed initially to gain the infant's attention, they must be replaced as quickly as possible with more meaningful and natural stimuli (the baby's bottle or the caregiver's face or voice) to promote the infant's interaction with the environment.

Discrimination   Discrimination behaviors include responding differently to significant caregivers, familiar and unfamiliar voices, and favorite toys and showing preferences for particular people, objects, and activities. For example, babies who fuss when a pediatrician picks them up and calms down when their mothers hold them are displaying discrimination behaviors. These responses indicate that the infants are learning about the characteristics of various stimuli.

Recognition   These responses indicate that an infant is able not only to discriminate differences between stimuli, but to recognize familiar stimuli. Behaviors include recognizing a familiar object, such as putting the bottle in the mouth; turning toward the caregiver in anticipation of a familiar game; responding to his or her name; stopping an activity when told no; following simple directions like "give me a kiss"; and performing simple actions in games, such as raising the arms for "so big" and imitating vocalization; responding with gestures to "bye bye," or "up"; and pointing to a common object or picture when it is named (Barraga, 1976; Hall & Bailey, 1989; Northern & Downs, 1991).

cookie. This hand-over-hand approach should be used with sensitivity to the infant's reactions. Some infants dislike having their hands manipulated and are threatened by the lack of control. Others become passive and learn to wait for the adult's hand on theirs as a prompt to initiate an action. Another term for hand-over-hand guidance is coactive manipulation (MacFarland, 1995).

Hand-under-hand guidance (the placement of an adult's hand under a child's hand) is a less intrusive approach (MacFarland, 1995). Although this method may be easily used with older children, it is more difficult to use with infants because it assumes that the infants are motivated to keep their hands on top of the adult's hands. Strategies for implementing hand-over-hand and hand-under-hand guidance are presented in Chapter 8, "Developing Meaningful Interventions." Systematic interventions are required to give infants with visual impairments and additional disabilities experiences to develop a sense of control over the social environment and to help their caregivers engage in enjoyable interactions with the infants and to develop confidence in their caregiving abilities.

Massage of Infants

Recently, massage has become a popular intervention with infants with multiple disabilities, including those who are visually impaired. The therapeutic value of massage has been recognized for centuries and is common, particularly with infants in other cultures (McClure, 1989). Massaging infants has been promoted by the International Association of Infant Massage Instructors and as a strategy to encourage social interaction and emotional attachment between caregivers and infants. A review of relevant research (Schneider, 1996) indicated that massage has positive effects on infants who are premature, were prenatally exposed to cocaine, and have motor disabilities. In general, the infants gained weight and their caregivers' interactions with them were more positive after massage. Through massage, caregivers learn to interpret their infants' signals, of, for example, pleasure and displeasure, drowsiness, and alertness. Massage is a method of predictable sensory stimulation for infants that builds an intimate relationship between infants and their caregivers. Infant-caregiver interaction is enhanced by activities that are pleasurable to both infants and caregivers.

SUGGESTIONS FOR INTERVENTIONS TO ASSIST CAREGIVERS

Early interventionists should assist caregivers in identifying their infants' communicative behaviors and cues indicating a readiness for interaction, games, or play routines that both the babies and adults enjoy and natural ways of responding contingently to infants' behaviors that the infants will perceive (Klein, Chen, & Haney, in press). Through careful observations, caregivers can become accurate and responsive interpreters of their infants' behaviors and develop mutually enjoyable interactions. In other words, the caregivers will learn to identify the types of sensory stimulation that their infants prefer and the ways to provide stimulation that are elicited by the infants' actions. The following are suggestions that interventionists can offer caregivers to promote interactions with their infants and to increase contingency experiences:

1. *Identify and Interpret Infants' Cues*

    Observe the infant and identify the infant's range of behaviors and nonverbal cues. For example, what does the infant do when he or she is alert, tired, hungry, wants interaction, or needs to rest? Some infants use subtle cues (such as a change in muscle tone), while others use clear signals (like crying or quiet attentiveness). Some behaviors (for example, a facial grimace of an infant with spastic cerebral palsy that may indicate pleasure or displeasure) are difficult to interpret without careful observation and knowing the infant well.

2. *Identify When the Infant Is Active or Alert and Ready for Interaction*

    Observe the infant's behavioral states (discussed in Chapter 3) during the daily routine. Note when the infant is alert (the time of day and during which activities) to take advantage of those opportunities for learning and interaction. For example, some infants are more interactive after lunch, whereas others prefer to nap.

3. *Respond Contingently to the Infant's Behaviors*

    Identify an infant's interest on the basis of subtle nonverbal signals (such as a calm, quiet, or alert state; hand movements or body orientation toward the object or person; or quiet vocalizations). Respond to these signals in a way that supports the infant's interaction and promotes turn taking; for example, move the object to touch the infant's hand, touch or pick up the infant, and imitate the infant's vocalizations.

4. *Identify the Infant's Preferences for Stimulation*

   Identify whether the infant responds to visual, auditory, tactile, olfactory, or kinesthetic stimuli during natural situations. Does the infant prefer brightly colored, shiny, or high-contrast objects or toys with lights? Does the infant attend to familiar voices, songs or other music on audiotape, or toys that make sounds? Does the infant enjoy tickling games, massage, or touching and handling objects? Does the infant seem interested in the odors of foods, soaps, and lotions? Does the infant enjoy finger plays, movement, or rough-and-tumble games? Observe the infant's responses to a variety of sensory cues by, for instance, having the adult tap his or her fingers on the highchair tray to encourage the infant to pick up small crackers; having the infant smell the shampoo before putting it on his or her hair; gently rocking the baby before putting him or her in a hammock; or having the adult clap his or her hands before holding them out for the infant to anticipate being picked up.

5. *Provide Contingent Sensory Stimulation*

   Carefully observe the infant's behaviors and provide preferred sensory stimulation that is contingent on the infant's particular actions. For example, when the baby vocalizes, respond consistently by imitating the sound and touching the infant; after diapering the baby, wait for the baby to reach out before picking him or her up; wait for the infant to look at the red puppet before making it dance; and wait for the infant to move his or her body before pushing the swing. In addition, provide toys and adaptive switches that the infant can activate easily to produce vibration, lights, movement, or music.

6. *Create Individualized Games that Both the Caregiver and Infant Enjoy*

   Identify opportunities within the daily routine that are natural times for playing individualized games, such as peek-a-boo using a washcloth during bathtime; riding the horsey while the infant is sitting on caregiver's lap; or tickling the tummy when the baby is being diapered.

7. *Use Favorite Activities*

   Begin with activities that are familiar to and preferred by the infant to provide opportunities for contingent stimulation and for the infant to realize that he or she can influence the adult's response. During familiar activities (like massage, riding horsey, rough-and-tumble or movement games, or mealtimes), pause and wait for the infant to indicate, through a body movement or vocalization, that he or she wants the activity to continue. Once the infant is familiar with the massage routine, the caregiver may pause to see whether the infant anticipates the next step in the routine or in some way requests that the massage continue. Begin the horsey ride and then pause and wait for the infant to request "more horsey ride." Learning experiences that are contingent, or dependent, on an infant's behavior are activities that naturally follow the infant's signals and interest and involve his or her active participation. Mealtime can become a contingency experience for an infant who loves to eat. The infant will be motivated to request another spoonful of applesauce by opening his or her mouth, saying "more," or signing MORE. The infant can also indicate a choice between applesauce and apple juice by reaching for the spoon rather than the cup.

8. *Decrease Hand-Over-Hand Guidance, or Coactive Manipulation*
After physically manipulating the infant through an activity a few times, guide the infant through the initial movement and then wait for a behavior to indicate an expectation of what will occur next. For example, place the infant's hand on a switch, remove your hand, wait for an indication (such as a finger movement) that the infant wants to activate the switch, and then provide the assistance. This strategy will be effective only if the infant likes the activity, so it is essential to choose a preferred sensory event (auditory, tactile, or visual). Furthermore, the switch should be the easiest type for the infant to activate, given his or her motor ability. Similarly, with other familiar activities, stop after initially positioning the infant and wait for the infant to indicate what will happen next. For example, place the infant on a large ball; wait for the infant's behavior, such as patting the ball, before bouncing the infant on the ball. If the infant does not respond, assist the infant to pat the ball. As physical guidance is gradually decreased, the infant will discover that he or she can elicit a reaction from the environment or make something happen.

9. *Provide Opportunities to Make Choices*
Offer choices during natural situations, such as between food or drink or between two toys. At first, an infant may choose to participate or not to participate in a specific activity at a particular time or to eat

or not to eat the particular food that is offered. When possible, the caregiver's responsiveness to the infant's preferences will assist the infant in learning that he or she can affect the environment. Next, an infant may develop an understanding that he or she can make a choice between a preferred and a disliked object like food. Finally, an infant will be able to choose between two preferred objects or activities. Through these experiences, the infant will learn that his or her behaviors can elicit a response from the caregiver.

THE COMPLEXITY OF THE CAREGIVING ENVIRONMENT

The caregiving environment of an infant may be composed of a number of adults or older children who contribute to the infant's care. Families vary along many dimensions, including size and form, cultural background and values, socioeconomic status, and educational level. Families also vary in their styles of interaction, the roles and responsibilities of members, and where they are in the family life cycle (Turnbull & Turnbull, 1997). The characteristics of a particular family influence not only the nature of caregiving and child-rearing practices, but the members' attitudes toward the infant's disability and expectations of early interventionists. For example, a single parent's concerns (such as being isolated and totally responsible for the infant's care) are likely to be different from those of a mother and father who live with a large extended family. The caregiving concerns of a family at a subsistence level will be different from those of a family who has more socioeconomic resources (McCollum & McBride, 1997).

Although an early interventionist may interact mainly with one family member and the infant, he or she should find opportunities to obtain a wider perspective on the family's concerns and resources related to the infant's care and development. For instance, the infant may usually receive a bath from grandmother and may be fed by an aunt, mother, or an older sibling. Therefore, suggestions for intervention need to be tailored to fit the family's structure, routines, and caregiving responsibilities. For example, in some households encouraging communication with infants during meals is not an appropriate suggestion because these families believe the purpose of mealtimes is to eat food, not to engage in social interactions.

CONCLUSION

Early interventionists need to recognize the tremendous amounts of energy and emotion that families devote to early intervention services for their infants who have multiple disabilities and visual impairments. They serve as a resource by offering observations and information that assist families in negotiating the complicated maze of medical and intervention systems. However, they need to understand the primary role of the family in an infant's development and the infant's influence on the family to work more effectively with infants and their families. By doing so, early interventionists can help families support their infants' development by enhancing the caregiving environment and the family's interactions with the infant.

REFERENCES

Ainsworth, M. D. S. (1969). Object relations, dependency, and attachment: A theoretical review of the infant-mother relationship. *Child Development, 40,* 969–1025.

Ainsworth, M. D. S., Blehar, M. C., Waters, E., & Wall, S. (1978). *Patterns of attachment.* Hillsdale, NJ: Lawrence Erlbaum.

Als, H., Tronick, E., & Brazelton, T. B. (1980). Affective reciprocity and the development of autonomy: The study of a blind infant. *Journal of the American Academy of Child Psychiatry, 19,* 22–40.

Aydlett, L. A. (1993). Assessing infant interaction skills in interaction-focused intervention. *Infants and Young Children, 5*(4), 1–7.

Badger, E., Edwards, S., & Burns, S. (1981). A cognitive-linguistic intervention model for mother-infant pairs: Birth-to-three. *Infant Mental Health Journal, 2,* 95–107.

Baird, S. M., Mayfield, P., & Baker, P. (1997). Mother's interpretations of their infants with visual impairments and other disabilities during interactions. *Journal of Visual Impairment & Blindness, 91,* 467–483.

Barraga, N. (1976). *Visual handicaps and learning. A developmental approach.* Belmont, CA: Wadsworth.

Blasco, P. M., Hrncir, E. J., & Blasco, P. A. (1990). The contribution of maternal involvement to mastery performance in infants with cerebral palsy. *Journal of Early Intervention, 14,* 161–174.

Blehar, M. C., Leiberman, A. F., & Ainsworth, M. D. S. (1977) Early face-to-face interaction and its relation to later infant-mother attachment. *Child Development, 48,* 182–194.

Brinker, R. P., & Lewis, M. (1982). Discovering the competent handicapped infant: A process approach to assessment and intervention. *Topics in Early Childhood Special Education, 2,* 1–16.

Bromwich, R. (1981). *Working with parents: An interactional approach.* Baltimore, MD: University Park Press.

Brown, J. V., & Bakeman, R. (1980). Relationships of human mothers with their infants during the first year of life: Effects of prematurity. In R. W. Bell & W. P. Smotherman (Eds.), *Maternal influences and early behavior* (pp. 353–373). Jamaica, NY: Spectrum.

Buckhalt, J. A., Rutherford, R. B., & Goldberg, K. E. (1978). Verbal and nonverbal interaction of mothers with their Down's syndrome and normal infants. *American Journal of Mental Deficiency, 82,* 337–343.

Burlingham, D. (1974). To be blind in a sighted world. *Psychoanalytic Study of the Child, 34,* 5–29.

Butterfield, E. C., & Siperstein, G. N. (1972). Influences of contingent auditory stimulation upon nonnutritional sucking. In J. Bosma (Ed.), *Oral sensation and perception: The mouth of the infant* (pp. 313–334). Springfield, IL: Charles C Thomas.

Calhoun, M. L., & Rose, T. L. (1988). Social reciprocity interventions with infants with severe retardation: Current findings and implications for the future. *Education and Training of the Mentally Retarded, 23,* 340–343.

Calhoun, M. L., Rose, T. L., & Prendergast, D. (1991). *Charlotte Circle Curriculum Guide.* Tucson, AZ: Communication Skill Builders.

California Infant Mental Health Work Group. (1996). *Executive summary: Recommendations for screening, assessment, service delivery and training related to the promotion of infant social and emotional mental health for all providers of education, health and human services to infants, toddlers and their families.* Sacramento, CA: Author.

Carnegie Corporation of New York. (1994). *Starting points. Meeting the needs of our youngest children.* New York: Author.

Chen, D. (1996). Parent-infant communication: Early intervention for very young children with visual impairment or hearing loss. *Infants and Young Children, 9*(1), 1–12.

Chen, D., & Dote-Kwan, J. (1998). Early intervention services for young children with visual impairments and other disabilities and their families. In S. Sacks & R. Silberman (Eds.), *Educating students with visual impairments and other disabilities* (pp. 303–338). Baltimore, MD: Paul H. Brookes.

Chen, D., Friedman, C. T., & Calvello, G. (1990). *Learning together. A parent guide to socially based routines for visually impaired infants.* Louisville, KY: American Printing House for the Blind.

Chen, D., & Haney, M. (1995). An early intervention model for infants who are deaf-blind. *Journal of Visual Impairment & Blindness, 89,* 212–221.

Chen, D., Haney, M., Klein, M. D., & Alsop, L. (1998). Learning how to PLAI. In *The Canadian Deaf-Blind and Rubella Association Conference Proceedings*, August 12—15, 1998, Mississauga, Ontario, Canada. Brantford, ON: Canadian Deaf-Blind and Rubella Association.

Clark, G., & Seifer, R. (1983). Facilitating mother-infant communication: A treatment model for high-risk and developmentally-delayed infants. *Infant Mental Health Journal, 4*, 67–82.

Clark, G. N., & Seifer, R. (1985). Assessment of parents' interactions with their developmentally delayed infants. *Infant Mental Health Journal, 6*, 214–225.

Crawley, S. F., & Spiker, D. (1983). Mother-child interactions involving two-year-olds with Down syndrome: A look at individual differences. *Child Development, 54*, 1312–1323.

DeCasper, A. J., & Carstens, A. A. (1981). Contingencies of stimulation: Effects on learning and emotion in neonates. *Infant Behavior and Development, 4*, 19–35.

Dote-Kwan, J. (1995). Impact of mothers' interactions on the development of their young visually impaired children. *Journal of Visual Impairment & Blindness, 89,* 47–58.

Dote-Kwan, J., & Chen, D. (1995). Learners with visual impairments. In M. C. Wang & M. C. Reynolds (Eds.), *Handbook of special and remedial education: Research and practice* (2nd ed., pp. 205–228). Oxford, England: Elsevier Science.

Dunst, C. J., Cushing, P. J., & Vance, S. (1985). Response-contingent learning in profoundly handicapped infants: A social systems perspective, *Analysis and Intervention in Developmental Disabilities, 5*, 33–47.

Dunst, C. J., & Lesko, J. (1988). Promoting the active learning capabilities of young children with handicaps. *Early Childhood Intervention Monograph* (Vol. 1). Morganton, NC: Family, Infant and Preschool Program, Western Carolina Center.

Erikson, E. H. (1963). *Childhood and society* (2nd ed.). New York: W. W. Norton.

Ferrell, K. A., & Muir, D. W. (1996). A call to end vision stimulation training. *Journal of Visual Impairment & Blindness, 90*, 364–366.

Field, T. M. (1978). The three R's of infant-adult interactions: Rhythms, repertoires and responsivity. *Journal of Pediatric Psychology, 3*, 131–136.

Field, T. M. (1979). Games parents play with normal and high-risk infants. *Child Psychiatry and Human Development, 10*, 41–48.

Field, T. M. (1982). Interaction coaching for high-risk infants and their parents. In H. A. Moss, R. Hess, & C. Swift (Eds.), *Prevention in human services* (pp. 5–24). New York: Haworth Press.

Fincham, F. D., & Cain, K. M. (1986). Learned helplessness in humans: A developmental analysis. *Developmental Review, 6*, 301–333.

Fraiberg, S. (1974). Blind infants and their mothers: An examination of the sign system. In M. Lewis & L. A. Rosenblum (Eds.). *The effect of the infant on its caregiver* (pp. 215–232). New York: John Wiley & Sons.

Fraiberg, S. (1977). *Insights from the blind.* New York: Basic Books.

Freeman, P. (1985). *The deaf-blind baby: A programme of care.* London, England: William Heinemann Medical Books.

Glass, P. (1993). Development of visual function in preterm infants: Implications for early intervention. *Infants and Young Children, 6*(1), 11–20.

Goldberg, S. (1977). Social competency in infancy: A model of parent-infant interaction. *Merrill-Palmer Quarterly, 23,* 163–177.

Greenberg, M., Calderon, R., & Kusche, C. (1984). Early intervention using simultaneous communication with deaf infants. *Child Development, 55,* 607–616.

Greenspan, S. I., & Greenspan, N. T. (1985). *First feelings: Milestones in the emotional development of your baby and child from birth to age four.* New York: Viking Penguin.

Hadadian, A. (1996). Attachment relationships and its significance for young children with disabilities. *Infant-Toddler Intervention, 6,* 1–16.

Hall, A., & Bailey, I. L. (1989). A model for training vision functioning. *Journal of Visual Impairment & Blindness, 83,* 390–396.

Hanson, M. J., & Hanline, M. F. (1985). An analysis of response-contingent learning experiences for young children. *Journal of the Association for Persons with Severe Handicaps., 10,* 31–40.

Holdgrafer, G., & Dunst, C. J. (1986). Communicative competence: From research to practice. *Topics in Early Childhood Special Education, 6,* 1–22.

Hyvarinen, L. (1988). *Vision in children: Normal and abnormal.* Meaford, ON. Canada: Canadian Deaf-Blind and Rubella Association.

Klein, M. D., Chen, D., & Haney, M. (in press). *PLAI: An early curriculum: Facilitating caregiver-infant interactions.* Baltimore, MD: Paul H. Brookes.

Klein, B., Van Hasselt, V. B., Trefelner, M., Sandstrom, D. J., & Brandt-Snyder, P. (1988). The parent and toddler training project for visually impaired and blind multihandicapped children. *Journal of Visual Impairment & Blindness, 82,* 59–62.

Kogan, K. L., Tyler, N., & Turner, P. (1974). The process of interpersonal adaptation between mothers and their cerebral palsied children. *Developmental Medicine and Child Neurology, 16,* 518–527.

Lewis, J., & Goldberg, S. (1969). Perceptual-cognitive development in infancy: A generalized expectancy model as a function of the mother-infant interaction. *Merrill-Palmer Quarterly, 15,* 81–100.

Lewis, M. (1978). The infant and its caregiver: The role of contingency. *Allied Health and Behavioral Sciences, 1,* 469–492.

Lewis, M., Sullivan, M., Brooks-Gunn, J. (1985). Emotional behavior during the learning contingency in early infancy. *British Journal of Developmental Psychology, 3,* 307–316.

Londerville, S., & Main, M. (1981). Security of attachment, compliance and maternal training methods in the second year of life. *Developmental Psychology, 17,* 289–299.

Lueck, A. H., Chen, D., & Kekelis, L. (1997). *Developmental guidelines for infants with visual impairments. A manual for early intervention.* Louisville, KY: American Printing House for the Blind.

Maestas y Moores, J. (1980). Early linguistic environment: Interactions of deaf parents with their infants. *Sign Language Studies, 26,* 1–13.

MacFarland, S. Z. C. (1995). Teaching strategies of the van Dijk curricular approach. *Journal of Visual Impairment & Blindness, 89,* 222–228.

Mahoney, G. (1983). A developmental analysis of communication between mothers and infants with Down syndrome. *Topics in Early Childhood Special Education, 3,* 63–76.

Mahoney, G. (1988). Communication patterns between mothers and mentally retarded infants. *First Language, 8,* 157–171.

Mahoney, G., Boyce, G., Fewell, R. R., Spiker, D., & Wheeden, C. A. (1998). The relationship of parent-child interaction to the effectiveness of early intervention services for at-risk children and children with disabilities. *Topics in Early Childhood Special Education, 18,* 5–17.

Mahoney, G., Finger, I., & Powell, A. (1985). The relationship of maternal behavioral style to the developmental status of organically impaired mentally retarded infants. *American Journal of Mental Deficiency, 90,* 296–302.

Mahoney, G., & Powell, A. (1984). *The transactional intervention program.* Woodhaven, MI: Woodhaven School District.

Mahoney, G., Robinson C., & Powell, A. (1992). Focusing on parent-child interaction: The bridge to developmentally appropriate practices. *Topics in Early Childhood Special Education, 12,* 105–120.

Maier, S. F., & Seligman, M. E. P. (1976). Learned helplessness: Theory and evidence. *Journal of Experimental Psychology: General, 105,* 3–46.

McClure, V. S. (1989). *Infant massage. A parent handbook for loving parents* (rev. ed.). New York: Bantam Books.

McCollum, J. A. (1984). Social interaction between parents and babies: Validation of an intervention model. *Child: Care, Health, and Development, 10,* 301–315.

McCollum, J. A., & McBride, S. L. (1997). Ratings of parent-infant interactions: Raising questions of cultural validity. *Topics in Early Childhood Special Education, 17,* 494–519.

McCollum, J. A., & Stayton, V. (1985). Infant/parent interaction: Studies and intervention guidelines based on the SIAI model. *Journal of the Division for Early Childhood, 9,* 125–135.

McGinnes, J., & Treffrey, J. (1982). *Deaf-blind infants and children: A developmental guide.* Toronto: University of Toronto Press.

Michael, M. G., & Paul, P. V. (1991). Early intervention for infants with deaf-blindness. *Exceptional Children, 57,* 200–210.

Nielsen, L. (1992a). *Educational approaches for visually impaired children.* Copenhagen, Denmark: SIKON.

Nielson, L. (1992b). *Space and self.* Copenhagen, Denmark: SIKON.

Northern, J. L., & Downs, M. P. (1991). *Hearing in children* (4th ed.). Baltimore, MD: Williams & Wilkins.

Power, D., Wood, D., Wood., H., & MacDougall, J. (1990). Maternal control over conversations with hearing and deaf infants and young children. *First Language, 10,* 19–35.

Resnick, M. B., Armstrong, S., & Carter, R. L. (1988). Developmental intervention program for high-risk infants: Effects of development and parent-infant interaction. *Developmental & Behavioral Pediatrics, 9,* 73–78.

Richards, N. B. (1986). Interaction between mothers and infants with Down syndrome: Infant characteristics. *Topics in Early Childhood Special Education, 6,* 54–71.

Rogers, S., & Puchalski, C. B. (1984). Social characteristics of visually impaired infant's play. *Topics in Early Childhood Special Education, 3,* 52–56.

Rogow, S. (1983). Social routines and language play: Developing communication responses in developmentally delayed blind children. *Journal of Visual Impairment & Blindness, 77,* 1–4.

Rowland, C. (1983). Patterns of interaction between three blind infants and their mothers. In A. E. Mills (Ed.), *Language acquisition in the blind child* (pp. 114–132). San Diego, CA: College Hill.

Rowland, C. (1984). Preverbal communication of blind infants and their mothers. *Journal of Visual Impairment & Blindness, 78,* 297–302.

Sameroff, A. J. (1982). The environmental context of developmental disabilities. In D. Bricker (Ed.), *Intervention with at-risk and handicapped infants: From research to application* (pp. 141–152). Baltimore, MD: University Park Press.

Sameroff, A. J. (1987). The social context of development. In N. Eisenberg (Ed.), *Contemporary topics in developmental psychology* (pp. 273–291). New York: John Wiley & Sons.

Sameroff, A. J., & Chandler, M. (1975). Reproductive risk and the continuum of caregiving causality. In F. Horowitz, M. Hetherington, S. Scarr-Salapatek, & G. Seigel (Eds.), *Review of Child Development Research* (Vol. 4, pp. 187–244). Chicago: University of Chicago Press.

Schneider, E. F. (1996). The power of touch: Massage for infants. *Infants and Young Children, 8*(3), 40–55.

Seligman, M. (1975). *Helplessness: On depression, development, and death.* San Francisco: W. H. Freeman.

Spence, M. (1991). Newborns' responsiveness to contingent stimulation: Implications for early intervention. *Infant-Toddler Intervention, 1,* 245–253.

Spencer, P., Bodner-Johnson, B., & Gutfreund, M. (1992). Interacting with infants with a hearing loss: What can we learn from mothers who are deaf? *Journal of Early Intervention, 16,* 64–78.

Stevenson, M. B., Leavitt, L. A., & Silverberg, S. B. (1985). Mother-infant interaction: Down syndrome case studies. In S. Harel & N. J. Anastasiow (Eds.), *The at-risk infant: Psycho/social aspects* (pp. 389–395). Baltimore, MD: Paul H. Brookes.

Sullivan, M. W., & Lewis, M. (1990). Contingency intervention: A program portrait. *Journal of Early Intervention, 14,* 367–375.

Sullivan, M. W., & Lewis, L. (1993). Contingency, means-end skills, and the use of technology in infant intervention. *Infants and Young Children, 5*(4), 58–77.

Tannock, R. (1988). Mothers' directiveness in their interactions with their children with and without Down syndrome. *American Journal of Mental Retardation, 93,* 154–165.

Teplin, S. W. (1995). Visual impairment in infants and young children. *Infants and Young Children, 8*(1), 18–51.

Thomas, A., & Chess, S. (1977). *Temperament and development.* New York: Brunner/Mazel.

Turnbull, A. P., & Turnbull, H. R. (1997). *Families, professionals and exceptionality. A special partnership* (3rd ed.). Upper Saddle River, NJ: Prentice Hall.

Urwin, C. (1983). Dialogue and cognitive functioning in the early language development of three blind children. In A. E. Mills (Ed.), *Language acquisition in the blind child* (pp. 142–161). San Diego, CA: College Hill Press.

Utley, B., Duncan., D., Strain, P., & Scanlon, K. (1983). Effects of contingent and noncontingent visual stimulation on visual fixation in multiply handicapped children. *Journal of the Association for Persons with Severe Handicaps, 8*(3), 29–42.

VandenBerg, K. A., & Hanson, M. J. (1993). *Homecoming for babies after the neonatal intensive care nursery. A guide for professionals in supporting families and their infants' early development.* Austin, TX: PRO-ED.

Walker, J. (1982). Social interactions of handicapped infants. In D. Bricker (Ed.), *Intervention with at-risk and handicapped infants: From research to application* (pp. 217–232). Austin, TX: PRO-ED.

Walker, J. A., & Kershman, S. M. (1981, April). Deaf-blind babies in social interaction: Questions of maternal adaptation. Paper presented at the biannual meeting of the Society for Research in Child Development, Boston.

Wasserman, G. A., Allen, R., & Soloman, C. R. (1985). At-risk toddlers and their mothers: The special case of physical handicaps. *Child Development, 56,* 73–83.

Wasserman, G. A., Lennon, M. C., Allen, R., & Shilansky, M. (1987). Contributions to attachment in normal and physically handicapped infants. *American Academy of Child and Adolescent Psychiatry, 26,* 9–15.

Watson, J. S. (1972). Smiling, cooing, and the "game." *Merrill-Palmer Quarterly, 18,* 323–339.

Watson, J. S. (1979). Perception of contingency as a determinant of social responsiveness. In E. Thoman (Ed.), *The origins of social responsiveness* (pp. 33–64). Hillsdale, NJ: Lawrence Erlbaum.

Watson, J. S., & Ramey, C. T. (1972). Reactions to response contingent stimulation early in infancy. *Merrill-Palmer Quarterly, 18,* 219–227.

Wedell-Monnig, J., & Lumley, J. (1980). Child deafness and mother-child interaction. *Child Development, 51,* 766–774.

3

Meeting the Intervention Needs of Infants

Deborah Chen

In recent years, researchers and service providers have reported an increase in the number of infants who are visually impaired and have additional disabilities. The combination of a visual impairment with another disability places an infant's early development at even greater risk than if the infant has only a visual impairment and requires skilled early intervention practices. Early interventionists have the professional responsibility to acquire knowledge of the potential influence of various disabilities on early development and skills that will assist families in promoting their infants' development. In working with infants who have multiple disabilities, an early interventionist has three primary tasks:

- to become familiar with the diagnoses and learning needs of an individual infant
- to develop a process for gathering and sharing information with families and other professionals
- to implement strategies with each family that address the specific learning needs of the infant and fit the family's concerns and values

To assist early interventionists in their work, this chapter discusses relevant research on infants with visual impairments and additional disabilities; describes common diagnoses that occur with visual impairment before age 36 months, identifies typical interventions that are used with these diagnoses, and presents implications for early intervention practices with infants who have other disabilities in addition to visual impairments. Because of their association with visual impairment and multiple disabilities, mental retardation, prematurity, seizure disorders, cerebral palsy, hearing loss, and autism are reviewed. The goal of this chapter is to provide basic information that will enable early interventionists to work effectively with infants who have multiple disabilities, their families, and other service providers.

INFANTS WHO ARE VISUALLY IMPAIRED AND HAVE ADDITIONAL DISABILITIES

Infants who are visually impaired and have additional disabilities are an extremely diverse group. First, they include children with many different diagnoses, such as, retinopathy of prematurity (ROP; changes to the retinas of premature infants caused by damage to the blood vessels of the eyes from prolonged exposure to oxygen), cortical visual impairment, optic nerve hypoplasia, cataracts, or refractive errors (Bishop, 1991; Ferrell et al., 1990; Hoon, 1996; see also the Appendix). The source of vision loss may be a problem in the eye, optic nerve, or brain or related to damage to the central nervous system (Teplin, 1995), as discussed in Chapter 4. Second, the term *visual impairment* includes a range of vision loss. One infant who is visually impaired may be legally blind and have some functional vision, whereas another may have no light perception. Third, common disabilities that are associated with visual impairment differ widely; they include developmental disabilities or mental retardation, cerebral palsy, hearing loss, autism, seizures, and other medical needs (Bishop, 1991; Hatton, Bailey, Burchinal, & Ferrell, 1997; Teplin, 1995). Fourth, there is great variation in the severity of each of these other disabilities, in how they interact with a visual impairment, and the effects of the co-occurrence of two or more disabilities on early development.

Given the heterogeneity of the population, it is not surprising to find little research on the effects of visual impairment with additional disabilities on early development. Two studies have reported that the combination of visual impairment with another disability has significant developmental consequences. Ferrell et al.'s (1990) retrospective study involving interviews with parents revealed that infants with visual impairments and additional disabilities attained selected developmental milestones later than did infants with visual impairments and no other disabilities (Ferrell et al., 1990). About half the infants with additional disabilities had cerebral palsy, seizures, or other neurological problems, and other disabilities included hearing loss, multiple disabilities, and developmental delays. Hatton et al.'s (1997) study found that mental retardation or developmental delay (MR/DD) occurred in 40 percent of the infants and young children with visual impairments and that these infants had not only lower developmental levels but slower developmental rates than did the children with visual impairment alone. All the children with MR/DD had 20/200 vision or worse, and 50 percent to 60 percent had 20/800 vision or worse; none had vision between 20/70 and 20/199. The findings of these two studies suggest that a severe central nervous system disorder may be the underlying cause of visual impairments and developmental delays in children with multiple disabilities. They support the impressions of early interventionists that infants with visual impairments and additional disabilities have more significant developmental delays than do infants who are visually impaired alone.

Infants with severe and multiple disabilities are more likely to have visual impairment than is any other group of infants receiving early intervention services. The combination of visual impairments and additional disabilities in infancy is associated with a number of causes that occur prenatally (before birth) or perinatally (at birth) (See the Appendix to Chapter 4 for more information about many of these conditions). During pregnancy, so-called TORCH infections (*t*oxoplasmosis, syphilis and *o*ther infections, *r*ubella, *c*ytomegalovirus, and *h*erpes) and other infections may affect fetuses and result in neurological impairments, visual impairments, hearing loss, and/or developmental delay (Hutchinson & Sandall, 1995; Lowenthal, 1997). Birth complications involving the loss of oxygen (hypoxia) and being born too soon and too small (prematurity) can have negative effects on infants' vision and other areas of development. Hypoxia may cause cortical visual impairment (Good et al., 1994), seizures, cerebral palsy, and severe mental retardation (McCormick, 1989). Extreme prematurity may result in visual impairment that is due to ROP, cortical visual impairment, refractive errors, and other eye problems (Glass, 1993; Hoon, 1996), as well as mental retardation, cerebral palsy, hearing loss, and various medical needs (Goldson, 1996). The increase in the number of infants whose multiple disabilities include visual impairment is associated with medical advances in neonatal intensive care (Trief, Duckman, Morse, & Silberman, 1989) that have increased the survival rate of infants with low birthweights (Goldson, 1996) and infants who are medically fragile.

Studies of young children who are visually impaired have indicated that 40 percent to 70 percent of them have additional disabilities (Bishop, 1991; Dietz & Ferrell, 1993; Ferrell, 1998; Hyvarinen, 1988; Kirchner, 1989). Conversely, research on children with severe or profound disabilities has reported that 42 percent to 90 percent of them have visual impairments (Cress et al., 1981; Jacobson & Janicki, 1985). Infants with cerebral palsy, Down syndrome, and other genetic conditions associated with mental retardation have a higher incidence of refractive errors, cortical visual impairment, and other ophthalmological problems than do those without disabilities (Capute & Accardo, 1996; Hoon, 1996; Rogers, Roizen, & Capone; 1996; Wesson & Maino, 1995).

BEGINNING INTERVENTION WITH INFANTS WITH VISUAL IMPAIRMENTS AND DEVELOPMENTAL DELAYS

Early interventionists should begin their work with an infant and his or her family by obtaining a view of the infant from available reports, interviews with parents and other caregivers, and observations and interactions with the infant. By reviewing records, the early interventionist gains information about the infant's developmental levels; whether the infant and family have received other services; and if so, what interventions have been used previously. It is helpful to review the records about the infant before one meets the family so as to have some knowledge about the infant and family and thus to be able to plan for the visit with them. First, the family's primary concerns about their infant's developmental needs should be identified. These concerns may have been documented on the Individualized Family Service Plan; if not, the early interventionist may need to inquire about the family's concerns, questions, and observations about the infant. Next, information about the infant's preferences and interests should provide a basis for developing meaningful interventions to address developmental needs. When possible, the early interventionist should schedule observations to coincide with the infant's waking periods.

By interviewing caregivers and observing the infant, the early interventionist and the caregivers can identify factors that influence the infant's ability to receive and understand sensory input: internal factors (such as health, energy level, and other disabilities) and environmental factors (including lighting; distractions; type of stimuli; and speed, frequency, and mode of presentation). These factors should be taken into account when developing, implementing, and evaluating intervention activities. Early interventionists should also discuss the infant's visual impairment and other disabilities with the caregiver to share information; to clarify questions and define terminology; and to learn from the caregiver about the child's diagnoses. Additional information about conducting interviews with the family appears in Chapter 8.

The questions listed in the sidebars throughout this chapter are intended to guide an early interventionist in reviewing reports, interviewing families, and observing infants with visual impairments and additional disabilities. The questions in Sidebar 3.1 pertain to all infants and focus on the infant's visual impairment, areas of strength, and general intervention needs. Additional lists of questions presented in the rest of this chapter focus on other areas of need related to high-risk factors or specific disabilities. The early interventionist should select those questions from each list that are appropriate for an individual infant. This information will provide a starting point for developing interventions and will contribute to a comprehensive picture of an individual infant who is visually impaired and has additional disabilities.

The sections that follow discuss specific diagnoses or disabilities that commonly occur with visual impairment in infants, as well as special interventions that they require and implications for early intervention practice. These disabilities include mental retardation or developmental delay, prematurity, seizure disorders, physical disabilities (including cerebral palsy), deaf-blindness, and autism. The remainder of the chapter discusses the crucial role of teamwork in providing early intervention services.

Sidebar 3.1 QUESTIONS TO GUIDE PRACTICE WITH INFANTS WHO ARE VISUALLY IMPAIRED AND HAVE ADDITIONAL DISABILITIES

1. What are the family's concerns and priorities regarding the infant's developmental needs?

2. What services are being provided to the infant and family?

3. When is the infant most alert and attentive?

4. What are the infant's favorite toys and activities?

5. What are the infant's strengths and interests?

6. What are the infant's primary intervention needs?

7. What are the infant's diagnoses, and how do they affect learning and development?

8. Are these conditions stable or likely to deteriorate?

9. What is the type and severity of the infant's visual impairment?

10. Are there any medical concerns or interventions regarding the visual impairment?

11. Have corrective lenses been prescribed? If so, does the infant wear them? If not, why not? If corrective lenses have not been prescribed, why not?

12. If the infant has low vision, how is the infant using his or her functional vision? What strategies are needed to promote the use of vision?

13. If the infant is blind, how does the infant use his or her other senses to gain information? What strategies are needed to promote the infant's access to information?

MENTAL RETARDATION OR DEVELOPMENTAL DELAY

The group of infants who have visual impairments and are identified as mentally retarded is a heterogeneous one. For example, one infant may have cortical visual impairment, spastic cerebral palsy, seizures, and developmental delays; another may be totally blind, have a severe hearing loss, and be mentally retarded; and still another may have Down syndrome and myopia (nearsightedness), low muscle tone, and developmental delays. As was noted earlier, in one study mental retardation or developmental delay was found in 40 percent of infants and children with visual impairments (Hatton et al., 1997).

In the medical field, the diagnosis of mental retardation is made when an infant has significant cognitive limitations and is usually associated with specific conditions, such as Down syndrome; congenital infections; birth trauma; and postnatal brain injuries (including meningitis, severe head injury, and near-drowning). Mental retardation frequently occurs with another disability, such as cerebral palsy or autism (Accardo & Capute, 1996). In addition, many children who are mentally retarded have visual impairments (Ellis, 1986).

The diagnosis of mental retardation is not usually reliable until after age 3, except in a minority of cases in which severe developmental delays are apparent. Consequently, the diagnosis of developmental delay is usually used for infants and younger children who show delays on developmental milestones. Developmental delay is a criterion for eligibility for early intervention services under the Individuals with Disabilities Education Act (IDEA), Part C (see Chapter 1). However, the term *delay* can be misleading, especially for a family, if the child's development will never catch up with that of children of the same age (Thomasgrad & Shonkoff, 1993).

Although the use of IQ scores is problematic during infancy as a predictor of later development (Thomasgrad & Shonkoff, 1993) and there are many controversies regarding the use of IQ tests to identify older children who have mild mental retardation or learning disabilities (MacMillan & Reschly, 1998), the definition of mental retardation by the American Association on Mental Retardation (AAMR) provides a framework for recognizing the intensity of interventions that a child will need. Children with IQs of 50–75 (mild mental retardation) need intermittent supports, children with IQs of 35–50 (moderate mental retardation) require limited supports, children with IQs of 20–35 (severe mental retardation) need extensive supports, and children with IQs below 20 (profound mental retardation) require pervasive supports (Luckasson et al., 1992). Given the combination of issues related to the diagnosis of mental retardation during infancy and prenatal and birth factors associated with neurological damage, it is likely that infants with visual impairments who are identified as mentally retarded will demonstrate significant developmental delays and require extensive supports.

Down Syndrome

Down syndrome is the most common genetic cause of mental retardation and affects about 30 percent of all children who are severely retarded. It is caused by an extra chromosome—trisomy 21—in addition to the two normal 21st chromosomes (Rogers et al., 1996). In the first year, it is likely that families of infants with Down syndrome will be involved in medical interventions, especially related to congenital heart problems and gastrointestinal malformations. In addition, infants with Down syndrome are prone to respiratory infections, and some may have infantile spasms. Once medical issues are stabilized, however, infants with Down syndrome will benefit from early learning experiences to promote their development (Hanson & Lynch, 1995).

The majority of these infants have hearing losses, visual problems, and hypotonia, so service providers from several disciplines and a team approach to early intervention are necessary. An occupational therapist or physical therapist will be needed to assist with feeding, to increase muscle tone, and to develop gross motor skills. A teacher who is certified in the field of blindness and visual impairment may be needed to promote visual or compensatory skills. A teacher in the field of deafness and hearing impairment will provide help with hearing aids, listening skills, and sign language development (if that is a priority for the family). A speech and language therapist will assist with the infant's speech and language development and with augmentative communication modes, if needed. An early interventionist with training in early childhood special education will provide developmentally appropriate activities and strategies to enhance the infant's development in motor, communication, play, and social interaction. The specific intervention needs of an infant with visual impairment and mental retardation will depend on the type and severity of his or her vision loss, the level of developmental delay, and other associated disabilities.

Implications for Practice

Families may have questions about the meaning of "developmental delay." Will an infant "catch up" in his or her development? Is the infant's developmental delay related to his or her visual impairment? These are complicated questions that are difficult to answer. Early interventionists can assist families in understanding that the term *developmental delay* indicates that an infant is not demonstrating behaviors that are typical for his or her age. Some of these infants will catch up with typically developing peers, whereas others may always acquire skills at a slower rate and never catch up with typically developing peers. In the latter case, these infants may eventually be diagnosed as having a "developmental disability" caused by mental retardation, cerebral palsy, autism, mental retardation, or other neurological disorders.

Visually impaired infants who are developmentally delayed and have other disabilities will need even more time than infants who are visually impaired without other disabilities to acquire early skills. They will need carefully planned learning opportunities. Early interventionists should assist families in identifying the infant's strengths and learning needs, as discussed in the previous section on beginning intervention with infants who are visually impaired and have additional disabilities. As with all infants who have disabilities, it is critical for infants who are visually impaired and developmentally delayed to participate actively in meaningful learning experiences. In this way, early intervention services will support their optimal development.

PREMATURITY

Prematurity places infants at risk for a variety of problems, including visual impairments and other disabilities. Infants who are born before 36 weeks gestational age are considered premature, but infants who are less than 32 weeks are more likely to experience significant developmental delays. A full-term baby is about 40 weeks (38–42 weeks) gestational age; infants who are 24–26 weeks of gestation are called micropremature infants (Goldson, 1996). The combination of gestational age (period from conception to delivery) and birth weight is an indicator of developmental outcome.

Being born too early and very small are high-risk factors for poor and delayed development. Infants with low birth weights, less than 3 pounds, 5 ounces (1500 grams), are at risk of respiratory distress, intraventricular hemorrhage (bleeding in the brain), apnea (breathing pauses), infections, feeding problems, and visual impairments. Premature infants who weigh under 3 pounds, 5 ounces, are usually hospitalized for two to three months after birth. Infants with extremely low birth weights, less than 1 pound, 10 ounces (750 grams) are prone to respiratory distress syndrome (immature lung disease), intraventricular bleeding, feeding problems, infections, retinopathy of prematurity (ROP), and hearing loss (Howard, Williams, Port, & Lepper, 1997). ROP may be caused by the need for long-term oxygen therapy (owing to apnea) that affects the fragile capillaries that supply the retina (Teplin, 1995). In the past 10 years, the expected survival rates of the smallest infants have increased to 50 percent; however, more than 45 percent of these children will require special education services, and the majority will have multiple disabilities (Hack et al., 1994; La Pine, Jackson, & Bennett, 1995).

Adjustment for Prematurity

To determine the appropriate developmental expectations for a premature infant, the age of the infant is corrected for prematurity until the infant is usually 24 months old. Adjusted ages are calculated by subtracting the time that the infant did not have in utero; thus, an infant who was born 3 months early, would at age 12 months, really be 9 months corrected age or adjusted for prematurity. This month-for-month ratio is usual during the first year. In the next year, the ratio is half a month correction for each month of prematurity; hence, a 20 month old who was 3 months premature would be 18 1/2 months adjusted age (Bernbaum & Batshaw, 1997). These corrections may be helpful in assessing infants' developmental progress, particularly infants who had low or very low birth weights. However, given these infants' multiple developmental challenges, the formula for correcting for prematurity may be less valid for infants who are micropremature, had extremely low birth weights, and have significant disabilities.

Early Behavioral Organization

Prematurity and very low birth weights place infants at a high risk for developmental delays and other disabilities. The development of these infants, according to Als (1982, 1986), is influenced by the interdependence of five subsystems: physiological (respiration, temperature), motor (tone, posture, movement), and state behavior (i.e., whether the infant is alert, active, quiet, drowsy, or fussy). When premature and high-risk infants are discharged from the hospital, they are still working on acquiring self-regulation. Although their physiological systems are stable, overstimulation will have a negative effect. Interventions during the first few months at home should support the infants in maintaining physiological stability while facilitating self-regulation abilities (VandenBerg & Hanson, 1993). Caregivers should notice physiological changes (such as changes in respiration, color, or muscle tone) that indicate the infants' need to rest and help the infants achieve self-regulation, state control (i.e., the ability to control their states with minimal physiological changes and the maintenance of posture and tone). Quiet holding and cuddling are optimal forms of physical contact at this time. Once infants have developed self-regulation, they can respond to and initiate interactions. Learning is enhanced by identifying the infants' signals of pleasure and by providing repeated activities that the infants enjoy and are predictable and responsive environments.

Behavioral States

Recognition of infants' behavioral states is essential not only for early interventionists and caregivers of premature infants, but for caregivers of other infants who have severe and multiple disabilities. Careful identification of these states will assist caregivers in responding to the infants' indications of stress or availability for interaction. After about age 3 months, typical infants are less state dependent; that is, their behaviors are not controlled by particular state conditions (Colombo & Horowitz, 1987). Infants who are at risk for developmental delays demonstrate inconsistent state patterns during the first months (Thoman & Whitney, 1990). An infant's behavioral state is influenced by internal factors (health; central nervous system status; nutrition; medication; and sensory, motor, and cognitive abilities) and by the external influences of the environment and social interactions (Thoman & Whitney, 1990). (See Sidebar 3.2 for a description of typical behavioral states of infants.)

An extensive study examined the behavioral states of children with severe and multiple disabilities, including infants and young children with visual impairments and additional disabilities (Guess, Seigel-Causey, Roberts, Guy, & Rues, 1993). It found that these children were frequently awake and alert but inactive during the day, and that there were infrequent social interactions and direct intervention activities to

---

Sidebar 3.2   TYPICAL BEHAVIORAL STATES OF INFANTS

Drowsy   The infant's eyes may be open, but the eyelids appear "heavy," or the eyes may open and close repeatedly. Vocalizations may occur.

Dazed-tuned out   The infant is awake but has no orientation to auditory, visual, or tactile stimuli; the eyes may appear glassy or dull. The infant may have brief body-limb movements or startles.

Quiet and alert   The infant's eyes are open, and there is some orienting or focusing on auditory, visual, or tactile stimuli. He or she may have motor movements, such as brief body or limb movements, or slight startles.

Active and alert   The infant attempts to engage or interact with other persons (for example, the infant looks at his or her mother's face or vocalizes) or the environment (for instance, the infant reaches for a toy or bangs the table) using a visual, auditory, or tactile modality.

Fussy and irritable   The infant's vocalization and/or facial expressions have a "complaining" or uncomfortable quality, but the infant is not crying.

Crying and agitated   The infant intensely vocalizes, cries, or screams or grimaces or frowns with or without intense vocalization. He or she exhibits increased tension or intense motor activity.

Engaging in repetitive-stereotypical behavior   The infant is actively engaged in movements that are stereotypical, repetitive, and rhythmic, such as moving the head from side to side, waving the arms, sucking or mouthing, rocking, and flapping the hands.

Source: Based on M. D. Klein, D. Chen, and M. Haney, *Project PLAI Curriculum: Facilitating Caregiver-Infant Interactions* (Northridge: California State University at Northridge, Department of Special Education, 1996), adapted from B. Brazelton, "Neonatal Behavioral Assessment Scale," *Clinics in Developmental Medicine* (No. 88). (London: Spastics International Medical Publisher, 1984); and D. Guess, E. Siegel-Causey, S. Roberts, B. Guy, and J. Rues, "Analysis of State Organization Patterns Among Students with Profound Disabilities," *Journal of the Association for Persons with Severe Handicaps, 18* (1993), 93–108.

promote the children's active-alert states. Furthermore, these children exhibited divergent state patterns; some children had extended drowsy state periods during the day, others had frequent periods of crying or repetitive or agitated behavior, and still others had high levels of alertness (Guess et al., 1993). The results suggested that early interventionists and caregivers of infants with severe and multiple disabilities should involve infants more actively in meaningful activities during the inactive-alert state to expand their periods of active alertness.

Implications for Practice

Premature and extremely low birth weight infants are medically fragile and underdeveloped, both physically and neurologically. During the first six months, they are developing self-organization to tolerate feeding, sleeping, and handling. Their behavioral states may not be easily recognized. Caregivers and early interventionists should attend to the infants' state, health status, developmental status, maturity level, and behavioral cues.

Because these babies are easily overstimulated, sensory experiences should be introduced gradually and sensitively to avoid overstimulation and with careful attention to the infants' cues. The infants should receive one sensory experience at a time (auditory, visual, tactile, or kinesthetic) until they can handle more. For example, holding a baby quietly provides a single sensory experience, whereas holding, rocking, and stroking a baby while singing stimulates many senses. Even positive social stimulation that an infant enjoys (such as rocking a baby while talking and engaging in eye contact) may be stressful. Cues of increased stress in infants include changes in color, yawns, averted gaze, hiccups, frowns, sneezes, increased startle, wide eyes, arching, jerking, and crying. Stimulation should be reduced when a baby is stressed. On the other hand, interactions should be initiated when a baby shows cues of being organized and available, including relaxed hands and feet, hands to mouth, sucking, and being quiet (VandenBerg & Hanson, 1993). Premature infants take more time to react to stimulation and to control their behaviors.

When infants are premature, looking behaviors should be encouraged to promote selective attention to environmental stimuli and the processing of sensory information (Glass, 1993). The infants should be encouraged to look at stimuli that will help them learn about the environment. The human face is the most significant social visual stimulus for all babies and is highly likely to elicit visual attention if the infants have sufficient vision. Responding to and recognizing a caregiver's face has profound emotional influences on both an infant and his or her caregiver. With premature infants, nonsocial visual stimuli should be simple, three-dimensional objects, like the baby's bottle. If older infants with visual impairments (including some cases of cortical visual impairment) do not attend to familiar faces or favorite toys, then high-contrast objects and black-and-white patterns may be used to elicit their visual

---

Sidebar 3.3   QUESTIONS TO GUIDE PRACTICE WITH PREMATURE INFANTS WHO ARE VISUALLY IMPAIRED AND HAVE ADDITIONAL DISABILITIES

1. How premature was the infant at birth, and how old is the infant now?
2. How is the infant's health and development?
3. What are the infant's medical needs, and how do they affect the infant's ability to learn?
4. Are there any restrictions or physical limitations on the infant because of his or her medical needs?
5. What medical treatment or other interventions are recommended?

---

attention. However, once they are attending visually to these artificial objects, more natural visual stimuli should be introduced (Glass, 1993).

Knowledge of when an infant was born and his or her current age provides information on how long the infant has been out of the hospital and a basis for developmental expectations. Some infants are healthy and have few medical needs, whereas other are not. Knowledge of an infant's condition will help an early interventionist understand the family's concerns and priorities, interpret the infant's behavior, and evaluate possible intervention practices. The first few months or even years may be overwhelming for many families who receive many referrals to take their infants for additional tests. The early interventionist can assist families in developing their priorities and creating a schedule and can accompany them to certain evaluations when appropriate. Sidebar 3.3 presents questions related to prematurity to guide early intervention practices with an individual infant who is visually impaired and premature.

SEIZURE DISORDERS

"A *seizure* is an alteration of motor or sensory function, behavior, or consciousness caused by a discharge of electrical activity in the brain. *Epilepsy* is recurrent seizures" (Vining & Freeman, 1996, p. 511). Factors that cause neurological damage (including congenital infections, birth trauma, fetal distress, abnormal chromosomes, head injuries, and infections in infancy, such as meningitis) place infants at risk for seizures (Howard et al., 1997). Statistics suggest that children with seizure disorders or epilepsy are at risk for other disabilities, including mental retardation, speech disorders, learning disabilities, minimal brain dysfunction, and other neurological impairments (Sillanpaa, 1992). Children with mental retardation, cerebral palsy, spina bifida (a neural tube defect), and hydrocephalus (accumulation of cerebrospinal fluid in the brain) have an increased risk of seizure disorders (Wallace, 1990).

The Commission on Classification of the International League Against Epilepsy (1989) categorizes seizures as partial or focal (originating in one part of the brain), generalized (involving both hemispheres of the brain), and unclassified. Generalized seizures include absence, atypical absence, myoclonic, atonic, tonic, clonic, and tonic-clonic types. Partial seizures may be simple (no loss of consciousness) or complex (loss of consciousness). Children with multiple disabilities are more likely to have mixed seizure disorders involving both partial and generalized seizures (Brown, 1997; Heller, Alberto, Forney, & Schwartzman, 1996). Table 3.1 presents the common classifications of seizure disorders based on the commission's classification and a review of the current literature on symptoms and related characteristics (Brown, 1997; Brunquell, 1994; Epilepsy Foundation of America, 1994; Vining & Freeman, 1996).

When children are classified as *status epilepticus,* they have seizures that last longer than 30 minutes and are unconscious during that time (J. K. Brown & Hussain, 1991, cited in Brown, 1997). *Status epilepticus* occurs most frequently before age 3. Children are at the greatest risk of further neurological damage when seizures last 15 minutes or more. The earlier an infant develops a seizure disorder, the worse the developmental prognosis. Infantile spasms usually occur between 6 and 24 months. They have negative consequences for development and the majority of children who have them are mentally retarded (Bobele & Bodensteiner, 1990, cited in Batshaw & Perret, 1992; Vining & Freeman, 1996)

Seizure disorders are associated with certain syndromes that may involve visual impairment and mental retardation (Brown, 1997; Vining & Freeman, 1996). *Tuberous sclerosis* involves acne, white birthmarks and beige-colored areas, infantile spasms, severe mental retardation, and retinal abnormalities. *Sturge-Weber* syndrome involves abnormal blood

Table 3.1. CLASSIFICATION OF SEIZURES TYPES

Types of Seizures	Symptoms	Characteristics
Generalized		
Absence (petit mal)	Blank stare, dazed look, blinking, chewing. Starts and ends suddenly. Lasts for a few seconds.	Usually in 4–15 year olds. May occur frequently in one day.
Atypical absence	More gradual onset and longer in duration than absence seizures. May be confused after seizure.	Associated with tonic-clonic, myoclonic, and atonic seizures.
Myoclonic (minor motor)	Sudden brief increase in muscle tone, abrupt jerking or muscle contractions in part or throughout body.	Typically develop between 6 months and 11 years. Infantile spasms (6–24 months).
Infantile spasms	Jackknifing of the body several times consecutively.	May occur frequently. The majority of children have poor developmental outcomes.
Atonic (akinetic, drop attacks)	Abrupt loss of muscle tone results in loss of consciousness. Lasts about 10 seconds.	
Tonic	Stiff contraction of muscles; limbs may be stiff.	
Clonic	Rapid contraction and relaxation of muscles.	
Tonic-clonic (grand mal)	Loss of consciousness. Rigidity for 30–60 seconds (tonic), followed by rapid jerking (clonic), shallow breathing; possible incontinence; may last minutes.	The most common type of generalized seizure. Occurs at any age. May occur frequently (several times a day) or seldom (once a year).
Partial or focal seizures		
Simple partial	Depends on the focal area of the brain.	Commonly begins between 4 and 12 years. May have an aura (changes in vision or sensations).

(continued on next page)

Table 3.1. *(continued)*		
Types of Seizures	**Symptoms**	**Characteristics**
With motor symptoms (Jacksonian)	Twitching of arm or leg and gradual involvement of other parts of the body.	
With autonomic symptoms	Face may become flushed or pale, pulse may increase.	
Complex partial (psychomotor or temporal lobe)	Blinking, facial grimacing, lip smacking, groaning, chewing, and aimless movement. May last between 30 seconds and 5 minutes.	Resembles absence seizures. May experience an aura. May laugh or seem angry or fearful. May experience odors, tastes, or hallucinations. Infrequent occurrence, less than a few times daily.

vessels that result in a port wine birthmark on the face, cortical atrophy on one side of the brain and calcifications in the temporal and occipital areas, partial seizures, and mental retardation. *Aicardi syndrome* occurs in girls and involves infantile spasms, absence of the corpus callosum (connection of white matter between the two hemispheres of the brain), abnormalities of the eye, and severe mental retardation. Children with multiple disabilities frequently have complex seizure disorders that require medication for an extended period (Brown, 1997).

Medications

Anticonvulsants are the universal treatment for seizure disorders. In some cases, surgical procedures may be considered if medications are not effective and the seizures are interfering with a child's development, and in some cases, a special diet (high in fats and low in carbohydrates, may be used) (Brown, 1997). Medication is usually prescribed if an infant is at risk for the recurrence of a seizure when the EEG is abnormal and there are other neurological abnormalities. Other risk factors may include the type of seizure, occurrence of seizures at night, febrile seizures (with high fever), and a family history of seizures (Heller et al., 1996). The literature indicates that physicians should be guided by the following framework when prescribing medication to treat a child's seizure disorder:

1. Choose the medication that is the most effective for a particular type of seizure disorder and has the least likelihood of producing side effects. . . .
2. The medication should be increased until seizures are controlled or until clinical toxicity is seen in the child. . . .
3. The child should be monitored. . . .
4. If a child's seizures have not been controlled after a single medication, or at the most two, have been tried, referral to an epilepsy center is warranted. (Vining & Freeman, 1996, pp. 518–519)

Identifying the appropriate medication and correct dosage takes time and careful monitoring by a physician. The dosage of a medication needs to be adjusted to control seizures and decrease side effects. The infant's blood should be tested a few times annually to determine whether the infant is receiving the appropriate dosage. Common side effects of anticonvulsants include drowsiness, tremors, dizziness, nystagmus, ataxia, and gastrointestinal problems (*Physicians' Desk Reference,* 1995). For example, Dilantin may cause nystagmus, swollen gums, and difficulty with balance and coordination (ataxia); phenobarbital may result in hyperactivity, drowsiness, and decreased cognitive performance; Zarontin is associated with vomiting and dizziness; Tegretol may cause drowsiness and ataxia; Klonopin may cause ataxia, sedation, and salivation; Depakene may cause drowsiness and an upset stomach; and ACTH may cause cataracts and brittle bones.

Implications for Practice

Early interventionists and caregivers of infants who are visually impaired and have seizure disorders should be familiar with the side effects of the prescribed medications, since the majority of anticonvulsants will affect infants' states and ability to attend to the environment (Wallace, 1990). Caregivers should follow instructions for administering particular medications and record the frequency of seizures to determine the effectiveness of the medications. The status of an infant's seizure disorder should influence intervention priorities; that is, the emphases for an infant who has recurring and uncontrolled seizures will differ from those for an infant whose seizures are less severe and controlled. In the former case, the family's priority is likely to be identifying potential medical interventions. In the latter case, the focus will turn to the infant's learning and development. Early interventionists and caregivers should find out about the types of seizure disorders the infants have, the symptoms, what they should do when a seizure occurs (Howard et al., 1997), and whether there are any triggers or restrictions because of the seizure disorder. (Sidebar 3.4 presents the first aid procedures for responding to a tonic-clonic seizure in an infant.) In addition, they should assist families in observing the effects of medications in infants and in providing feedback to physicians regarding the effects of the medication. (Sidebar 3.5 lists questions related to seizure disorders to

Sidebar 3.4   RESPONDING TO A GENERALIZED TONIC-CLONIC SEIZURE IN AN INFANT

- Remain calm and note when the seizure began to monitor its duration.
- Remove possible harmful objects and position the infant safely.
- Do not restrain the infant.
- If possible, lay the infant on his or her side with hips raised and head to the side to allow saliva or vomit to drain from the mouth.
- Do not provide any liquids or put any objects in the mouth.
- Call 911 if the duration of the seizure is more than 5 minutes or there are multiple consecutive seizures.
- After the seizure is over, assess whether first aid or medical attention is needed.
- Change the infant's clothing if the infant is soiled.
- Allow the infant to rest.

Source: *Seizure Recognition and First Aid* (Landover, MD: Epilepsy Foundation of America, 1994).

Sidebar 3.5   QUESTIONS TO GUIDE PRACTICE
WITH INFANTS WHO ARE VISUALLY IMPAIRED
AND HAVE A SEIZURE DISORDER

1. What kind of seizure disorder does the infant have?
2. What behaviors indicate that the infant is having a seizure?
3. What medication does the infant take for the seizure disorder, and when should it be administered?
4. Are there any side effects of the medication that should be kept in mind?
5. Is the infant being monitored by a physician?
6. Are there certain situations or times when the infant is likely to have a seizure?
7. Is there a particular stimulation that is likely to trigger a seizure?
8. How should one respond when the infant has a seizure?
9. Are there any restrictions for the infant because of the seizure disorder?
10. When is the infant most alert?

guide early intervention practices with individual infants who are visually impaired and have a seizure disorder.)

CEREBRAL PALSY AND OTHER PHYSICAL DISABILITIES

Physical disability is the broad term indicating a problem in the motor system that affects movement and motor skills. There are several causes of physical disability in infancy, including arthrogryposis multiplex (congenital stiffness in joints and deformity of limbs), cerebral palsy (a disorder of movement and posture due to damage in the motor areas of the brain), limb deficiency (partial loss or absence of a limb), osteogenesis imperfecta (a congenital disease resulting in brittle or improperly formed bone, weak muscles, and loose joints), and spina bifida (a defect in the closure of the spine). Cataracts are associated with osteogenesis imperfecta, and ocular anomalies are associated with arthrogryposis multiplex. However, up to 64 percent of children with cerebral palsy (depending on the type) has a visual impairment (Robinson, 1973, cited in Batshaw,

1997). Because cerebral palsy is the most common physical disability in infancy and has the highest incidence of visual impairment, this section will focus on infants with visual impairments and cerebral palsy.

Cerebral palsy refers to a variety of disorders in movement and posture caused by a nonprogressive abnormality in the developing brain (Nelson, 1996; Pellegrino, 1997). Children with cerebral palsy are at risk of a variety of additional disabilities, including visual impairment, hearing loss, seizure disorders, and severe mental retardation. Visual problems include nystagmus, optic atrophy, myopia (nearsightedness); strabismus (eye turns), amblyopia (loss of vision related to disuse because of strabismus), optic nerve atrophy, visual field defects, and cortical visual impairment (Capute & Accardo, 1996; Pellegrino & Dormans, 1998). Infants who have cerebral palsy as a consequence of prematurity may also be visually impaired because of ROP.

Cerebral palsy is considered a developmental disability because it occurs in infants and young children and affects their developmental outcomes. The four main types of cerebral palsy are based on the location of the neurological abnormality: *pyramidal or spastic* (high muscle tone or hypertonic), caused by damage to the motor cortex or pyramidal system; *extrapyramidal or choreathetoid or dyskinetic* (fluctuating muscle tone), caused by problems in the basal ganglia; *ataxia* (impaired balance and coordination), associated with damage to the cerebellum; and *mixed-type,* caused by extensive brain injury that results in multiple disabilities (Capute & Accardo, 1996; Nelson, 1996; Pellegrino, 1997). (See Table 3.2 for additional information on the types of cerebral palsy.)

A specific diagnosis for cerebral palsy usually occurs after 12 months of age, when the infant develops certain motor symptoms (Berkow, 1992, cited in Heller et al., 1996). However, there are many early diagnostic signs. In the first few months, infants with cerebral palsy may sleep a lot, be irritable, have difficulty sucking or swallowing, and show little interest in the environment, and have abnormal muscle tone. By the end of the first year, they may show persistent primitive delays in motor development, abnormal signs (clenched fists, early hand dominance), and abnormal muscle tone and movement (Capute & Accardo, 1996; Pellegrino, 1997). Some infants who display these symptoms, especially if the symptoms are mild, do not develop cerebral palsy (Nelson, 1996).

Table 3.2 TYPES OF CEREBRAL PALSY

Types and Incidence	Primary Characteristics	Additional Characteristics
Pyramidal	Spasticity. Increased tone, rigid "clasped-knife" quality, then resistance gives way suddenly. Difficulty initiating movement.	Contractures may occur. Seizures and orthopedic problems are more common in spastic cerebral palsy.
Spastic diplegia	Affects legs more than arms.	Associated with strabismus.
Hemiplegia	Affects one side of the body, usually the arm more than the leg.	Associated with seizure disorders, severe visual field loss (hemianopsia), cortical visual impairment, retardation of growth.
Double hemiplegia	Affects all four limbs. Usually one side more than the other and the arms more than the legs.	
Spastic quadriplegia	Affects all four limbs. The legs are more affected than the arms. The body and face may be affected.	Associated with seizure disorders, mental retardation, eye turns (strabismus), and articulation problems (dysarthria).
Extrapyramidal	Abrupt involuntary movements. Limbs rigid ("lead pipe rigidity") but bend with steady pressure. Difficulty maintaining posture and controlling movement.	Contractures are less likely to occur than in pyramidal cerebral palsy. When the child is asleep, tone seems normal.
Choreoathetoid	Often affects head, neck, facial muscles, and arms. Sudden, involuntary limb movements.	Usually starts after age 18 months. Drooling and difficulty sucking, swallowing, and speaking.

(continued on next page)

Table 3.2 *(continued)*		
Types and Incidence	**Primary Characteristics**	**Additional Characteristics**
Rigid	Constant or intermittent resistance to passive movement, especially slow movement.	May occur alone or with spastic or athetoid cerebral palsy.
Atonia	Floppy, low muscle tone (hypotonia).	Usually the first symptom in an infant who develops other types of cerebral palsy. Hypotonia occurred in utero if the newborn is spastic.
Ataxia	Uncoordinated movement and poor balance.	The rarest type of cerebral palsy; seldom occurs alone.

Interventions for Infants with Cerebral Palsy and Other Motor Problems

Children with cerebral palsy and other motor problems may receive occupational or physical therapy; adaptive equipment; braces and other orthotic devices; medications; orthopedic surgery; and, in some cases, neurosurgery to improve their movement and muscle tone (Capute & Accardo, 1996; Pellegrino, 1997). With older children, physical therapists usually focus on providing interventions to assist gross motor skills, sitting, movement, and walking, whereas occupational therapists work on fine motor skills; the use of the hands; and adaptive skills, such as feeding and dressing. In early intervention, however, occupational therapists and physical therapists have similar roles and responsibilities; since these traditional roles overlap, the term *developmental therapists* has been coined to refer to occupational therapists and physical therapists who work with infants (Harris & Tada, 1983).

The following four treatment approaches—*neurodevelopment treatment* (NDT), *the Rood sensorimotor approach, proprioceptive neuromuscular facilitation* (PNF), and *sensory integration* (SI) *therapy*—influence the work of developmental therapists with infants who have cerebral palsy and other neurological problems:

1. NDT is one of the most commonly used approaches by pediatric physical therapists based on the work of the Bobaths that began over 40 years ago in England. NDT draws from normal neuromotor development. The goal is to facilitate normal postural tone and movement patterns, inhibit abnormal reflex patterns, and prevent related complication like contractures or deformity (B. Bobath, 1967; K. Bobath, 1980). The approach stresses appropriate positioning and handling to increase normal movement patterns. NDT is used with infants and other children with cerebral palsy or severe and multiple disabilities and with those who are mentally retarded, blind, or deaf (Harris & Tada, 1983). The principles of NDT are still used, although there have been some changes, including an emphasis on the infants' active participation in purposeful movement during functional activities (Bly, 1991; Heriza & Sweeney, 1995).

2. *The Rood sensorimotor approach* was developed by Rood in the United States at about the same time as the Bobaths were working in England. Rood's approach is based on the twofold nature of muscle systems that allow for both movement and the maintenance of body posture (Rood, 1956). Muscles are exercised in developmental positions to stimulate the normal function. The aim of the Rood approach is to use sensory stimulation to activate movement and postural responses at an autonomic level. Prolonged stimuli (such as pressure at joints) are provided to promote stability, and rapidly changing stimulation (vibration or tapping) is used to achieve movement (Harris & Tada, 1983). Both exteroceptive (stimuli outside the body) and proprioceptive (stimuli produced within the body) types of sensory stimulation are used, such as tactile stimulation, ice, stretching, resistance, vibration, and pressure (Heriza & Sweeney, 1995).

3. PNF was developed by Knott and Voss (1968) in the 1950s in the United States. It is based on normal neuromotor development. The aim is to increase functional movement and coordination through a full range of movement. A characteristic of PNF is the use of spiral and diagonal movement patterns of the limbs and body and a developmental sequence of movement skills in movement patterns. Like the Rood approach, PNF stresses the interaction between mobility and stability.

This approach also stresses the repetition of movement patterns and sensory cues, such as using visual or auditory stimuli to encourage infants to lift their heads (Harris & Tada, 1983; Heriza & Sweeney, 1995).

4. SI was originated by Ayres (1972) in the 1970s in the United States. The purpose of SI is to enable children to process and understand sensory information by providing specific sensory input that will elicit purposeful responses. SI emphasizes the tactile (touch), vestibular (balance and posture), and proprioceptive (unconscious awareness of body position) systems. Examples of activities to assist infants' integration of sensory input include swinging for vestibular stimulation, swaddling young infants for tactile input, and pushing a weighted stroller for proprioceptive stimulation. Originally, SI was developed to promote the academic development of preschool and older children with learning disabilities. It was later incorporated into occupational and physical therapy treatment with infants and older children who are mentally retarded or autistic or have cerebral palsy or other neurological problems (Heriza & Sweeney, 1995), and is now viewed as an important intervention with infants who have difficulty in social interactions (Williamson & Anzalone, 1997).

Another, controversial approach—patterning—is used by some parents of infants and young children who have severe motor and neurological impairments, particularly infants who were born normal and then suffered a trauma (such as near-drowning) resulting in severe and multiple disabilities. *Patterning* involves the passive movement and exercise of a child's arms and legs in an attempt to program undamaged brain areas to assume the functions of the damaged areas (Zigler, 1981). For families, this approach demands considerable time, effort, and several individuals to perform the many hours of patterning exercises with a child.

Implications for Practice

An early interventionist is likely to have more consistent contact with infants with physical disabilities and their families than is an occupational or physical therapist. Early interventionists should therefore gather specific information about the therapeutic approaches that are being implemented by physical or occupational therapists, so they can collaborate closely with the therapists, other service providers, and families in implementing intervention activities with infants. For example, all service providers should know how to position and handle infants to decrease abnormal tone and increase normal movements and how to put on or remove braces and orthotic devices and use adaptive equipment (such as specialized seats) and other devices. Teachers who are certified in the field of blindness and visual impairment should provide information on the infants' functional vision, if appropriate, or compensatory strategies for infants who are blind (for example, ways to alert the infants when they are going to be moved and strategies for helping the infants search for desired objects). Early interventionists with a background in severe and multiple disabilities can share information with physical and occupational therapists and teachers certified in the field of blindness and visual impairments on the infants' interests, signals, responses to sensory stimulation, and responses to adaptive equipment. In addition, they can share ways to communicate with infants who are visually impaired and have multiple disabilities and identify additional adaptive devices that may be needed to promote the infants' interactions.

For a variety of reasons, some infants with severe and multiple disabilities may not be receiving physical or occupational therapy services or may not have even had evaluations. Their families may be unaware of the requirements of IDEA, Part C, and do not know that they can request physical or occupational therapy; may not speak the same language as their service coordinators or other program staff; or, given the shortage of occupational therapists and physical therapists, a decision may have been made that these services are not a priority for individual infants. In these cases, early interventionists may need to work with the families and service coordinators for the benefit of the infants. In some cases, the infants may, in fact, need physical or occupational therapy and in others, consultation by these service providers with the families and early interventionists is sufficient.

Whatever the situation, an early interventionist should find out about the specific type and severity of an infant's cerebral palsy because interventions will vary accordingly (Finnie, 1990). Sidebar 3.6 presents a list of questions related to cerebral palsy to guide early intervention practices with an individual infant who is visually impaired and has physical disabilities. A general rule of intervention is to place an infant in as

Sidebar 3.6   QUESTIONS TO GUIDE PRACTICE WITH INFANTS WHO ARE VISUALLY IMPAIRED AND HAVE PHYSICAL DISABILITIES

1. What type of motor difficulties does the infant have—a type of cerebral palsy or abnormal tone?

2. How will these motor problems affect the infant's motor development?

3. How should the infant be positioned for sitting, lying down, and bearing weight?

4. How should the infant be handled and moved?

5. For the infant with low vision, what positions will allow him or her to use functional vision?

6. For the infant with low vision, how can we work on the infant's motor and visual needs during daily activities?

7. For the infant who is blind, what compensatory strategies need to be used for this infant to gain information?

8. What positions will allow the infant to manipulate objects?

9. What types of adaptive equipment does the infant need?

normal a position as possible to normalize muscle tone, and to inhibit abnormal reflexes. Interventions focus on *positioning* or providing symmetrical placement and support to inhibit abnormal reflexes and postures, and *handling,* or preparing the infant for movement and positioning. For example, an infant with spastic cerebral palsy who has an asymmetrical tonic neck reflex (ATNR) will extend his or her arm and leg on the side to which the head is turned while flexing the limbs on the other side. This reflex interferes with the development of purposeful looking, reaching, social interaction, eating, and play. Activities should be introduced and performed directly in front of the infant to discourage triggering the ATNR (Howard et al., 1997). The early intervention team for an infant with low vision and spastic cerebral palsy should include a physical or occupational therapist to implement appropriate interventions, such as positioning and handling, and the use of assistive devices and equipment; a teacher certified in the field of blindness and visual impairments to identify where objects should be presented within the child's visual field without eliciting an abnormal reflex or extensor pattern; and an early interventionist with a background in severe and multiple disabilities to implement activities that promote all areas of the infant's development.

An infant who is hypertonic (has too much muscle tone) should be positioned on the stomach over a small pillow or wedge on his or her side to decrease or break up spasticity (so the trunk is supported and the hips and knees are flexed at a 90-degree angle); and repositioned frequently to decrease the chance of contractures. Moreover, moving the infant suddenly or quickly or laying him or her on the back increases spasticity and should be avoided (Watkins, 1989).

Infants who are hypotonic (have too little muscle tone) need handling to increase their tone and positioning for support. These infants may benefit from tactile, auditory, visual, and other environmental stimulation that will increase their alertness and tone. Many infants who have severe visual impairments have hypotonia but do not have cerebral palsy. This low tone seems to be related to the absence of sufficient vision to motivate head movements that contribute to the development of the ability to shift weight and the development of the muscles of the trunk and arms (Bureau of Education for Exceptional Students, 1986). Low tone affects the posture, balance, coordination, and locomotion of children who are visually impaired. Early interventionists, teachers who are certified in the field of blindness and visual impairment, and orientation and mobility instructors should consult with physical or occupational therapists regarding the specific intervention needs and strategies for each infant with visual impairment and cerebral palsy or other motor problems.

INFANTS WHO ARE DEAF-BLIND

The term *deaf-blind* indicates that an infant has impairments in both primary avenues for receiving information and learning—vision and hearing. The combination of these sensory impairments have profound implications for early intervention services. Fortunately, the majority of these children have either some vision or some hearing (Fredericks & Baldwin, 1987). Infants who are deaf-blind include those with mild-to-profound vision and hearing losses; those with cortical visual impairment and/or central auditory processing disorders; those who are hard of hearing and blind; those who have low vision and are deaf; those who are totally blind and have profound hearing losses; those who are hard of hearing and have low vision; and those with medical needs, severe developmental delays, and other physical disabilities (Chen, 1993; Chen & Haney, 1995; Michael & Paul, 1991). There are over 70 syndromes in which visual impairment and hearing loss occur together (Regenbogen & Coscas, 1985).

There are no data on the distribution of characteristics in infants who are deaf-blind. Data are available on the school-age population. According to Outlette (1984, reported in Fredericks and Baldwin, 1987), 6.1 percent were deaf and blind, 3.4 percent were deaf and had severe visual impairments, 48 percent were blind and had severe hearing losses, and 42.4 percent had severe hearing losses and severe visual impairments. These statistics indicate that almost 94 percent of school-age children who are deaf-blind have some functional vision or hearing. More recent data from the 1990s (Edwards, Goehl, & Gordon, n.d.) also indicated that a majority of the deaf-blind population (from birth to age 21) have some usable vision or hearing.

Implications for Practice

Given the heterogeneity of the population, early intervention strategies with infants who have both visual impairment and hearing loss will depend on the learning needs of the individual infants. However, the development of communication is a focus that is common among all intervention programs reported in the literature on infants and young children who are deaf-blind. Specific strategies have been identified to promote interaction with caregivers (Chen & Haney, 1995), the development of early communication (Chen, 1995a; van Dijk, 1967a,b), the increased use of available vision and hearing (Michael & Paul, 1991), and all areas of development (P. Freeman, 1985; McGinnes & Treffry, 1982; Watkins, 1989). Early communication strategies include interpreting infants' signals; developing predictable routines; using touch, object, and other anticipatory cues; developing familiar games; and adapting signs (Chen, 1995a; P. Freeman, 1985; McGinnes & Treffry, 1982; Watkins, 1989). In addition, a movement-based approach, commonly called *coactive movement,* is another specific intervention associated with the education of young children who are deaf-blind (van Dijk, 1967a,b; Writer, 1987). These communication strategies are discussed in Chapter 9.

Because few programs have early interventionists who are trained to work with infants who are deaf-blind, the intervention team for such a child may involve, at a minimum, the caregiver, an early interventionist, a teacher who is certified in the field of blindness and visual impairment, and a teacher who is certified in the field of deafness and hearing impairments. On this team, the caregiver would provide information on the infant's preferences, interests, and communication and on the family's concerns and priorities. The teacher who is certified in the field of blindness and visual impairments would provide information on the infant's visual impairment and on strategies for developing the functional use of vision, if appropriate; for developing the infant's tactile exploration; or for adapting signs (placement in the visual field or adapted for tactile recognition), as needed. The early interventionist with a background in early childhood special education would provide information on the infant's play, communication, and other developmental skills; intervention strategies (such as the use of object cues); and developmentally appropriate activities (like early games) in which to infuse intervention strategies. The teacher who is certified in the field of deafness and hearing impairments would provide information on the infant's hearing loss, care and use of hearing aids, and strategies for developing listening skills and using signs, as appropriate. Sidebar 3.7

**Sidebar 3.7   QUESTIONS TO GUIDE PRACTICE
WITH INFANTS WHO ARE DEAF-BLIND**

1. What type and degree of hearing loss does the infant have?

2. Have hearing aids been prescribed? If so, what needs to be known about their care and management? Does the infant wear the aids? If the infant is not wearing the hearing aids, why not? If hearing aids have not been prescribed, why not?

3. If the infant has some hearing and is wearing hearing aids, how is he or she responding to sound? What strategies are needed to promote the infant's use of hearing?

4. How does the infant communicate? What strategies are needed to support the infant's development of communication?

presents a list of questions related to hearing loss to guide early intervention practices with an individual infant who is deaf-blind.

AUTISM

Autism is a spectrum disorder (a complex continuum of symptoms) that results in abnormal development before age 3 and has significant consequences for a child's social and language development. About one-third of infants with autism display normal development during the first year and then lose social and communication skills (B. J. Freeman, 1993; Mauk, 1993). Diagnoses of autism during the second year are becoming more common, and the number of young children with autism has increased. It is not known whether an actual increase in children with this disorder, more awareness of the characteristics of autism, or better diagnostic procedures has resulted in this growth (Feinberg & Beyer, 1998). An infant with autism may demonstrate the following behaviors:

- unusual responses to stimuli (such as engaging in self-stimulatory and repetitive movements like rocking and hand flapping or being hyper- or hyposensitive to sensory stimuli)
- restricted development of communication (for example, the absence of vocalization, repetitive imitation of sounds, limited use of gestures, or poor response to requests)
- atypical social development (including poor or absent eye contact; lack of interest in early games, toys, physical contact, and other children or significant caregivers; and delayed social smile) (B. J. Freeman, 1993; Smith & Lovaas, 1998)

The majority of children with autism have some mental retardation, although the range is broad. Additional disabilities may include hearing loss, seizure disorder, and difficulty processing sensory information (visual, auditory, and tactile). Children with certain disabilities, such as Rett syndrome, severe blindness, and deaf-blindness, may display autistic-like behaviors (Gense & Gense, 1994; Mauk, 1993). Certain etiologies including congenital rubella, Cornelia de Lange syndrome, Down syndrome, Rett syndrome, and viral infections, have been associated with autism (Fisher et al., 1999; B. J. Freeman, 1993).

The diagnosis of autism is extremely complex, particularly if an infant has another disability, and requires skilled clinicians. No one symptom is indicative of autism. An accurate diagnosis involves a multidisciplinary approach to gathering comprehensive information about the infant's history and conducting systematic observations (Fisher et al., 1999; Volkmar, 1993). The *Diagnostic and Statistical Manual of Mental Disorders* (American Psychiatric Association, 1994) provides the most commonly used criteria for diagnosing autism and a category of "autistic-like" *pervasive developmental disorder not otherwise specified* (PDD-NOS) for children whose behaviors do not meet those for autism (Farber, 1996). Diagnostic criteria for autism fall into four main categories:

1. problems in social interaction
2. limitations in communication
3. severely restricted, repetitive, and stereotypic behaviors, interests, and activities
4. onset before age 3 (American Psychiatric Association, 1994).

In addition, the *Diagnostic Classification of Mental Health and Developmental Disorders of Infancy and Early Childhood* (Zero to Three, 1994) includes a category, *multisystem developmental disorder* (MSDD), to characterize very young children who demonstrate significant problems in communicating, developing social emotional relationships, processing sensory information, and organizing sensory information to plan and execute required movements for an activity. MSDD was recently conceptualized by clinicians in the field of infant mental health as a diagnosis for very young children whose difficulties in social emotional relationships may be secondary to sensory processing and motor problems.

Interventions for Infants with Autism

Before age 36 months, an infant with autism is eligible for early intervention services under IDEA, Part C. A number of intervention approaches that have been used with preschoolers (3–5 year olds) with autism are being implemented with younger children as well (Feinberg & Beyer, 1998). First, the *TEACH Approach (Treatment and Education of Autistic & Communication Handicapped Children),* developed at the University of North Carolina, structures the environment (by, for example, using picture or object cues to identify activities in the schedule and clearly identifying activity areas in a room) so a young child will anticipate, recognize, and participate in familiar routines (Lord, Bristol, & Schopler, 1993). Skills are introduced through direct teaching and one-to-one instruction with gradual generalization to group activities and other situations. Some *TEACH* strategies are reminiscent of the calendar box and picture and object cues used with children who are deaf-blind (see Jurgens, 1977; Rowland, Schweigert, & Prickett, 1995).

Second, the *Intensive Behavioral Intervention* (IBI), developed by Lovaas at the University of California, Los Angeles, has been requested by many parents of infants and preschoolers with autism (Feinberg & Beyer, 1998). IBI uses behavioral methods to obtain a child's attention, cooperation, and response. The child's behaviors are shaped by reinforcing successive approximations, discrete trial learning (stimulus-response-reinforcer), and prompting and fading prompts. Self-stimulatory and other undesirable behaviors are ignored, or alternative behaviors are reinforced. Initially, primary reinforcers (food and sensory stimulation) are used; then social and more natural reinforcers are introduced, when possible. This approach requires extensive parental training and may involve up to 40 weeks of one-to-one instruction for two to three years. As the child shows progress, procedures become less structured and are used in everyday settings (Smith & Lovaas, 1998). The expense of the IBI approach (which may be over $30,000 a year) and the requests of families to have that intervention included in their Individual Family Service Plans are of great concern to state agencies nationwide because of budget limitations. Early intervention programs receive an average of $5,000 to $8,000 a year to provide sevices to an infant (Feinberg & Beyer, 1998).

In early intervention programs with infants with autism, a third approach has been derived from the field of infant mental health. On the basis of 20 years of clinical practice with young children with severe disorders in communication and relationships, Greenspan and Wieder (1997) proposed the following integrated and systematic approach to assist families in promoting the development of their infants with autism:

1. The basic needs of the family for shelter, medical care, food, clothing, and emotional security must be addressed.

2. Early interventionists promote trusting relationships by assisting caregivers to recognize their infants' cues and to use appropriate interactional strategies that will elicit positive responses from the infants. For example, an infant may be hypersensitive to touch and respond negatively to the caregiver's contact. The infant's irritability may be interpreted as rejection by the caregiver. However, the infant may respond positively if the caregiver uses firm pressure, rather than light touch, when handling him or her.

3. Interventions focus on expanding interactions between infants and caregivers by providing a variety of strategies to engage the infants and elicit responses.

4. Interventions emphasize interactions that match an infant's developmental level to promote the next developmental level. For example, if an infant is not demonstrating purposeful communication, then strategies would focus on promoting intentional communication for high-preference activities.

5. Specific intervention techniques are implemented, such as behavioral approaches (Smith & Lovaas, 1998) or an interactive "floor time" approach (Greenspan, 1992a,b). The floor time approach involves structured social interaction and play sessions in which many developmentally appropriate and common strategies are used to promote early communication (Wieder, 1997; Greenspan, 1992a,b). These strategies include following the infant's interest, interpreting the infant's actions as meaningful, playing "dumb" to elicit an infant's requests, using cause-and-effect toys, creating simple problems, encouraging choices, and creating familiar games (see Chapter 9 for further explanation).

Implications for Practice

Early interventionists need to examine the characteristics of these current approaches to identify strategies that may be useful for encouraging learning in particular infants who are visually impaired and have autism or autistic-like behaviors. First, it is likely that these infants will benefit from structured activities, predictable environments, and direct instruction from adults. Second, infants who are autistic have difficulties processing sensory information and may be over- or understimulated by what they see, hear, taste, touch, or smell. Similar responses to sensory input have been observed in young children with visual impairments and

Sidebar 3.8   QUESTIONS TO GUIDE PRACTICE WITH INFANTS WHO ARE VISUALLY IMPAIRED AND AUTISTIC

1. What symptoms of autism does the infant exhibit?
2. How does the infant interact with and respond to a familiar caregiver?
3. Does the infant participate in games with the caregiver?
4. How does the infant communicate?
5. How does the infant interact with toys?
6. How does the infant respond to various sensory stimuli: touch (being touched, touching various textures, and handling objects), sound (voice and music), and vision (patterned objects, different colors, and pictures)?
7. What are the infant's main difficulties?
8. What specific interventions are recommended?

multiple disabilities (Morse, 1991). Some young children with autism who are developmentally delayed and those with multiple disabilities and visual impairments demonstrate "stimulus overselectivity" by focusing on an irrelevant aspect of a stimulus and ignoring the rest. For example, an infant may become distracted by the stripes on a container and neglect to play with the blocks in it. Therefore, sensory input for these infants should be carefully selected and organized to encourage attention and understanding. Third, specific interventions are needed to enhance interactions between caregivers and infants and to promote early communication by infants. When infants with visual impairments demonstrate disturbances in social interactions, communication, and responses to sensory stimuli, early interventionists and teachers who are certified in the field of blindness and visual impairment may need to collaborate with occupational therapists, speech and language therapists, and specialists in autism to provide optimal early intervention programs. Sidebar 3.8 presents a list of questions related to autism to guide early intervention practices with an individual infant who is visually impaired and autistic.

THE NEED FOR TEAMWORK

The complicated needs of infants who are visually impaired and have additional disabilities underscore the requirement for both interagency and interdisciplinary approaches to providing early intervention services. Federal legislation requires interagency and interdisciplinary coordination among various agencies and specialists serving infants with disabilities and their families at the state, local community, and program levels (Harbin & McNulty, 1990; Lowenthal, 1992; Woodruff & McGonigel, 1988). Depending on state regulations and local resources, an infant with a visual impairment and additional disabilities may have a primary early interventionist from one of many areas of special education (early childhood special education, visual impairment, hearing loss, or severe disabilities) and will probably receive services from multiple service providers (Chen & Dote-Kwan, 1998). Even though a service coordinator is identified on each Individual Family Service Plan, effective coordination remains a challenge in providing early intervention services. In reality, some infants and families may be receiving regularly scheduled yet separate visits from different service providers who do not communicate with each other, and some families may not even know why these professionals are visiting their homes. As illustrated in the accompanying vignette "Creating a Team for Lupita" and the vignette "Sam and His Early Intervention Team" presented later in this chapter, whether services involve just two service providers or several, most families find an uncoordinated model extremely unhelpful and disruptive to their family life.

CREATING A TEAM FOR LUPITA
Pamela Haag Schachter

I met 8-month-old Lupita and her family in my position as a consultant from a federally funded project. The Garcia family's life was centered in Lupita's bedroom, where her suction machine, oxygen, nebulizer, feeding pump, and apnea monitor were set up and in frequent use. Lupita's 2-year-old brother's toys were there, as was the couch where Mrs. Garcia slept at night, so she would immediately hear if Lupita needed suctioning. I sat in Lupita's bedroom and listened as Mr. and Mrs. Garcia told me the story of Lupita's traumatic birth and severe deprivation of oxygen as she was being born. Mrs. Garcia's tears displayed the grief she was still struggling with as she told me that the physicians had told her that Lupita could not see or hear and would never know her mother.

I inquired naively about what services Lupita and the family were receiving, and Mrs. Garcia answered by handing me an inch-thick pile of business cards. I began to sort through the cards to try to understand who was doing what and when each service provider came to the house. Mrs. Garcia did not know why all these people were coming or when to expect them. She did not know what they could do for Lupita and clearly had no idea of any goals or objectives that might have been written in an Individual Family Service Plan.

Following the first home visit, I began to call the professionals who were visiting Lupita. They included a visiting nurse from the family's health insurer, a nurse sent to provide occasional respite care, an occupational therapist, an early interventionist specializing in infants with multiple disabilities, a general infant development specialist, a teacher in the field of blindness and visual impairments, and a teacher in the field of deafness and hearing impairments. Not one of these professionals was aware that all the others were also visiting Lupita and her family.

I contacted the service coordinator assigned to the Garcia family and tried to explain tactfully that despite all the services, the family's urgent needs were not being met. Mrs. Garcia did not know what intervention could do for Lupita, how she could be involved in her daughter's treatment, or how to get the increased respite care that she so desperately needed. As I spoke to many of the professionals involved, I was overwhelmed by the lack of coordination between them and their seeming indifference. Each believed that as long as he or she was seeing Lupita and working in the assigned developmental area or body part, then all was well. The professionals seemed defensive, and my questions about the services being provided were taken as a condemnation. My frustration grew as I struggled to convince the service coordinator that Lupita's services were totally unco-

ordinated and had not even begun to address her unique needs as a child with dual sensory impairments. As professionals, we allowed our own agendas to interfere with the appropriate delivery of services.

Eventually, the service coordinator and I agreed to call a meeting of all Lupita's service providers. Choosing a date and time was difficult, and a few providers did not attend. The meeting began with introductions, clarifying the role of each provider and his or her service and schedule. We began to debate the relative value of each service, a process that only reinforced territorialism and fragmented services. Finally, the administrator who was hosting the meeting turned to Mrs. Garcia and asked her what she thought would help Lupita and the family. It was an important turning point.

Mrs. Garcia explained her urgent need for sleep and time with her 2-year-old son. She expressed concern about her ability to communicate with her daughter, asked how she could help her move her arms and legs, and wondered aloud if Lupita could see anything. The service providers in the room began to respond in a compassionate and professional manner, some suggesting that their services were a duplication or could be done on a consultant basis. The teacher of infants who are deaf asked to increase her services, as did the teacher of infants who are visually impaired. The service coordinator pledged to increase respite services, asking Mrs. Garcia how many hours a month she thought she needed. Paperwork was begun for a referral for physical therapy. Future team meetings were scheduled because everyone agreed that Lupita's complex needs required a coordinated approach.

Team Models

As was discussed in Chapter 1, there are three team models in early intervention services: multidisciplinary, interdisciplinary, and transdisciplinary (McCollum & Hughes, 1988; Woodruff & McGonigel, 1988). In the traditional multidisciplinary model, there is no planned sharing or overlap in assessment or intervention procedures among the various disciplines. In the interdisciplinary model, the results of assessments are discussed, interventions may be planned jointly, and discipline-specific interventions are implemented by each service provider. In the transdisciplinary model, service providers of various disciplines collaborate to conduct assessments and to plan and implement interventions. Families are active members of the transdisciplinary team, and interventions are integrated into the daily routines. Furthermore, role release—the willingness to share information about discipline-specific practices to help team members implement interventions and to teach team members to perform specific interventions—is at the heart of the transdisciplinary model (Orelove & Sobsey, 1987).

A survey of 10 early childhood special education programs found that multidisciplinary teams were used frequently for conducting assessments, interdisciplinary teams were common for implementing interventions, and transdisciplinary teams were the least common (McCollum & Hughes, 1988).The challenges of limited time and resources, skeptical attitudes, and traditional practices hinder the widespread implementation of a true transdisciplinary model (Chen, 1993). However, the transdisciplinary approach is essential for providing effective early intervention services to families and their infants with disabilities, especially those with significant disabilities.

Research on the early childhood special education services of different disciplines (special education, occupational therapy, special therapy, and speech and language therapy) in center-based settings has identified the need for a continuum of consultative models for different situations (McWilliam, 1995). Therapists in this study advocated the increased use of an integrated therapy model approach that integrates discipline-specific objectives and interventions into a child's daily activities and naturally occurring situations (Hill, Dobson-Burk, & Smith, 1989; McWilliam, 1995; Rainforth & Salisbury, 1988). This model increases opportunities for primary service providers, specialized consultants, and families to share their knowledge and skills. Moreover, it facilitates the use of the transdisciplinary approach and supports meaningful outcomes by building on the strengths and interests of young children in creating motivating interventions (Brown & Lehr, 1993; Campbell, 1991; Chen, 1995). The vignette "Sam and His Early Intervention Team" demonstrates this approach.

SAM AND HIS EARLY INTERVENTION TEAM
Deborah Chen

Sam is 18 months old and receives home-based intervention services. His diagnoses include anophthalmia (no eyeballs), hypotonia (low tone), and severe developmental delay. Sam is totally blind and seems to recognize his parents' voices. He vocalizes to get attention; is beginning to grasp objects, such as his bottle; can sit independently; and is beginning to stand with support.

Sam and his mother receive weekly home visits from a teacher who is certified in the field of blindness and visual impairments through the school district, and they go to weekly occupational therapy sessions funded by the family's health insurance at a nearby center. This teacher and occupational therapist have changed from a multidisciplinary approach to implementing an interdisciplinary model. Previously, each saw Sam and his mother individually and never shared information. Sam's mother, Mrs. Smith, found these services to be time consuming and confusing for both Sam and herself. Sometimes the two service providers made suggestions that were different or even contradicted each other. For example, the teacher suggested a walker to assist Sam in his movement and exploration, whereas the occupational therapist did not recommend a walker at this time. The teacher was using touch and object cues (for example, having Sam touch the chair before sitting him in it) to support Sam's development of communication and understanding of activities, whereas the occupational therapy used different touch cues during Sam's therapy session (like patting Sam on his bottom before sitting him in a chair).

Mrs. Smith asked these service providers to share their observations and findings of assessments and to develop interventions together. The occupational therapist shared specific techniques for increasing Sam's muscle tone, for positioning him, and for encouraging his manipulation of toys. The teacher showed techniques to encourage Sam to search for objects and explore them tactilely and demonstrated some touch and object cues that she and Mrs. Smith had developed with Sam during caregiving and vocal play routines. Together, the team developed specific techniques for Sam's special learning needs, such as, using consistent touch cues and selecting communication and positioning strategies that everyone would use in his or her interactions with Sam.

In six months, Sam will attend the center-based infant program that provides a transdisciplinary model. His classroom teacher will be an early childhood special education teacher who will work closely with the specialized consultants: occupational therapist, teacher of children with visual impairments, speech and language therapist, and orientation and mobility instructor to develop and implement Sam's program. The consultants will see Sam in the classroom setting, share observations and strategies with each other, and identify ways of integrating their discipline-specific objectives within the context of the daily schedule.

Creating a Team

Although there is great variation in models of service delivery, many early intervention programs provide home-based services, and some also provide center-based services. Depending on their learning needs and the discipline of their primary service providers, infants with visual impairment and additional disabilities and their families frequently receive services from multiple service providers, such as an infant development specialist or early childhood special educator, occupational therapist or physical therapist, a credentialed teacher of children who are visually impaired, credentialed teacher of children who are hearing impaired, and an orientation and mobility specialist. In addition, not all these service providers work for one school district or agency. It is essential that service coordinators, as well as program and agency administrators, provide opportunities for true collaboration.

The effectiveness of a transdisciplinary team approach is enhanced if service providers have discipline-specific competencies and skills that they contribute to the process. Each member of the team should have a particular contribution to make. At the same time, service providers need to realize when additional expertise is necessary and where to find help. To facilitate a team process, service providers should recognize the unique and shared interventions provided by the different disciplines serving infants with multiple disabilities and then identify strategies for developing a coordinated approach for providing meaningful transdisciplinary interventions within the infant's and family's daily routine. To help define the role and responsibilities of each member, each service provider may reflect on the following set of questions:

1. What is your discipline's role and responsibility in serving infants and their families in the specific early intervention program?

2. What services do you provide?

3. What do you view as the unique services provided by your discipline?

4. What training does your discipline require to provide these services to infants with multiple disabilities?

5. What professional competencies are needed for your discipline to work effectively with infants whose multiple disabilities include visual impairment?

6. What strategies do you use to integrate your discipline-specific objectives into an infant's daily routine?

7. What strategies do you use to develop an effective team approach in serving an infant whose multiple disabilities include visual impairment?

On the basis of their responses to these questions, service providers can identify and share similarities and differences across their disciplines.

Specific roles and responsibilities in a particular team depend on each program's or agency's characteristics and each service provider's philosophy and professional background. For example, depending on their training, an occupational therapist, a teacher who is certified in the field of blindness and visual impairments, and an early childhood special educator may have strong backgrounds in facilitating fine motor and play skills. The occupational therapist is usually the expert on feeding strategies, although some speech and language therapists also have that expertise. Similarly, a speech and language therapist, early childhood special educator, and teacher who is certified in the field of deafness and hearing impairments all focus on the early development of communication and may be familiar with a variety of nonsymbolic modes of communication. Although conducting functional vision assessments is usually the responsibility of the teacher who is certified in the field of blindness and visual impairments, some occupational therapists may also have been trained in this area. The opportunity to share individual perspectives on roles and responsibilities and to agree on primary responsibilities should create a sense of collegial support; mutual recognition of each other's contributions; and, in the end, provision of more effective services.

In addition to defining roles and responsibilities, there has to be a process for sharing information, planning, and implementing meaningful interventions. This process can be established by formulating ground rules for the process and maintaining communication among team members by sharing reports, resources, and progress. Specific strategies involve interagency meetings, shared staff meetings, joint home visits, family interviews, joint assessments for program planning, family-directed goals, and infusing objectives within daily routines.

CONCLUSION

Effective early intervention services for infants with visual impairments and other disabilities require a transdisciplinary approach involving the family and service providers from selected disciplines. The primary early interventionist serving an individual infant who is visually impaired and has other disabilities should be knowledgeable about the infant's diagnoses, the effects of these diagnoses on early development, interventions being provided by other service providers, and the family's concerns and priorities.To meet the multiple learning needs of these infants, team members must have additional time and opportunities to share information, to receive and provide cross-disciplinary training, and to develop true collaboration with families. Only in this way will these infants and their families receive individualized, coordinated, and meaningful early intervention services.

REFERENCES

Accardo, P. J., & Capute, A. J. (1996). Mental retardation. In A. J. Capute and P. J. Accardo (Eds.), *Developmental disabilities in infancy and childhood. Vol II: The spectrum of developmental disabilities* (2nd ed., pp. 211–219). Baltimore, MD: Paul H. Brookes.

Als, H. (1982). Toward a synactive theory of development: Promise for the assessment and support of infant individuality. *Infant Mental Health Journal, 3,* 229–243.

Als, H. (1986). A synactive model of neonatal behavioral organization: Framework for the assessment of neurobehavioral development in the premature infant and for support of infants and parents in the neonatal intensive care environment. *Physical and Occupational Therapy in Pediatrics, 6*(3–4), 3–55.

American Psychiatric Association. (1994). *Diagnostic and statistical manual of mental disorders* (4th ed.). Washington, DC: Author.

Ayres, A. J. (1972). *Sensory integration and learning disorders.* Los Angeles: Western Psychological Services.

Berkow, R. (1992). *The Merck manual of diagnosis and therapy.* Rahway, NJ: Merck, Sharp & Dohme Research Laboratories.

Bernbaum, J. C., & Batshaw, M. L. (1997). Born too soon, born too small. In M. L. Batshaw (Ed.) *Children with disabilities* (4th ed., pp. 115–139). Baltimore, MD: Paul H. Brookes.

Bishop, V. E. (1991). Preschool visually impaired children: A demographic study. *Journal of Visual Impairment & Blindness, 85,* 69–74.

Bly, L. A. (1991). A historical and current view of the basis of NDT. *Pediatric Physical Therapy, 3,* 131–135.

Bobath, B. (1967). The very early treatment of cerebral palsy. *Developmental Medicine and Child Neurology, 9,*373–390.

Bobath, K. (1980). A neurophysiological basis for the treatment of cerebral palsy. *Clinics in Developmental Medicine* (No. 75), 77–87.

Bobele, G. B., & Bodensteiner, J. B. (1990). Infantile spasms. *Neurologic Clinics, 8,* 633–645.

Brazelton, T. B. (1984). Neonatal behavioral assessment scale. *Clinics in Developmental Medicine,* (No. 88). London: Spastics International Medical Publisher.

Brown, F., & Lehr, D. H. (1993). Making activities meaningful for students with severe multiple disabilities. *Teaching Exceptional Children, 25,* 12–16.

Brown, J. K., & Hussain, J. H. (1991). Status epilepticus. II. Treatment. *Developmental Medicine and Child Neurology, 33,* 97–109.

Brown, L. W. (1997). Seizure disorders. In M. L. Batshaw (Ed.) *Children with disabilities* (4th ed., pp. 553–593). Baltimore, MD: Paul H. Brookes.

Brunquell, P. J. (1994). Listening to epilepsy. *Infants and Young Children, 7*(1), 24–33.

Bureau of Education for Exceptional Students. (1986). *Volume A-K: Movement analysis and curriculum for visually impaired preschoolers.* Tallahassee: Florida Department of Education.

Campbell, P. H. (1991). Evaluation and assessment in early intervention for infants and toddlers. *Journal of Early Intervention, 151,* 36–45.

Capute, A. J., & Accardo, P. J. (1996). Cerebral palsy. The spectrum of motor dysfunction. In A. J. Capute & P. J. Accardo (Eds.), *Developmental disabilities in infancy and childhood. Vol II: The spectrum of developmental disabilities* (2nd ed., pp. 81–100). Baltimore, MD: Paul H. Brookes.

Chen, D. (1993). Early intervention. In J. W. Reiman & O. A. Johnson (Eds.), *Proceedings from the National Symposium on Children and Youth Who Are Deaf-blind* (pp. 37–44). Monmouth, OR: Teaching Research.

Chen, D. (1995). The beginnings of communication: Early childhood. In K. M. Huebner, J. G. Prickett, T. R. Welch, & E. Joffee (Eds.), *Hand in hand.*

Essentials of communication and orientation and mobility for your students who are deaf-blind (pp. 185–218). New York: AFB Press.

Chen, D., & Dote-Kwan, J. (1998). Early intervention services for young children with visual impairments and other disabilities and their families. In S. Sacks & R. Silberman (Eds.), *Educating students with visual impairments and other disabilities* (pp. 303–338). Baltimore, MD: Paul H. Brookes.

Chen, D., & Haney, M. (1995). An early intervention model for infants who are deaf-blind. *Journal of Visual Impairment & Blindness, 89,* 213–221.

Colombo, J., & Horowitz, F. D. (1987). Behavioral state as a lead variable in neonatal research. *Merrill-Palmer Quarterly, 334,* 23–427.

Commission on Classification and Terminology of the International League Against Epilepsy. (1989). Proposal for revised classification of epilepsies and epileptic syndromes. *Epilepsia, 30,* 389–399.

Cress, P., Spellman, C. R., DeBriere, T. J., Sizemore, A. C., Northam, J. K., & Johnson, J. L. (1981). Vision screening for persons with severe handicaps. *Journal of the Association for the Severely Handicapped, 6,* 41–50.

Dietz, S., & Ferrell, K. A. (1993). Early services for young children with visual impairment: From diagnosis to comprehensive services. *Infants and Young Children, 6*(1) 68–76.

Edwards, L. E., Goehl, K. S., & Gordon, L. A. (n.d.) *Profiles: Individuals with deaf-blindness.* Terre Haute, IN: Indiana State University, Blumberg Center for Interdisciplinary Studies in Special Education, Indiana Deaf-Blind Services Project.

Ellis, D. (1986). *Sensory impairments in mentally handicapped people.* San Diego: College Press.

Epilepsy Foundation of America. (1994). *Seizure recognition and first aid.* Landover, MD: Author.

Farber, J. M. (1996). Autism and other communication disorders. In A. J. Capute & P. J. Accardo (Eds.), *Developmental disabilities in infancy and childhood. Vol II: The spectrum of developmental disabilities* (2nd. ed., pp. 347–364). Baltimore, MD: Paul H. Brookes.

Feinberg, E., & Beyer, J. (1998). Creating public policy in a climate of clinical indeterminacy: Lovaas as the case example du jour. *Infants and Young Children, 10*(3), 54–66.

Ferrell, K. A. (1998). *Project PRISM: A longitudinal study of the developmental patterns of children who are visually impaired. Executive summary. CFDA 84.0203C-Field-initiated Research HO23C10188.* Greeley, CO: University of Northern Colorado.

Ferrell, K. A., Trief, E., Dietz, S. J., Bonner, M. A., Cruz, D., Ford, E., & Stratton, J. M. (1990). Visually impaired infants research consortium (VIIRC): First year results. *Journal of Visual Impairment & Blindness, 84,* 404–410.

Finnie, N. R. (1990). *Handling the cerebral palsied child at home* (3rd. ed.). New York: Dutton.

Fisher, E., Van Dyke, D. C., Sears, L., Matzen, J., Lin-Dyken, D., & McBrien, D. M. (1999). Recent research on the etiologies of autism. *Infants and Young Children, 11*(3), 1–8.

Fredericks, H. D. B., & Baldwin, V. L. (1987). Individuals with sensory impairments: Who are they? How are they educated? In L. Goetz, D. Guess, & K. Stremel-Campbell (Eds.), *Innovative program design for individuals with dual sensory impairments* (pp. 3–12). Baltimore, MD: Paul H. Brookes.

Freeman, B. J. (1993). The syndrome of autism: Update and guidelines for diagnosis. *Infants and Young Children, 6*(3), 1–11.

Freeman, P. (1985). *The deaf-blind baby. A programme of care.* London, England: William Heinemann Medical Books.

Gense, M. H., & Gense, D. J. (1994). Identifying autism in children with blindness and visual impairments. *RE:view, 26,* 55–62.

Glass, P. (1993). Development of visual function in preterm infants: Implications for early intervention. *Infants and Young Children, 6*(1), 11–20.

Goldson, E. (1996). The micropremie: Infants with birth weight less than 800 grams. *Infants and Young Children, 8*(3) 1–10.

Good, W. V., Jan, J. E., DeSa, L., Barkovich, A. J., Groenveld, M., & Hoyt, C. S. (1994). Cortical visual impairment in children. *Survey of Ophthalmology, 38,* 351–364.

Greenspan, S. I. (1992a). *Infancy and early childhood: The practice of clinical assessment and intervention with emotional and developmental challenges.* Madison, CT: International Universities Press.

Greenspan, S. I. (1992b). Reconsidering the diagnosis and treatment of very young children with autistic spectrum or pervasive developmental disorder. *Zero to Three, 10,* 1–9.

Greenspan, S. I., & Wieder, S. (1997). An integrated developmental approach to interventions for young children with severe difficulties in relating and communicating. *Assessing and treating infants and young children with severe difficulties in relating and communicating* (pp. 5–18). Washington, DC: Zero to Three: National Center for Infants, Toddlers, and Families.

Guess, D., Seigel-Causey, E., Roberts, S., Guy, B., & Rues, J. (1993). Analysis of state organization patterns among students with profound disabilities. *Journal of the Association for Persons with Severe Handicaps, 18,* 93–108.

Hack, M., Taylor, G., Klein, N., Eiben, R., Schatschneider, C., & Mercuri-Minich, N. (1994). School-age outcomes in children with birthweights under 750 grams. *New England Journal of Medicine, 331,* 753–759.

Hanson, M., & Lynch, E. (1995). *Early intervention: Implementing child and family services for infants and toddlers who are at risk or disabled* (2nd ed.). Austin, TX: PRO-ED.

Harbin, G., & McNulty, B. (1990). Policy implementation: Perspectives on service coordination and interagency coordination. In S. Meisels & A. Shonoff (Eds.), *Handbook of early intervention* (pp. 700–721). New York: Cambridge University Press.

Harris, S. R., & Tada, W. L. (1983). Providing developmental therapy services. In S. G. Garwood and R. R. Fewell (Eds.), *Educating handicapped infants. Issues in development and intervention* (pp. 343–368). Rockville, MD: Aspen.

Hatton, D. D., Bailey, D. B., Burchinal, M. R., & Ferrell, K. A. (1997). Developmental growth curves of preschool children with visual impairments. *Child Development, 68,* 788–806.

Heller, K. W., Alberto, P. A., Forney, P. E., & Schwartzman, M. N. (1996). *Understanding physical, sensory, & health impairments.* Pacific Grove, CA: Brookes/Cole.

Heriza, C. R., & Sweeney, J. K. (1995). Pediatric physical therapy: Part II. Approaches to movement dysfunction. *Infants and Young Children, 8*(2), 1–14.

Hill, E. W., Dobson-Burk, B., & Smith, B. A. (1989). Orientation and mobility for infants who are visually impaired. *RE:view, 21,* 47–60.

Hoon, A. H., Jr., (1996). Visual impairments in children. In A. J. Capute & P. J. Accardo (Eds.), *Developmental disabilities in infancy and childhood. Vol. II: The spectrum of developmental disabilities* (2nd ed., pp. 461–478). Baltimore, MD: Paul H. Brookes.

Howard, V. F., Williams, B. F., Port, P. D., & Lepper, C. (1997). *Very young children with special needs: A formative approach for the twenty-first century.* Upper Saddle River, NJ: Merrill.

Hutchinson, M. K., & Sandall, S. R. (1995). Congenital TORCH infections in infants and young children: Neurodevelopmental sequelae and implications for intervention. *Topics in Early Childhood Special Education, 15,* 65–82.

Hyvarinen, L. (1988). *Vision in children: Normal and abnormal.* Meaford, ON, Canada: Canadian Deaf-Blind and Rubella Association.

Jacobson, J. W., & Janicki, M. P. (1985). Functional and health status characteristics of persons with severe handicaps in New York State. *Journal of the Association for Persons with Severe Handicaps, 10,* 51–60.

Jurgens, M. R. (1977). *Confrontation between the young deaf-blind child and the outer world. How to make the world surveyable by organized structure.* Amsterdam, The Netherlands: Swets & Zeitlinger.

Kirchner, C. (1989). National estimates of prevalence and demographics of children with visual impairments. In. M. C. Wang, M. C. Reynolds, & H. L.

Walberg (Eds.), *Handbook of special education: Research and practice. Vol. 3, Low incidence conditions* (pp. 135–153). Oxford, England: Pergamon Press.

Klein, M. D., Chen, D., & Haney, M. (1996). *Project PLAI curriculum: Facilitating caregiver-infant interactions.* Northridge: California State University, Northridge, Department of Special Education.

Knott, M., & Voss, D. E. (1968). *Proprioceptive neuromuscular facilitation: patterns and techniques* (2nd ed.). New York: Harper & Row.

La Pine, T. R., Jackson, J. C., & Bennett, F. C. (1995). Outcome of infants weighing less than 800 grams at birth: 15 years' experience. *Pediatrics, 96,* 479–483.

Lord, C., Bristol, M. M., & Schopler, E. (1993). Early intervention for children with autism and related developmental disorders. In E. Schopler, M. Van Bourgondien, & M. M. Bristol (Eds.), *Preschool issues in autism,* New York: Plenum Press.

Lowenthal, B. (1992). Interagency collaboration in early intervention: Rationale, barriers and implications. *Infant-Toddler Intervention, 2,* 103–112.

Lowenthal, B. (1997). HIV infection: Transmission, effects on early development and interventions. *Infant-Toddler Intervention, 7,* 191–200.

Luckasson, R., Coulter, D. L., Polloway, E. A., Reiss, S., Schalock, R. L., Snell, M. G., Spitalnik, D. M., & Stark, J. A. (1992). *Mental retardation: Definition, classification, and systems of supports* (9th ed.). Washington, DC: American Association on Mental Retardation.

MacMillan, D. L., & Reschly, D. J. (1998). Overrepresentation of minority students: The case for greater specificity or reconsideration of the variables examined. *Journal of Special Education, 32,* 15–24.

Mauk, J. E. (1993). Autism and pervasive developmental disorders. *Pediatric Clinics of North America, 40,* 567–578.

McCollum, J. A., & Hughes, M. (1988). Staffing patterns and team models in infancy programs. In J. B. Jordan, J. J. Gallagher, P. L. Hutinger, & M. B. Karnes (Eds.), *Early childhood special education: Birth to three* (pp. 129–146). Reston, VA: Council for Exceptional Children.

McCormick, M. C. (1989). Long-term follow-up of infants discharged from neonatal intensive care units. *Journal of the American Medical Association, 261,* 24–31.

McGinnes, J. M., & Treffry, J. A. (1982). *Deaf-blind infants and children. A developmental guide.* Toronto, ON, Canada: University of Toronto Press.

McWilliam, R. A. (1995). Integration of therapy and consultative special education: A continuum in early intervention. *Infants and Young Children, 7*(4), 29–38.

Michael, M., & Paul, P. (1991). Early interventions for infants with deaf-blindness. *Exceptional Children, 57,* 200–210.

Morse, M. (1991). Visual gaze behaviors: Considerations in working with visually impaired multihandicapped children. *RE:view, 23,* 5–15.

Nelson, K. B. (1996). Epidemiology and etiology of cerebral palsy. In A. J. Capute & P. J. Accardo (Eds.), *Developmental disabilities in infancy and childhood. Vol II: The spectrum of developmental disabilities* (2nd ed., pp. 73–79). Baltimore, MD: Paul H. Brookes.

Orelove, F. P., & Sobsey, D. (1987). *Educating children with multiple disabilities: A transdisciplinary approach.* Baltimore: Paul H. Brookes.

Outlette, S. (1984). Deaf blind population estimates. In D. Watson, S. Barrett, & R. Brown (Eds.), *A model service delivery system for deaf-blind persons* (pp. 7–10). Little Rock: University of Arkansas.

Pellegrino, L. (1997). Cerebral palsy. In M. L. Batshaw (Ed.) *Children with disabilities* (4th ed., pp. 499–593). Baltimore, MD: Paul H. Brookes.

Pellegrino, L., & Dormans, J. P. (1998). Definitions, etiology, and epidemiology of cerebral palsy. In L. Pellegrino & J. P. Dormans (Eds.), *Caring for children with cerebral palsy: A team approach* (pp. 3–30). Baltimore, MD: Paul H. Brookes.

Physicians' Desk Reference (49th ed.). (1995). Oradell, NJ: Medical Economics Data.

Rainforth, B., & Salisbury, C. L. (1988). Functional home programs: A model for therapists. *Topics in Early Childhood Special Education, (7),* 33–45.

Regenbogen, L. S., & Coscas, G. J. (1985). *Oculo-auditory syndromes.* New York: Masson.

Rogers, P. T., Roizen, N. J., & Capone, G. T. (1996). Down syndrome. In A. J. Capute & P. J. Accardo (Eds.), *Developmental disabilities in infancy and childhood. Vol II: The spectrum of developmental disabilities* (2nd ed., pp. 221–244). Baltimore, MD: Paul H. Brookes.

Rood, M. S. (1956). Neurophysiological mechanisms utilized in the treatment of neuromuscular dysfunction. *American Journal of Occupational Therapy, 10,* 220–225.

Rowland, C., Schweigert, P. D., Prickett, J. G. (1995). Communication systems, devices, and modes. In K. M. Huebner, J. G. Prickett, T. R. Welch, & E. Joffee (Eds.), *Hand in hand. Essentials of communication and orientation and mobility for your students who are deaf-blind* (pp. 219–259). New York: AFB Press.

Sillanpaa, M. (1992). Epilepsy in children: Prevalence, disability, and handicap. *Epilepsia, 33,* 444–449.

Smith T., & Lovaas, O. I. (1998). Intensive and early behavioral intervention with autism: The UCLA young autism project. *Infants and Young Children, 10*(3), 67–78.

Teplin, S. W. (1995). Visual impairment in infants and young children. *Infants and Young Children, 8*(1), 18–51.

Thoman, E. B., & Whitney, M. P. (1990). Behavioral states in infants: Individual differences and individual analyses. In J. Colombo & J. W. Fagen (Eds.), *Individual differences in infancy* (pp. 113–135). Hillsdale, NJ: Lawrence Erlbaum.

Thomasgard, M., & Shonkoff, J. P. (1993). Mental retardation. In C. H. Zeanah, Jr. (Ed.). *Handbook of infant mental health* (pp. 250–259). New York: Guilford Press.

Trief, E., Duckman, R., Morse, A. R., & Silberman, R. K. (1989). Retinopathy of prematurity. *Journal of Visual Impairment & Blindness, 83*, 500–504.

van Dijk, J. (1967a). The first steps of the deaf-blind child towards language. *International Journal for the Education of the Blind, 15,* 112–114.

van Dijk, J. (1967b). The non-verbal deaf-blind child and his world: His outgrowth toward the world of symbols. *Proceedings of the Jaarverslag Instituit voor Doven, 1964–1967* (pp. 73–110). Sint-Michielsgestel, The Netherlands: Instituit voor Doven.

VandenBerg, K. A., & Hanson, M. J. (1993). *Homecoming for babies after the neonatal intensive care nursery: A guide for professionals in supporting families and their infants' early development.* Austin, TX: PRO-ED.

Vining, E. P. G., & Freeman, J. M. (1996). Epilepsy and developmental disabilities. In A. J. Capute & P. J. Accardo (Eds.), *Developmental disabilities in infancy and childhood. Vol. II: The spectrum of developmental disabilities* (2nd. ed., pp. 511–520). Baltimore, MD: Paul H. Brookes.

Volkmar, F. R. (1993). Autism and the pervasive developmental disorders. In C. H. Zeanah, Jr. (Ed.), *Handbook of infant mental health* (pp. 236–249). New York: Guilford Press.

Wallace, S. J. (1990). Risk of seizures (Annotation). *Developmental Medicine and Child Neurology, 32,* 645–649.

Watkins, S. (1989). *The INSITE model. Home intervention for infant, toddler, and preschool aged multihandicapped sensory impaired children* (Vols. 1 & 2). Logan, UT: Hope.

Wesson, M. D., & Maino, D. M. (1995). Oculovisual findings in children with Down syndrome, cerebral palsy, and mental retardation without specific etiology. In D. M. Maino (Ed.), *Diagnosis and management of special populations* (pp. 17–54). St. Louis, MO: Mosby Year Book.

Wieder, S. (1997). Creating connections: Intervention guidelines for increasing interaction with children with multisystem developmental disorder (MSDD). In *Assessing and treating infants and young children with severe difficulties in relating and communicating* (pp. 19–27). Washington, DC: Zero to Three: National Center for Infants, Toddlers, and Families.

Williamson, G. G., & Anzalone, M. (1997). Sensory integration: A key component of the evaluation and treatment of young children with severe difficulties in relating and communicating. In *Assessing and treating infants and young children with severe difficulties in relating and communicating* (pp. 29–36). Washington, DC: Zero to Three: National Center for Infants, Toddlers, and Families.

Writer, J. (1987). A movement-based approach to the education of students who are sensory impaired/multihandicapped. In L. Goetz, D. Guess, & K. Stremel-Campbell (Eds.), *Innovative program design for individuals with dual sensory impairments* (pp. 191–223). Baltimore, MD: Paul H. Brookes.

Woodruff, G., & McGonigel, M. (1988). Early intervention team approaches: The transdisciplinary team. In J. B. Jordan, J. J. Gallagher, P. L. Hutinger, & M. B. Karnes (Eds.), *Early childhood special education: Birth to three* (pp. 163–181). Reston, VA: Council for Exceptional Children.

Zero to Three/National Center for Clinical Infant Programs. (1994). *Diagnostic classification: 0–3. Diagnostic classification of mental health and developmental disorders of infancy an early childhood.* Washington, DC: Author.

Zigler, E. (1981). A plea to end the use of patterning treatment for retarded children. *American Journal of Orthopsychiatry, 51,* 388–390.

PART II

Assessment: The Foundation of Intervention

In many ways, assessment provides the foundation for service delivery. To plan and provide essential services for a child, the early interventionist in collaboration with the family should identify what the child needs. Obtaining accurate, comprehensive information about an infant's overall medical condition and existing disabilities is critical in this process. The chapters that follow provide information on the assessment of visual impairment and hearing loss because of the complex impact that these impairments have on a child's ability to form concepts, develop language, and social skills. Assessing infants who have disabilities involves (a) a careful review of available records, (b) gathering information from families, (c) systematic observation of the infant in typical activities and structured situations, and (d) sharing perspectives with the family and other members of the infant's early intervention team. This way the early interventionist can obtain information about the infant's medical needs and disabilities, identify the family's priorities and concerns about their child's development, identify the infant's strength and interests, select intervention priorities with the family and other service providers, and coordinate the intervention activities with service providers from various disciplines.

4

Clinical Vision Assessments for Infants

Deborah Orel-Bixler

Until about 25 years ago, it was thought that infants could see little. Textbooks for ophthalmologists in 1960 stated that infants could see light and dark but could not see patterns. Over the past 20 years, the development of vision has been studied intensively by developmental and experimental psychologists and vision care practitioners. It is now known that the visual system of infants is relatively mature at birth and rapidly develops in the early postnatal years (Teller & Movshon, 1987).

DEVELOPMENT OF THE VISUAL SYSTEM

Of all the human organs, the eye is the most fully developed at birth. Formation of the eye begins at 22 days of fetal life and develops from an outpouching of the developing brain. By six weeks after conception, the ocular structures and differentiation of the brain are fairly well developed. Therefore, teratogenic factors (drug abuse, infection, and medications) that occur in the first trimester of pregnancy often result in ocular defects. The eye of the newborn is two-thirds the size of the adult's. It undergoes its most rapid growth during the first year of life and finally reaches the length and size of the adult's eye by adolescence. At birth, the anterior structures of the eye (such as the cornea, lens, and iris) are more developed than the posterior structures (including the retina). (See the diagram of the eye in the Appendix to this chapter.) In the retina, the photoreceptors, consisting of rods (responsible for night vision) and cones (responsible for day vision, detail vision, and color vision), are all present at birth but are immature in size and spacing. The inner layers of the retina differentiate further after birth. In particular, the fovea (central area of the retina specialized for acute vision) is immature and develops later than the peripheral retina. The optic nerve, which conveys information from the eye to the brain, is almost full size at birth. Myelination of this visual pathway to speed the neural connection rate is not complete until age 2. The lateral geniculate nucleus (a midbrain relay station) has the full complement of neurons present at birth, but the neurons enlarge and establish more connections to other neurons with age. The visual cortex of the brain has all the neurons of one's lifetime present at birth, but these neurons migrate to superficial layers of the brain and their neural connections increase.

The anatomical and physiological developments of the visual system are accompanied by a rapid improvement in visual capabilities. Most aspects of visual function reach adult levels during the first year of life. Visual fixation is evident at birth, and accurate fixation is achieved by 6 to 9 weeks. The newborn's eye movements change from saccadic, or steplike, fixational movements to smooth-pursuit eye movements by age 2 to 3 months (Aslin, 1987). Optokinetic nystagmus (OKN) and the vestibular ocular reflex (VOR; reflexive eye movements induced by spinning) are involuntary eye movements that are important for providing stability of visual images on the eye when objects in the world move (OKN) or the infant moves (VOR). OKN is present at birth but is immature until age 3 months. The newborn is unable to suppress the VOR until age 2 months. Accommodation, the ability to focus the intraocular lens of the eye for near viewing, is present at birth but inaccurate until age 2–3 months (Banks, 1980). Fortunately, the small pupils of the newborn permit a relatively large depth of focus or range over which visual objects remain clear without focusing effort. The average refractive error of newborns is hyperopic (farsighted) because of the strong optical power of the lens and cornea and short axial length of the eye. The incidence of astigmatism ranges from 15 percent to 30 percent (Fulton et al., 1980). The prevalence of hyperopia and astigmatism decreases with age (Abrahamsson, Fabian, & Sjöstrand, 1988). The refractive error in the majority of infants disappears by 9 to 12 months (Baldwin, 1990).

Visual capabilities improve rapidly during the first year of life. Contrast sensitivity, the ability to detect differences in the brightness of or subtle shades of gray in large objects is adultlike by age 10 weeks (Norcia, Hamer, & Tyler, 1990). Infants have measurable color discrimination as early as age 2 weeks, although they need more saturated (brighter) colors and larger target areas than do adults to discriminate colors. Color vision improves over the first 3 months of life (Brown, 1990). Visual acuity, the ability to discern fine details, reaches adult levels by age 6 to 8 months (Norcia & Tyler, 1985). Stereopsis, the ability to discern fine-depth, or three-dimensional, vision, has a rapid onset at age 3 months and reaches near-adult levels in most infants by age 6 months (Birch, Gwiazada, & Held, 1982). The extent of the peripheral visual field of infants increases rapidly after age 2 months. By 1 year of age, the upper visual field reaches adult size, but the lateral and lower visual fields are still smaller than the adult size (Mohn & van Hof-van Duin, 1986a).

EARLY IDENTIFICATION OF VISUAL PROBLEMS

Any hindrance to normal visual developmental processes should be detected early and remedied. Vision screening at birth and during the first 6 months of life is important. Unfortunately, primary care physicians usually limit their visual assessments to ocular media clarity, which does not detect strabismus (eye turns) and amblyopia (unilateral loss of vision) (Campbell & Charney, 1991). For this reason, the current recommendation by both the American Academy of Optometry and the American Academy of Ophthalmology is for complete eye examinations to be given to all infants at 6 to 8 months of age, followed by examinations at age 2 1/2. The basic components of a vision examination include the infant's medical and family history; evaluation of the alignment and binocularity of the eyes; determination of refractive error (focus of the eyes); quantification of visual capabilities, including visual acuity, color vision, contrast sensitivity, depth perception and visual fields; and assessment of the health of the eyes.

Table 4.1   PREVALENCE OF VISION PROBLEMS IN SEVERAL STUDIES OF CHILDREN WITH AND WITHOUT DISABILITIES (PERCENTAGE)

Status	Percentage with Vision Problem		
	Refractive error	Strabismus	Other
Nondisabled	15–30	2–4	—
Cerebral palsy	21–76	15–60	1–25
Mental retardation	52	16–40	21
Down syndrome	42–73	23–44	33
Fragile X syndrome	59	30–50	13

Source: Based on data from M. D. Wesson and D. M. Maino, "Oculovisual findings in children with Down Syndrome, cerebral palsy, and mental retardation without specific etiology, in D. M. Maino (Ed.), *Diagnosis and Management of Special Populations* (St. Louis: Mosby Year Book, 1995), 17–54.

The infant with severe or multiple disabilities is at a greater risk of vision disorders, since there is a high prevalence of visual impairments in the population with multiple disabilities (Edwards, Price, & Weisskopf, 1972; Harcourt, 1974; Jan, Freeman, & Scott, 1977; Landau & Berson, 1971; Orel-Bixler, Haegerstrom-Portnoy, & Hall, 1989) as listed in Table 4.1. Several studies have indicated that children with more severe disabling conditions have more severe vision problems (Landau & Berson, 1971; Mohn & van Hof-van Duin, 1986b).

Children with cerebral palsy who have refractive errors are three times more likely to be farsighted than nearsighted. Other ocular anomalies that are associated with cerebral palsy include nystagmus (12%), optic atrophy (8%), visual field defect (5.6%), cortical visual impairment (3.6%), cataract (2.2%), fundus anomaly (6.1%), microphthalmos (5.9%), and corneal opacity (2.2%) (Wesson & Maino, 1995).

It is important to detect these problems early to provide proper intervention. Conditions that are not correctable through medical or optical means must be understood so that appropriate vision rehabilitation and educational programs can be implemented. The examination techniques for infants with severe or multiple disabilities are the same as for infants without disabilities but may require some modification of the testing procedure.

Most aspects of the vision examination rely on objective measures that require the examiner to be not only fast and flexible, but also patient. Any behavior-based testing techniques should be tailored to the developmental level of the individual infant or child. For example, young children with cerebral palsy and limited motor abilities may need more time to respond if the task requires pointing. If pointing proves to be too formidable, then mere observation of the child's looking behavior or fixation pattern should be substituted. The examiner should establish rapport with and determine the appropriate reinforcement to motivate the child. A visually impaired infant may respond only to auditory reinforcement, not to the visual reinforcement of an examiner's smile. The examination should be scheduled with consideration of medications and dosage times for infants and children who take seizure medications, in particular, to ensure maximum alertness. Scheduling the examination in the morning or after nap time often ensures a more attentive and alert infant. The examiner should be receptive to parents' or guardians' suggestions regarding modifications of the testing procedures. For example, when a child is asked to locate a visual target from between two locations, a parent may note that it is easier for the child to indicate yes or no regarding the presence or absence of a single target presented sequentially, rather than to choose between two targets presented simultaneously. A more thorough history is often required to gather information about the infant's or child's disabilities in areas other than vision, such as motor limitations or hearing problems, since these disabilities may affect the vision procedures of the examination.

THE VISION EXAMINATION

The vision examination of infants includes the following components:

- taking a history that includes taking the medical and ocular histories of the infant and the family
- using confrontation tests to evaluate the infant's fixation and eye-movement behavior
- determining refractive error or the focusing error of the eyes
- assessing the infant's visual fields or peripheral vision

- evaluating the health of the anterior and posterior structures of the eyes
- measuring the infant's visual capabilities, such as visual acuity, by qualitative or quantitative methods
- measuring contrast sensitivity (the ability to detect differences in brightness and color vision)
- referring the infant for other diagnostic tests, such as an electroretinogram, to assess the health of the eyes or neuroimaging to assess the health of the central nervous system
- meeting with the parents or guardians to explain the findings, recommend treatment and follow-up, and refer the infant for early intervention services.

History

Taking an accurate medical and ocular history of an infant requires the careful review of several aspects of the infant's pre- and postnatal course. Information gathered from the infant's parents or guardians includes the reason for the examination; signs and symptoms, including the family's and pediatrician's observations; the family's history of vision or medical problems; and the child's pre-, peri- and postnatal course or complications.

Chief Complaint or Reason for the Examination

The first question concerns the chief complaint or reason for the eye examination to clarify the nature of the presenting problem. Parents, grandparents, or other family members are usually concerned about the infant's visual inattention, that is, the baby's failure to make eye contact, respond to familiar faces, or fixate and follow objects with his or her eyes. The early presence of nystagmus (repetitive, usually rapid, and involuntary movements or rotation of the eyes) or wandering eye movements generally prompts an early vision assessment. A difficult prenatal or neonatal course, such as prematurity, is another indication of the need for an early eye examination. Parents want to know first what the infant can "see" and then if anything can be done (treatment or intervention strategies) if the infant cannot see well or at all.

The following ocular conditions can result in poor vision and lead to visual inattention in infants:

- opacities of the ocular media, including bilateral cataracts or corneal opacities associated with congenital glaucoma
- disorders of the retina, such as achromatopsia, congenital stationary night blindness, Leber's congenital amaurosis, albinism, retinal degenerations associated with rare syndromes and metabolic disorders, retinopathy of prematurity, vitreous hemorrhage, and macular lesions
- optic nerve disorders, such as optic nerve hypoplasia and optic nerve atrophy
- disorders of the brain, including cortical visual impairment.

All these conditions can be diagnosed with a vision examination, but not all present obvious signs to the parents, other than visual inattention. (See the Glossary for more information on these conditions.)

Signs and Symptoms

The signs during infancy that a parent may recognize and that may indicate a severe vision-threatening problem are listed in Sidebar 4.1. These signs should prompt a visit to the infant's pediatrician (Teplin, 1995) and eye care professional.

The specific behaviors of an infant that suggest poor vision may include staring at lights, nystagmus, eye poking, failure to smile, or disinterest in the visual environment. The apparent visual difficulty may be present only under specific conditions, such as dim or bright illumination. The infant may become upset when a night light is turned off or when he or she is taken out into bright sunlight. If the infant has older siblings, the parents can compare his or her development to the older children's achievement of visual milestones. Often the open-ended question, "How well does your baby see?" prompts the parents to recall these specific behaviors of concern.

Patients' Medical History

The etiology of childhood visual impairment can be categorized into pre-, peri-, and postnatal factors (see Sidebar 4.2). Up to two-thirds of all cases of visual impairment in children can be attributed to prenatal (preceding birth) factors, and of these factors, genetic causes account for half of the cases. Inheritance patterns include dominant, recessive, and X-linked traits. Careful inquiry into the family's history of systemic

---

Sidebar 4.1   SIGNS OF A VISION PROBLEM

The following are signs that may indicate a vision problem in infants and that parents should be able to recognize. Infants who exhibit any of these signs should be examined by their physician and an eye care professional.

- Absence of eye contact by age 3 months
- Poor visual fixation or following by age 3 months
- Insufficient accuracy in reaching for objects by age 6 months
- Failure of the eyes to move together or the constant crossing of one eye after about age 4 months
- Horizontal or vertical rapid eye movements (nystagmus)
- Absence of a clear black pupil (hazy cornea, a whitish pupil, or a marked asymmetrical "red-eye" appearance in a flash photograph)
- Constant tears when the infant is not crying
- Great discomfort in reaction to bright light (photophobia)
- Constant redness of the white conjunctiva
- Sagging of an eyelid that blocks the pupil
- Visible irregularities in the shape, size, or structure of the eyes (keyhole pupil)

Source: Based on S. W. Teplin, "Visual Impairment in Infants and Young Children," *Infants and Young Children,* 8(1) (1995), 18–51.

and ocular disorders, particularly whether any family members have poor vision, ocular abnormalities, or inheritable conditions that affect the eyes, aids in the diagnosis of the disorder. Inquiries about prenatal factors also include complications or problems during the pregnancy. The clinician may need to ask specific questions about the frequency of prenatal examinations; the mother's history of using drugs, including alcohol, tobacco, caffeine, and anticonvulsants; and aspects of the mother's health, such as anemia, diabetes, blood pressure, and infection.

Inquiries about perinatal factors (at the time of birth) include whether the delivery was pre-, post-, or at term and vaginal or Cesarean; the duration of labor; and whether there was any evidence of fetal distress (meconium staining or fetal heart rate monitoring). Inquiries about

---

Sidebar 4.2 ETIOLOGY OF CHILDHOOD VISUAL IMPAIRMENT

The factors listed here that occur prenatally, perinatally, or postnatally may each cause visual impairment in infancy or early childhood.

Prenatal Factors

Genetic

Other: infection, preeclampsia

Perinatal Factors

Prematurity

Complications of delivery (neonatal asphyxia)

Infection (meningitis and ophthalmia neonatorum)

Postnatal Factors

Trauma (nonaccidental injury)

Infection

Raised intracranial pressure and tumors

Source: Based on J. Elston, "Epidemology of Visual Handicap in Childhood," in D. Taylor (Ed.), *Pediatric Ophthalmology* (Boston: Blackwell Scientific, 1990), 3–60.

postnatal factors (occurring after birth) include the newborn infant's birth weight, Apgar scores, any difficulty feeding, and jaundice.

The trend in childhood visual impairment is that fewer impairments are attributed to environmental causes and more are attributed to pre- and perinatal factors. Overall, genetics is the predominant cause of visual impairment. Fortunately, knowledge of the gene locus of eye diseases is increasing with more sophisticated technology (Elston, 1990).

Developmental History of the Infant

The pediatrician must determine whether the infant who is visually impaired has a generalized delay in development or a systemic syndrome of which poor vision is only one manifestation (Isenberg, 1994). Although specific questions about early milestones can be asked, often just asking the open-ended question, "Do you or your child's pediatrician have any concerns about the child's health and general development?" addresses the specific areas of concern.

Developmental delay exists when the infant or child does not reach developmental milestones at the expected age, with allowance for the broad variations in typically developing children (see Illingworth, 1978; Shalowitz & Gorski, 1990; Simeonsson & Sharp, 1992 for indicators of developmental delay). The causes of developmental delay may include prenatal factors, such as the mother's abuse of drugs that leads to the retardation of intrauterine growth, as well as postnatal factors, such as a drug-abusing mother's ongoing difficulties that impair her ability to nourish and nurture her baby through each developmental stage (First & Palfrey, 1994).

The motor development of infants with visual impairments is not markedly different from that of fully sighted infants in the first few months of life. Postural milestones, such as independent sitting and standing, can be achieved within expectations for sighted infants (Fraiberg, 1977). There are, however, qualitative differences in motor development. It has been reported that an infant who is blind sits in a "frozen attitude" (Sonksen, 1983) and that his or her self-initiated mobility is delayed. Even blind infants "look" at their hands by bringing them to their faces by 16 weeks, but reaching out is delayed beyond the norm of age 3 to 4 months (Reynell & Zinkin, 1975). Whereas sighted infants localize a part of the body that has been "touched" with their eyes by age 7 months, infants who are blind may take up to 2 years to do so (Sonksen, 1983). In general, infants who are blind are slow to localize sounds by reaching out to touch them; instead, they tend to remain motionless in response to sounds. In the area of language development, both sighted and visually impaired infants start to babble at the same age, but there are mixed findings as to whether both achieve the 10–20 word vocabulary at the same age (Warren, 1994).

According to Robinson, Jan, and Kinnis (1987), 64 percent of 455 infants they studied with congenital visual impairments had additional major disabilities (see Table 4.2). Walker, Tobin, and McKennell (1991) reported 56 percent of 285 visually impaired children had other permanent illness or disability. In another report, 68 of 100 children with visual impairments were at the 75th percentile level of development or less for their age (Zinkin, 1979).

A complete vision examination with specialized tests can answer some questions about an infant's visual capabilities. Other diagnostic

Table 4.2 PERCENTAGE OF 576 CONGENITALLY BLIND INDIVIDUALS WITH ASSOCIATED DISABILITIES (1945–84)

Associated Disabilities	Average Percentage with Disability
None	36.1
Mental retardation	37.1
Cerebral palsy	15.6
Epilepsy	13.3
Hearing loss	13.7
Heart defect	11.8
No information	21.5

Source: Based on data from G. C. Robinson, J. E. Jan, and C. Kinnis, "Congenital Ocular Blindness in Children: 1945 to 1984," *American Journal of Diseases of Children, 147* (1975), 1321–1324.

tests (including an MRI, ERG, and genetic workup) can answer questions about the etiology of the visual disorder. With an accurate diagnosis, the prognosis for most disorders except for cortical visual impairment can be given with some certainty.

While taking the history, the astute clinician makes observations of the infant's or child's interactions with the parent or parents and the environment as he or she plays. The vision examination for infants and children is best approached as an extension of this play. In addition, it is preferable to avoid shining bright lights into an infant's eyes as the first interaction. An adequate supply of noisy and quiet toys (including the examiner's face) is usually all that is needed to engage and maintain the infant's visual interest.

Confrontation Tests

The first battery of tests in the vision examination are confrontation tests that assess an infant's fixation and eye-movement behavior.

Versions

This test is an observation of the infant's eye movements as the infant fixates and follows a toy that is moved in front of the eyes in different fields of gaze. The toy is moved from the midline of the infant's vision (straight ahead) to the extreme right and left along a horizontal path; up and down along a vertical path; and into the upper-right, upper-left, lower-right, and lower-left quadrants. The clinician looks for any restriction of eye movement, since both eyes should move in concert and to the same extent. This eye movement test evaluates the function of the six extraocular eye muscles in various directions of gaze and gives information about the function of the cranial nerves III, IV, and XI and supranuclear (brain structures other than the motor neurons) control of eye movements.

Hirschberg Test

The Hirschberg test is an objective measure to detect the presence of an eye turn (strabismus). It is based on evaluating the symmetry of images from a penlight reflected on the corneas of both eyes. The light reflexes from the penlight should be centered in each eye or slightly nasal (toward the nose) when the penlight is held straight ahead and each eye fixates with the fovea. If the reflex in one eye is decentered (displaced from the central position) with respect to the other, then the eye with the decentered reflex may have a strabismus. For example, if the reflex in the right eye is displaced nasally (toward the nose), it implies that the eye is exotropic (turned outward). Conversely, if the image of the penlight in the right eye is displaced temporally (toward the ear) compared to the left eye, it implies that the right eye is esotropic (turned inward). (A *tropia* is a deviation in the alignment of the eyes that the individual is not able to control.)

A strabismus is a misalignment of the eyes resulting in the failure to achieve or maintain binocular vision when both eyes are viewing. It is defined in terms of frequency (constant or intermittent occurrence), laterality (occurring only in one eye, unilaterally, or alternating between the two eyes), direction (esotropia or inward eye turn; exotropia, or outward eye turn; hypertropia, or upward eye turn; and hypotropia, or downward eye turn), and concomitancy (whether the eye turn remains the same or varies in different directions of gaze). An accommodative esotropia is an inward eye turn that increases in magnitude when the infant attempts to focus for near viewing. Accommodative esotropia is usually accompanied by a hyperopic (farsighted) refractive error. Hyperopic refractive errors may be overcome by focusing effort to provide clear vision. In infants with accommodative esotropia, the amount of hyperopia is too large to allow for clear vision and aligned eyes simultaneously. Corrective lenses to correct the hyperopia are usually sufficient to eliminate the eye turn.

Monocular Fixation

The evaluation of the pinpoint reflection of light on the cornea from a penlight shined on each eye tests for monocular fixation by noting whether the infant's fixation on the penlight target is central or eccentric (that is, uses another part of the eye to view the target), steady or unsteady, and maintained or not maintained. During this test, one eye is occluded (covered), and the fixation of the uncovered eye on a penlight is recorded. If the penlight reflection is centrally located on the infant's cornea, then fixation is assumed to be with the fovea and is recorded as C for central fixation. Next, the penlight is slowly moved and the infant's ability to follow the light is observed. If the eye maintains an alignment with the penlight, then fixation and following are recorded as S for steady. Whether the eye can maintain fixation is observed when the occluder is removed from the other eye. If the previously fixating eye continues to fixate on the penlight, then fixation is recorded as M for maintained. If all the foregoing conditions are met, CSM fixation is recorded in the chart as an abbreviation for central, steady, and maintained fixation (von Noorden, 1975).

When a unilateral strabismus is present, the deviating eye often does not maintain fixation when the preferred eye is uncovered. Infants with a strabismus or decreased vision in one eye often do not show central fixation. Eccentric fixation occurs when infants view with the nonfoveal part of the retina. Infants with macular lesions from colobomas, toxoplasmosis scars, or dragging of the macula region with retinopathy of prematurity may show eccentric fixation. Since visual acuity is maximal at the fovea, any eccentric fixation implies reduced vision. It is important to note that the loss of visual acuity is not always accompanied by eccentric fixation, so central fixation does not imply normal visual acuity.

Nystagmus is a repetitive, usually rapid, and involuntary movement or rotation of the eye. The movement is either oscillatory or with slow and fast phases in alternate directions. It is important to quantify the nystagmus in terms of its amplitude (the extent of the eye excursion), frequency (the rate of the side-to-side movement), manifest or latent (whether the nystagmus is present when both eyes are open, that is, manifest, or elicited only when one eye is covered, that is, latent). The presence of a null point (position of the eyes where the nystagmus is damped or minimal) should be noted. Often the infant adopts a head turn or eye turn for which the nystagmus is minimal or absent. If the nystagmus diminishes as the infant converges the eyes for near fixation, this fact should be noted.

Sensory nystagmus in infancy occurs with bilateral disruption of central vision if the visual defect is congenital or acquired during the first two years of life (Cogan, 1956). In congenital nystagmus, the onset of nystagmus occurs usually between age 8 and 12 weeks (Jan, Farrell, Wong, & McCormick, 1986). Acquired nystagmus appears about one month after the loss of vision and develops only when the vision loss occurs before age 2 if damage occurs to the ocular or anterior structures of the visual pathway. If central vision can be restored, the nystagmus may disappear. With longer delays in vision rehabilitation, the nystagmus becomes irreversible. The presence of roving eye movements indicates severely reduced vision, usually worse than 20/200. There have been reports that jerky nystagmus implies vision between 20/70 to 20/200. However, the absence of nystagmus does not imply good vision, particularly since nystagmus is absent in cortical visual impairment.

Although the presence or absence of nystagmus alone cannot predict visual function, Jan et al. (1986) reported that nystagmus can be used to ascertain the age at onset of visual impairment. Slow, large-amplitude nystagmus accompanies the loss of vision in the first 6 months of life. Vision loss acquired before age 1 is generally followed by nystagmus within 4 weeks, whereas vision loss after 1 year does not cause nystagmus. In Jan et al.'s (1986) study, roving nystagmus gradually disappeared between 2 and 12 months of age in most children who developed useful vision. The notable exception to this time frame was that the children with cortical visual impairment developed no nystagmus, despite the presence of subnormal vision from birth.

Cover Test

The unilateral cover test, also known as the cover-uncover test, involves observing an infant's fixation as the other eye is covered to test for the presence of strabismus. After the infant's attention is attracted with a small, noisy toy, an occluder or cover paddle is introduced briefly over the right eye while the left eye is observed for any movement or refixation. The cover is removed, and the process is repeated by covering the left eye and observing the fixation of the right eye. In each instance, the fixation of the uncovered eye should remain steady and no movement should be elicited. When an esotropia (inward eye turn) is present, the deviating eye moves outward when the other eye is covered. When an exotropia (outward eye turn) is present, the deviating eye moves inward when the cover is introduced in front of the nondeviating eye. The cover-uncover test is repeated several times to determine whether strabismus exists, which eye has the strabismus, and whether the strabismus is constant or intermittent.

The alternate cover test is an observation of the infant's fixation when each eye is alternately covered. It assesses the eye posture when the eyes are not permitted to be used together. The cover is placed over the right eye and is quickly moved to the left eye and back. The movement of the right eye is observed. The test is repeated with the cover placed over the left eye and quickly moved to the right eye and back. Any inward movement of the eye when it is uncovered indicates the tendency for the eyes to assume an outward posture (exophoria) when they are not actively being used together. Any outward movement of the eyes with uncovering indicates an inward posture to the eyes (esophoria). A *phoria* is the relative direction assumed by the eyes when one eye is covered, thus preventing binocular fixation.

The magnitude of an eye turn can be quantified with a prism, a wedge of glass that moves the visual image on the retina, and is expressed in prism diopters. Eye turns exceeding 20 prism diopters are cosmetically noticeable to laypersons. Medical records may include the following abbreviations: RET for a constant right esotropia; LXT for a constant left exotropia; RH(T) for an intermittent; right hypertropia; XP for exophoria; and EP for esophoria.

The infant or child may assume a head posture to minimize or even mask the presence of a strabismus. Observation of the head posture of an infant or child may provide an insight into which eye muscle is affected. Head turns to the right or left imply a problem with the horizontal eye muscles; a posture with the chin up or down implies problems with the vertical eye muscles; and a head tilt to the left or right shoulder implies a problem with the oblique eye muscles.

Base-out Prism Test

This test is an observation of the infant's eye movements when a base-out prism is alternately placed in front of each eye. The base-out prism moves the image of the object viewed through that eye, causing temporary diplopia (double vision). If the innate ability to see singly is intact, the eye behind the prism reflexively moves to place the image again on the fovea and achieve clear, single vision. If an eye turn is present, the eye behind the prism makes no attempt to refixate. Small amounts of an eye turn (microtropia) can be detected with this test.

Pupillary Test

A pupillary test, the observation of a pupil's response to illumination for integrity of the visual pathway, has four components: the direct illumination test (shining a light into an eye and observing the pupil's constriction), the consensual illumination test (shining a light into one eye and observing the pupillary response in the other eye), the swinging-flashlight test (shining a light into one eye for a few seconds and then rapidly moving the light to the other eye), and the near reflex test (observing the pupil's constriction as fixation and focus are shifted from distance to near).

Pupillary responses to direct illumination are present at birth in full-term infants and premature infants of at least 30 weeks' gestation age. Consensual pupillary responses are present at birth (Isenberg, 1994). An eye that is totally blind from ocular or optic nerve disease usually has no pupillary reaction to light. If only one eye is blind, the affected eye has no pupillary response to direct illumination, but when the light is shifted to the unaffected eye, both pupils constrict. When one or both eyes have visual impairments associated with optic nerve disease, the swinging-flashlight test indicates that one eye is more affected than the other. The pupil's reactions to light are sluggish in infants with congenital retinal disorders but are usually normal in infants with cortical visual impairment.

Determination of Refractive Error

The determination of refractive error, or the focusing error of the eye, is achieved objectively with an instrument called a *retinoscope* in the procedure called *retinoscopy*. During retinoscopy, the examiner evaluates the movement of a light reflex generated in the infant's eye. If the eye is hyperopic (farsighted), the observed reflex in the eye moves "with" the movement of the examiner's light, that is, as the examiner's light is moved from right to left, the observed light reflex in the eye also moves from right to left. If the eye is myopic (nearsighted) the light reflex is observed to move "against" the movement of the examiner's light, or in the opposite direction, that is, as the examiner's light is moved from right to left, the observed light reflex in the eye moves from left to right. Spectacle lenses of different powers are held in front of the eye to attain a neutral light reflex, the point at which the light reflex does not move. The lens power at neutrality, minus the working distance of the examiner, yields the prescription for eyeglasses. The presence of astigmatism is detected by comparing the light reflex in the eye in two orthogonal directions (vertically and horizontally). No subjective response from the infant is necessary to determine refractive error and to prescribe corrective lenses.

Estimates of refractive error are determined before tests of visual function are performed, so an approximate spectacle correction can be used. The final prescription for eyeglasses, however, is determined with the use of eye drops that temporarily relax the infant's accommodation (ability to focus). The medication is used after all functional vision tests have been completed and preceding the ocular health evaluation.

In a study of 1,000 full-term newborn infants, hyperopia was found to be present in 43.9 percent, myopia in 16.7 percent, and astigmatism in 35 percent (Cook & Glassock, 1951). In premature infants, the most common refractive error is myopic (Dobson, Fulton, Manning, Salem, & Peterson, 1981). Premature infants with retinopathy of prematurity (ROP) have a higher incidence of myopia (25 percent) than do infants without ROP (13 percent). The incidence of high myopia (greater than

5.00 diopters) is 6.5 percent infants with ROP but only 1 percent in infants without ROP. Severe ROP and low birth weight are strong predictors of myopia (Quinn et al., 1990). The prevalence of significant refractive error in infants and children with severe and multiple disabilities ranges from 21 percent to 76 percent (Edwards et al., 1972; Harcourt, 1974; Jan et al., 1977; Landau & Berson, 1971; Orel-Bixler et al., 1989; Wesson & Maino, 1995).

Tests of Visual Fields

Although rigorous standard tests of visual fields—testing to measure the extent of the visual field and locate any blind spots—cannot be conducted with infants and young children because it is difficult to gain their attention and cooperation, useful information can be obtained from measuring confrontation visual fields. In dim room illumination, the examiner faces the infant or child and attracts his or her attention with a penlight toy. Then the central penlight is extinguished, and another examiner, hiding behind the infant, introduces another penlight toy silently from the far periphery in the infant's lateral (left and right), superior (upper), and inferior (lower) visual fields. The infant's refixation to the peripheral penlight toy provides an estimate of the extent of the visual field. An infant with full visual fields will rapidly turn his or her head or eye toward the peripheral target. Significant visual field loss, or hemianopsias, can be detected with this confrontation technique. Qualitative differences in the infant or child's response to the peripheral penlight from one field to the other should be verified by repeating the tests. After age 1 year, fully sighted infants have full visual fields. The development of visual fields is currently being studied.

Children with cerebral palsy or poor head and eye motor control may need additional time to respond, so the peripheral target should be moved in slowly. Sometimes other responses, such as the child smiling when the peripheral target is seen, can suffice to indicate that the child sees the target, rather than relying on a head or eye movement. Although the measurement of visual fields by this technique is crude, the field losses are likely to be functionally significant. Infants with hemianopsias may be startled when objects or persons suddenly appear in their visual fields without warning. The assessment of visual fields can indicate the best way to place educational materials when they are presented to a particular child to maximize his or her visually attending to them.

Assessment of Ocular Health

Gross inspection of the health of an infant's eyes and surrounding structures can be obtained using penlights, but the magnification provided by more sophisticated instruments yields more precise results.

Handheld Slit Lamp

A biomicroscope (slit lamp) is used to evaluate the anterior (front) structures of the eye, including the clarity of the ocular media (cornea and lens). It is particularly important in evaluating infants with nystagmus and possible albinism. In ocular albinism, transillumination defects of the iris can be seen with retroillumination (that is, light reflected back from the fundus shines through areas of pigment loss in the iris as a red glow). The slit lamp affords a magnified view for the evaluation of corneal opacities and cataracts.

Direct and Indirect Ophthalmoscopes

Different instruments are used to evaluate the posterior (back) structures of the eyes: the optic discs, retina, macula or fovea, and retinal vasculature. This evaluation generally requires the pupils to be dilated. The instruments used provide different magnified views. The binocular indirect ophthalmoscope (BIO) provides for stereoscopic (three-dimensional) high-resolution views into the infant's eye. Its advantages include the presence of stereopsis, a large field of view, minimal peripheral distortion, and the ability to evaluate the extreme peripheral retina, which is important in assessing ROP (Fingeret, Casser, & Woodcome, 1990). Views with the BIO are relatively independent of a child's refractive error or moderate opacification of the media. The examiner is able to maintain a comfortable evaluation distance (arm's length) from the infant and to hold a fixation target for the eye not presently being evaluated. That the infant may nurse or drink from a bottle during the evaluation increases his or her cooperation. The disadvantages of BIO include a lower magnification than direct ophthalmoscopy, with the loss of fine detail, and moderate glare or discomfort for the infant because of the brightness of the light source, as well as the examiner's need to steady the hand holding the condensing lens on the infant, which may be difficult for infants who are sensitive to touch.

The direct ophthalmoscope produces a magnified, well-detailed image of the retina. It can be used with nondilated pupils and is less bright, thereby increasing the infant's comfort. Media opacities degrade the view and allow an estimate of the extent of the infant's visual compromise (Fingeret et al., 1990). The primary disadvantage is the very close working distance of the examiner to the infant (cheek to cheek), the lack of stereopsis, dependence on refractive error for clarity and magnification, and the small field of view. Dilation of the pupils is most often necessary for the best view.

An assessment of ocular health is easiest to obtain when the infant is comfortable nursing or being bottle fed. Singing by the examiner may have a calming effect. An examination with sedation or anesthesia may be necessary if an adequate evaluation cannot be obtained but is necessary because of the infant's history and the findings of other examinations.

Handheld Tonometer

This device is used to measure the intraocular pressures (IOP) of each eye, which is important in the diagnosis of glaucoma. Measuring intraocular pressure is not a routine part of the eye examination of an infant or toddler, since IOP measures are difficult to obtain and often unreliable (American Academy of Ophthalmology, 1992). Intraocular pressure should be assessed in rare instances when glaucoma is suspected because of other ocular signs (corneal edema, increased corneal diameter, or myopia) or other risk factors for glaucoma are present. Most often, the measurement of IOP in infants and toddlers must be done under sedation or anesthesia.

Assessment of Visual Capabilities for Newborns to 2 Year Olds

Visual Acuity Tests

Visual acuity is a threshold measure of the eye's ability to detect fine detail or fine resolution. Clinically, it is measured with optotypes (usually letters or symbols arranged on a chart) and expressed in terms of the Snellen fraction or 20/20 notation. The numerator in 20/20 notation is the test distance, or the distance from the eye to the visual target, and the denominator is the letter size for which the detail in the visual target subtends one minute of arc at the eye. People with 20/20 vision will be able to detect each line in the letter E, for example, even though each line encompasses only 1 minute of arc at the eye. In more practical terms, people with 20/200 visual acuity have a 10-fold reduction in vision such that they would need to be 20 feet from a letter to identify it, whereas those with normal vision could be 200 feet from the same letter and still identify it.

Indirect Tests of Visual Acuity

In routine clinical applications, indirect tests to make assumptions about visual acuity are used primarily with infants from birth to age 2. For example, when a constant strabismus is present in one eye, visual acuity is presumed to be reduced in the strabismic eye. When the eye turn alternates between the eyes, visual acuity is likely to be equal in both eyes. However, actual measures of acuity and fixation preference do not show a strong association. For the infant with severe or multiple disabilities, inferences about visual function based on the presence of strabismus are not accurate.

For an infant with suspected vision loss or visual impairment, the presence of involuntary eye movements; optokinetic nystagmus (OKN) and the vestibular ocular reflex (VOR), may be used to infer visual function. OKN is an involuntary eye movement elicited by motion in the environment. In clinical testing, black-and-white stripes on a rotating cylinder elicit slow following eye movements at the same rate as the movement of the stripes, followed by a fast saccadic eye movement in the opposite direction. An OKN response indicates that some pattern vision is present (the stripes were seen by the infant), but the lack of response has uncertain significance. In VOR testing, the infant's fixation is evaluated after inducing the VOR reflex (a horizontal nystagmus induced by spinning). The infant is held at arm's length in front of the examiner, and after several rotations the spinning is discontinued and the examiner assesses the infant's eye movements. In infants with normal vision, there are only one or two beats of nystagmus after the spinning stops, but in infants with severe visual impairment or severe cerebellar disease, the nystagmus is prolonged.

These indirect tests of visual function are only qualitative assessments of visual function. Quantitative measurement of visual acuity is possible with preferential looking and visual evoked potential tests (see Teller & Movshon, 1987, for a review).

Preferential Looking Tests

In the preferential looking (PL) test, grating targets (black-and-white stripes of different widths) are presented with a gray square of equal luminance on a gray background. The infant's fixation is observed through a peephole on the stimulus card. The narrowest stripe on which the infant reliably fixates is judged to be the estimate of visual acuity. Early laboratory studies with preferential looking used rigorous psychophysical testing protocols and two alternative forced-choice paradigms to ensure that the infant's performance was different than predicted by chance alone. Laboratory studies reported that a single estimate of acuity required an average of approximately 15 minutes of test time and 60 trials, which made it impractical for clinical settings (Gwiazda, Brill, Mohindra, & Held, 1978). A more rapid procedure, the acuity-card procedure, was later developed specifically for applications in clinical settings.

In the acuity-card procedure (McDonald, Ankrum, Preston, Sebris, & Dobson, 1986; McDonald, Sebris, Mohn, Teller, & Dobson, 1986), the tester's task on each trial is to judge, on the basis of the quality and consistency of the infant's looking behavior, whether the infant can see the grating. When the stripes are wide and easily seen and the infant is clearly looking in the direction of the grating, then only two presentations of the grating are needed. As the infant's acuity limit is approached, the looking behavior becomes less consistent, and the tester may need to show the grating cards several times to determine whether the infant is consistently looking at the grating. The tester uses the infant's overall looking behavior on a small number of presentations to judge whether the grating was visible to the infant. Grating patterns are expressed in terms of spatial frequency, or the number of cycles (pairs of light-and-dark bars) of the grating per degree of visual angle. The acuity estimate is given in cycles/degree. The grating acuity (c/deg) is converted to Snellen notation by using the conversion that a grating with 30 cycles/degree is equivalent to one minute of the arc of the visual

angle, or 20/20. It is important to note that this mathematical translation of grating acuity into Snellen notation is not appropriate for some
eye disorders with accompanying low vision. The ideal way to report
an infant's visual acuity with PL techniques is to reference it to age-
matched norms.

The development of grating acuity during the first few years of life
has been investigated by several groups using forced-choice preferential looking (FPL) techniques (Dobson & Teller, 1978), FPL acuity cards
(McDonald, Ankrum et al., 1986; McDonald, Sebris et al., 1986), and
the acuity-card procedure (Mayer et al., 1995). The studies generally
agree that PL grating acuity develops from approximately 1 cycle/degree
at age 1 month and improves to 6 cycles/degree by age 6 months with
little measurable improvement from 6 to 12 months. Preferential-looking
grating acuity does not reach adult levels until approximately age 3 years
(Mayer et al., 1995). In premature infants, the development of acuity
is predictable from postterm (corrected) age, rather than from postnatal age (Getz, Dobson, & Luna, 1992). For example, if an infant is
born 4 weeks prematurely and is tested at 20 weeks postnatally, his or
her acuity data should be compared to the normative data of a 16 week
old, rather than a 20 week old, at least during the first year of life.

The advantages of the acuity-card procedure is the portability of
the testing cards and flexibility in testing; the examiner can interact
with the infant between presentations to maintain interest. In infants
with eye turns or nystagmus whose horizontal eye position is difficult to
judge, the test cards can be rotated so that vertical head and eye movements are generated. The disadvantages of PL techniques include the
bias of the tester; the cards' lack of durability, such that smudges can be
more interesting than the gratings; and edge or brightness artifacts of
the fine grating targets that could lead to an overestimation of acuity. A
major disadvantage of PL techniques is that one cannot conclude that
a grating that is not preferentially fixated is not resolvable to an infant.
Therefore, a PL-derived acuity probably represents a conservative measure of visual threshold. There have been some reports that PL grating
acuities underestimate the vision loss in people with amblyopia compared to measures obtained with optotypes. Currently, there is no "conversion factor" for PL grating acuity to optotype acuity for infants. The
PL measure is compared to age-matched norms. If the measure for a

3 month old falls outside the normal range, the infant is diagnosed as visually impaired, but a numerical value for acuity is not given.

Successful applications of PL acuity techniques have been reported for several clinical populations, including infants and children with congenital cataracts and aphakia (Mauer, Lewis, & Brent, 1989), retinopathy of prematurity (Dobson et al., 1990), Leber's congenital amaurosis (Mayer, Fulton, & Hansen, 1985), and infants with neurological impairment and multiple disabilities (Bane & Birch, 1992; Mohn & van Hof-van Duin, 1986b).

Visual Evoked Potential Test

The visual evoked potential (VEP) is an electrical signal generated in the occipital region of the cortex in response to visual stimulation (Sokol, 1976). To measure visual acuity, the VEP is recorded while the infant watches grating patterns presented on a television monitor. The VEP is recorded through five recording sensors that are attached to the infant's scalp with a water-soluble paste. Its signals are amplified and computer analyzed. In the sweep VEP technique, 20 stripes of different sizes are displayed on a video monitor during each 10-second recording trial. The amplitude (magnitude) of the VEP decreases progressively as the width of the stripes decreases. Visual acuity is determined from an extrapolation of the amplitude of the VEP versus the width of the stripe (Norcia & Tyler, 1985).

In pediatric applications, VEP tests are usually performed in a darkened room to provide minimum distraction. Attention to the video monitor is achieved by dangling small fixation toys on the video screen and speaking or singing to the infant or child being tested. The examiner uses a pause–resume remote control to start and stop the VEP recording during lapses in fixation. Electrical artifacts caused by the infant's excessive movements can be eliminated with appropriate data analysis techniques. The VEP is a noninvasive test that does not require an infant or young child to be sedated to obtain reliable results.

As determined by the VEP test, visual acuity develops rapidly during the first year of life, and adult levels of grating acuity are reached as early as 6 to 8 months of age (Norcia & Tyler, 1985; Orel-Bixler & Norcia, 1987). The rate of acuity development is much more rapid with the VEP than with behavioral measures with preferential looking (PL)

| Table 4.3 | MEAN EXPECTED VALUES FOR MONOCULAR GRATING ACUITY IN INFANTS AND TODDLERS UP TO AGE 2 | | | |
Age (months)	VEP (c/deg)	PL (c/deg)	VEP (20/20 notation)	PL (20/20 notation)
1	5	0.94	20/120	20/638
2.5	7.8	2.16	20/77	20/278
4	12	2.68	20/50	20/224
6	18	5.65	20/33	20/106
9	23	6.79	20/26	20/88
12	25	6.42	20/24	20/93
18		8.59		20/70
24		9.57		20/62

Source: Based on data from A. M. Norcia and C. W. Tyler, "Spatial Frequency Sweep VEP: Visual Acuity During the First Year of Life," *Vision Research, 25* (1985), 1399–1408, and D. L. Mayer, A. S. Beiser, A. F. Warner, E. M. Pratt, K. N. Raye, and J. M. Lang, "Monocular Acuity Norms for the Teller Acuity Cards Between Ages One Month and Four Years," *Investigative Ophthalmology and Visual Science, 36* (1995), 671–685.

Note: To convert acuity in c/deg to 20/20 notation the following conversion was used: 600 divided by the value in c/deg yields the denominator in 20/20 notation. For example, 5 c/deg; 600/5 = 120; or 20/120.

techniques (see Table 4.3). In a study by Hamer, Norcia, Tyler, and Hsu-Winges (1989), the sweep VEP technique had relatively small test-retest variability and a narrower standard deviation range in comparison to PL techniques. The 99 percent confidence limits and interocular differences (differences in the acuity of the two eyes) for the sweep VEP were two to four times smaller than PL measures. Likewise, monocular VEP grating acuities were higher than PL acuities by a factor of 2 to 10. Therefore, the sweep VEP technique may be more highly sensitive to detecting visual acuity deficits in infants than many PL techniques.

VEP in Clinical Populations   The VEP test has been shown to be a sensitive indicator of early acuity losses in studies of infants with strabismus (Day, Orel-Bixler, & Norcia, 1988). The VEP test has been used to monitor changes in the vision of the amblyopic and fellow eye during patching therapy (Odom, Hoyt, & Marg, 1981) and to record the acuity of infants with congenital cataract after early surgical interventions (Beller, Hoyt, & Marg, 1981). Several studies have reported that the VEP measure of visual function can be useful in the clinical management of nonverbal patients, including children with multiple disabilities (Mackie, McCulloch, & Saunders, 1995; Orel-Bixler et al., 1989); a diverse group of children with ocular disorders with and without accompanying visual impairment (Gottlob et al., 1990); and children with visual impairments (Bane & Birch, 1992).

Validation studies using the sweep VEP have reported good correlations between VEP grating acuity and optotype (Snellen) acuity in fully sighted adults and children (Orel-Bixler, 1989) and in children with various visual impairments, including strabismus and amblyopia (Gottlob et al., 1990; Orel-Bixler, 1989). Sweep VEP grating and optotype acuities were well correlated in amblyopia, in spite of substantial absolute differences between the two measures in observers with significant amblyopia (Orel-Bixler, 1989). There was good agreement among observers regarding VEP and optotype acuity with optotype acuity better than 20/60, but an increasing discrepancy accompanied poorer acuity. A discrepancy by a factor of 2.5 was found, with grating measures giving better acuity than optotypes. Thus, a measured grating acuity of 6 cycles/degree, which is mathematically equivalent to a 20/100 grating acuity, is expected to yield an optotype acuity of approximately 20/250. Several other studies have indicated that visual acuities measured with grating targets are higher than those measured with optotypes in adults and children with amblyopia (Selenow, Cuiffreda, Mozlin, & Rumpf, 1986) children with significant ocular structural anomalies (Mayer, Fulton, & Rodier, 1984). A better prediction of optotype acuity from the VEP grating acuity can be made by taking this systematic overestimation into account.

VEP Studies with Cortical Visual Impairment Cortical visual impairment (CVI) is a loss of vision secondary to damage to the geniculostriate pathways and is characterized by reduced vision, the absence of OKN, and normal findings on ocular examinations and intact pupillary responses to light (Barnett, Manson, & Wilner, 1970). CVI results from hypoxic insults, meningitis, encephalitis, metabolic disturbances, head trauma, or hydrocephalus. The recovery of vision is often protracted and only partial, although in some cases, recovery is complete and rapid. For this reason CVI, rather than cortical blindness, is the more appropriate term (Whiting et al., 1985). The most common cause of CVI is generalized cerebral hypoxia in the striate, parietal, and premotor regions and vascular lesions of the striate cortex.

Several studies have evaluated VEP responses to flashes of light, rather than gratings, in CVI. The findings have varied, probably because of the inherent difficulty in interpreting flash VEPs and the larger variations in waveform and amplitude than in pattern VEPs. The studies have often been limited to single case reports or studies of small populations of people with CVI and have reported both normal and abnormal flash VEP responses or VEP responses that improved with time (Aduchi-Usami, 1991). McCulloch, Taylor, and Whyte (1991) used the VEP to determine visual prognosis following perinatal asphyxia (impaired exchange of oxygen and carbon dioxide during birth). In this study, flash VEPs were recorded from 25 asphyxiated infants. Sixteen infants had normal or only transient abnormalities of the VEP, and with follow-up, all these infants developed normal vision. The remaining nine infants who had abnormal flash VEPs never developed normal vision. The VEP findings in CVI remain controversial, since subjective measures of visual function cannot be determined for comparison with the VEP measures and the lesions that cause CVI are not often localized exclusively to the striate cortex (Aduchi-Usami, 1991).

There have been several clinical applications of VEPs with children. The VEP is noninvasive and requires some expertise, but it can be applied to a population that cannot communicate or cooperate with standard assessments of visual function. As Taylor and McCulloch (1992) summarized in their review, the major applications of VEPs with infants have been done to quantify visual impairment with measures of visual acuity or contrast sensitivity or to quantify abnormalities in flash or pattern VEPs. Early detection of visual impairment allows infants to be referred to early intervention programs. The flash VEP may help establish the prognosis for visual recovery for specific pediatric disorders, including perinatal asphyxia in full-term neonates and acute-onset cortical visual impairments, and in some cases, contribute to the differential diagnoses. The VEP can help monitor infants who are at risk of visual complications either from diseases (for example, hydrocephalus) or as a complication of therapeutic interventions (such as neurosurgery) to help detect and avoid long-term sequelae of such therapies on the developing nervous system. VEPs have become an indispensable tool in pediatric ophthalmology and neurology and will probably play an increasingly important role in the future, primarily because of the difficulty of assessing visual system function in young or medically fragile children and the VEP's sensitivity to subclinical damage in this aspect of the central nervous system (Taylor & McCulloch, 1992).

Although VEP and PL techniques provide quantitative measures of visual acuity in infants, due to time constraints in some clinical practices, qualitative measures may have to suffice. The relative advantages and disadvantages of visual acuity tests for infants should be considered (see Table 4.4).

Other Visual Functions: Contrast Sensitivity and Color Vision

In addition to visual acuity, other visual functions need to be assessed, including contrast sensitivity and color vision. These functions can be evaluated using the same PL and VEP techniques that are used to measure visual acuity.

Contrast Sensitivity

Contrast sensitivity is the ability to detect differences in brightness or subtle shades of gray. This ability is used to detect real-world spatial targets under a variety of luminance conditions. Some visual anomalies are revealed only under low- or moderate-contrast conditions. A wide range of vision disorders affect contrast sensitivity but spare visual acuity. Tests measuring contrast sensitivity have been applied clinically in diagnosing such visual disorders as glaucoma, amblyopia, and optic neuropathies (Regan, 1988). Contrast sensitivity can predict performance in everyday tasks, such as reading (Rubin & Legge, 1989) and mobility (Marron & Bailey, 1982).

The development of contrast sensitivity has been studied with the VEP. The contrast sensitivity for coarse targets for a 10 week old was only a factor of 2 lower than for adults (Norcia et al., 1990). Preferential looking measures of contrast sensitivity with grating targets (Adams & Courage, 1996) and happy-face targets (Fisher, Orel-Bixler, & Bailey,

TABLE 4.4   COMPARISON OF VISION TESTS FOR INFANTS

Method	Procedure	Advantages	Disadvantages
Qualitative tests			
Fixation and following	Assess fixation	Practical	Lacks precision
VOR test	Assess involuntary eye movements		No acuity estimate
Optokinetic nystagmus			
Fixation preference			
Quantitative tests			
Preferential looking techniques (PL)	Observe fixation preference with acuity card procedure	Portability Ease of use Accessibility	Limited durability Tester's bias Requires cooperation Grating acuity measure
Visual evoked potential (VEP)	Record the electrical response generated in the visual cortex of the brain following visual stimulation	Objective test Expect higher acuity than PL, smaller interocular differences and smaller standard deviation Repeated measurement	Requires technician Cost Testing duration Grating acuity measure

Source: Based on S. W. Teplin, "Visual Impairment in Infants and Young Children," *Infants and Young Children,* 8(1), (1995), 18–51.

1995) have shown a slower rate of development than have VEP studies; adultlike values are not reached until 1 to 2 years of age in most children.

Color Vision

VEP studies have indicated that infants as young as 2 weeks have the functional pathway needed to relay information on color discrimination from the eyes to the brain (Allen, Banks, & Norcia, 1993). These findings do not imply that neonates have mature color vision, since behavioral measures of color discrimination have shown that mature color vision develops later (Adams, Mauer, & Davis, 1986). Unfortunately, it is not yet possible to conduct routine clinical assessments of color vision in infants under 2 years old (Pease & Allen, 1988), but behavioral tests for color vision are under development. These tests use face targets in a preferential looking paradigm to evaluate access color vision in infants (Ventocilla, Orel-Bixler, & Haegerstrom-Portnoy, 1995).

Congenital red-green color vision deficiencies are inherited in an X-linked manner and occur in 8–10 percent of the male population and less than 0.05 percent of the female population in the United States (Krill, 1977). The probability for an inherited color vision defect can be inferred from information about the family's history of color vision problems. Since the color vision defect is carried on the X-chromosome, the mother is a carrier if her father has the defect, and there is a 50 percent chance that each son will have the color defect. Fathers with color vision defects cannot pass the defects on to their sons, but all daughters are carriers. For a girl to have an inherited red-green defect, both her father and her maternal grandfather must have a color vision defect.

Blue-yellow color vision defects occur in up to 0.007 percent of the U.S. population and most frequently accompany eye disease (Krill, 1977). Dobson et al. (1996) suggested that premature infants with significant ROP have blue-yellow color vision defects. Acquired color vision defects (red-green or blue-yellow) can occur with optic nerve disorders, retinal disorders, and patholgoy of the central nervous system.

It is important to measure color vision because many educational materials for reading and mathematics are color coded. Changes in color vision can precede a loss of visual acuity or visual fields and may serve as an early warning signal of the presence of disease.

Other Diagnostic Tests

Electroretinogram (ERG)

The ERG is a measure of the bioelectrical response generated in the retina in response to stimulation by light (Fishman & Sokol, 1990). It is recorded with a contact lens electrode under both light- (photopic) and dark-adapted (scotopic) viewing conditions using single and multiple (flicker) flash presentations. The amplitude (size of the response) and latency (time for the response to occur) of the ERG components are compared to normative data. In general, the interpretation of electro-physiological responses depends upon comparisons with age-matched norms. It may be difficult to interpret the results when an infant has clinically abnormal vision yet a recordable ERG. Often serial testing is necessary for a conclusive diagnosis (Fulton, Hartmann, & Hansen, 1989).

The ERG is valuable in the differential diagnosis of vision impairments in infants and children whose common presenting feature is reduced vision and nystagmus. Infants with Leber's congenital amaurosis, achromatopsia, albinism, and congenital stationary night blindness all have nystagmus, but the ERG can differentially diagnose the specific disorder. The photopic and scotopic ERG is extinguished in Leber's congenital amaurosis. The flicker and single flash photopic ERG is absent in achromatopsia, and infants with this condition have no color vision. In all forms of albinism, including oculocutaneous albinism, the scotopic ERG is supernormal. In congenital stationary night blindness, the b-wave is absent in the scotopic ERG. Abnormal ERG findings may precede any changes in ocular health in retinitis pigmentosa and cone-rod dystrophies.

ERG testing is not necessary with other disorders that cause nystagmus and visual impairments in infants when the findings of the ocular health examination are abnormal. For example, nystagmus and visual impairment in infancy may be associated with ocular abnormalities or media opacities, including bilateral congenital cataracts or corneal opacities, macular scarring, vitreous hemorrhage, and ROP. Similarly, optic nerve hypoplasia and optic nerve atrophy are accompanied by visual impairment and nystagmus, but with careful examination, the anomalies of the optic disc are detectable. Fundus signs and nystagmus are absent in infants with visual impairments that are due to CVI and delayed visual maturation. Little information is gained from an ERG regarding suspected CVI, delayed visual maturation, and optic nerve anomalies; rather, referrals for VEP tests and neuroimaging would be recommended.

Neuroimaging
The introduction of X-ray computed tomography (CT) in 1972 launched a new era in imaging technology and provided a safer and

more sensitive way to image soft tissue and bone that was also far superior to the previous techniques of plain X-rays of the orbits and skull (McCrary, 1991). CT can provide images of fine anatomical details of the orbit, oculomotor nerves and muscles, and the central nervous system. Magnetic resonance imaging (MRI) uses nuclear magnetic resonance to produce tomographic images (Kamholtz & Abrahams, 1992). Available since the early 1980s, MRI is now accepted as the most sensitive and among the most specific diagnostic imaging tools available for most neuro-ophthalmic applications (McCrary, 1991).

Neuroimaging studies are indicated in the workup of a child who may be blind when the diagnosis is still uncertain after a careful history, clinical examination, and electrophysiological testing have been performed (Fulton, Hansen, & Lambert, 1994). CT is the preferred imaging technique for the diagnosis of complex ocular trauma and suspected nonaccidental injury because of its excellent imaging of the orbit and bony anatomy (Zimmerman & Bilanuik, 1994). Calcium deposits within intracranial and intraorbital masses, particularly retinoblastoma, are readily detected with CT (McCrary, 1991). As Brodsky, Baker, and Hamed (1996) recommended, neuroimaging studies are indicated in the following groups: (1) infants with congenital nystagmus and optic nerve hypoplasia, to look for anomalies in the central nervous system; (2) infants or children with congenital nystagmus and optic atrophy, to rule out hydrocephalus or a congenital suprasellar tumor (a tumor above the *sella turcica* of the middle cranium, which is near the pituitary gland); and (3) infants or children with an uncertain diagnoses of congenital nystagmus and the possibility of spasmus nutans (nystagmus associated with head-nodding movements), to rule out chiasmal gliomas (slow-growing tumors located at the crossing of the optic nerves and optic tracts in the midbrain) or other suprasellar tumors.

Neuroimaging is not usually indicated for children with retinal disorders unless there are other neurological abnormalities or developmental delays (Fulton et al, 1994). For example, the ERG is severely reduced in the retinal disorder Leber's congenital amaurosis, which may later be accompanied by optic atrophy. Other causes of optic atrophy show a normal ERG. Generally, neuroimaging studies are warranted in all infants with optic atrophy or optic nerve hypoplasia (Brodsky et al.,

1996). Optic nerve atrophy is a clinical sign but not a diagnosis. Children of any age who exhibit nystagmus and optic atrophy should have CT or MRI scans to rule out associated conditions.

Neuroimaging is valuable in revealing the structural abnormalities of the central nervous system and is critical to the diagnosis of CVI in infants and children. However, the findings with neuroimaging cannot predict visual function or visual potential. In a study of 30 infants with CVI, all but two had abnormalities in the neuroimaging studies, but none of the abnormalities demonstrated with neuroimaging correlated with the degree of visual recovery in these infants except for abnormalities of the optic radiations (Lambert, Hoyt, Jan, Barkovich, & Flodmark, 1987). Areas that appear nonfunctioning on MRI and CT scans may have some residual function. For example, a 20 month old whose lack of the occipital and parietal lobes was confirmed by neuroimaging could nonetheless use vision to reach for small objects (Summers & MacDonald, 1990). Neuroimaging has many applications for the diagnosis of syndromes of the visual system, but also gives useful information for prognostic and genetic counseling.

Consultation with Parents or Guardians

The final aspect of the vision examination is a discussion of the findings with the parents or guardians in laypersons' terms. The clinician should discuss the treatment or intervention plan, follow-up schedule, prognosis, need for rehabilitation services, and consultation with other medical professionals, if necessary.

When the diagnosis includes visual impairment, the parents want to know what the infant can see. Many people equate visual impairment with the lack of light perception, so the clinician needs to explain how the infant can use the vision he or she has. Often a demonstration of the visual impairment can be simulated with blurring lenses (to simulate nearsightedness and astigmatism) or by showing the letter size required at the visual acuity threshold. Visual field losses can be demonstrated by having the parents look through field-restricting cardboard tubes. A brief summary report given at the time of the examination should be followed by a more detailed report (see the sample reports of Jessica's and Aaron's visual examinations at the end of this chapter). This report may also include specific recommendations for maximizing the child's use of vision, as is done in Jessica's report. The parents will want to know if anything can be done regarding treatment or intervention. They may ask what the future holds and about educational options for their child. Finally, they will want to know what to do next. The clinician should provide information about available resources, such as early intervention programs, educational services from a teacher certified in the field of blindness and visual impairment, and services from an orientation and mobility instructor, as appropriate.

Early identification of the visual impairment is important. The earlier the identification of causative factors of visual impairment, the better the prognosis for any therapeutic interventions. The infant's visual system is still developing, and the reversal of amblyogenic factors may prevent the occurrence of visual deficits before they become embedded. Parents can provide toys and visual stimulation to match the infant's visual abilities and participate actively in enabling their infant's optimal visual development.

SAMPLE VISUAL EXAMINATION REPORT FOR JESSICA

Special Visual Assessment

Child's Name: Jessica   **Age:**   2 years, 9 months

History: Jessica has been diagnosed with cerebral palsy and cortical visual impairment associated with birth asphyxia and cerebral hemorrhages. Her mother had preeclampsia and seizures resulting in a coma during the pregnancy. Jessica's maternal grandmother reported that Jessica was injured in an automobile accident when she was 8 months old and had surgery for a hematoma 5 months after the accident. Jessica reportedly has had stomach problems since birth and takes Pepto Bismol as needed. She receives physical and speech therapy.

Reason for Examination: To provide information about visual functioning.

Refractive Status:

Current spectacles: none

Retinoscopy with cycloplegia: **Right Eye:**   +4.25 -3.00 × 180

                                      Left Eye: +4.75 -3.25 × 180

Binocular Status: A very large, alternating exotropia was noted (Jessica's eyes turn outward alternately). Jessica's eyes were often in an up gaze. She did not reliably fixate on objects. No restrictions of eye movements were noted on versions (she can move her eyes in all directions).

Ocular Health: Normal direct, consensual, and accommodative pupil responses were present in each eye. Clear ocular media, maculae, and fundii were noted in each eye. The optic nerves appeared normal in size and color. The retinal periphery was unremarkable. Jessica's ocular health appeared normal, which is consistent with her diagnosis of cortical visual impairment.

Visual Acuity: Jessica was able to detect a penlight, but did not appear to detect a black-and-white striped doll moved silently and directly in front of her face. No formal behavioral tests of vision could be done because of Jessica's lack of fixation and lack of a visual response.

Sweep Visual Evoked Potential: Both eyes viewing at 50 cm with current prescription of 1.25 cy/deg or predicted optotype acuity 20/1515

The visual evoked potential (VEP) uses black-and-white gratings (stripes) as the target to measure visual acuity (the ability to see fine details). In persons with low vision, the VEP grating acuity measure is higher than the acuity measured by letters or symbols. A conversion factor is used to "predict" the letter acuity from the grating acuity measure, and this predicted optotype acuity measure should be used in setting guidelines for educational materials. The VEP acuity findings are quite discrepant from the behavioral estimates of Jessica's vision. Although the VEP indicates that information is being relayed to the visual cortex, it cannot tell us exactly what Jessica perceives. On the basis of measures from other children with cortical visual impairment who have been able to complete both VEP and behavioral acuity tasks, the predicted acuity measure from the VEP should represent an upper boundary on Jessica's visual function and her behavioral responses, the lower boundary.

Behavioral Impressions: Jessica is nonverbal and nonmobile and was carried into the examination by her grandmother. The grandmother reported that Jessica sees lights, can track her fingers when she moves them, and responds to her speech. Jessica had stomach distress during the examination, and when it was most severe, her eyes rolled upward and she did not respond. She was able to lift her head and push up on her arms when she was laid on the floor.

Summary and Recommendations: Jessica has a moderate hyperopic refractive error (farsightedness) with significant astigmatism. She has an alternating outward eye turn and poor fixation. Jessica has significant visual impairment from cortical visual impairment, but her ocular health appears normal. We cannot be certain that eyeglasses to correct her refractive error will have any benefit visually because of her severe visual impairment. However, since this refractive error would decrease the visual abilities of a normally sighted child, we have recommended eyeglasses for full-time wear.

Jessica did not respond visually to the acuity targets used to obtain a behavioral measure of her visual acuity or an assessment of her visual fields. Objective measures with the VEP indicated pattern vision (20/1515), but it is severely reduced from normal (by a factor of 75). Educational materials, pictures, and toys should be large, with high-contrast primary colors (rather than pastels), and pictures should be outlined with thick marking pens. To make it easier for Jessica to locate toys and objects, the contrast should be enhanced between the object and its background. For example, place dark-colored toys on a light-colored mat, or vice versa. These objects should be paired with auditory or tactile cues, since hearing is her strength. The objects should be at least 4 inches high if viewed at 1 foot, and 8 inches high if viewed at 2 feet. Jessica's education should emphasize auditory, tactile, and olfactory learning. Jessica is legally blind and qualifies for educational services for children with visual impairments. She should be evaluated for educational services for her visual impairment and multiple disabilities. We would like to reevaluate Jessica's vision after she has worn her glasses for about 6 months.

General recommendations for educational materials for children with cortical visual impairment are summarized as follows:

1. *Use high-contrast and primary colors.* Present visual objects and toys that are high in contrast, and use colors as cues whenever possible. For example, when Jessica is eating, place light-colored cereal and milk in a dark-colored bowl. Place dark-colored food, such as raisins, on a light-colored placemat to increase the contrast. Concrete steps or light-colored stairs can be painted with a dark, wide line of nonslippery paint on the edges. Outline simple shapes with colors since the perception of form may be facilitated with the use of colors.

2. *Use all senses; add verbal and tactile clues to visual presentations.* Present objects that Jessica can feel, smell, and see. For example, when she is eating, place an apple, banana, and orange on the table and let her choose which she would like to eat. Ask her to feel, smell, and look at the fruit before she chooses. Tell her the names of the three fruits before and during the presentation.

3. *Simplify the environment and eliminate crowding.* Present only a few objects at a time with spacing between objects. Objects placed close together may "blend" together for children with cortical visual impairment, and because of the "crowding" together, the objects in the middle may be difficult to see or may disappear.

4. *Use repetition and constancy.* It often takes repetition and constancy of objects being presented for the child to "see" them. Use familiar objects or symbols. Repeat presentations of the same objects on many occasions.

5. *Use movement.* Often children with cortical visual impairment "see" better when they are moving or things around them are moving. Choose toys that move. As Jessica begins to scoot and crawl, encourage her to explore. Try moving objects back and forth to increase their visual interest. Remember to tell her what the objects are and let her feel, smell, and taste them when it is appropriate.

SAMPLE VISUAL EXAMINATION REPORT FOR AARON

Special Visual Assessment

Child's Name: _Aaron_   **Age:** _4 months_

History: Aaron has been diagnosed with familial exudative vitreoretinopathy as reported by Dr. X. The macula of the right eye is involved in the retinal fold. The macula of the left eye appeared completely flattened at his follow-up evaluation when he was 3 months old. Aaron has also been examined by Dr. Y, but results of the examination were not available for our review. Aaron was born full term with a birthweight of 9 pounds, 7 ounces. There is no family history of visual impairment. Aaron receives services from Ms. Z, a counselor with an early intervention program, Off to a Good Start, of the Blind Babies Foundation.

Reason for Examination: To provide information about visual functioning.

Refractive Status:

Retinoscopy with cycloplegia:	**Right Eye:**	unable to judge reflex due to retinal fold
	Left Eye:	-6.25 -3.50 × 090
Prescription written:	**Right eye:**	plano
	Left eye:	-4.75 -2.50 × 090

Binocular Status: A variable, right esotropia (inward eye turn) was noted. Aaron appeared to fixate on a penlight and the television monitor during VEP testing with the left eye. No fixation response was noted with the right eye. No nystagmus was noted.

Ocular Health: The corneal diameter of the right eye appears about 1 mm smaller than in the left eye. Aaron has been diagnosed with familial exudative vitreoretinopathy involving the right eye more than the left. The right eye has a severe retinal fold that includes the macula. The macula of the left eye appeared flat to the disc margin. Temporal lens opacities were noted in each eye, but the lenses appeared clear along the visual axis.

Visual Acuity:

Sweep Visual Evoked Potential grating acuity measure: Both eyes viewing at 50 cm: 1.4 cycles/degree or "predicted" optotype acuity 20/1350.

Left eye viewing at 50 cm with −8 DS lens: 3.5 c/deg or "predicted" optotype acuity 20/520.

The visual evoked potential (VEP) uses black-and-white gratings (stripes) as the target to measure visual acuity (the ability to see fine details). In persons with low vision, grating acuity consistently overestimates visual acuity compared to the acuity obtained when measured using letters or symbols. Therefore, a conversion factor is used to "predict" the letter acuity from the grating acuity measure. This predicted acuity measure should be used in setting guidelines for educational materials. The VEP indicates pattern detection. During the VEP testing, Aaron appeared to fixate on the television monitor. He often stopped sucking on his bottle when the grating pattern appeared and resumed sucking when the gratings disappeared at the end of the 10-second trial.

Contrast Sensitivity:

Sweep VEP contrast sensitivity: 11.3% Michelson contrast without spectacle correction, 4.5 percent Michelson contrast with a −8 DS lens held in front of the left eye. Normal values are 0.5 percent, indicating that Aaron's ability to detect subtle shades of gray is reduced by a factor of 10 from normal.

Summary and Recommendations: Aaron has familial exudative vitreoretinopathy affecting the right eye more than the left. The right eye has a severe retinal fold involving the macula. The macula in the left eye appears flat. The refractive error of the right eye could not be determined because of the retinal fold along the visual axis. The refractive error of the left eye showed significant myopia with astigmatism. The myopia decreased significantly after cycloplegia, indicating that an accommodative (focusing) response was present before cycloplegia. With this amount of myopia, objects farther than 5 inches from Aaron's eyes will be out of focus. Although his vision is reduced because of the FEVR, such a large amount of optical defocus may also affect his vision. We have recommended a trial period using eyeglasses with a follow-up. The prescription written purposely undercorrects his myopia to place his eyes in focus for objects within arm's reach (closer than 50 cm or 20 inches).

Aaron's visual acuity (ability to see details), as measured with the VEP, was 20/1350 without spectacle correction. With a −8 DS trial lens held in front of the left eye, the VEP measure of acuity was 20/520. This improvement with spectacle correction is not surprising, since his eyes are in focus for 5 inches or closer without glasses, and the VEP monitor was placed at 20 inches for testing. His contrast sensitivity (ability to detect differences in brightness) was reduced by a factor of 10 from normal as measured with the VEP. The VEP indicates that Aaron has pattern vision, and observations of his fixation during the VEP testing also suggest that he has pattern vision.

To make it easier for Aaron to locate toys and objects, the contrast should be enhanced between the object and its background. For example, place dark-colored toys on a light-colored mat, or vice versa. These objects should be paired with auditory or tactile cues, since hearing is his strength.

Aaron is legally blind and qualifies for educational services to children with visual impairment, including services from a teacher who is certified in the field of blindness and visual impairment. He should continue services with the early intervention program Off to a Good Start.

We would like to reevaluate Aaron's vision after he has worn his eyeglasses for 2 months. He should continue to receive regular eye examinations.

APPENDIX

Causes of Visual Impairments and Refractive Errors That Occur in Children with Additional Disabilities

Irene Topor

There are several categories of visual conditions that affect children with additional disabilities. This section discusses causes of visual impairment related to brain trauma and dysfunction, damaged or underdeveloped optic nerves that connect the eye and brain, prematurity, infections and hereditary syndromes, and refractive errors. Figure 4.1 provides a cross section of the eye and the visual pathway from the eye to the optic nerve is provided to assist in the location of eye problems that cause visual impairments.

Neurological visual impairment is a leading cause of vision loss. It is becoming more prevalent among children with visual and additional disabilities because of the nature of the vision loss. Neurological abnormalities of the visual pathway and/or visual centers of the brain without eye disease cause the vision impairment.

Figure 4.1   CROSS-SECTION OF THE EYE

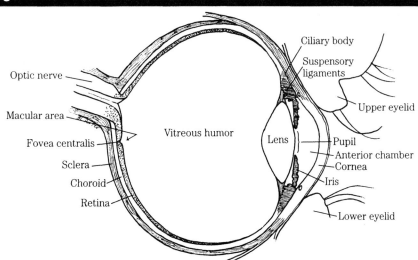

Credit: Barbara Porter

Neurological visual impairment is caused by lack of oxygen during or after the birth process, hydrocephalus, trauma/shaken baby syndrome, intrautero drug exposure, meningitis, seizure disorders or trauma to the brain causing bleeding. According to Takashita (1996), a child with neurological visual impairment may function in one of three ways:

- *Cortical blindness*   There is no or minimal functional vision owing to damage to the occipital lobe and/or posterior visual pathway (behind the lateral geniculate body). Magnetic resonance studies will reveal damage to the occipital cortex.
- *Delayed visual maturation*   The results of the MRI do not reveal abnormalities (Hoyt, Jastrzebski, & Marg, 1983). During the first months of life, no apparent functional vision is observed. Visual function generally improves by 2 to 3 years of age. The child may have nystagmus. The delayed visual function may be related to abnormalities of the anterior visual pathway.
- *Cortical visual impairment (CVI)*   Most children will have indications of visual function. An MRI will reveal abnormalities in the posterior visual pathway.

Nystagmus will not be present unless the child has an additional visual problem like nearsightedness that is causing the nystagmus (Jan & Groenveld, 1993). He or she may respond to objects in the peripheral field and high-contrast, rotating, and moving targets. The child's use of peripheral vision may be just as functional as his or her use of central vision. The use of the tactile sensory system may be initiated if vision is either unreliable or difficult to use. Some children will be assisted by additional light, but others may appear sensitive to the presence of bright light in the environment (Jan, Groenveld, Sykanda, & Hoyt, 1987). Vision often improves with time; a child with CVI may demonstrate visual functioning that fluctuates from day to day (Crossman, 1991). Children with CVI may not look blind or visually impaired, leading adults to believe that they are seeing more than they really can. There may be an absence of postural differences that are often seen in children with visual impairments; that is, a blank stare or other nonfunctional visual behavior is used instead of the head-down position of children who need to be reminded to keep their heads up. Children may benefit from using touch and auditory cues to stimulate attention.

Children with CVI are attracted to colors, especially yellow and red. Environmental factors, such as unusual odors, a high noise level, or hot-cold temperature extremes may affect the child's overall functioning.

Optic nerve atrophy and **hypoplasia** affect the optic nerve, a bundle of fibers that transmit signals from the retina to the brain. In optic nerve atrophy, the optic nerve has been damaged in some way; in optic nerve hypoplasia the nerve has not developed. Tumors of the visual pathways, an inadequate supply of blood or oxygen before or shortly after birth, trauma, hydrocephalus, heredity, and rare degenerative diseases have been identified as causes of optic nerve atrophy (Blind Babies Foundation, 1998). These conditions often occur in children whose brains are impaired in other ways. Children with optic nerve atrophy may have some vision or may be blind, depending on how much of their optic nerve is intact or has been damaged.

In optic nerve hypoplasia, one of the most prevalent types of visual impairments among young children (Hatton, Bailey, Burchinal, & Ferrell, 1997), a child's optic nerve fails to develop properly because of something that happened early in pregnancy. This condition has been associated with the mother's diabetes, alcohol abuse, and use of anti-epileptic drugs and young age (age 20 or under), as well as the mother's exposure to a toxic substance or change in genes. Children with optic nerve hypoplasia may have other disabilities, such as cerebral palsy or growth problems, since the optic nerve is located close to the pituitary gland, which is responsible for physical growth.

Infants who are born at a gestational age of less than 36 weeks and weigh less than 1,500 grams (3.5 pounds) are at the greatest risk of other medical problems, including visual impairments. Although some premature babies can be considered healthy, others may weigh as little as 500 grams and are at risk of breathing, eating, motor, cognitive, hearing, and visual problems. Babies who are born prematurely are at risk of ROP, a condition in which abnormal blood vessels grow inside the eye (Barr, 1990). The two most important factors in the development of retinopathy of prematurity are degree of prematurity and birth weight. The more premature the baby and the lower the birth weight, the more likely the baby will develop ROP. In the vast majority of babies with ROP, the blood vessels that grew abnormally go away, and the eye heals completely on its own before the babies are 1 year old. Sometimes the abnormal blood vessels scar the retina when they heal; if so, the child will be at risk of a lazy eye or nearsightedness. In fewer cases, the retina detaches, meaning that the child will have poor vision, but detached retinas occur in only 5% of all babies who are at risk of developing ROP. Premature infants who are also affected by bronchopulmonary dysplasia may have additional visual impairments, including strabismus and refractive errors (Harvey, Dobson, & Luna, 1997).

Other common causes of visual impairments among children with additional disabilities are congenital infections. **TORCH syndrome** is an acronym denoting toxoplasmosis, other infections (such as syphilis), rubella, cytomegalovirus (CMV), and herpes (McDonough, 1994). A newborn may be visually impaired and have other disabilities if his or her mother had a particular infection during pregnancy.

Toxoplasmosis occurs in 1–4 infants per 1,000 live births. It is characterized by inflammation of the retina and choroid that causes scarring. Microorganisms found in animal feces and raw meat may cause toxoplasmosis, so pregnant women should not expose themselves to this risk, by, for example, eating rare meat or emptying used kitty litter. The effects on an infant's vision may include blind spots or the loss of central vision or visual fields.

CMV is a common virus that may not affect the mother, but can damage a child's brain before birth and cause mental retardation and hearing and visual impairments. The most common eye disorder resulting from CMV is chorioretinitis, which occurs in approximately one-quarter of affected infants. Lesions destroy the normal retinal and choroidal structures (vessels that nourish the other part of the retina).

Rubella, or **German measles,** is a contagious viral infection that can cause hearing loss, cataracts, glaucoma, decreased visual acuity, colobomas, strabismus, and constricted visual fields.

Neonatal herpes is a rare disorder that may cause an infant's eyes to become infected, with the symptoms recurring for some time.

Other common causes of visual impairments among children with additional disabilities are syndromes or hereditary disorders. There are many hereditary syndromes that affect children's visual function; some of the more common ones are **CHARGE association, Down syndrome** (trisomy 21), **Laurence-Moon Biedl,** and **Duane's syndrome.**

In a complete and comprehensive eye assessment, a child is exam-ined for **refractive error,** that is, to determine if the child has **astigma-tism, myopia (nearsightedness),** or **hyperopia (farsightedness)** (Bailey, 1997). Refractive errors are caused by irregularities in the shape and curvature of the cornea (astigmatism) or the eyeball being too long (myopia or nearsightedness) or too short (hyperopia or farsightedness), thus affecting how light rays are bent (refracted) and producing a blurry image on the retina (Teplin, 1995). Many children benefit from wearing prescription eyeglasses to correct a refractive error. If a child is physi-cally involved and there is concern that he or she may not tolerate wearing eyeglasses, the early intervention team can brainstorm to de-termine if the child can start by wearing the eyeglasses for a shorter time and then slowly increase the time he or she wears them. Children may tolerate lenses for longer periods if the lens prescription is not ini-tially given at full strength. A weaker prescription can allow children to adjust slowly to the new images that they are seeing. The full prescrip-tion can be offered after members of the early intervention team agree that the children have adjusted to wearing the eyeglasses and may tol-erate learning to see an even clearer image.

REFERENCES

Abrahamsson, M., Fabian, G., & Sjöstrand, J. (1988). Changes in astigmatism between the ages of 1 and 4 years: A longitudinal study. *British Journal of Ophthalmology, 72,* 145–150.

Adams, R. J., & Courage, M. L. (1996). Monocular contrast sensitivity in 3- to 36-month-old human infants. *Optometry & Vision Science, 73,* 546–551.

Adams, R. J., Mauer, D., & Davis, M. (1986). Newborns' discrimination of chromatic from achromatic stimuli. *Journal of Experimental Child Psychology, 41,* 267–281.

Aduchi-Usami, E. (1991). Visually evoked cortical potentials in cortical blind-ness. In J. R. Heckenlively & G. B. Arden (Eds.), *Principles and prac-tice of clinical electrophysiology of vision* (pp. 578–580). St. Louis: Mosby Year Book.

Allen, D., Banks, M. S., & Norcia, A. M. (1993). Does chromatic sensitivity develop more slowly than luminance sensitivity? *Vision Research, 33,* 2553–2562.

American Academy of Ophthalmology (1992). *Preferred practice pattern: Comprehensive pediatric eye evaluation.* San Francisco: Author.

Aslin, R. N. (1987). Motor aspects of visual development in infancy. In P. Salapatek & L. Cohen (Eds.), *Handbook of infant perception* (Vol. 1, pp. 43–113). New York: Academic Press.

Bailey, I. L. (1997). Optometric care for the multihandicapped child. *Journal of Low Vision and Neuro-Optometric Rehabilitation, 11,* 12–20.

Baldwin, W. R. (1990). Refractive status of infants and children. In A. Rosenbloom & M. Morgan (Eds.), *Principles and practice of pediatric optometry* (pp. 104–152). Philadelphia: J. B. Lippincott.

Bane, M. C., & Birch, E. E. (1992). VEP acuity, FPL acuity, and visual behavior of visually impaired children. *Journal of Pediatric Ophthalmology and Strabismus, 29,* 202–209.

Banks, M. S. (1980). The development of visual accommodation during early infancy. *Child Development, 51,* 646–666.

Barnett, A. B., Manson, J. I., & Wilner, E. (1970). Acute cerebral blindness in children. *Neurology, 20,* 1147.

Barr, C. (1990). *Retinopathy of Prematurity: Parents' Newsletter.* Louisville, KY: Visually Impaired Preschool Services.

Beller, R., Hoyt, C. S., & Marg, E. (1981). Good visual function after neo-natal surgery for congenital monocular cataracts. *American Journal of Ophthalmology, 91,* 559–565.

Birch, E. E., Gwiazada, J., & Held, R. (1982). Stereoacuity development for crossed and uncrossed disparities in human infants. *Vision Research, 22,* 507–513.

Blind Babies Foundation. (1998). *Pediatric visual diagnosis visual fact sheets.* San Francisco: Author.

Brodsky, M. C., Baker, R. S., & Hamed, L. M. (1996). In *Pediatric neuro-ophthalmology* (pp. 302–465). New York: Springer-Verlag.

Brown, A. M. (1990). Development of visual sensitivity to light and color vision in human infants: A critical review. *Vision Research, 30,* 1159–1188.

Campbell, L. R., & Charney, E. (1991). Factors associated with delay in diagnosis of childhood amblyopia. *Pediatrics, 87,* 178–185.

Cogan, D. G. (1956). Neurology of the ocular muscles. Springfield, IL: Charles C Thomas.

Cook, R. C., Glassock, R. E. (1951). Refractive and ocular findings in the newborn. *American Journal of Ophthalmology, 34,* 1407–17.

Crossman, H. L. (1991). Visual improvement in the multi-handicapped child with cortical visual impairment: *Transactions of the VIIth International Orthoptic Congress* (pp. 2.6–6.6). Nuremberg, Germany.

Day, S. H., Orel-Bixler, D. A., & Norcia, A. M. (1988). Abnormal acuity development in infantile esotropia. *Investigative Ophthalmology & Visual Science, 29,* 327–329.

Dobson, V., Fulton, A. B., Manning, K., Salem, D., & Peterson, R. A. (1981). Cycloplegic refractions of premature infants. *American Journal of Ophthalmology, 91,* 490–495.

Dobson, V., Quinn, G. E., Abramov, I., Hardy, R. J., Tano, B., Siatkowski, R. M., Phelps, D. L. (1996). Color vision measured with pseudoisochromatic plates at five-and-a-half years in eyes of children from the CRYO-ROP study. *Investigative Ophthalmology and Visual Science, 37*(12):2467–74.

Dobson, V., Quinn, G. E., Biglan, A. W., Tung, B., Flynn, J. T., & Palmer, E. A. (1990). Acuity card assessment of visual function in the cryotherapy for retinopathy of prematurity study. *Investigative Ophthalmology & Visual Science, 31,* 1702–1708.

Dobson, V., & Teller, D. Y. (1978). Visual acuity in human infants: A review and comparison of behavioral and electrophysiological studies. *Vision Research, 18,* 1469–1483.

Edwards, W. C., Price, W. D., & Weisskopf, B. (1972). Ocular findings in developmentally handicapped children. *Journal of Pediatric Ophthalmology, 9,* 162–167.

Elston, J. (1990). Epidemiology of visual handicap in childhood. In D. Taylor (Ed.), *Pediatric Ophthalmology* (pp. 3–6). Boston: Blackwell Scientific.

Fingeret, M., Casser, L., & Woodcome, H. T. (1990). *Atlas of primary eye-care procedures.* Norwalk, CT: Appleton & Lange.

First, L. R., & Palfrey, J. S. (1994). The infant or young child with developmental delay. *New England Journal of Medicine, 330,* 478–483.

Fisher, S., Orel-Bixler, D., & Bailey, I. (1995). Mr. Happy contrast sensitivity: A behavioral test for infants and children [abstract]. *Optometry & Vision Science, 72,* 204.

Fishman, G. A. & Sokol, S. (1990). Electrophysiologic testing in disorders of the retina, optic nerve, and visual pathway. *Ophthalmology Monographs 2.* San Francisco: American Academy of Ophthalmology.

Fraiberg, S. (1977). *Insights from the Blind.* London, England: Souvenir Press.

Fulton, A. B., Dobson, V., Salem, D., Mar, C., Peterson, R. A., & Hansen, R. M. (1980). Cycloplegic refractions in infants and young children. *American Journal of Ophthalmology, 90,* 239–247.

Fulton, A. B., Hansen, R. M., & Lambert, S. R. (1994). Workup of the possibly blind child. In S. J. Isenberg (Ed.), *The eye in infancy* (pp. 547–560). St. Louis, MO: Mosby Year Book.

Fulton, A. B., Hartmann, E. E, & Hansen, R. M. (1989). Electrophysiological testing techniques for children. *Documenta Ophthalmologica, 71,* 341–354.

Getz, L., Dobson, V., & Luna, B. (1992). Grating acuity development in two-week to three-year-old children born prior to term. *Clinical Vision Science, 7,* 251–256.

Gottlob, I., Fendick, M. G., Guo, S., Zubcov, A. A., Odom, J. V., & Reinecke, R. D. (1990). Visual acuity measurements by swept spatial frequency visual-evoked-cortical potentials (VECPs): Clinical application in children with various visual disorders. *Journal of Pediatric Ophthalmology and Strabismus, 27,* 40–47.

Gwiazda J., Brill, S., Mohindra, I., Held, R. (1978). Infant visual acuity and its meridional variation. *Vision Research, 18,* 1557–1564.

Hamer, R. D., Norcia, A, M., Tyler, C. W., & Hsu-Winges, C. (1989). The development of monocular and binocular VEP acuity. *Vision Research, 29,* 397–408.

Harcourt, B. (1974). Strabismus affecting children with multiple disabilities. *British Journal of Ophthalmology, 58,* 272–280.

Harvey, E. M., Dobson, V., & Luna, B. (1997). Long-term grating acuity and visual-field development in preterm children who experienced bronchopulmonary dysplasia. *Developmental Medicine and Child Neurology, 39,* 167–173.

Hatton, D., Bailey, D. B., Burchinal, M. R., & Ferrell, K. (1997). Developmental growth curves of preschool children with vision impairments. *Child Development, 68,* 788–806.

Hoyt, C. S., Jastrzebski, G., & Marg, E. (1983). Delayed visual maturation in infancy. *British Journal of Ophthalmology, 67,* 127–130.

Illingworth, R. S. (1978). Child development. In J. O. Forfar & G. C. Arneil (Eds.), *Textbook of pediatrics.* Edinburgh, Scotland: Churchill Livingstone.

Isenberg, S. J. (1994). Workup of common differential diagnostic problems. In S. J. Isenberg (Ed.), *The eye in infancy* (pp. 73–86). St. Louis, MO: Mosby Year Book.

Jan, J. E., Farrell, K., Wong, P. K., & McCormick, A. Q. (1986). Eye and head movements of visually impaired children. *Developmental Medicine and Child Neurology, 28,* 285–293.

Jan, J. E., Freeman, R. D., & Scott, E. P. (1977). *Visual impairment in children and adolescents.* New York: Grune & Stratton.

Jan, J. E., & Groenveld, M. (1993). Visual behaviors and adaptations associated with cortical and ocular impairment in children. *Journal of Visual Impairment & Blindness, 87,* 101–105.

Jan, J. E., & Groenveld, M., Sykanda, A., & Hoyt, C. (1987). Behavioral characteristics of children with permanent cortical visual impairment. *Developmental Medicine and Child Neurology, 29,* 571–576.

Kamholtz, R. G., & Abrahams, J. J. (1992). Magnetic resonance imaging of the orbits and extraorbital visual system. In T. J. Walsh (Ed.), *Neuroophthalmology: Clinical signs and symptoms* (pp. 277–322). Philadelphia: Lea & Febiger.

Krill, A. E. (1977). Congenital color vision defects. In A. E. Krill & D. B. Archer (Eds.), *Krill's hereditary retinal and choroidal diseases: Vol II. Clinical characteristics* (p. 355–390). Hagerstown, MD: Harper & Row.

Lambert, S. R., Hoyt, C. S., Jan, J. E., Barkovich, J., & Flodmark, O. (1987). Visual recovery from hypoxic cortical blindness during childhood. Computed tomographic and magnetic resonance imaging predictors. *Archives of Ophthalmology, 105,* 1371–1377.

Landau, L., & Berson, D. (1971). Cerebral palsy and mental retardation: Ocular findings. *Journal of Pediatric Ophthalmology, 8,* 245–248.

Mackie, R. T., McCulloch, D. L., & Saunders, K. J. (1995). Comparison of visual assessment tests in multiply handicapped children. *Eye, 9,* 136–141.

Marron, J. A, & Bailey, I. L. (1982). Visual factors and orientation-mobility performance. *American Journal of Optometry and Physiological Optics, 59,* 413–426.

Mauer, D., Lewis, T. L., & Brent, H. P. (1989). The effects of deprivation on human visual development: Studies of children treated for cataracts. In F. J. Morrision, C. E. Lord, & D. P. Keating (Eds.), *Applied developmental psychology. Vol 3: Psychological development in infancy.* New York: Academic Press.

Mayer, D. L., Beiser, A. S., Warner, A. F., Pratt, E. M., Raye, K. N., & Lang, J. M. (1995). Monocular acuity norms for the Teller Acuity Cards between ages one month and four years. *Investigative Ophthalmology and Visual Science, 36,* 671–685.

Mayer, D. L., Fulton, A. B., & Hansen, R. M. (1985). Visual acuity of infants and children with retinal degenerations. *Ophthalmic Paediatrics and Genetics, 5,* 51–56.

Mayer, D. L., Fulton, A. B. & Rodier, D. (1984). Grating and recognition acuities of pediatric patients. *Ophthalmology, 91,* 947–953.

McCrary, J. A. (1991). Magnetic resonance imaging applications in ophthalmology. *International Ophthalmology Clinics, Neuro-Ophthalmology, 31,* 101–115.

McCulloch, D. L., Taylor, M. J., & Whyte, H. E. (1991). Visual evoked potentials and visual prognosis following perinatal asphyxia. *Archives of Ophthalmology, 109,* 229–233.

McDonald, M., Ankrum, C., Preston, K., Sebris, S. L., & Dobson, V. (1986). Monocular and binocular acuity estimation in 18- to 36-month-olds: Acuity card results. *American Journal of Optometry & Physiological Optics, 63,* 181–186.

McDonald, M., Sebris, S. L., Mohn, G., Teller, D. Y., & Dobson, V. (1986). Monocular acuity in normal infants: The acuity card procedure. *American Journal of Optometry & Physiological Optics, 63,* 127–134.

McDonald, J. T. (1994). *Stedman's concise medical dictionary* (2nd ed.). Baltimore, MD: Williams & Wilkins.

Mohn, G., & van Hof-van Duin J. (1986a). Development of the binocular and monocular visual fields of human infants during the first year of life. *Clinical Vision Science, 1,* 51.

Mohn, G., & van Hof-van Duin, J. (1986b). Preferential looking in normal and neurologically abnormal infants and pediatric patients. *Documenta Ophthalmologica Proceedings Series, 45,* 64–69.

Norcia, A. M., Hamer, R. D., & Tyler, C. W. (1990). Development of contrast sensitivity in the infant. *Vision Research, 30,* 1475.

Norcia, A. M., & Tyler, C. W. (1985). Spatial frequency sweep VEP: Visual acuity during the first year of life. *Vision Research, 25,* 1399–1408.

Odom, J. V., Hoyt, C. S., & Marg, E. (1981). Effect of natural deprivation and unilateral eye patching on visual acuity of infants and children: Evoked potential measurements. *Archives of Ophthalmology, 99,* 1412–1416.

Orel-Bixler, D. A. (1989). *Subjective and visual evoked potential measures of acuity in normal and amblyopic adults and children.* Unpublished doctoral dissertation, University of California at Berkeley.

Orel-Bixler, D. A., Haegerstrom-Portnoy, G., & Hall, A. (1989). Visual assessment of the multiply handicapped patient. *Optometry & Vision Science, 69,* 530–536.

Orel-Bixler, D. A., & Norcia, A. M. (1987). Differential growth of acuity for steady-state pattern reversal and transient pattern onset-offset VEPs. *Clinical Vision Science, 2,* 1–9.

Pease, P., & Allen, J. (1988). A new test for screening color vision: Concurrent validity and utility. *American Journal of Optometry & Physiological Optics, 65,* 729–738.

Quinn, E. A., Dobson, V., Repka, M. X., Reynolds, J., Kivlin, J., Davis, B., Buckley, E., Flynn, J. T., & Dalmer, E. A. (1990). Development of myopia in infants with birth weights less than 1251 grams: The cryotherapy for retinopathy of prematurity cooperative group. *Ophthalmology, 99,* 329–340.

Regan, D. (1988). Low contrast visual acuity test for pediatric use. *Canadian Journal of Ophthalmology, 23,* 224–227.

Reynell, J., & Zinkin, P. (1975). New perspectives for the developmental assessment of young children with severe visual handicap. *Child: Care, Health, & Development, 1,* 61–69.

Robinson, G. C., Jan, J. E., & Kinnis, C. (1987). Congenital ocular blindness in children: 1945 to 1984. *American Journal of Diseases of Children, 147,* 1321–1324.

Rubin, G. S., & Legge, G. E. (1985). Psychophysics of reading: VI-The role of contrast in low vision. *Vision Research, 29,* 79–91.

Rutstein, R. P., Wesson, M. D., Gotlieb, S., & Biasini, F. J. (1986). Clinical comparison of the visual parameters in infants with intrauterine growth retardation vs. infants with normal birth weight. *American Journal of Optometry & Physiological Optics, 63,* 697–701.

Selenow, A., Cuiffreda, K. J., Mozlin, R., & Rumpf, D. (1986). Prognostic value of laser interferometric visual acuity in amblyopia therapy. *Investigative Ophthalmology & Vision Science, 27,* 273–277.

Shalowitz, M. U., & Gorski, P. A. (1990). Developmental assessment in the first year of life. In J. A. Stockman, III (Ed.), *Difficult diagnosis in pediatrics* (pp. 3–14). Philadelphia: W. B. Saunders.

Simeonsson, R. J., & Sharp, M. C. (1992). Developmental delays. In R. A. Hoekelman, S. B. Friedman, N. M. Nelson, & H. M. Seidel (Eds.), *Primary pediatric care* (2nd ed., pp. 867–870). St. Louis: Mosby Year Book.

Sokol, S. (1976). Visually evoked potentials: Theory, techniques, and clinical applications. *Survey of Ophthalmology, 21,* 18–44.

Sonksen, P. (1983). Vision and early development. In K. Wybar & D. Taylor (Eds.), *Paediatric Ophthalmology* (pp. 85–95). New York: Dekker.

Summers, C. G., & MacDonald, J. T. (1990). Vision despite tomographic absence of occipital cortex. *Survey of Ophthalmology, 35,* 188–190.

Takashita, B. (1996). *Neurological vision impairment: Cortical vision impairment, delayed visual maturation, cortical blindness.* Paper presented at the annual conference of the California Trnascribers and Educators of the Visually Handicapped, San Diego.

Taylor, M. J., & McCulloch, D. L. (1992). Visual evoked potentials in infants and children. *Journal of Clinical Neurophysiology, 9,* 357–372.

Teller, D. Y., & Movshon, J. A. (1987). Visual development. *Vision Research, 26,* 1483–1506.

Teplin, S. W. (1995). Visual impairment in infants and young children. *Infants and Young Children, 8* (1), 18–51.

Ventocilla, M., Orel-Bixler, D. A., & Haegerstrom-Portnoy, G. (1995). Pediatric color vision screening: AO HRR vs. Mr. Color [abstract]. *Optometry & Vision Science, 72,* 203.

von Noorden, GK. (1975). Ocular motor effects on vision: Clinical aspects. In G. Lennerstrand & P. Bach-y-Rita (Eds.), *Basic mechanisms of ocular motility and their clinical implications* (pp. 417–423). Oxford, England: Pergamon.

Walker, E., Tobin, M., & McKennell, A. (1992). Blind and Partially Sighted Children in Britian: The RNIB Survey. Royal National Institute for the Blind, Vol. 2, London: HMSO publications, pp. 65–71.

Warren, D. H. (1994). *Blindness and children. An individual differences approach.* New York: Cambridge University Press.

Wesson, M. D., & Maino, D. M. (1995). Oculovisual findings in children with Down syndrome, cerebral palsy, and mental retardation without specific etiology. In D. M. Maino (Ed.), *Diagnosis and management of special populations* (pp. 17–54). St. Louis, MO: Mosby Year Book.

Whiting, S., Jan, J. E., Wong, P. K. H., Flormark, O., Farrell, K., & McCormick, A. Q. (1985). Permanent cortical visual impairment in children. *Developmental Medicine & Child Neurology, 27,* 730–739.

Zimmerman, R. A., & Bilaniuk, L. T. (1994). Pediatric head trauma. *Neuroimaging Clinics of North America, 4,* 349–366.

Zinkin, P. (1979). The effect of visual handicap on early development. In *Visual handicap in children* (Vol. 16, pp. 132–138). London, England: Spastics International Medical Publications.

CHAPTER

5

Functional Vision Assessments and Early Interventions

Irene Topor

An infant who has a visual impairment and additional disabilities will benefit most from early intervention services when the parents, other caregivers, and teachers understand the kind of eye condition that is causing the infant's visual impairment and ability to use vision. The eye condition is diagnosed during a clinical vision examination by a pediatric ophthalmologist or optometrist, who may also prescribe other treatments, such as eyeglasses or contact lenses (see Chapter 4). Following the clinical vision examination, the infant's ability to use vision should be assessed by a professional in the field of visual impairments—that is, a teacher of children who have visual impairment or a low vision specialist—by evaluating the infant's visual capabilities in the environments in which he or she spends most of the time. This is a functional vision assessment.

A functional vision assessment is a systematic way of observing and assessing an infant's ability to use vision for certain tasks under different conditions and in both familiar and unfamiliar settings. It builds on the findings of the clinical eye examination to describe how the infant's responses vary with motivation, levels of alertness, and environmental conditions, such as the time of day and lighting and contrast conditions. It highlights the infant's areas of strength and needs in using vision as the basis for identifying priorities for learning.

157

In some cases, the functional vision assessment may be completed first, to supply evidence that the infant has visual difficulty and that a clinical eye examination is needed. Usually, it is conducted after the clinical eye examination has been conducted and the medical eye report has been written and received.

As described in detail in Chapter 4, the clinical vision assessment is conducted by an eye care professional whose primary purpose is to gather information about how the eye looks, how healthy it is, and how well it is working. The principal objectives of the examination are to identify (diagnose) any visual impairments or refractive errors, give a prognosis of the eye condition, determine the visual acuity and extent of the visual fields, recommend surgery, prescribe eyeglasses or contact lenses for correction, and to prescribe medications. (See the Appendix to Chapter 4 for an illustration of the anatomy of the eye and descriptions of the common visual impairments and refractive errors that occur in children with visual and multiple disabilities.)

The clinical vision assessment provides important information for teachers, parents, and other caregivers. This information, accompanied by the results of the functional vision assessment, will provide the best overall vision programming for the infant.

This chapter focuses on the functional vision assessment and intervention strategies for an infant with visual and additional disabilities. The assessment differs from an assessment for children who are older or have only a visual impairment in that it depends on the maturity of the infant's visual system; the infant's developmental level, language and communication, physical ability and motivation; and the importance of the visual tasks.

The chapter begins with a detailed discussion of the functional vision assessment for an infant, including the components, contexts, adaptations, procedures, and materials commonly used. It also presents assessment considerations specific to young children who have visual and multiple disabilities. This section emphasizes the family's role in identifying the extent to which an infant uses vision to learn about the world. The next section discusses how the results of the clinical and functional assessments are used together to affect early intervention, including specific interventions and adaptations that promote an infant's use of vision within the context of interactions with his or her parents, teachers, and caregivers and everyday routines, as well as environmental adaptations that foster the effective use of vision. Finally, selected resources for teachers who are certified in the field of blindness and visual impairment are provided throughout the chapter.

THE BASICS OF THE FUNCTIONAL VISION ASSESSMENT

Purposes

A functional vision assessment has three primary objectives or purposes. The first is to supplement the clinical information with a broad picture of the infant's physical characteristics that may relate to vision. For example, if the parents or early interventionist notice that the infant shuts his or her eyes in a brightly lit room or see one eye drift inward toward the nose, this information can be reported to an eye care specialist who can explore the causes and may prescribe treatment.

The second purpose is to assess the infant's range of visual function so that learning objectives can be established. Many infants with visual and additional multiple disabilities, especially those with neurological impairments, vary in their use of vision and in their attention throughout a typical day. The functional vision assessment attempts to identify these variations by noting the conditions under which the infant uses vision with more efficiency and those under which he or she uses senses other than vision to obtain information. For example, a parent may observe the infant looking and reaching for a small item of food when it is always placed on the left side of the tray. Therefore, the parent may move the food to other locations on the tray and tap his or her finger near the food to redirect the infant's gaze. Or the parent may place a placemat of a contrasting color under the food, on the right side of the tray, to attract the infant's attention to it. Whatever the conditions, the purpose is to collect information about a variety of behaviors under a variety of conditions. Toward this end, the functional vision assessment should take place in several settings, at several times of day, and during various routine activities.

The third objective is to draw upon the observations of the functional vision assessment to teach the parents to help the infant develop alternate ways to obtain the information required to meet a need. These techniques may be visual, such as environmental adaptations of contrast, lighting, or changing the time of day when the material is presented. Alternately, they may be tactile if the infant has not learned how to use his or her vision functionally or does not have sufficient vision. For instance, a infant who is not able to locate a favorite toy consistently using vision may be taught to search with his or her hands to find the desired object.

When to Conduct the Assessment

The functional vision assessment should be conducted when the infant with a visual impairment is first enrolled in an early intervention program, when there are changes in the infant's visual and/or medical condition, and when there are changes in the types of tasks or environments in which the infant participates. One example is when an infant makes the transition from a home-based to a center-based program, and the activities in the center are different than those in the home. Another example is when an infant receives new medication, such as for seizures, and appears to behave differently. The new behavior may include differences in visual functioning that can be identified in an assessment.

Considerations for Infants

As was stated previously, a functional vision assessment for an infant differs from an assessment for older children. An infant may not understand what is requested and usually cannot respond with speech, so the assessment techniques must be tailored accordingly. The results are often based upon observations of an infant's physical responses to a toy, another person, or an event made by parents, teachers, and caregivers. Eye movements or head turning, movement of an arm and hand toward a toy, changes in the breathing rate, a change in the frequency of body movement, or vocalizations may be used as indications of an infant's visual response.

Components of the Assessment

The functional vision assessment consists of the following activities and assessments:

- gathering background information about the infant's medical and developmental history, including chronic medical conditions and seizures that affect the infant's ability to use vision
- screening visual acuity to determine if there is a need for further assessment in this area
- assessing eye movements
- assessing near-point vision (within the distance of the infant's arm)
- assessing intermediate and distance vision (16 inches to 3 feet and beyond)
- assessing visual fields
- assessing color vision
- assessing environmental considerations

Each of these components will be discussed separately in the sections that follow. Samples of completed reports of a functional vision assessment and follow-up are presented at the end of this chapter. They can be consulted for illustrations of the material described in the text.

GATHERING BACKGROUND INFORMATION

The early inverventionist or vision professional conducting the assessment first gathers background information about the infant's medical conditions and developmental status that could influence the infant's ability to use vision (see, for example, the Vision Screening Questionnaire in the Appendix). This information should include a brief summary of the most recent findings from a clinical vision assessment.

Questions to Ask
the Ophthalmologist or Optometrist

The first step in this activity is to obtain information and explanations from the ophthalmologist or optometrist who examined the infant. The following list of questions should be considered at this stage. (A blank questionnaire appears in the Appendix.) Note that the parents and service providers should be able to answer the first seven questions based on the clinical vision report. If the written report does not provide this information, the early interventionist or the vision professional conducting the functional vision assessment will need to discuss the results with the optometrist or ophthalmologist.

1. What vision tests were conducted?

Several grating acuity tests are available for use with infants, including the LEA grating paddles and the Teller Acuity Cards (see Chapter 4 for more information on clinical assessment tests). These tests require a gaze preference to lines on a card. The ophthamologist or optometrist takes a case history; diagnoses the ocular disease; and assesses refractive error, accommodative abilities, visual acuity, visual fields, contrast sensitivity, color vision, ocular motility, and binocular vision. In some cases, the infant may be given a visual evoked response (VER) or electroretinogram (ERG) to determine if the brain is processing information in the visual cortex or if the retina is receiving and transmitting information.

2. What were the results of the test or tests?

Request a simple explanation of the test results in terms that you understand.

3. How did the test go? How was the infant during the testing situation? How reliable are the results?

4. What do the results mean in terms of the infant's ability to see clearly?

5. With this vision loss, would this infant benefit from eyeglasses or contact lenses?

6. What can the infant be expected to see with and without the eyeglasses or contact lenses?

7. Are more tests needed? If so, when and what kind?

The next six questions may not be answered by the clinical eye examination report and will likely require additional information from the optometrist or ophthalmologist.

8. What is the best way to assess an infant with visual and additional disabilities?

9. When should the infant be retested?

If questions remain about the infant's vision, the infant should be seen at least once every six months to determine if his or her vision has changed, or if eyeglasses or contact lenses have been prescribed, to see if their strength and fit are appropriate.

10. How can the infant be prepared for further testing, for example, for recognition acuity tests that require a matching or verbal response or tests conducted at distances beyond 16 inches.

11. Can the early interventionist participate in further testing; such as recognition acuity tests?

12. To gain a better understanding of the infant's vision loss, can the parents and the early interventionist look at the forced-choice preferential looking cards from the viewpoints of the tester and the infant?

13. If the infant is wearing contact lenses or glasses, when does he or she need to be checked for a new prescription?

Questions to Ask Parents

The role of the parents in assessing their infant's vision cannot be emphasized too strongly. The collaboration of medical and educational personnel with the parents provides the most comprehensive information about an infant. Parents are usually the first to suspect that their infants, especially preverbal or nonverbal infants who cannot describe their own visual needs and experiences, have a vision problem.

The screening questions listed in this section are intended to capture the parents' understanding of their infant's medical, health, and vision statuses. (A blank questionnaire appears in the Appendix.) Although some of these questions may appear redundant with the questions directed to the ophthalmologist or optometrist, remember that a functional vision assessment may be conducted before a clinical eye examination. In such cases, before scheduling an appointment with the eye care professional, the early interventionist and parents should review what they already know about the infant's vision. The early interventionist administering these questions need not be a certified teacher of visually impaired children. However, if the parents express significant concerns about the infant's ability to use vision, a referral to an eye care specialist and a certified teacher of visually impaired children is important to identify the further steps the family should take to ensure that the infant gets appropriate care.

This list of questions covers many aspects of what will be tested during the functional vision assessment. The questions are used to gather information about the parents' impression of their infant's vision and visual functioning. The dialogue between the questioner and the parents increases the parents' participation and involvement. The discussion should help the parents observe their infant's use of vision at different times during the day and increase the teacher's knowledge of how the infant uses vision; since the family has many more opportunties to make observations.

The initial questions consider medical and health information about the infant.

1. What have you been told by medical professionals (such as the pediatrician or family physician) about your infant's vision?

Look for diagnoses that may indicate that the infant is at risk of visual impairment. Ask the parents whether the infant has ever had a vision test. Is so, what kind of test? If the infant was premature, has an ophthalmologist checked whether the infant has retinopathy of prematurity? If the infant had other complications that were due to prematurity, he or she may be at a greater risk of visual difficulties.

2. Is your infant taking any medications? What medical issues would affect your infant's ability to learn to use vision?

Antiseizure medications may have an effect on how an infant uses vision to perform tasks. Sometimes infants who are taking high doses of antiseizure medications do not appear to use vision because they are tired and sleep often, and they are rarely visually attentive. Side effects of the medication may cause the infant to have abnormal eye movements and/or the decreased ability to use both eyes together. To observe how an infant uses vision during a task ask the parents to defer giving the medications (but only with the physician's consent) one time before the observation. In some cases, it may not be practical to defer medication because the infant may have increased seizure activity. If antiseizure medications interfere with the infant's ability to attend to stimuli visually, suggest that the parent discuss the situation with the doctor. Differences in the infant's use of vision may occur in situations unrelated to the medication. These differences may be related to the infant's level of alertness, motivation to look at something, and/or environmental conditions in which the infant can use vision.

3. Do your infant's eyes look normal?

The infant's eyes should look clear, be free of discharge, and have distinct colors. For example, the iris (usually colored brown, green-hazel, or spot) should be pigmented with color throughout. The pupil (the black hole in the middle of the iris) should be a complete closed curve, and the white part of the eyes (sclera) should be white, not yellow or red. The lids should not droop (ptosis conditions). The eyes should be free of redness, encrustation, or infection. Nystagmus, involuntary movement of the eyes, should not be present.

4. Have you noticed if one of the infant's eyes turns inward, outward, upward, or downward? If so, when does this occur?

Eye muscle imbalance (strabismus) can cause vision problems if left untreated. Children do not outgrow crossed eyes. If an infant's eyes are not moving together by 6 to 8 weeks of age, the parent should consult an eye health care professional.

5. Does anyone in the family have a vision problem, such as amblyopia, or "lazy eye"; farsightedness; nearsightedness; astigmatism; or color deficiency?

Early identification of amblyopia, lazy eye, is essential. Lazy eye can be treated in babies as young as 2 months of age. The earlier the treatment, the better the chances the infant will have to develop binocular vision. In cases of extreme farsightedness or nearsightedness and/or astigmatism, the infant's vision can be corrected with eyeglasses or contact lenses. Although color deficiency cannot be treated and is more prevalent for boys than for girls, the family may be alerted to the genetic tendency for boys to have blue-green color deficiency if a male relative has an identified color deficiency.

In addition to general medical and health information, the parents' general observations of the infant's use of vision is useful. The following questions address these areas of concern.

6. What is your impression of your infant's vision?

Parents often have a sense about their child's vision that may differ from what medical professionals have told them. Parents should be urged to share their thoughts and concerns with the TVI.

7. What does your infant like to look at?

Research indicates that infants are first attracted to features of the human face, black-and-white concentric designs, stripes that alternate black and white, and brightly colored toys. Looking away from (Isenberg, 1989) any of these stimuli (gaze aversion) is a reason to refer the child to an eye care professional.

8. What kinds of things do you think your infant sees, and in what activities does he or she use vision?

Ask the parents to name their infant's areas of strength and preferences for visual stimuli. For example, ask whether the infant appears to use vision to

- notice if room lights are on or off
- gaze and reach for a bottle, cup, or food when eating
- follow a moving toy
- search for an item that has been dropped
- follow and move toward a ball that has been rolled across the room
- look at objects that he or she places into and takes out of a container
- look at himself or herself in a mirror that is displayed in the crib.

9. Does your infant seem to respond to your face or to brightly colored toys? If so, how far away, or how close, and in what positions does he or she notice them?

Have the parents note the infant's "visual sphere" or area in which he or she appears to attend visually to stimuli and then loses visual attention. Research indicates that babies as young as 6 months see at distances to 20 feet (albeit not with the best detail) (Isenberg, 1989). Interest in visual events beyond 1 foot is considered typical at young ages. If the infant appears to see toys on one side of his or her body but not the other when the head is stable, then a visual difficulty (like limited visual fields) may be present.

10. Does your infant use both eyes to look at objects or at your face when close to him or her (about 4 inches away)?

It is important to note the infant's use of his or her eyes at this distance. Both eyes "converging" together at this distance is considered typical for the infant whose vision is developing normally.

11. What does the infant do when you look at him or her from about 8 to12 inches?

Ask the parents to note the infant's responses to primary caregivers and other family members. Determine if the infant responds differently when a person looks at, smiles, and talks to him or her, rather than just looks at the infant and smiles. Note whether the infant is using both eyes and a head position when looking at the caregiver.

12. What toys does your infant prefer? Toys that make sounds? Toys that are bright and colorful? Shiny toys?

Find out what toys are available to the infant. Note what colors attract the infant's attention. If a variety of toys are available and the infant responds well only to sound-making toys, determine whether the infant can see them or if the sound simply adds to the infant's enjoyment of these toys. Does the infant respond to seeing the spoon or bottle during feeding times.

13. Does your infant swipe at, reach for, or grasp colorful objects that are close to him or her? If so, please explain.

The parents should note the infant's reaching and grasping behaviors. At 3 months of age, the baby should be swiping (even though inaccurately at first) at interesting toys, such as mobiles. Poor reach-and-grasp behaviors could indicate a visual difficulty and delayed development of eye-hand coordination.

14. How does your infant respond if many toys are presented at the same time, for example, several toys on a quilt during playtime? Will he or she notice a favorite toy?

This item indicates whether the infant has difficulty attending when "visual clutter" is present. Infants with cortical visual impairment or neurological impairments may have difficulty attending to more than one stimulus at one time if too many stimuli are presented at once.

15. Does your infant use both eyes to follow a moving object crossing from the one side of the body to the other (such as from left to right)?

At 2 months of age, babies use both eyes to follow objects that move horizontally, vertically, circularly, and diagonally. The lack of coordinated eye movements that follow a visually attractive object or face may indicate a visual difficulty.

16. Does your infant recognize people when they enter a room, when no auditory cue is given (such as the person signalling his or her presence by calling out the infant's name or the sound of footsteps)? How far away is the person when the child visually recognizes his or her presence?

After they answer these questions, parents often think about other ways in which their infants use vision to localize, fixate, track, scan, and shift gaze at distances beyond 6 feet (these terms are defined in the section on the assessment of near-point vision). They may say, for example, "My baby appears to see her own image in a mirror when working with the physical therapist, but when close to the mirror, doesn't appear to know that the reflection is of her."

If the parents are unable to answer the questions up to this point, the early interventionist will need to help them structure observations of the infant's responses to visual stimuli and to model for the parents, how to observe their baby. The following additional questions are examples of how this may be accomplished. Note that some of the responses related to these questions involve suggestions for intervention for the infant:

17. Does your infant look out the windows of a car, bus, or train when you take him or her on an outing?

The parents may notice their infant using vision during a car ride. Parents often comment that they had not realized that their baby noticed the "golden arches" of a McDonald's or seemed visually aware of a bright red landmark such as a red gas station emblem at places routinely passed along a route. Information pertaining to this question also gives early interventionists more insight into how an infant uses distance vision to gain information about the environment.

18. Have you noticed your infant squinting when playing in bright sunlight? What is his or her reaction to an outside source of light or from lighting in an indoor environment?

This question addresses an infant's potential sensitivity to light (photophobia). Parents and other caregivers should understand that they can easily adapt a situation that may be potentially uncomfortable for an infant because of glare that causes discomfort or interferes with the performance of a task visually. Some infants have only light perception; their first visual response observed may well be defensive blinking to a bright light. Such children may later be taught to turn toward a diffused source of light, such as a window (light projection).

19. Describe your infant's coloring or drawing skills (if applicable). Obtain a sample, if possible. How does your infant use vision to perform these tasks? Does he or she experiment with many colors? Does he or she choose to color or draw on much of the space, or are colors limited to certain areas on the page (such as right or left corner, center of the page, or upper or lower areas of the page)?

These observations provide early interventionists with insight into how the infant uses near vision for eye-hand tasks. The early interventionist may need to explain that it is developmentally appropriate for an infant to choose one color or use much space in coloring. Also, if parents have been hesitant to expose their infant to this type of task, early interventionists can determine if the family needs assistance in finding ways to set up situations so that their infant can experience more eye-hand coordination tasks. Early interventionists should also discover whether there is a history of color deficiency in the family. If the mother's father or brother has a history of color deficiency, the infant may also be at risk of the same type of color deficiency, in addition to any primary visual condition. Special considerations may be needed in adaptations of toys (like using bright, warm colors, such as reds, oranges, and yellows and limiting greens and blues) and environmental conditions. The process of discovering which colors are most discernible for the infant with a color-perception deficit is ongoing. Records can be kept to determine if there is a pattern of which colors are most discernible and which colors are least attractive to the infant.

20. Some infants with visual impairments hold their hands near or against their eyes in unusual ways. For example, some wave a hand in front of one or both eyes, whereas others press a hand against an eye. Have you noticed your infant doing this, and if so, when do you see this behavior most often?

Parents often ask questions about their infant's eye pressing. Some of the more common questions are these: "Is eye pressing harmful?" "Should I stop it?" "Are there times when my baby's hand waving or eye pressing is appropriate? Consultation with medical specialists is necessary to determine when to redirect the child from these behaviors, since they may initially have adaptive value. Waving hands in front of the eyes may mean that the infant is interested in light and shadows. Eye poking, however, can be self-injurious, causing an eye to sink into the orbit and leading to permanent disfigurement. Encouraging the development of manual activities to give the infant something else to do with his or her hands may be more motivating. If the infant is poking an eye during story time, the parent may want to give him or her something to hold that is mentioned in the story or engage the infant in turning the pages. During music time, the infant may shake a musical toy to accompany a melody heard on a tape or record.

21. Does your infant appear to tilt his or her head in an unusual way to look at things?

A head tilt may mean that the infant has a visual field loss. An infant may prefer to use one eye to look at a picture in a book. By turning his or her head all the way to the right to use an area of vision that is undamaged the child may be able to discriminate details and colors. Children whose eyes move rapidly from side to side or up and down (nystagmus) may slow down this movement by placing the eyes to the right or left side, temporarily to get a better image of a picture. Parents may need to be taught that it is fine for their infant to tilt the head or move the eyes to one side to get a better image of the material.

22. How does your infant locate things he or she drops on the floor? Please give an example. Does the infant use vision to locate lost objects? How?

Parents can give early interventionists information about how their infants use vision to solve problems, scan, and use the eyes and hands together to complete an activity. If vision is not routinely used to complete a daily activity when something needs to be retrieved, environmental strategies and adaptations may need to be tried to improve the infants' use of vision.

23. Is your infant more hesitant to explore or move about unfamiliar places, such as open spaces or stairs, than familiar places? Please describe.

It is likely that an infant will move more freely in familiar places but that he or she may need to be taught to use vision when experiencing an unfamiliar environment. Movements up and down stairs require different skills than movement in open spaces. For each kind of movement, vision is a learned process. Infants with diagnosed visual impairments need instruction in how to use vision in new, unfamiliar environments to ensure that they do not miss incidental information that may be obvious to their caregivers or infants who do not have visual impairments.

The following questions apply to infants who use eyeglasses or contact lenses or are implementing a patching program.

24. Does your infant wear the eyeglasses all the time? If not, why not?

25. Has your infant's response to wearing eyeglasses changed at any time?

26. Does your infant move the eyeglasses forward on the nose or look over them?

27. How long has your infant had the present pair of eyeglasses or contact lenses?

28. Does your infant wear the patch the prescribed length of time recommended by the eye care specialist?

Parents often wonder whether eyeglasses are helpful to their infants. If infants do not appear to benefit from wearing eyeglasses, parents are sometimes hesitant to require the infants to wear them. Patch programs are sometimes prescribed to strengthen the functioning of the weaker eye. Patching may frustrate children if there are large differences in the right and left eyes' ability to see. If infants are required to use their weaker eye for up to four hours a day, they may attempt to remove the patch. Parents feel guilty when they repeatedly have to replace the patch on their infants' eye. Some may eventually stop the patch programs entirely because of the infants' adverse reactions to it. Interventions for parents include asking them under what circumstances they would feel most comfortable reinforcing their infants for wearing the patch for short periods throughout a routine day. The early interventionist may recommend that patching occur during less visually strenuous times and allow the infant to use the better eye for more visually strenuous activities, such as fine motor tasks or moving about an unfamiliar playground. The parents' goal, with support, would be to assist the infant gradually to wear the patch for the amount of time prescribed by the eye care specialist.

For many infants there are benefits to wearing corrective lenses (eyeglasses or contact lenses), even if the infants are visually impaired and have additional disabilities. Although an infant may not attain 20/20 vision even with correction, affording him or her an opportunity to see with the best correction possible is desirable under conditions when using vision is the most reliable way to complete tasks. If an infant does not want to wear eyeglasses consistently, several possible reasons should be checked before deciding that the infant should stop wearing them.

Check the fit of the eyeglasses or contact lenses. Are they too tight? For example, do the frames rub against the nose or behind the ears causing red marks? Do the eyeglasses slide down the infant's nose? Are the contact lenses causing corneal abrasions? Do the contact lenses appear to be moving about the eye or eyes—for example, are they lodged above the upper or lower eyelids? If the answer to any of these questions is yes, an optician experienced in fitting children with eyeglasses or contact lenses should be consulted to improve the fit.

Also find out whether the prescription of the eyeglasses or contact lenses is correct. The parent or the early interventionist can ask the ophthalmologist's technician or optician to recheck the prescription, to ensure that the correct prescription has been placed in each eye. Busy laboratories may inadvertently switch prescriptions or mistakenly provide someone else's prescription to the infant.

29. What types of communication systems does your infant use? Vocalization (sounds and words), picture or communication boards, gestures or body language, touch cues, objects or textures, sign language, or other methods? (Refer to Chapter 9 for a discussion of these modes of communication.)

After the early interventionist has gathered all the information pertaining to the foregoing questions, she or he must then ask the parents about their daily schedules.

30. Describe your infant's indoor and outdoor activities on a typical day. Include the weekend schedule if it differs from the weekday schedule. (A format and form for interviewing families about daily activities is provided in Chapter 8.)

31. Of the activities in your infant's schedule, which ones—for example, playing, eating, or moving—would you like to focus on to enhance his or her use of vision more efficiently?

Ask the parents what they want their infant to be able to do visually during typical times. A parent may respond, "I want my baby to look at me." The early interventionist can address this concern during daily routines, such as, feeding, diaper changing, or picking up the infant from the crib and during face-to-face games throughout the day. Playing games like peek-a-boo while changing an infant's diaper encourages the child to look toward the parent.

Another comment may be, "I want my baby to entertain herself so I can get something done." Perhaps the infant has enough vision to enjoy looking at herself in a mirror that could be mounted nearby when the mother is preparing a meal or cleaning an area of the house. Mobiles with interesting black and white designs can be positioned so that they are within the infant's visual field.

"Family mealtimes would be much easier if he could feed himself." Parents can be encouraged to allow the infant to sit with the family in a highchair or other supportive chair. The infant might not eat at this time, but could be positioned in such a way that smells, sights, and sounds would be nearby. Family members could include the infant by commenting about the food items and speaking the infant's name to draw his or her attention to the discussion. If the infant does not appear to be visually interested in the social event, the parents can be taught to give visual or auditory stimulation by using different facial expressions, voices, or music in response to the infant's movement of his arms and legs or vocalizations.

"My child doesn't appear to like her bathtime. How can I help her enjoy this daily experience?" Check the size of the bathing area. Is the infant secure in the tub, or is she frightened about its openness? The infant's dislike of bathtime may be reduced if she feels the security of the caregiver's hands and arms and sides of a small tub. Also, the caregiver can be taught that using the washcloth as an object cue for playing peek-a-boo can enhance face-to-face interactions if the infant responds to the movement or smell of the washcloth against her face. If the infant vocalizes, the caregiver can respond to the vocalizations and combine it with encouraging the visual gaze to his or her face or other available toys in the tub. (See Chapters 3 and 8 for additional discussions of early exchanges.)

THE COMPONENTS OF THE FUNCTIONAL VISION ASSESSMENT

An example of a report that presents the findings of a functional vision assessment appears at the end of this chapter in the initial and follow-up reports on Bonita Juarez.

Visual Acuity Testing

The forced-choice looking procedure (such as the Teller Acuity Cards) is one such test instrument that can be used with infants. This test measures near-point visual acuity with behavioral responses and can be used with preverbal or nonverbal infants. The technique is based on the assumption that infants will attend to a patterned stimulus in preference to a plain one. With the Teller Acuity Cards, each card contains a black-and-white grating located to the left or to the right of a central peephole. Initially, the tester holds a card with larger stripes. The infant will show a preferential fixation to the right or left side of the card, which reverses when the card is rotated by 180 degrees. The tester shows the infant cards with progressively smaller stripes and uses the presence or absence of consistent preferential fixation as an indication of whether the infant can resolve the grating on each card. Acuity is estimated by the smallest stripe pattern that the tester judges the infant can discriminate. The test must be adapted for infants with visual impairments (Trueb, Evans, Hammel, Bartholomew, & Dobson, 1992), but it is quickly used, easily learned by the tester, and applicable to a wide age range of children. The test is useful for infants with nystagmus (involuntary movement of the eyes in a horizontal direction), but in this case, the cards should be held vertically instead of horizontally, as stated in the directions.

This procedure is not sensitive to identifying all visual difficulties (such as nearsightedness). The ability to stabilize the head is necessary for the infant to make a preferential gaze. Sometimes an infant may anticipate where lines on the cards may appear and may deceive the tester who expects a true preferential gaze. This test provides a reliable measurement of acuity for children with "mild to severe ocular or neurological abnormalities as in healthy children, even though children with abnormalities are more difficult to test" (Getz, Dobson, Beatriz, & Mash, 1996).

Eye Movement

An informal assessment of an infant's ability to move the eyes together smoothly in one direction across the midline of the visual field involves observing how the infant's eyes move when watching a bouncing ball or a pinwheel, scanning pictures in a book, or following the movement of a caregiver's head. The observer should note whether the infant moves just the eyes or the head and eyes together during these activities. A formal assessment of eye movement is usually done in a physician's office. The physician directs a high-intensity light, observing how the infant's eye moves in response to the stimulus.

Near-point Vision

Informal activities are selected on the basis of interviews with parents and early interventionists to determine which toys, objects, or events are motivating to the infant. The feature common to all these activities is that the infant must use vision within a distance of 8 to 12 inches (near point). There are six visual behaviors that teachers, parents, and caregivers should look for as they describe how the infant uses vision during these activities:

- *localizing*   searching and locating an object or a person against a background
- *fixating*   focusing directly on an object or a person
- *scanning*   systematically examining an area from a display of three or more objects, pictures, people, or events
- *tracking*   following the movement of an object, person, or event
- *shifting gaze*   looking back and forth from one object or person to another
- *eye-hand coordination*   reaching out to touch something or pick up an object

The evaluator will observe the infant's visual functioning as he or she locates small objects, pushes a switch to activate a toy, visually follows bubbles blown by a caregiver, or scans pictures in a book under both high- and low-contrast conditions and different levels of illumination.

Additional observations of visual performance during typical routines, such as locating a snack on a highchair tray, looking at family photographs, or playing peek-a-boo with a pet, can be used to describe how an infant uses vision for tasks that occur within arm's reach. Near-point activities can also include informal observations of eye-hand coordination, such as scribbling and coloring; completing a puzzle; or swiping, reaching, or grasping for a colorful toy suspended on a toy gym, should be included in the informal observations of the functional vision assessment.

If an activity typically occurs outdoors, the infant should be observed in that environment, making note of the conditions (like bright sunlight, an overcast day, or a shaded area). The tester may alter the conditions (provide more light or give the infant outdoor sunglasses) to determine if visual responses differ and report any effect on the infant's behaviors. The formal measure of visual acuity most commonly used is the forced-choice preferential looking procedure.

Intermediate and Distance Vision

In assessing intermediate and distance vision, the evaluator observes an infant during activities that require the use of vision at distances of 16 to 36 inches (intermediate), and beyond 3 feet (distance). Assessments would include observing the infant watching a familiar person walk across his or her visual field from left to right, watching a movie or television screen, and identifying objects at a distance or identifying a favorite location from a car.

Sometimes it is possible to estimate distance acuity with toys that are motivating and familiar to an infant. The toys should be measured in height and width before placing them at different distances from the infant. Placing the objects at distances of 3 feet and beyond, in low- and high-contrast conditions, can be used to estimate an infant's ability to see detail. This method of assessing functional visual acuity is effective if an infant has the mobility to seek out the object. Table 5.1 gives the approximate functional visual acuity for an infant who can see an object of the specified size, at the given distance from the infant to the object. The chart does not account for levels of illumination or contrast, and the evaluator should note the environmental conditions.

A infant's use of vision in an outdoor environment should be considered, especially if the infant regularly accompanies the family on trips to the grocery store, the mall, or local restaurants. The evaluator should note if the infant visually recognizes landmarks in the environment at 3 feet or beyond during outings to favorite places.

Visual Fields

An infant's ability to respond visually to movement and form in the central and peripheral fields of vision should be assessed through informal activities. Color and detail are perceived as the infant uses vision for tasks at different distances within the central visual field. A variety of informal tests can be used to assess areas of clarity or deficiency.

An approximate measure of the infant's visual fields can be measured with the following procedure. One person holds a toy in front of

Table 5.1 APPROXIMATE FUNCTIONAL VISUAL ACUITY FOR DIFFERENT SIZES OF OBJECTS AND DISTANCES

Functional visual acuity is measured in natural environments. The objects used as text targets should be familiar and motivating to the child; their size is measured at their widest point or will be equal on all sides. The objects are placed at sequentially greater distances, and the child's response is observed. This table assists the examiner in estimating the child's functional visual acuity, given the size of the object and the greatest distance at which the infant appears to see it.

Size of Object	Distance from Child				
	2 feet	4 feet	6 feet	8 feet	20 feet
1/4 inch	20/200	20/100	20/67	20/50	20/20
1/2 inch	20/400	20/200	20/133	20/100	20/40
3/4 inch	20/600	20/300	20/200	20/150	20/60
1 inch	20/800	20/400	20/267	20/200	20/80

the infant as a fixation target. Another person, standing, moves an object similar in size, form, and color on the end of a stick into different quadrants of the infant's visual fields. The target comes from behind the infant's ear to in front of the second person's nose. The moving target should be kept at about 13 inches from the infant at all times. It can be presented several times on the infant's right and left sides at different heights along the perimeter of the infant's face. Eye movement may indicate a response to the moving target, even if no verbal response is given.

Other informal measures to determine an infant's preferred visual field include observing how the infant responds to approaching people and rolling balls of different sizes and colors. Rolling the balls toward the infant from the right, left, and center may help to determine if and when the infant looks at them. The color and size of each ball should be noted, as well as the speed with which the ball was rolled (slowly or quickly along the visual pathway). If the infant is amenable, the eyes should be alternately covered so that each eye is tested separately, as with the visual acuity test, to identify which eye is being used to detect an object in a particular visual field.

It is often difficult to assess the extent of an infant's visual fields when the infant has visual and multiple disabilities, especially if he or she is has restricted physical movement. Many infants with visual and multiple disabilities have low- or high muscle tone and are difficult to assess in one position to obtain information about their visual fields. The educational assessment and observations of infants over time and in many environments may give parents and teachers information about the way in which the infants use their eyes and head to turn to look at objects, events, and people in fields where vision is useful for them.

Color Recognition

An infant's ability to recognize color may be informally assessed by observing the infant's preferences for two similar objects of different color (Erin, 1996). First, two objects of the same color are presented and covered with a sheet of paper. Then, they are exposed. After several presentations, one object is replaced with another of a different color. If the infant has color recognition, it may be inferred, the new object will draw his or her attention.

Color perception may be hard to detect clinically, but caregivers can report the infant's color preferences for toys, food, and attraction to people's clothing. It is therefore important to know which eye conditions show a predisposition to color deficiency, so that the caregivers of infants with those conditions are alerted to watch carefully for any color preferences. Gathering background information about the family's history of color deficiency is also important, since infants (especially boys) have an increased likelihood of color deficiency when there is a history of this condition in the family. (See Chapter 4 for more information on color vision deficiencies.)

Environmental Considerations

Environmental considerations in vision assessment should include color and contrast, lighting, space (distance), and time (Utley, 1993). These parameters are noted during the near, intermediate, and distance assessment portions of the functional vision assessment.

Contrast

An infant's contrast sensitivity, or ability to detect differences of brightness (for example, seeing and grasping a toy against a background or finding a food item on a highchair tray) should be observed during typical activities like mealtimes, grooming time in the bathroom, or outdoor walks in the park. One way to make it easier for an infant to see is to increase the contrast between the target object and its background and to reduce the number of items around the object. The infant may need a more exaggerated difference between an object and its background for visibility. Black and white provide a good contrast, but often routine activities involve objects that are not black or white. Dycem, a nonslip background material often used by occupational therapists, works well when creating a contrast between an infant's finger foods and the background. Dycem is made in red and bright blue. When crackers, cereals, and other foods are placed on a blue dycem background, the ability to localize, fixate, and reach and grasp for small food items is remarkably improved for many infants. It is always important to experiment with the sizes and colors of objects (such as different-colored cups and spoons and placing articles of clothing on different-colored backgrounds) to increase visual choice-making behavior. Highlighting light switches with a contrasting color on the walls or bands of tape outlining switchplates helps to distinguish light switches against walls. Another way to use contrast, for example, to indicate a toy storage area in the infant's room, is to place a contrasting piece of carpet in front, so the infant recognizes where to locate toys.

The Hiding Heidi Low Contrast "Face" test (Hyvarinen, 1995–96) is a formal measure of contrast sensitivity. This test detects an infant's ability to recognize a face as it appears at six different levels of contrast. The evaluator notes an infant's typical response to a face (like widening the eyes, breathing, quieting, arching the eyebrows, smiling, or babbling to or reaching for an object). A blank card is presented on top of one of six Hiding Heidi faces, each of which has a different level of contrast. The evaluator asks, "Where is Heidi hiding?" as each card is moved in opposite directions across the child's midline. If the infant responds to the face and not the blank card, it is inferred that he or she sees Hiding Heidi at that level of contrast.

Strategies for increasing the infant's awareness include providing high-contrast cues on the faces of caregivers if the infant is not sensitive to low-contrast situations. For more information on such strategies, see the section on Interventions, Strategies, and Considerations later in this chapter, as well as Chapter 8.

Lighting

Lighting conditions during informal activities and formal testing should be noted: natural or artificial illumination and the type of artificial lighting, such as incandescent, fluorescent, halogen, or full spectrum. Some research has found that prolonged exposure to blue light wavelengths (such as of cool-white fluorescent tubes) may cause damage to the eyes (Kitchel, 1998). Blue light is commonly found in schools, stores, and public places. Other fluorescent bulbs are available to replace regular cool white fluorescent tubes that emit the full spectrum of light, rather than ultraviolet and blue-end spectrum wavelengths. The quantity, type, direction, and position of illumination are critical to visual performance. Dimmers, diffusers, and light filters may decrease the amount and direction of light needed by some infants. Kitchel (1998) identified the pericube, a silver egg-crate type of grid that replaces the acrylic lenses found on many fluorescent tubes, as one such filter.

Some infants are sensitive to light and may experience pain and discomfort from bright or direct light or glare. Others need more lighting to see optimally. The evaluator can experiment with different sources of light, such as gooseneck lamps, including those with full-spectrum lighting, that can be directed on tasks and positioned to avoid glare. Full-spectrum lighting combines the red-orange spectrum with the blue spectrum to make the illumination more calming to infants. If an infant appears to be more responsive in a brighter lighting condition indoors, the evaluator can alter the testing environment to see if an area lit more strongly will encourage more visual behavior during an activity.

The issue of light sensitivity should also be considered. If an infant is sensitive to light (as are some infants with cortical visual impairment) or gazes toward bright lights, the evaluator may find it more difficult to draw conclusions about the infant's ability to use vision in environments where lighting changes as a natural part of the indoor-outdoor environment. Parents can observe their infant's reaction to lighting conditions when the infants wear caps or visors to protect their eyes from glare and bright sunlight or sunglasses designed for small faces (NoIR, 1998, produces sunglasses for young children).

An infant's sensitivity to light may be more apparent in a clinical setting. Infants who are taking medication to prevent seizures (or whose anterior pathway of the brain is damaged) may demonstrate unusual responses to a physician's penlight. For example, their pupils may become larger, rather than smaller, or may constrict and then dilate without a reintroduction of the penlight. Parents can report if these responses typically occur after the infant receives medication for seizures or if the infant's ocular reflexes appear different in the clinical environment. In addition, infants may not track lights or shift gaze between two lights because of their lack of motivation.

Caregivers and early interventionists should report on the infant's visual behaviors during changes in light in a variety of environments. An infant may take a long time to adjust visually to lighting conditions when going from one environment to another if the lighting changes from very bright to dim, or vice versa. Lenses to block ultraviolet rays may be considered to help the infant adapt to these changes in lighting. Infants with visual and multiple disabilities can benefit from a sun lens evaluation in which some protection is afforded them from bothersome sunrays that may diminish visual acuity and function.

Space and Distance

Space or distance considerations refer to the way the infant is positioned throughout the day and with the physical arrangement of the visual environment. Infants who cannot move themselves into different positions need the assistance of others to reposition them, so they learn to view the world from different angles. In addition, the presentation of objects and people need to be at the infant's eye level. Caregivers should consider presenting familiar objects in different ways, so the infant begins to discriminate the object visually from its back and sides, in addition to its front. Visual landmarks within a space provide visual orientation for objects that are out of reach, which can give constant orientation to an infant who is not able to move.

Another consideration when adapting the physical space of the environment is to position the infant so that he or she does not maintain an asymmetrical tonic neck reflex. An asymmetrical tonic neck reflex is elicited when the infant turns his or her head to one side, causing the face-side arm and leg to extend (stiffen) and the other side to flex (bend). Geniale (1991) suggested ways to position infants with cerebral palsy that may affect the position of the head and eyes for looking at items of interest at different distances. The key to proper positioning is for the early interventionist first to consult the physical therapist for suggestions about how to position the infant so he or she is supported in the trunk-neck and head areas. A physical therapist can look for the key patterns of an infant's abnormal movements and recommend ways to position the infant and describe directions of movement or preferred movement patterns. When well supported during an activity, an infant has the best opportunity to use vision as a reinforcer, rather than as an additional challenge. Next, the early interventionist should discuss with the parents what equipment is available to them to create a situation in which the infant is in a supported position to encourage looking behaviors. If the available equipment is easily used during an activity and vision is a skill that can be encouraged in this activity, the early inverventionist should continue to work with the physical and occupational therapists to monitor the stability of the infant's head-neck and trunk and to use vision as the infant engages in and completes the routine task.

Infants who cannot see detail or small objects well at a distance may be helped by moving closer to an object, such as a television screen, to make it more visible. Even with corrective lenses, moving closer to an object may make the detail of the object more easily seen. If possible, one can also increase the size of the objects. Pictures, designs, and wall hangings in the infant's bedroom should be placed at the infant's eye level.

Time

Infants lose anticipatory time when moving through space or may not recognize a familiar person until the person is within a few feet of them. Thus, they have no time to consider a personal greeting and appear to be slow or inattentive before they initiate a greeting (Erin, 1991). They may be receiving only small pieces of information because of their visual impairments and need to be taught to attend to important information about the world. For example, an infant may be more interested in a small piece of lint on the floor than the visual appeal of a toy that is a few feet away.

Accuracy and speed of performing an activity decreases when an infant has a visual impairment. According to Brennan, Peck, and Lolli (1992), detecting, recognizing, and then acting upon an object require more time for a child with a visual impairment and can be especially difficult and time consuming for an infant with multiple disabilities. The physical demands of the prolonged use of vision may cause eye fatigue and reduce the infant's speed, accuracy, and attention. More time should be given to the infant who is visually impaired and has additional disabilities to locate and obtain objects.

SPECIAL CONSIDERATIONS IN ASSESSING FUNCTIONAL VISION

Specific characteristics of infants with visual and additional disabilities should be considered when conducting a functional vision assessment. These characteristics include the maturity of the visual system, the infant's developmental level, language and communication ability, physical ability, motivation, and the importance of visual tasks.

The maturity of the visual system may vary among children of similar chronological ages. Particularly during infancy and early childhood, the neurological system changes rapidly. Prematurity, brain dysfunction, normal developmental variations, and individual experiences may affect it. As an infant learns to respond to the visual world, changes in his or her ability to use vision often occur.

Some infants' visual systems mature slowly, which may result in an early prognosis of limited vision in an infant who later demonstrates increased visual function. Delayed visual maturation (the inability to use vision at birth) may be overcome by age 24 to 36 months, according to Takashita (1996). It is not known what characteristics lead to recovery in the visual system during the first two years of life. Parents are often confused when their infant seems to use vision, but if the ophthalmologist stated earlier that the infant has a severe visual impairment that will not lead to any useful visual function. In reality, the infant's neurological system has matured since then, and the visual world is more meaningful to him or her.

There is a critical period of visual development during which an infant can learn to use vision; thereafter, the development of visual learning is less effective (see Development of the Visual System in Chapter 4). According to Tavernier (1993), that period peaks in humans during the first year of life and diminishes gradually until age 6. Thus, impairments to the visual system during this early period, even if corrected, can permanently influence a child's visual learning.

The visual development of children varies widely. Therefore, medical and functional assessments of visual function in infants or neurologically delayed children should be considered to be descriptions at one point in time, rather then long-term diagnoses and prognoses.

The developmental level of an infant is another consideration when assessing his or her functional vision. The use of vision varies with an infant's developmental level, whether or not the visual system is impaired. The lack of responsiveness to typical materials (such as silverware on a table, colorful toys, or bright pictures in books) may simply mean that the materials do not have meaning or a connection for an infant at a particular time. This lack of responsiveness may make it difficult to determine whether a visual impairment is present or whether the lack of response is related to cognitive difficulties in distinguishing important visual information. Hatton, Bailey, Burchinal, and Ferrell (1997) found that children with visual impairments and developmental delay–mental retardation had lower developmental age scores and slower rates of growth in development than did children with visual impairments alone. However, for children with additional disabilities including visual impairment, the amount of functional vision and mental retardation–developmental disability did not interact. These results indicate that the two factors of visual impairment and developmental delay had additive, not multiplicative, effects on development during early childhood. Therefore, it is important to assess an infant's visual functioning in addition to overall developmental functioning, for the purpose of educational programming.

Another consideration that may influence the outcome of a functional vision assessment is the infant's ability to express or understand language. When a child does not have the language to make a choice or to describe what he or she sees, the results of an assessment need to be based on observations of behaviors or physical responses, such as turning the head, moving to or away from objects, and shaping the hand to anticipate a toy when reaching.

The physical stamina of an infant may limit the time he or she can spend on a task, even if the task is understood. Infants may be offered alternate response options during an assessment; for example, having the evaluator or other adult model a task and allowing the infant to respond by pointing, selecting, or indicating yes or no by blinking the eyes. If there are physical disabilities and limitations in stamina that inhibit an infant's ability to respond, extended observations and interviews with caregivers can provide a more complete picture of visual function for infants whose responses are limited.

USING THE COMBINED RESULTS OF FUNCTIONAL AND CLINICAL VISION ASSESSMENTS

Information from the clinical eye examination and the functional vision assessment can be used together in three ways. First, the information from both evaluations together provides a more comprehensive picture of what the infant's eye condition is and under what conditions he or she will best utilize visual behaviors. The ophthalmologist is able to diagnose and treat eye conditions and associated refractive errors. The parents and early interventionist describe how the infant is using vision under different circumstances; for example, with a patch, eyeglasses, or surgery (according to the ophthalmolgist's treatment); during different activities and routines; and under different conditions. Sometimes the ophthalmologist may believe that lenses will be of little or no benefit to the infant, even if he or she has a need for them. The parents can provide the ophthalmologist with information from the functional vision assessment concerning the infant's visual curiosity. They may comment about how close the infant appears to move his or her head to faces, pictures, or a television screen. They may also state that the infant does not appear to be interested in objects, people, or events beyond, for example, a 3-foot distance. Given concrete examples of what the infant is doing or attempting to do visually, the ophthalmologist may be more enthusiastic about prescribing eyeglasses, if only on a trial basis.

The early interventionist and parents can carefully observe the infant to see what differences wearing the eyeglasses make for him or her. Some infants may benefit from wearing lenses with weaker prescriptions than those the ophthalmologist prescribed. They may be used to seeing the world in images that are not easily discriminated when wearing new eyeglasses. In one case, a 9-month-old baby with aphakia was not tolerating her strong lenses. Her mother also had a visual impairment and could not easily recognize when the infant was wearing the eyeglasses, which was not often during the baby's waking hours. The pediatric ophthalmologist decreased the strength of the prescription, and the baby gradually tolerated the lenses, which were prescribed at full strength a year later.

Behavioral observations by the parents and early interventionist can serve a second purpose. For example, the parents or early interventionist can assess whether a drooping eyelid does, in fact, interfere with the infant's ability to use an eye. A trained professional can give the forced-choice preferential looking test to determine if the acuity of each eye is similar or different for an infant with ptosis. If there are concerns about the infant's inability to use an eye, these concerns can be reported to the ophthalmologist. In some instances, temporary sutures can be used to raise the drooping eyelid. A more permanent solution to keeping the eyelid up may be used when the infant is older.

Another way that the results of the assessments can be used together is to discuss the implications of the eye condition in terms of the infant's present level of visual functioning (the results of the functional vision assessment). For example, if an infant is diagnosed with cortical visual impairment, the ophthamologist may discuss that condition as one in which an infant's vision fluctuates. The parents may become more at ease when they realize this behavior is one characteristic of cortical visual impairment, rather than the deterioration of their infant's visual functioning. If an infant is diagnosed with delayed visual maturation, the parents and early interventionist should expect to see a gradual improvement of visual functioning when the child is 2 to 3 years old. They can use this information in planning their assessment and instruction; for instance, they can look for times and places when the infant may appear to use vision for an activity and can determine the infant's best visual function compared to his or her normal visual function (Erin, 1996).

The results of both assessments can be used as written communication tools to encourage dialogue between the parents, early interventionist, and ophthalmologist. The clinical evaluation is an explanation of what the ophthalmologist has determined about the infant's vision at one point in time. For example, he or she may attain visual acuity outcomes that differ from those the early interventionist attained when testing the infant at home. The results may differ because unlike the clinical vision assessment, which is made in one place and at one point in time, the functional vision assessment is an ongoing process, occurring over several sessions and in different environments, to determine the infant's best visual functioning. The infant may become accustomed to the symbols that the early interventionist is using and the way that the early interventionist gives the test. The early interventionist can share the information that the familiarization process of test symbols and procedures is successful for an infant. The parents and early interventionist may also have additional questions about the visual functioning of the infant during a functional vision assessment. These questions can then be directed to the opthalmologist for an explanation.

INTERVENTIONS, STRATEGIES, AND CONSIDERATIONS

Once the functional vision assessment is completed, the early interventionist needs to consider strategies to help the infant make the best use of his or her functional vision in daily activities. If an infant has an eye condition that would prevent him or her from seeing in a typical way, the infant may need to be taught to understand what he or she is viewing. The first step is to share the results of the functional vision assessment with the family. Then the family's routine of activities should be observed to evaluate how the infant uses vision during various activities and the environmental cues that affect his or her use of vision in these activities. Figure 5.1 provides a format for recording these observations, with two examples of completed forms in different areas for the same child (a blank form is provided in the Appendix).

The early interventionist should talk about ways in which he or she can assist the family to encourage the infant's use of vision and educate the parents about how vision is learned. This information will be useful to the parents as they modify their efforts during interactions with their infant. The early interventionist needs to encourage consistency of instruction in the vision area throughout the family's daily routine.

What to Teach

The focus of the early interventionist is to encourage the child to make the best use of his or her functional vision in his or her daily life. There are six basic visual behaviors that interventionists and parents need to foster and promote with the infants to develop their use of vision:

- *localizing*   searching for and locating an object or a person against a background
- *fixating*   focusing directly on an object or a person
- *scanning*   systematically examining an area from a display of three or more objects, pictures, people, or events
- *tracking*   following the movement of an object or person
- *shifting gaze*   looking back and forth from one object or person to another
- *eye-hand coordination*   reaching out to touch something or pick up an object

---

Figure 5.1   SAMPLE COMPLETED FUNCTIONAL VISUAL ASSESSMENT FORMS

The form presented here provides a useful format for the parent or early interventionist to record a child's visual responses during typical activities. A column is provided to record the probable factors that may have affected the child's inability to use vision (for example, glare from light, an object placed outside the child's visual field, or an object presented too quickly). Another column allows the team working with the child to record their ideas. The team must decide whether to instruct the child to use vision for a step in the activity or substitute another way that the child can accomplish the step if it is not possible for him or her to use vision.

These two completed examples illustrate how the form is filled out, and the type of information that may be included. These are only examples and do not cover the range of activities or responses that may be observed and recorded.

Daily Routines and Factors Affecting Use of Vision

Example 1

Child's name: __Monica__   Date: __January 26, 1999__

Assessment area: __Bathroom__

Lighting: __Artificial illumination around mirror and ceiling-mounted track__
__lighting; brightly lit__

Activity: __Bathing__

Visual aids (such as a slant board, magnification, and colored filters):
__Plastic-bathing container placed within the tub to provide defined space__
__and more security for the child.__

Steps in Activity	Child's Action*	Factors Affecting the Use of Vision	Teaching Strategies and Adaptations
Child is undressed	–	Check lighting level, security, features of bathing area	Provide object cues, such as a washcloth, contained area within tub for bathing (red)
Child looks at caregiver as different body parts are cleaned with washcloth	incon	Distance of caregiver from child (may need to be closer), direction of illumination	Verbally cue child by responding to child's vocalizations, face-to-face contact, play peek-a-boo with washcloth
Child plays with caregiver and toys in tub	incon	Motivation to interact with toy, color preferences, size of toy; toy has physical contact with child	Verbal prompt to accompany movement of toy in water, splashing action of water to increase looking
Child is removed from water and towel dried	–	Body movement change was quick; decreased opportunities to use vision	Caregiver sings song indicating the end of the bathing routine; baby gazes into mirror to see clean face

* Child's Action =   + (independent)   – (needed help)   incon (inconsistent)

Comments

(continued on next page)

Daily Routines and Factors Affecting Use of Vision

Example 2

Child's name: __Monica__   Date: __February 1, 1999__

Assessment area: __Kitchen__

Lighting: __Natural lighting occurring through a window on the east side of__
__house, curtains drawn to inhibit light from fully illuminating room; overhead__
__incandescent light fixture with two 40-watt white bulbs overhead, 10 feet__
__above eye level__

Activity: __Eating breakfast__

Visual aids (such as a slant board, magnification, colored filters): __None__

Steps in Activity	Child's Action*	Factors Affecting the Use of Vision	Teaching Strategies and Adaptations
Child is seated in highchair, ready and motivated to eat	+	Support for neck, trunk, and head needed as prerequisite for looking	
Child fixates on mom and food, shifts gaze as mom places cracker on highchair tray	+	Mom's distance from chair and position relative to chair when she places cracker on tray	
Child reaches for pieces of cracker on tray	Child overreaches for cracker pieces −	Color-contrast of cracker upon background of highchair tray	Change color background; adjust lighting
When offered a spoonful of oatmeal, child opens mouth and eats cereal	+	Size, color of spoon, color-contrast of oatmeal against spoon, angle at which mom presents spoon	
Child is offered a bottle, reaches for it, and begins to drink liquid	Child overreaches for bottle −	Color and size of bottle, position and distance of mom when offering bottle, illumination	Try different color and size bottles; present within different visual field

* Child's Action =   + (independent)   − (needed help)   incon (inconsistent)

Comments: Child is within the birth to 12 months of age range

Each of these visual behaviors is considered a voluntary skill and is important in the development of vision.

Where and When to Teach

It is best to teach during the normal routine of the day's activities (bathing, eating, dressing, bedtime, games, and outings). The best time to help an infant learn to use vision is whenever a need naturally arises. Ferrell and Muir (1996) noted that stimulating vision without a context (for example, encouraging a child to follow a bright light) is based on questionable research and does not provide opportunities to integrate vision into the infant's functional routines.

Some activities (such as taking a bath, listening to music, or getting a massage) may not require the use of vision. Other activities (like watching cartoons, looking at a family member's face when engaging in play, or picking out a favorite cereal at the grocery store) may not require vision, but are made easier or more enjoyable with vision. If an infant seems to be having difficulty in an activity and if the use of vision could help participation, then the parent may want to offer ways to make what is seen more visible or encourage the infant to look.

Although special times may be set aside to work on using vision, it is just as important that infants receive assistance to see and make use of visual information throughout the activities in a typical day. Instruction that fits naturally into the infant's life and that is provided when and where needed is most beneficial, motivating, and reinforcing. Sidebar 5.1 identifies some additional considerations to guide the choice of activities that will encourage an infant's use of functional vision.

How to Teach

Like all skills, developing vision is learned, and just as people achieve some skills before others, vision use also tends to happen in a certain order. (See also Development of the Visual System in Chapter 4.) It begins with an interest in light. Then people attract an infant's attention. Finally, objects become more of a focus. Black-and-white patterns, bright colors, and high-contrast presentations are initially attractive to infants. When infants start to fix their attention, they usually begin with stationary targets. Then, they try to follow movement. Awareness usually begins with interest in large, simple items that are nearby. Later infants seek out more detail and complexity and examine what is beyond

Sidebar 5.1 SUGGESTIONS FOR DEVELOPING ACTIVITIES TO ENCOURAGE AN INFANT'S USE OF FUNCTIONAL VISION

- Identify activities in established routines that are already motivating and fun for an infant. Instruction in vision skills will be most successful if practiced while doing interesting and enjoyable activities. (Downing & Bailey, 1993; Topor & Bailey, 1995).

- Be sensitive to an infant's reaction to sensory stimuli—either hypersensitivity or hyposensitivity. For example, does the infant display an intense startle response; tactile defensiveness; or attraction to strong visual effects, such as light?

- Consider the effects of seizure medication on ocular and visual function. Select times for instructing the infant in visual skills when he or she is in an alert state.

- Identify which sensory channels the infant prefers for learning, including auditory, visual, tactile, gustatory, olfactory, kinesthetic, and proprioceptive. Consider an infant's sensory learning preferences before planning instruction in visual skills during routine activities (Erin, 1996).

- Consider the ways in which an infant communicates what he or she is seeing. Vocal sounds and body movements are two ways that infants communicate without using a symbolic communication system (Erin, 1995).

- Collaborate with physical and occupational therapists when developing a vision skill program, so that an infant's trunk, neck, and head are stable and well supported as he or she attempts to use vision during an activity (Geniale, 1991).

- Include instruction in vision skills in learning routines that are both functional and social. **Functional** refers to routines in which the infant is taught to do something so he or she is not totally dependent on another person to do the task for him or her (such as eating, dressing, and grooming). **Social** refers to routines that always require at least two persons and involve an interaction between two or more individuals (Erin, 1996).

- Consider the ways in which the environment can facilitate visual functioning. Look at the individual environmental modifications that the infant may need in the areas of color, contrast, lighting, space or distance, and time. Alter as many of these conditions as necessary to encourage the infant's looking behaviors. For example, increase or reduce the lighting, enhance contrast by changing the background color when a toy is presented, and reduce the number of items and present them closer to the infant (Utley, 1993).

- Observe typical children during learning routines to see which visual skills are included in the steps of an activity. For example, during an eating task, localization and fixation or holding a steady gaze on a cracker is necessary to find the cracker, reach for it, and grasp it before placing it in the mouth and eating

(continued on next page)

Sidebar 5.1   SUGGESTIONS FOR DEVELOPING ACTIVITIES TO ENCOURAGE AN INFANT'S USE OF FUNCTIONAL VISION *(continued)*

it. Singing a greeting song during an opening circle in a playgroup or school setting requires visual scanning to look from one classmate to another as each child's name is mentioned in the song (Downing & Bailey, 1990).

- A chain of skills normally performed in the same order during many activities is a skill cluster (Erin, 1996). Common visual skill clusters are looking, reaching, and grasping and localizing, tracking, and grasping. Encouraging a visual behavior before the desired paired responses of reaching and grasping occur will result in improved responses to paired activities (Goetz & Gee, 1987).

- Determine the "critical moment," or time when visual behaviors are important for making the performance of a step in a routine more efficient or enjoyable for the infant (Goetz & Gee, 1987).

- Use cues or prompts (physical or tactile, auditory, or augmentative) are used to teach the infant when it is important to use a visual skill during an activity. A tap on the table in front of the infant gives him or her a sound cue to direct his or her visual gaze in that direction. A flashlight beam directed on a toy shows the infant to look toward the toy. Visual skills can be shaped to a desired outcome (performance of a paired skill), but a reinforcer must be present to maintain the response. Cues-prompts and environmental modifications can be systematically changed to find the best combination of instructional strategies to encourage the infant's looking behaviors (Utley, 1981).

their immediate reach. Initially, they show preference for what is familiar. Later they develop interest in what is new or different.

Think about what motivates a particular infant. How an infant presently tries to use his or her vision often provides clues about where to start teaching. Remember that some infants can detect that something is present (for instance see a shape or a bright color), but have no idea what they are viewing. Thus, when an infant is looking at something, the parents should not assume that he or she automatically understands what it is. Understanding what one sees is a process that occurs over time as one grows from an infant to a young child.

The experience of learning what one sees requires interaction. A parent can guide learning by making sure that the infant is an active participant in daily routines and is able to make use of what he or she sees. Infants with visual impairments and additional disabilities may need encouragement to reach out, explore, and manipulate items. If they can hear, telling them what they are experiencing can help make meaningful connections. For instance, an infant may not be able to see clearly the features of an object. However, if a parent is consistent in using words, presenting activities, and supporting the infant's response to actions, the infant may learn to associate what he or she sees with the words that the parent uses to describe meaningful objects and activities. Parents need to give their infants plenty of time to make sense of what they see as they learn about objects.

For example, a pet turtle may be detected only as movement at a certain height above the floor. Yet if the infant touches this "movement" and interacts with it, and the parent consistently identifies the turtle as a turtle, the visual detection of this "movement" can become recognized as the pet turtle. The infant may not be able to clearly see the turtle, but can still "recognize" the turtle.

Some infants may not be able to "recognize the turtle" or respond to the game the parents are attempting to play. In this case, contingency games (interactive opportunities that can be mutually satisfying and sustained) may facilitate the development of their use of vision (Chen & Haney, 1995). For example, the father of an infant with low vision and additional impairments waits for the infant to look at him, and each time she does, he rewards her by kissing her stomach. This process requires repetition and that the child be motivated by the "reward." (For more information on developing intervention strategies to use with children with visual and additional disabilities, see Chapter 8.)

The important aspects of teaching an infant to use available vision are consistency, use of cues and prompts, repeating information in contingency games and routines, and using a positive approach while providing many regular opportunities to encourage the use of vision. To gain and direct an infant's attention, cues and prompts may be built into the task (see Sidebar 5.1). The materials and setting contain natural cues, and some infants quickly learn to initiate a visual skill based on the materials alone. It is important to observe the infant in a routine before selecting a cue or prompt, to determine where additional prompting is needed. For instance, if an infant picks a snack from two different choices and prefers one to the other, he or she may be motivated to learn what differentiates the two snacks. A parent can assist the infant to get what he or she wants by making sure that the two snacks look different in shape, size, or color (such as a red apple versus animal crackers) or by placing them on two different-colored plates. Again, the early interventionist may need to teach the parent to use prompts and cues to encourage the infant to use his or her vision.

The system of least prompts (Chen & Dote-Kwan, 1995; Utley, Goetz, Gee, & Sailor 1981) has been successfully used in teaching children with visual impairments and additional disabilities. The order with which a parent uses the prompts may vary, especially if the infant responds less favorably, for example, to an auditory, rather than to a tactile, prompt. A verbal prompt assumes that the infant understands words as references because the sound is not produced from the same source as the object. If the infant does not understand that the words direct visual attention to something beyond the parent's immediate vicinity, then an auditory prompt originating with the referent itself or a nonverbal prompt will be more effective.

The following example illustrates a typical sequence of least prompts. When an infant is hungry, the parent offers him or her snacks to eat. Animal crackers and sliced apples are placed on two different colored plates (natural cue). If the infant gives no response or an incorrect response (throws the cookie or apple), then the least intrusive prompt is provided and the infant is again given the opportunity to respond. A prompting hierarchy would follow this sequence:

- *Visual or tactile prompts*   The parent guides the infant to touch the cookies and apples to prompt visual orientation.
- *Gestural prompts*   The parent points to the cookies and apples.
- *Indirect verbal prompts*   The parent says, "Cookies taste good," "apples taste good."
- *Direct verbal prompts*   The parent says, "Get a cookie," "get an apple."
- *Modeling the desired behavior*   The parent demonstrates eating a cookie or apple.
- *A physical prompt*   The parent touches the infant's hand or elbow to encourage the infant to choose a cookie or apple.

- *Physical guidance*   The parent uses hand-under-hand or hand-over-hand assistance to help the infant select a cookie or apple.

When the infant responds with the desired behavior, the intrusiveness level of the prompt (such as a physical prompt) is maintained and then faded to less assistance (for instance, a model or verbal prompt) to encourage the infant to become less dependent on prompts. As another example, consider an infant with severe visual, hearing, and motor disabilities. Mealtimes offer a different kind of experience to increase visual awareness. The infant may not be aware that she is gavage fed. A section of the tube is used to let her know that she is going to be fed, by first showing her the tube as a means of facilitating visual orientation to it. A pat on the stomach can be used as a touch cue to let her know that it is time to eat. The physical therapist should already have worked with the family to determine which position and stabilizing equipment for eating is most helpful for the infant. Cues and prompts are used temporarily but as much as needed during the infant's acquisition of a new task. They should be faded as soon as the infant can use vision to succeed at one step of a task.

CONCLUSION

Many opportunities arise throughout a routine day to encourage infants with multiple disabilities to use their vision. Looking and discovering the world through vision can be fun. Parents and other caregivers should be enthusiastic about what there is to see in the world, provide interesting things to look at, and plenty of time to explore. Look for typical times and places to practice using different visual skills. Looking, finding, following, shifting attention between objects, and picking up or pointing can all happen during daily routines and activities. Professionals can give parents recommendations for adaptations of materials and activities, modifications of the environment, and special training techniques to help parents improve their infants' visual skills.

For some infants, the functional use of vision may not be a realistic outcome, despite all of the best efforts. In these cases, early interventionists should continue to support parents with techniques that would encourage their infants to use their senses of hearing, touch, and taste to learn about the world.

EXAMPLES OF A FUNCTIONAL VISUAL ASSESSMENT AND A FOLLOW-UP ASSESSMENT

The following examples include the reports for a functional vision assessment and a follow-up assessment of the same child, conducted approximately one year later. This is one possible format to use in compiling and reporting the information collected during a functional vision assessment. The information was obtained in an objective manner, which is an important component of the process.

SAMPLE FUNCTIONAL VISION ASSESSMENT FOR BONITA

Child's Name: Bonita Juarez

Date of Birth: 9-2-96

Assessment date: 7-24-97

Chronological age: 10 months

Adjusted age: 8 months

Assessment team: Irma Tote, teacher of children with visual impairments; Mr. and Mrs. Juarez; and Pat Clark, the early interventionist.

Ophthalmological/Optometric Information: According to Sandra and Isaiah Juarez (the mother and father), Dr. Pushman recently examined Bonita and determined that she was "not blind." A six-month return date was recommended. Prior to discharge as a newborn at Phoenix Children's Hospital, Bonita was found to have an abnormal magnetic resonance imagery (MRI) test. She did not have any evidence of retinopathy of prematurity. She evidenced no blink to threat; horizontal and vertical tracking; or recognition of objects, such as her bottle. A left lateral gaze was held throughout the testing session, and it was hypothesized that Bonita may have noticed the movement of red yarn within her peripheral visual fields, rather than have sustained a visual fixation on the yarn.

Background Information: Bonita was born at 32 weeks gestation, with a diagnosis of hypoxic ischemic encephalopathy. Her twin sister experienced the same early birth, but had no complications. Mr. and Mrs. Juarez are concerned that Bonita appears to look to her left more than her right side. A follow-up evaluation at Phoenix Children's Hospital by A. J. Prospt, a licensed pediatric physical therapist, noted that Bonita was not visually focusing or tracking objects. At times, she appeared to focus briefly, though would not follow objects and did not visually guide her reach for objects. Overall, she had abnormal neuromotor presentation with low muscle tone and restriction in range of motion in movement. Decreased visual function may have inhibited Bonita's motor development. Bonita is not taking any medications for seizures at this time.

Setting: The Juarez family preferred to bring Bonita to the early intervention center in Saguaro, Arizona, for the functional vision assessment. There was limited natural lighting available in the room where the assessment occurred. Overhead fluorescent light bulbs provided artificial lighting conditions throughout the center. We conducted the assessment in a large playroom. A large red therapy mat and other play equipment was housed throughout the room.

Results of the Functional Vision Assessment

Pupillary Response Bonita's pupils constricted slowly when a penlight was presented at 8 inches from each eye. She presented with a right eye that turned inward.

Eye Movements Bonita maintained the left gaze that has been noted by others. She did, however, show some ability to fixate on caregivers' faces when in their arms with her right eye closer to their faces. When switched to the other side, so her left eye was closer to her father's face, it was difficult for Bonita to hold fixation, and she became fussy after a few moments in this position.

Near Vision The Teller Acuity Cards, Forced Choice Preferential Looking Cards, were used to assess Bonita's visual acuity at 55 centimeters without correction. Both eyes: 20/470. We did not assess each eye separately. Bonita's ability to resolve detail is not what we would expect of an infant of her adjusted age, and this may, in part, be a factor in Bonita's ability to engage in looking behaviors. Bonita, however, did lie in a prone position and looked at a large yellow-and-red train (yellow is her favorite color) from her left side to her midline at 6 inches without disengaging from it. In a supported sitting position on her mother's leg, she watched the same train move from midline to her left side, at an 8-inch distance but did not appear to follow it any further once the train reached her midline. Interestingly, when Bonita was propped in a sitting position the 1/8-inch-wide string-rope attached to the train attracted her attention as I placed it on her left side next to her hand. She intentionally grabbed the string and was assisted by her mother to pull the train toward her body. An assistive technology toy that makes a sound when gently pushed with a hand movement or touch of the head was demonstrated for Bonita. She used her left hand to push down the large yellow button that was made more visible by the blue plastic setting in which it was mounted. Bonita also used her head to push down the yellow button to activate the toy.

Distance Vision Was not tested today.

Visual Fields It appears as though Bonita may be more restricted in using her right visual field than her left, but does appear to detect motion and movement on her right side as observed when her mother and father displayed their faces without an auditory prompt.

Summary Bonita shows evidence of being able to fixate on her caregivers' faces when positioned so she can primarily use her left eye. When attempting to use vision while in different positions in space, Bonita appears to be attempting to localize, fixate, and even reach and grasp toward large colorful objects. She indicated that she may understand cause and effect when she pushed the yellow button on the assistive technology toy. She also saw a thin, white piece of rope attached to a toy train against a blue mat background, which indicates that color and contrast may improve her ability to see detail at near distances.

Recommendations

Ophthalmological/Optometric
1. Question for Dr. Pushman: Would Bonita benefit from medical intervention for the right eye? Also, Bonita should have a full eye examination to determine if she has a refractive error (need for eyeglasses).

Educational
1. As discussed in *Cortical Visual Impairment Presentation, Assessment and Management* (Crossman, 1992) there is a possibility for Bonita to recover the ability to see over time. Therefore, it is essential that her caregivers provide Bonita with opportunities to use vision with the following ideas in mind:

a. Movement of an object is frequently more easily detected than a stationary object. Bonita may turn in the direction of a gently agitated object or follow an object as it is brought in from the periphery .

b. Colors, such as red and yellow, are more easily seen than others at first.

c. Large toys and other objects should be presented in Bonita's right and left visual fields, starting at 45 degrees from the periphery and perhaps accompanied by an auditory cue or a light to engage Bonita's looking responses. Bonita should be reinforced for what she is looking at, for if she is not interested in the toy or object, she will not be interested in looking.

d. Visual fluctuations should be considered. If Bonita does not appear to be seeing on a particular day, visual training should not be attempted because it will only lead to frustration.

e. Bonita should be positioned so that all her available energy can be directed at responding visually. Today, Bonita indicated that with support and assistance, she was able to use vision in prone and supported sitting positions besides a supine or back-lying position when in the arms of her father and mother.

f. A visual field loss may be more evident as Bonita starts to look at more stimuli. Currently, it appears as though she is responding to objects on her left side more than her right. Allow Bonita to practice finding interesting toys that are slightly to the right of her midline to improve her ability to use vision on her right side.

g. Provide Bonita with mobiles of visually interesting objects, like a comb, brush, and cup, that she may see frequently in the home. Use other objects that are red and yellow and have reflective surfaces and faces. The goal is for Bonita to use her hands and/or feet to move, reach for and/or grasp these objects to indicate that she is using vision to guide her hand or foot behavior, and repeat the actions to indicate that she is developing cause-effect behaviors.

h. Allow Bonita to look at her own reflection for short periods when in side-lying or prone positions with the mirror 6–8 inches from her face.

i. Minimize or eliminate possible backgound noise; keep the environment uncluttered and free from too many visual distractions. Bonita may find too much visual input overwhelming and close her eyes or "switch off."

2. Another functional vision assessment should be conducted in the Juarez home. Bonita's participation in typical routines will provide more information about her use of vision in a familiar environment. At that time, Pat Clark and Irma Tote will discuss how the parents can use cues and prompts to encourage Bonita to use vision.

Conclusions: Bonita is an engaging baby and has the potential to develop her visual functioning if encouraged through interaction with caregivers and opportunities to see and play with toys that are interesting to her. I have no doubt that this loving family will do everything they can to develop Bonita's visual functioning. It was a pleasure working with you.

Sincerely,

Irma Tote and the team

FUNCTIONAL VISION ASSESSMENT FOLLOW-UP

Child's Name: Bonita Juarez

Date of Birth: 9–2-96

Chronological age: 23 months

Adjusted age: 21 months

Date of follow-up: 10–27–98

Team present: Josie Bunton, parent adviser; Esther Juarez, grandmother; Irma Tote, teacher of visually impaired children

Reason for referral: Bonita needed an updated functional vision assessment. She was last tested on 7–24–97. She now lives with her paternal grandparents and has made progress in all developmental areas.

Updated background information: Esther reported that Bonita moved to her home in August 1998. Since that time, her biting behavior (not noted at last functional vision assessment 7/97) has diminished. She commented that she appears to be calmer and does not cry as often. She is eating "home-cooked food" and enjoys the different flavors and textures. Though Bonita still has some bad days, her new skills have become more and more prominent. She is commando crawling to toys that she wants. Esther commented that Bonita really knows her way around her home and allows her freedom to move wherever she desires (within safety limits). Bonita helps dress herself by moving an arm outward. Bonita is pulling herself to stand and starting to grab toys in her crib. Josie stated that these new behaviors became most evident when Bonita moved to her grandparents' home. Bonita has become more social and enjoys the company of her twin sister and brother who also live with the grandparents. Within the past year, Bonita reportedly had muscle surgery to correct the misalignment of the right eye. Esther believes that her left eye looks smaller than her right eye.

Setting: The grandparents' home in Saguaro, Arizona, was the setting for the evaluation. We were in a room with much floor space for Bonita to move around. Esther had placed a flowered sheet across the floor for Bonita to lie on as she played with her toys. The lighting was very dim, since no artificial or natural illumination was available. During the Teller Acuity testing, we requested more light, and Esther accommodated by bringing in a floor lamp. The lamp was left in the room for the remainder of the session. There were a variety of toys available for Bonita to choose from. Josie had also brought a bag of novel and attractive toys to share with Bonita today.

Tests: We administered the following tests in addition to observing Bonita in her natural environment: Teller Near Acuity System Cards, Informal Test of Visual Fields.

Results of the Functional Vision Assessment

Near Vision Bonita imitated Josie's clapping behavior, even when Josie had not provided a sound cue. Bonita repeated this action facing Josie at 2 feet. Bonita was very interested in a lollipop drum 12 inches in circumference with ribbons of red, blue, and green colors painted on the face of the drum. Esther commented that Bonita appears very attracted to bright colors. Bonita used the pompom to beat the drum in imitation of Josie's actions. Interestingly, Bonita displayed the following gaze pattern throughout the assessment: She turned her head and eyes to the left, squinted, and then moved back to the right side as if she was trying to focus or accommodate to look at a toy or face. When presented with a Sesame Street toy radio of 4 inches x 5 inches at midline, Bonita followed it to her left side, but appeared to lose it on her right side for about 3 inches. She then continued her eye movement when the radio went past this small area on her right side. Interestingly, Bonita did not appear to see the radio when it was moving within her peripheral right visual field, but when it was 45 degrees from the 180-degree horizontal plane on the right side, she reached out for it. A similar visual pattern of searching was observed when the lollipop drum was moved into her right peripheral visual field. The pompom was moved 8–10 inches from her on her right and left sides and Bonita retrieved it without difficulty even though it was placed on the flowered sheet background. Bonita affectionately hugged a 12-inch Winnie the Pooh ball with two hands to her chest and mouthed the ball. She also was very attracted to a vibrating ladybug that was red, black, and white. Josie said that this toy was a favorite, and Bonita held it, laid on it, and put her face on it as if to show her appreciation of the vibration. I asked if Bonita was interested in books, and Josie got out the *Where's Spot* from toy bag. Bonita intently stared at the pages. It appeared as though she was looking at the black print on the pages and at Spot, but this was the first time Josie had ever seen Bonita look at two-dimensional representations. It should be noted that Bonita assumed a variety of positions when looking, reaching, and grasping for favorite toys: sitting and lying on her tummy and on her back. She changed her body positions without the assistance of an adult. Just before Esther brought more light for the room, Bonita lay prone on a water toy and watched the green-blue and purple shapes slowly move inside the toy on her left side to midline.

The Teller Acuity Land System was administered at 55 centimeters without correction. Esther was kind enough to bring in a halogen floor lamp that changed the illumination significantly in this small room. Bonita sat in Josie's lap for the testing, and the results were as follows:

Both eyes: 20/260 or 2.4 cycles/cm
Right eye: 20/260 or 2.4 cycles/cm
Left eye: 20/470 or 1.3 cycles/cm

These results are considered reliable for both eyes together, but a minimal estimate for the left eye, since Bonita was losing interest by the time we tested the left eye. The results are an improvement from the 1997 testing. Although her acuity is still not what is expected of a child her chronological age, Bonita shifted gaze to the lines presented on the card. Acuity measures do not predict visual function, but do give us a sense of improvement of Bonita's ability to see detail compared to her Teller acuity test from over a year ago. An example of Bonita's visual curiosity occurred after the testing. She got off Josie's lap and sought out the vibrating red, black, and white ladybug that was 1 1/2 feet away.

Intermediate-distance Vision We built these activities into the near-play, so we could see Bonita find a favorite toy. Bonita viewed the 12-inch lollipop drum at 3 feet when it was 3 feet from her on her left side. She watched the Winnie the Pooh Bear Ball roll behind a chair on her left side at a 4–6-foot distance. Bonita was interested in looking at Josie's face at an intermediate distance when she talked to her and presented toys, such as the ladybug and drum. Occasionally, we observed Bonita taking a break by squinting her eyes while turning slightly to the right and then looking in back of her on the left side. She also patted her head. During this part of the assessment, I asked Esther if she had a solid-color sheet to cover the flowered one and discussed the benefits for Bonita of using a solid background underneath the toys. Included in these benefits was the increased chance that Bonita would more clearly see a toy against a solid background than one that was patterned. Esther brought out a black sheet and laid it upon the flowered one. We did not have time to see whether it improved Bonita's ability to discriminate toys more easily, but Josie will work with this adaptation in future visits.

Summary: Bonita has made evident progress in the motor and visual motor areas of development. In addition to her improved near acuity, as measured by the Teller Acuity Card System, she is motivated to commando crawl in an area familiar to her. Bonita's self-injurious behaviors have decreased to a light patting on the head. Bonita appears to have useful vision in her left peripheral visual field and left central visual field, as observed by how she visually approached and interacted with objects and people. Her right central visual acuity appears to be better for detail than her left eye, although she may have a scotoma or blind spot on her right side. She consistently loses an object to the right of her nose and then behaves as though she sees it when the object is past this spot. Her right peripheral visual field is more compromised than her left visual field (45 degrees off the 180-degree horizontal plane). Her functional vision profile sounds complex, but Bonita is motivated to use vision to play with toys, interact with people, and move in a familiar environment.

Recommendations

Ophthalmology, Optometry, Audiology
1. Ask ophthalmologist why Bonita's visual acuity tests differently for each eye? Does she have a blind spot in her right eye? If she has a lazy eye, what kind of treatment will improve its functioning?

2. Have the optometrist check Bonita's need for eyeglasses (refractive error) and consider a prescription if needed.

3. Schedule a hearing screening with an audiologist to rule out a mild hearing loss.

Educational
1. Play activity ideas for Esther and Josie:

a. Encourage Bonita to play with balls of different sizes and colors. Start at distances that are considered near and intermediate and then move to farther distances for rolling and returning balls. Present the balls from different directions to encourage scanning and tracking abilities during these activities.

b. Use a container that has separations like a muffin tin or egg carton. Increase the contrast within the separations. Show Bonita the carton. Hide it from her and place a snack of a contrasting color wrapper into one of the holes. Uncover the carton and have Bonita search each hole to find the snack. You can substitute a toy instead of snack as long as the toy is small enough to fit in each separation (scanning).

c. Allow Bonita to paint by using a Ziploc bag with a mixture of ketchup and mustard or yellow and red tempera paint and a couple of drops of blue food coloring in each bag that is sealed. Lay a bag flat on the table in front of Bonita and demonstrate how to mix colors by pressing with your finger or "drawing" on the bag. After the activity, keep the painting flat for a few days until dry and hang on the window or on the bulletin board. Bonita appeared to enjoy pressing a water-filled plastic toy filled with moving colorful shapes, such as fish. This activity would give her another way to press and watch the effects of her action (visual-motor).

2. Use vision in routines throughout the day:

a. Work with Esther to identify times throughout the day that Bonita is using vision. Esther commented that mealtimes are becoming more enjoyable since Bonita is eating more and more home-cooked food. Perhaps you could observe Bonita during a mealtime and record Bonita's ability to locate food items and engage in social routines during this activity. Discuss the ways she can improve Bonita's ability to discriminate, track, scan, and use her eyes and hands together. Follow up on the lighting-color and contrast cues that were incorporated into today's assessment by giving Bonita more light and improved contrast backgrounds for her toys. Teach Esther to use instructional prompts to encourage Bonita to look at interesting toys, events, and pictures in books.

b. Expose Bonita to a variety of two-dimensional pictures in books and photographs. She enjoyed *Where's Spot,* and you can highlight this dog by using black construction paper windows to focus Bonita's attention on the dogs. Ask Esther for photographs of the family and teach Bonita to associate the pictures with Esther and grandfather, mother, father, sister and brother, and teachers. The Tana Hoben books with black-and-white and white-and-black pictures are other materials that can be shared with Bonita.

Conclusions: It was a pleasure working with you. Bonita is making progress in the vision area in response to the physician's intervention, family nurturing, and early intervention services. Do not hesitate to call Irma at 770–4562 should you have further questions about Bonita's visual functioning.

REFERENCES

Brennan, V., Peck, F., & Lolli, D. (1992). *Suggestions for modifying the home and school environments. A handbook for parents and teachers of children with dual sensory impairments.* Watertown, MA: Perkins School for the Blind.

Chen, D., & Dote-Kwan, J. (1995). *Starting points: instructional practices for young children whose multiple disabilities include visual impairment.* Los Angeles: Blind Childrens Center.

Chen, D., & Haney, M. (1995). An early intervention model for infants who are deaf-blind. *Journal of Visual Impairment & Blindness, 89,* 213–221.

Crossman, H. L. (1992). *Cortical visual impairment: Presentation, assessment and management.* (Monograph Series No. 3). North Rocks 2151, Australia: North Rocks Press.

Downing, J., & Bailey, B. (1990). Developing vision use with functional daily activities for students with visual and multiple disabilities. *RE:view. 21,* 209–220.

Downing, J., & Bailey, B. (1993). *Helping young children with visual impairments make use of their vision.* Terre Haute: Blumberg Center for Interdisciplinary Studies in Special Education, Indiana State University.

Erin, J. (1991). *A unique learner. A manual for the instruction of the child with visual and multiple disabilities.* Austin, TX: Education Service Center No. XIII.

Erin, J. (1995). Children with multiple and visual disabilities. In M. Cay Holbrook (Ed.), *Children with visual impairments: A parents' guide.* Bethesda, MD: Woodbine House.

Erin, J. (1996). Functional vision assessment and instruction of children and youths with multiple disabilities. In A. L. Corn & A. J. Koenig (Eds.), *Foundations of low vision: Clinical and functional perspectives.* New York: American Foundation for the Blind.

Ferrell, K. A., & Muir, D. W. (1996). A call to end vision stimulation training. *Journal of Visual Impairment & Blindness. 90,* 364–366.

Geniale, T. (1991). *The management of the child with cerebral palsy and low vision—A neurodevelopmental therapy perspective* (Monograph Series No. 2. North Rocks 2151, Australia: North Rocks Press.

Getz, L. M., Dobson, V., Beatriz, L., & Mash, C. (1996). Interobserver reliability of the Teller acuity procedure in pediatric patients. *Investigative Ophthalmology & Visual Science, 37,* 180–187.

Goetz, L., & Gee, K. (1987). Teaching visual attention in functional contexts: Acquisition and generalization of complex visual motor skills. *Journal of Visual Impairment & Blindness, 81,* 115–117.

Hatton, D. D., Bailey, D. B., Burchinal, M. R., & Ferrell, K. A. (1997). Developmental growth curves of preschool children with vision impairments. *Child Development, 68,* 788–806.

Hyvarinen, L. (1995–96). *Vision testing manual.* Orlando, FL: Vision Associates.

Isenberg, S. J. (1989) *The Eye In Infancy.* Chicago: Yearbook Medical Publishers, Inc.

Kitchel, E. (1998). *Light and low vision.* Louisville, KY: American Printing House for the Blind.

Mohn, G. & van Hof-van Duin, J. (1986). Development of the binocular and monocular visual fields of human infants during the first year of life. *Clinical Vision Science, 1,* 51–64.

NoIR Medical Technologies. (1998). *Ultraviolet shields.* South Lyon, MI: Author.

Takashita, B. (1996). *Neurological vision impairment: Cortical vision impairment, delayed visual naturation, cortical blindness.* Paper presented at the Annual Conference of the California Transcribers and Educators of the Visually Handicapped, San Diego.

Tavernier, G. (1993). The improvement of vision by vision stimulation and training: A review of the literature. *Journal of Visual Impairment & Blindness, 87,* 143–148.

Topor, I., & Bailey, B. (1995). *A guide to helping young children with visual impairments make better use of their vision, Book 2.* Terre Haute: Blumberg Center for Interdisciplinary Studies in Special Education, Indiana State University.

Trueb, L., Evans, J., Hammel, A., Bartholomew, P., & Dobson, V. (1992). Assessing visual acuity of visually impaired children using the Teller acuity card procedure. *American Orthoptic Journal, 42,* 149–154.

Utley, B. (Winter, 1993). Assessing the instructional environment to meet the needs of learners with multiple disabilities including students who are deaf-blind. *Deaf-Blind Perspectives,* 5–8.

Utley, B., Goetz, L., Gee, K. M., & Sailor, W. (1981). *Vision assessment and program manual for severely handicapped and/or deaf-blind students* (Eric Document Reproduction Service No. ED 250–840). Reston, VA: Council for Exceptional Children.

6

Understanding Hearing Loss: Implications for Early Intervention

Deborah Chen*

In addition to vision, hearing is the other primary sense used for accessing information and for connecting us with others and the world around us. Therefore, it receives extensive treatment in this book. The importance of both vision and hearing in learning and early development is recognized by federal legislation. Part C of the Individual with Disabilities Education Act (IDEA) (see Chapter 1) requires that each infant who is eligible for early intervention services receive a multidisciplinary assessment. The Individualized Family Service Plan should contain a statement about the infant's present levels in a number of areas, including "physical development," which encompasses the infant's vision and hearing status.

Compared to visual impairment, hearing loss is a less obvious disability that may be undetected in infancy. Many infants who have a hearing loss and no other disabilities are not identified until about 1 (Mahoney & Eichwald, 1986) or 2 years old (Elssmann, Matkin, & Sabo, 1987), when it becomes evident that they have not developed speech. Hearing problems are more prevalent among infants with other disabilities than

---

*The list of questions to ask families as part of a functional hearing screening and their rationales were developed by Deborah Chen and Pamela Haag Schacter.

among infants without disabilities (Hayes & Northern, 1996). If an infant has a visual impairment or another disability, it is even more critical to evaluate the infant's hearing status to determine the infant's best avenues for learning.

A newborn who has a visual impairment, severe multiple disabilities, congenital facial anomalies, Down syndrome, or other high-risk criteria, usually receives a hearing test. However, even after a hearing problem is identified, it may take several months before the infant and family receive related intervention services (Kramer & Williams, 1993). Follow-up on an identified hearing loss in the case of an infant with severe and multiple disabilities may be delayed for several reasons:

- Because of the infant's multiple needs, addressing a hearing loss may not be viewed as a priority.
- Most early interventionists who work with infants who have visual impairments and multiple disabilities do not have a background in the area of hearing loss.
- Many professionals who do have a background in hearing loss are less experienced in working with infants who have multiple disabilities.
- Access to services to address an infant's hearing loss may not be readily available.

In many cases, the timeliness and quality of services to address the hearing loss of an infant with multiple disabilities depend on the resources of the individual service systems and the family's ability to negotiate these systems (Chen, 1997).

Given the influence of hearing loss on early communication, the requirements of federal legislation, the absence of universal hearing screening for infants in most states, the delay in identifying hearing loss in infants with multiple disabilities, and the lack of appropriate follow-up services, early interventionists must assume responsibility for ensuring that infants receive hearing evaluations and receive appropriate services if they need them. Concerns about infants' hearing status should be discussed with families and with other service providers, if available, who are knowledgeable about hearing loss, such as nurses, teachers who are certified in the field of deafness and hearing impairments, and speech and language therapists. Working together, relevant members of the program team should obtain information about how an infant is responding to sound. If they are concerned about the infant's responses, the service coordinator should assist the family in obtaining an audiological evaluation for the infant, particularly if he or she has not had one in the recent past.

If an infant has been identified as having a hearing problem, the early interventionist should be aware of the effects of the hearing loss on the infant's ability to understand speech and develop communication, work with the family and relevant service providers to address the infant's developmental needs related to the hearing loss, and learn how to promote listening skills if the infant has usable hearing. To assist early interventionists in these professional responsibilities, this chapter provides information on the hearing system, types and causes of hearing problems, characteristics of sounds, characteristics of hearing loss, risk factors and indicators of hearing loss, systematic procedures for conducting a functional hearing screening with infants who have multiple disabilities, and strategies for supporting the development of listening skills.

THE AUDITORY SYSTEM

Knowledge about the structure of the ear and how sound travels to the auditory nerve is needed to understand how hearing problems may occur, the different types of hearing problems that are found in infants, and the need for relevant interventions to address a hearing loss. As Figure 6.1 shows, the hearing system is composed of three sections: the conductive, sensorineural, and central auditory mechanisms. The outer (pinna, or ear lobe and ear canal) and middle ear (eardrum, or tympanic membrane and three ossicles or bones) make up the conductive mechanism. Sound waves enter the outer ear, funnel along the ear canal, vibrate the ear drum, or tympanic membrane (which divides the outer from the middle ear) and the three tiny bones—malleus, incus, and stapes—which, in turn, conduct sound vibrations to the oval window at the entrance of the fluid-filled inner ear. The ear drum and three tiny bones not only conduct the sound waves to the inner ear, but amplify them by about 30 dB. Problems in the middle ear affect this conduction and amplification process and cause a conductive loss.

Figure 6.1   CROSS-SECTION OF THE EAR

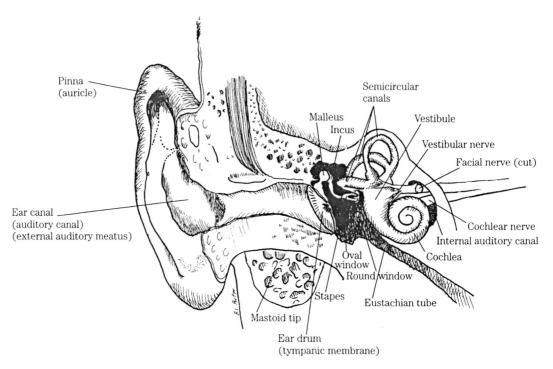

Credit: Barbara L. Porter

The sensorineural mechanism consists of the inner ear, or cochlea (sensory) and the VIIIth cranial nerve (neural). Mechanical sound vibrations from the bones are transformed by the hydraulic movement of the fluids into electrical impulses of the hair cells of the cochlea. These electrical impulses trigger neural impulses along the auditory nerve that are transmitted to the brainstem and brain, which make up the central auditory mechanism (Flexer, 1994; Niswander, 1987; Northern & Downs, 1991). Problems in the inner ear and along the auditory nerve cause a sensorineural loss. Problems in the brainstem and brain cause a central auditory-processing disorder. Thus, abnormalities along the auditory pathway from the outer ear, middle ear, inner ear, and auditory nerve can affect how sound is transmitted to the brain and, consequently, whether an infant can make sense of speech and other sounds.

Types of Hearing Problems

The conductive, sensorineural, and central processing mechanisms of the auditory pathway can also be grouped into two areas with different functions. The first area, the peripheral auditory pathway, involves the conductive and sensorineural mechanisms (outer, middle, and inner ear) and serves to receive sounds. The second area, central auditory system (brainstem and cortex), functions to interpret the meaning of sounds. The precise location of damage or problem in the auditory pathway determines the type of hearing problem that an infant will have. Hearing problems are classified as conductive, sensorineural, mixed, and progressive losses, or central auditory-processing disorders (Flexer, 1994; Northern & Downs, 1991).

A *conductive hearing loss* is caused by problems of the outer and/or middle ear that block the sound from being conducted to the inner ear. Sound conduction may be obstructed by middle ear infections (otitis media), the absence or closure of the ear canal (atresia), an abnormally small ear canal (stenosis), other malformations, a perforated tympanic membrane, and excess wax. An infant may experience a *fluctuating hearing loss* caused by a temporary blockage in the middle ear or recurrent episodes of otitis media (Kile, Schaffmeyer, & Kuba, 1994). A conductive hearing loss makes sounds softer and tends to affect low frequencies more severely than high frequencies. Most conductive losses may be remediated by medical intervention and/or amplification.

A *sensorineural loss* is caused by permanent damage to the inner ear, or cochlea. There are many causes, including viral or bacterial infections in utero (the TORCH infections, toxoplasmosis, syphilis, rubella, cytomegalovirus, and herpes); the lack of oxygen (anoxia) prenatally, during birth, or postnatally; malformations of the cochlea (dysplasia); other problems with the inner ear; and bacterial meningitis in very young children. (See the Appendix to Chapter 4 for more information about some of these conditions.) Compared to a conductive hearing loss, a sensorineural hearing loss can be more severe and usually affects the high frequencies more than the low frequencies. Sensorineural losses also result in difficulty in discriminating one sound from another. Depending on the severity of the hearing loss, in many cases, an infant will be able to detect sounds with amplification. However, the difficulty in discriminating between sounds will still exist although the discrimination of sounds can be improved through auditory training to develop listening skills.

A *mixed hearing loss* is caused by the presence of both conductive and sensorineural hearing losses. Once an audiologist identifies the type of hearing loss and recommends amplification and other educational interventions, a physician should diagnose the cause and recommend medical treatment, if warranted. The conductive part of the hearing loss can be corrected, but the sensorineural loss cannot be fully improved.

A *progressive hearing loss* is indicated when the hearing loss increases over time. Coordinated efforts by the family, physician, audiologist, and early interventionist with certification in the field of deafness and hearing impairments are necessary to monitor the status of the infant's hearing. In addition, a family needs support in adjusting to the infant's progressive hearing loss.

A *central auditory processing disorder* is indicated when an infant does not have a conductive or sensorineural loss but has difficulty understanding the meaning of sounds. Congenital brain damage and head trauma may cause central auditory-processing problems. Some infants with significant developmental delay and multiple disabilities may seem not to understand the meaning of different sounds even though hearing tests do not reveal any hearing loss. Current tests for central auditory-processing disorder involve recognition of spoken words, so this hearing problem is difficult to diagnose in infants who are preverbal or nonverbal. In any case, an infant whose peripheral auditory pathway is intact but has difficulty understanding speech will need specific interventions that emphasize contextual cues to help him or her understand sounds, focus his or her attention, and support early listening skills (Kile et al., 1994). Hearing aids are prescribed only for peripheral hearing losses (conductive and/or sensorineural)—never for central auditory processing disorders unless the individual also has a conductive or sensorineural loss.

Characteristics of Sounds

To understand the characteristics of hearing loss, it is first necessary to know something about sound. Sound is measured in two dimensions, frequency (pitch) and intensity (loudness). The pitch or frequency of a sound in measured in Hertz (Hz), or cycles per second (cps). This measurement refers to the vibration of sound waves. If a sound vibrates slowly, then a low-frequency sound is heard. If a sound vibrates quickly, then a higher frequency is heard. Most speech sounds fall within the range of 500–6,000 Hz (Bluestone, Stool, & Kenna, 1996, cited in Steinberg & Knightly, 1997).

A decibel (dB) is a measurement of loudness, or the intensity of sound. The intensity of a whisper is about 25 dB HL (hearing level), conversational speech is about 50 dB HL, an alarm of an alarm clock is about 80 dB HL, a food blender is about 90 dB HL, rock concerts are at least 110 dB HL, and the bang of a firecracker is about 140 dB HL (Berg, 1993, cited in Flexer, 1994). The degree of hearing loss is measured by decibel level; however, 0 dB does not indicate the absence of sound; the average softest sound heard by a normal hearing person is defined as 0 dB hearing level (HL). The decibel is a logarithmic scale, not a linear scale, so a 20 dB sound is 10×10, or 100 times louder than a sound at 0 dB. Consequently, if an infant has a 20 dB hearing loss because of an ear infection, he or she may be hearing 100 times less well than usual (Flexer, 1994).

A sound may be loud or soft in intensity, as measured by decibels, and of a high or low frequency, as measured by cycles per second (Watkins, 1989). Although the characteristics of speech sounds are complex, knowledge of their general characteristics provides an early interventionist with a means of interpreting an infant's responses, or lack of responses, to sounds of various intensity and frequency and to discuss observations with an audiologist. For example, the majority of vowel sounds are lower frequencies than are most consonants. If an infant attends to sound play vocalizations with vowel sounds (such as "uh-ooo" "ya-ya") but ignores the high-pitch sound of a plastic rattle, it is possible that hearing in the high frequencies may be affected. Similarly, if an infant seems to ignore his or her mother's voice when she whispers his or her name, but responds when she uses a louder voice, then a mild hearing loss may be suspected. In any case, atypical responses to sounds should be noted and discussed with an audiologist.

Characteristics of Hearing Loss

An early interventionist should understand the characteristics of an infant's hearing loss to identify and implement appropriate interventions

that address the infant's needs for communication. The slope, or configuration, of the hearing loss in addition to the severity will influence the
infant's ability to understand the meaning of sounds. Hearing losses
may be flat (a similar loss across the low-to-high sound frequencies) or
sloping (less loss in certain frequencies and more loss in others). For
example, an infant with a sloping loss that is worse in the higher frequencies will have more difficulty discriminating consonants than vowel
sounds. The degree of hearing loss ranges from slight or mild to moderate to severe to profound (Flexer, 1994; Northern & Downs, 1991); Sidebar 6.1 presents the definitions of each of these categories. *Deaf* is
defined as having a hearing loss that is greater than 70dB (severe and
profound losses) that prevents the process of spoken linguistic information even with amplification. *Hard-of-hearing* is defined as a hearing loss less than 70dB (mild, moderate, and moderately severe losses)
in the better ear.

Implications of Early Hearing Loss

All infants and young children are just starting to learn language, so even
a slight, mild, or fluctuating hearing loss caused by middle ear infections
can have a negative effect on their development of language (Kile et al.,
1994; Nozza, 1994). The consequences of a temporary hearing loss can
be even more detrimental to the early development of an infant who has
other disabilities (such as visual impairment and developmental delay).
Infants who are visually impaired may have distorted or limited access to
visual cues or no access at all. Thus, recognition of the caregiver, family
members, and objects and the anticipation of activities may depend on
other cues besides visual ones. Infants who are visually impaired and
have a developmental delay usually need additional time and repeated
experiences to obtain meaning from speech and other sounds. Hence,
even a mild hearing loss will influence these infants' early communication, cognitive, and social and emotional development.

An infant's ability to discriminate speech depends on many factors,
such as the clarity of the speech signal in contrast to environmental
sounds or background noise and the child's abilities and other disabilities. An optimal environment for young children to understand speech
requires that speech be at least 30 dB louder than background noise
(Northern & Downs, 1991; Watt, Roberts, & Zeisel, 1993). Research has

Sidebar 6.1   CLASSIFICATION OF DEGREES OF HEARING LOSS

The following classifications are used to categorize the degree of an infant's hearing loss:

Mild hearing loss   15 to 30 dB HL. An infant with a mild hearing loss may miss soft speech, subtle conversational cues, and voiceless consonants (s, p, t, k, th, f, sh). An undetected or untreated mild hearing loss in addition to visual impairment and other disabilities will have severe effects on the early development of communication of an infant with multiple disabilities. Some infants with a mild hearing loss will benefit from hearing aids.

Moderate hearing loss   30 to 50 dB HL. An infant with a moderate hearing loss will miss most conversational speech without amplification. In most cases, infants with a moderate hearing loss will benefit greatly from hearing aids because the loss is not too severe.

Moderately severe hearing loss   50 to 70 dB HL. An infant with a moderate-to-severe hearing loss may miss up to 100 percent of conversational speech without amplification. If the speaker is loud and nearby, some speech may be heard.

Severe hearing loss   70 to 90 dB HL. An infant with a severe hearing loss cannot understand any conversational speech without amplification. However, depending on his or her other abilities and disabilities, the infant may function as hard-of-hearing if he or she receives appropriate amplification and related early intervention services.

Profound hearing loss   90 dB HL or greater. The majority of infants with profound hearing loss have some available hearing but cannot hear sounds without amplification. Whether an infant with a profound hearing loss will benefit from amplification is determined by many factors, including the infant's abilities and other special needs, the family's values and priorities, and the availability of resources. These infants may need communication methods (such as manual signs) other than speech to support their development of communication and language.

found that for infants (aged 6–24 months) to detect speech, the speech signal must be 10 times louder or more intense than the level required by adults (Trehub, Bull, & Schneider, 1981, cited in Kramer & Williams, 1993). If infants with visual impairments and other disabilities have been identified as having mild, moderate, or severe hearing losses, caregivers and early interventionists should monitor the auditory environment to make sure that the infants have easy access to what is being said. Background sounds (such as from a television, radio, air conditioner, or heater) should be eliminated, when possible, or at least reduced (for example, by closing the windows and doors to decrease the noise of traffic and having the speakers move closer to the infant).

Risk Factors and Indicators

Early interventionists need to be familiar with the risk factors and indicators associated with hearing losses in infancy. The National Institutes of Health (1993) recommended that both the public and professionals should be educated about the high-risk factors for hearing loss; early behavioral indicators of hearing loss; and the ineffectiveness of crude measures, such as hand clapping, for evaluating infants' hearing. The Joint Committee on Infant Hearing (1994) recommended that infants (aged 29 days to 2 years) should receive additional clinical screenings for hearing loss if they have certain high-risk factors:

- caregivers' concerns regarding the infant's hearing or speech development
- bacterial meningitis and other infections
- a head trauma that results in unconsciousness or a skull fracture
- certain syndromes (CHARGE, Down Syndrome)
- ototoxic medications
- recurrent or persistent otitis media with effusion for at least three months (see Sidebar 6.2).

In addition, infants (aged 29 days to 3 years) should receive periodic hearing evaluations every six months until age 3 and afterward if they have any indicators associated with delayed-onset sensorineural hearing loss, such as a family history of childhood hearing loss, congenital infections (like TORCH), neurofibromatosis Type II, and neurogenerative disorders, or indicators associated with conductive hearing loss, such as recurrent or persistent otitis media with effusion (see Sidebar 6.2), deformities of the anatomy, disorders that influence the function of the eustachian tube, and neurogenerative disorders.

Many causes of visual impairment place an infant at risk for hearing loss as well as other disabilities, as shown in Sidebar 6.3. However, according to the Joint Committee on Infant Hearing (1990) about 9 percent of newborns are at a high risk of having hearing losses or about

Ear infections, or otitis media with effusion (OME), is common in all young children, especially during the first two years. OME causes fluid in the middle ear that results in a fluctuating or temporary, mild-to-moderate hearing loss, ranging from 15 to 40 dB (Bluestone & Klein, 1990a). This loss affects the infant's ability to discriminate differences in sounds (such as the spoken words: *shoe* and *chew, mama* or *papa, block* and *blocks, cracker* and *cracker?* may sound the same). With decreased hearing, even temporarily, the infant may have difficulty learning the meanings of different words, understanding the use of plurals, or hearing differences in intonation (Northern & Downs, 1991; Watt et al., 1993).

Risk factors   Colds and other respiratory illnesses increase an infant's risk of developing otitis media. Infants who have a cleft palate and certain syndromes, such as Down syndrome, Apert syndrome, Williams syndrome, or fetal alcohol syndrome, are at a high risk for ear infections (Bluestone & Klein, 1990b).

Prevention strategies   Service providers should practice common procedures for health and safety in center-based settings, such as washing hands consistently (both for children and staff) and cleaning toys and other objects that are handled frequently (American Public Health Association, 1992). The caregivers should avoid letting the infant lie down with a bottle because germs or liquid from the bottle can travel up the infant's eustachian tube and cause an ear infection (Watt et al., 1993).

Indicators of otitis media   Some infants may have otitis media and show no symptoms, while others may demonstrate one or more symptoms, including crying or irritability, pulling at the ear, discharge from the ear, fever, loss of appetite or energy, and decreased responses to sound (Hayes & Northern, 1996).

Treatment   Otitis media is usually treated by an antibiotic, and symptoms subside within three days. A physician may recommend ventilating or tympanotomy tubes if the infant has frequent ear infections. The infant's ears should be kept dry to avoid the possibility of new infection, so earplugs or cotton sealed with vaseline are needed for baths (Hayes & Northern, 1996; Watts et al., 1993). When an infant has an ear infection, an early interventionist may need to assist the family in seeking medical treatment, in monitoring the infant's response to the treatment, and in creating an environment that supports the infant's listening behaviors.

half the young children who are later found to have hearing losses. Some infants who are born in small hospitals may not be identified as being at risk, and follow-up programs are uncoordinated. Thus it is imperative that early interventionists play an active role in the ongoing monitoring of infants' hearing. More than one-third of the children who have hearing

Sidebar 6.3 HIGH-RISK FACTORS ASSOCIATED WITH HEARING LOSS OR VISUAL IMPAIRMENT IN VERY YOUNG CHILDREN

High-Risk Factors Associated with Hearing Loss

Family history

Prenatal exposure to maternal infections (toxoplasmosis, syphilis, rubella, cytomegalovirus, herpes)

Prematurity

Hypoxia

Cleft lip and palate

Craniofacial anomalies (malformations of pinna, ear canal, absent philtrum, or low hairline)

Hyperbilirubinemia level requiring transfusion

Apgar score of 3 or less at 5 minutes after birth

Prolonged medical ventilation (more than 10 days)

Certain syndromes (such as CHARGE, Down, fetal alcohol, Goldenhar, Hurler, Norrie, Refsum, Trisomy 13, Usher, and Waardenburg)

Childhood infections (bacterial meningitis, mumps, and measles)

Head trauma

Cerebral palsy

Certain neurodegenerative disorders (such as neurofibromatosis, Tay-Sachs, Niemann-Pick)

High-Risk Factors Associated with Visual Impairment

Family history

Prenatal exposure to maternal infections (toxoplasmosis, syphilis, rubella, cytomegalovirus, herpes, chicken pox, HIV)

Abnormal prenatal brain development

Prematurity

Hypoxia

Certain syndromes (such as CHARGE, Cri du chat, Down, fetal alcohol, Goldenhar, Hurler, Lowe, Marfan, Norrie, Refsum, Trisomy 13, and Usher)

Other congenital ophthalmological syndromes (such as optic nerve hypoplasia and Leber's congenital amaurosis)

Bacterial meningitis

Head trauma

Cerebral palsy

Certain neurodegenerative disorders (such as neurofibromatosis and Tay-Sachs)

Source: Joint Committee on Infant Hearing, "Position Statment," *Audiology Today, 33* (1994), 3–6; J. L. Northern and M. P. Downs, *Hearing in Children,* 4th ed. (Baltimore, MD: Williams & Wilkins, 1991); and S. W. Teplin, "Visual impairment in infants and young children. *Infants and Young Children, 8*(1), (1995) 18–51.

losses have other disabilities as well (Kile & Beauchaine, 1991). At least 1 out of every 5 children with multiple disabilities has a hearing loss (Sobsey & Wolf-Schein, 1991), and there are more than 70 syndromes (including Usher syndrome) in which hearing and vision losses are likely to occur together (Regenbogen & Coscas, 1985). It is common for most infants with Down syndrome to have conductive hearing losses, although some of these infants have sensorineural and mixed losses (Northern & Downs, 1991).

In addition to the risk factors, early interventionists should be aware of the potential physical and behavioral signs that may indicate that an infant has a hearing loss (see Sidebar 6.4). An infant who shows these signs should be referred to an audiologist (Chen, 1990; Gatty, 1996). Families are often the first to observe these indicators and to have questions about their infants' hearing. These concerns should be discussed with the families and should be taken seriously (Gatty, 1996).

FUNCTIONAL HEARING SCREENING

The purpose of *hearing screenings* is to identify infants who are likely to have hearing problems that will interfere with their early development and who should receive comprehensive audiological evaluations. The National Institutes of Health (1993) and the Joint Committee on Infant Hearing (1994) recommended universal screening not only for newborns with high-risk factors but for all infants by age 3 months through audiological tests, such as the auditory brainstem response or evoked otacoustic emissions, and at 6 months or later, by behavioral testing. As was discussed previously, the Joint Committee on Infant Hearing also recommended periodic audiological tests to monitor infants up to age 3 who are at risk of sensorineural or conductive hearing losses. These tests are described in Chapter 7. In an ideal world, all newborns would be screened for hearing loss through these clinical tests, and infants with high-risk factors would receive ongoing monitoring and periodic audiological evaluation. In reality, they are not.

Recently, early intervention agencies identified a review of infants' records, informal behavioral observations, and parents' reports as essential components of initial hearing evaluations, in addition to audiological tests, and mandated that these procedures should be implemented by

Sidebar 6.4 SIGNS OF A HIGH RISK FOR POSSIBLE HEARING LOSS

Atypical appearance of the face or ears:

- Cleft lip and palate
- Malformations of the head or neck
- Malformations of the ears, including the lack of an opening at ear canal (atresia)

Medical conditions:

- Frequent earaches or ear infections (otitis media)
- Discharge from the ears

Atypical listening behaviors:

- Makes few or inconsistent responses to sounds
- Does not seem to listen
- Does not respond to caregivers calling his or her name
- Shows a preference for certain types of sounds

Atypical vocal development:

- Has limited vocalizations
- Has abnormalities in voice, intonation, or articulation
- Shows a delay in language development

Other behaviors:

- Pulls on ears or puts hands over ears
- Breathes through mouth
- Cocks head to one side

Source: Adapted from D. Chen, "Functional Hearing Screening," in *Parents and Visually Impaired Infants,* edited by D. Chen, C. T. Friedman, and G. Calvello (Louisville, KY: American Printing House for the Blind, 1990), pp. 1–8; R. R. Fewell, "Working with Sensorily Impaired Children," in *Educating Young Handicapped Children: A Developmental Approach,* 2nd ed., edited by S. G. Garwood (Rockville, MD: Aspen Systems, 1983), pp. 235–280; C. G. Gatty, "Early Intervention and Management of Hearing in Infants and Toddlers," *Infants and Young Children, 9*(1), 1–13; and Joint Committee on Infant Hearing, "Position Statement," *ASHA, 33* (1990), 3–6.

qualified personnel, that is, those with appropriate training, knowledge, and skills (Early Education Unit, 1998). With the exception of nurses, speech and language therapists, and teachers who are certified in the field of deafness and hearing impairments, many service providers who work with infants who have multiple disabilities are not familiar with the characteristics of hearing loss or decreased hearing. In many cases, personnel with backgrounds in hearing loss are unlikely to have ongoing contacts with infants with multiple disabilities or visual impairments. Thus, early interventionists who serve infants with visual impairments and additional disabilities have a critical role in the initial identification and ongoing monitoring of infants who should be referred for audiological evaluations.

In this chapter, the term *functional hearing screening* is used to differentiate nonclinical procedures from audiological tests that are used in a hearing screening. An early interventionist has the responsibility and should possess the skills to implement a functional hearing screening procedure by

- conducting a comprehensive review of an infant's medical records
- interviewing the infant's family about their concerns and observations
- making careful observations of the infant's reactions to various sounds and familiar voices.

When possible, this information-gathering procedure should be implemented in collaboration with personnel who are trained in hearing loss. The resulting observations and concerns should be discussed with the service coordinator, and, if necessary, the family should be assisted in obtaining a referral to an audiologist for a clinical evaluation of the infant's hearing. The process of conducting a functional hearing screening is outlined in Figure 6.2, and these steps in a functional hearing screening are discussed in the sections that follow.

Review Medical Records

With the consent of the family and the approval of the program, an early interventionist should examine medical reports to identify the causes of the infant's disability, tests that have been conducted, and any recommendations for intervention or related services that have been made by

Figure 6.2 THE PROCESS OF FUNCTIONAL HEARING SCREENINGS

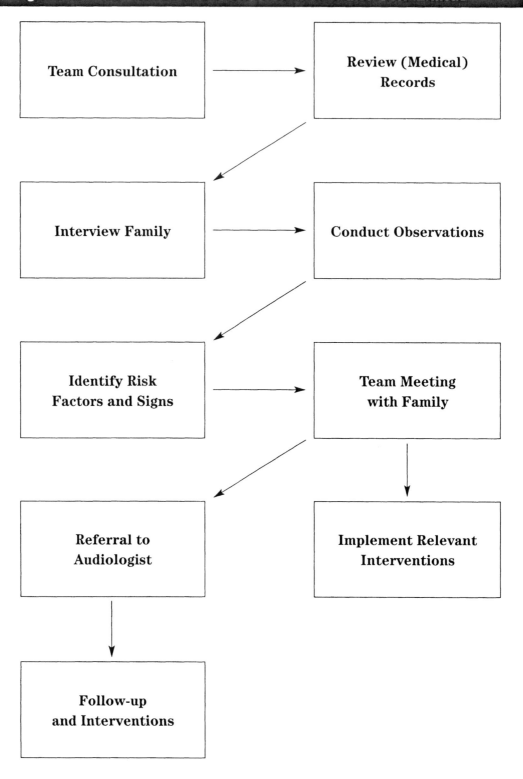

medical and other professionals. This review enables the early interventionist to determine whether the infant has had an audiological evaluation and, if so, the results and the audiologist's recommendations. If there is no record of an audiological evaluation, the early interventionist should note whether the infant has certain conditions that place him or her at risk of a hearing loss and any information about the infant's response to sounds and development of communication.

Referring to Sidebar 6.3, is there any indication of a risk factor in the infant's medical history associated with hearing loss? If the infant received an audiological evaluation, review the report to identify the types of hearing tests that were conducted, the results, the reliability of the results, and the recommendations of the audiologist. The interventionist can contact the audiologist if any necessary information is missing from the written report. Was a hearing loss identified? If so, what is the type and degree of loss? Were hearing aids recommended? If so, is the infant wearing them? If not, why not? If hearing aids were not recommended, why not? When was the last hearing test conducted? When should the infant receive another hearing test? Were any recommendations made regarding specific interventions to assist the infant's use of hearing or development of communication? How have these recommendations been implemented? A completed sample of answers provided from the medical records or by contacting the audiologist appears in Sidebar 6.5, and a blank version of the questions appears in the Appendix for the reader's use.

Gather Information from the Family

Parents and other family members are skillful observers of their infant's behaviors and response to a variety of sounds in everyday activities. In many cases, they are the first "screeners" of their infant's hearing and the first people to wonder whether there is a problem. The early interventionist should determine if family members have any concerns and whether they have received any information from physicians or other professionals about the status of the infant's hearing. The early interventionist should gather information about the family's observations by asking open-ended questions and clarifying observations. The purpose of the interview is to obtain detailed information about the infant's responses to different types of sounds (toys, environmental noises, and voices), the intensity (loudness) of the sounds to which the infant responds, and

Child's Name: ___Mai-ling Chin___   Age: ___12 months___

Audiologist: ___Dr. Roberts___   Date of Evaluation: ___6-21-99___

1. What kinds of hearing tests were conducted?
Behavioral Observation Audiometry (BOA)

2. What did the tests measure, and what were the results?
Bilateral severe-to-profound hearing loss

3. How did the test go—how was the baby during the testing situation? How reliable are the results?
Consistent responses to low and high frequency bands of noise at 70–80 dBHL. Eye widening and partial localization to sound.

4. When should the baby be retested?
In 3 months with hearing aids

5. What do the results mean in terms of the baby's ability to discriminate sounds?
Will be aware of loud environmental sounds

6. With this hearing loss, would this baby benefit from amplification?
Recommend binaural Phonak hearing aids

7. What do you think is the best way to get more information about this baby's hearing?
Gradually increase use of hearing aids

8. How can I help prepare this child for further testing?
Increase use of hearing aids

9. Can I participate in or observe future testing?
—

10. If present at the audiological evaluation exam—can we listen to sounds though the headphones to get an idea of the sounds that the infant can hear?
—

11. If the infant wears hearing aids, when will new ear molds be needed?

The interventionist should be able to answer questions 1 to 4 from a complete audiogram and audiological report. If the written report does not provide this information, the results will need to be discussed with the audiologist.

the infant's use of vocalization (babbling, intonation, and imitation). In this way, the early interventionist can gain a better understanding of how the infant is using hearing (Chen, 1990; Northern & Downs, 1991).

Ask specific questions about the infant's response to sound. What have the parents observed about the baby's responses to their voices, household noises, and other sounds? How loud are these sounds? How close do the parents have to be to the baby to get a response? Does the infant seem to prefer certain sounds? Specific questions to ask the family are listed here. A blank list of questions appears in the Appendix for the reader's use.

Questions About Medical and Health Information

1. What have you been told by medical professionals about your baby's hearing?

Look for diagnoses that are associated with hearing loss. Ask if the parents know whether a hearing test has ever been conducted. Parents may be unaware that the baby had a brainstem auditory evoked response test in the hospital. A thorough search of medical records will be necessary.

2. Has the baby had an ear infection? How frequently?

Frequent ear infections can cause a fluctuating level of hearing or a transient hearing loss that may affect the development of communication skills.

3. Is your baby often congested? Does he or she have frequent colds?

Babies who have frequent colds or are often congested may have fluid in the middle ear (without there being an infection) and are at a high risk for ear infections that can cause intermittent hearing loss.

Questions About the Parents' Observations

Note: If the parents are unable to answer these questions, you will need to structure situations to observe the infant's responses to sound.

4. What is your impression of the baby's hearing?

Parents are often the first to screen their babies' hearing and have questions about what medical professionals have told them. Encourage the parents to share their concerns with you.

5. What sounds seem to get your baby's attention? How does your baby respond to these sounds?

Note whether particularly high or low sounds or varied intonations get the baby's attention. Notice what the baby's reaction to sounds is, such as, increased movement, quieting, startle, or vocalization.

6. What does your baby do when you call his or her name?

Note the baby's responses to speech; they may be different from the responses to non-speech sounds. Notice how the parent says the baby's name. Does the parent vary intonation, volume, and pitch to engage the baby's attention?

7. How does the baby react to sudden loud noises (such as a telephone ringing, a car horn honking, or vacuum cleaner running)?

Note the baby's responses to loud environmental sounds. The lack of response may indicate a hearing problem. Babies with other neurological problems may have an exaggerated startle or lack of startle that may make these responses more difficult to interpret.

8. Does your baby seem to respond differently to your vocalizations when the radio or television is on?

Background noise makes it more difficult for a baby to hear speech, especially if he or she has a hearing loss. Furthermore, babies with cortical vision impairment or neurological impairments may have difficulty attending to more than one stimulus at a time.

9. Does your baby enjoy toys that "talk" or make noise?

Find out whether the baby has been exposed to these toys. If so, if the baby does not seem interested in them, ask questions to determine if the baby is not hearing them or if the sounds are loud and annoying to the baby.

10. Does your baby enjoy when you talk, coo, or sing to him or her?

Give examples of songs or games that are familiar to the parents or typical of the family. The lack of response to the parents' voices may indicate a hearing loss.

11. What words does your baby seem to understand?

Find out whether the baby seems to recognize any familiar words, for example, "bye-bye" and "mama."

Conduct Systematic Observations

Structured observations should be used as part of the screening process when the family members or service providers are concerned about the infant's hearing and after the infant has received an audiological evaluation. If an infant has been diagnosed as having a hearing loss and hearing aids are recommended, then systematic observations are needed to obtain information about how the infant is responding to sounds with amplification. The early interventionist should observe the infant both during routine situations and during activities that are structured to engage the infant's attention to different sounds. In addition, planning systematic observations involves identifying the sound stimuli (characteristics of sounds that are presented to the infant), context (environmental factors and activities) and the infant's responses (state, response behaviors, and the time between the sound and the infant's response), and any high-risk indicators that the infant displays that are associated with hearing loss. The findings from these observations should provide a general impression of the infant's hearing and should be discussed with relevant service providers to decide whether a referral to an audiologist is warranted. If the infant is referred for an audiological evaluation, the early interventionist should follow up on the recommendations and identify necessary interventions with the family and other service providers.

Routine Activities

Observe the infant and caregiver in a routine activity, such as eating a meal, having a bath, and playing, and note the infant's responses to environmental sounds—sounds that are typically part of the infant's home, such as the sounds of water running from a faucet, a telephone ringing, a blender running, and a radio playing. Note if there is background noise; the sounds from an air conditioner and heater for example, can be noisy. Pay attention to how the infant was positioned (for instance, in infant seat). Observe the distance and location of the source of sound from the infant in relation to the infant's eyes and ears and note whether the infant responded visually to the person and object, rather than aurally to the sound. Describe the infant's response.

Sidebar 6.6 lists some questions that can guide the early interventionists observations of the infant's responses to sounds that occur during routine activities. Figure 6.3 presents a sample completed form for recording observations of a routine activity.

Selected Sounds

Conducting a structured observation of the infant's responses to selected sounds requires the careful selection of sound stimuli and a keen

1. What type of activity was observed?
2. What sounds occurred?
3. Where was the source of sound located in relation to the infant?
4. How far away was the source of sound from the infant?
5. What were the infant's reactions? How long did it take to see his or her reactions?
6. Was the infant receiving any cues other than those provided by the sounds?
7. What are your impressions of the infant's responses to environmental sounds?

Figure 6.3   SAMPLE COMPLETED FORM FOR RECORDING OBSERVATIONS OF RESPONSES TO SOUNDS DURING A ROUTINE ACTIVITY

Observations of a Routine Activity for Responses to Sound

Name: __Maria__   Date of Observation: __February 2, 1999__

Date of birth: __December 5, 1997__

Context: __Maria is sitting in her high chair in the kitchen finishing her__ __bottle. She seems alert. Her mother is fixing her lunch.__

Participants: __Maria's mother, Mrs. Lopez__

Environmental Sounds	Distance and Location	Responses
Mrs. Lopez turned on the blender to puree food	About 4 feet from the right of the high chair	Maria startled.
Mrs. Lopez turned on the faucet to wash a bowl	About 5 feet from the right of the high chair	No change in behavior observed.
The telephone rang	About 4 feet from the left of the high chair	Maria moved her head from side to side.

observation of the infant's response to each sound. If the infant has some vision, the source of sound must be presented out of the infant's visual field.

Select the sound of stimuli from a variety of noisemakers, such as the infant's favorite toys that make sounds, a baby rattle, a xylophone, a squeaky toy, or noisemakers from the HEAR Kit (Downs, 1984). In addition to the responses to noisemakers and sound toys, the infant's response to a familiar voice should also be observed. If one service provider is conducting the screening, he or she should sit in front of the infant and provide an object (such as a toy or bottle) that does not make a sound to keep the infant quiet and attentive. Hold the sound toy or noisemaker out to the side, level with the infant's ear and about 36 inches from the ear. (Sounds should be presented to the right or left of the infant's head and slightly behind, out of the infant's visual field, if the infant has vision.) Remain in this position and count slowly and silently to 10, to be sure that the infant's response is not elicited by an arm movement and positioning of the test object. Observe the infant's typical behaviors; then create the sound stimuli. Remain in this position and repeat the procedure. After two trials, if the infant has reacted, let him or her handle the sound toy for a few seconds and then continue the screening.

Randomize presentations to the right or left side; that is, do not present sound in a predictable pattern by alternating the presentations to each side, such as right, left, right, left. Note the infant's responses and whether the sound stimuli were familiar or unfamiliar. For example, a caregiver calling the infant's name is a meaningful and familiar sound, whereas the sound of a bell may be unfamiliar and meaningless to an infant. Also note the duration of the sound presentation. For example, tapping a xylophone with a stick once makes a short sound, tapping it three times in succession makes a longer sound, and running the stick along the bars makes a sound that is longer in duration.

Environment and Context of the Observation

Assess the environment during both routine and structured observations and identify whether there is background noise or other sounds that may interfere with the infant's attention to speech and other target sounds. Place the infant in a position that is comfortable and that allows an unobstructed view of the infant's entire body. Some infants are more alert sitting in a high chair, infant seat, on their caregiver's laps, or in some other supported position. Pay attention to how the infant is positioned and where the stimuli are presented in relation to the infant's eyes and ears and note whether the infant responded visually to the person and object, rather than to the sound. Also note the distance (for example, 6 inches, 1 foot, or 3 feet) of the source and location of the sound (such as slightly behind to the right or to the left of the infant's head).

Characteristics of the Infant's Responses

Note the infant's state and attention to the activity and before sound stimuli are presented. Observe the infant's behavioral responses to each type of sound stimuli. Observations should include the infant's responses both to sound toys and to speech. Infants usually respond differently to sound toys than to familiar voices and may have different response times to various sounds. When caregivers call the infant using intonation and familiar words, infants with hearing are likely to display attention and recognition behaviors, including body movement, facial expression, or vocalization. For example, an infant may startle at the noise of a blender in the kitchen, turn quickly toward the sound of a telephone, or take a few seconds to respond to the caregiver calling his or her name. Observe the infant's response time to each type of sound stimuli. Some infants respond quickly within 2 seconds, while others take 5 to 10 seconds. The responses of infants who are visually impaired may also be influenced by their additional disabilities or other medical needs. For example, the responses of infants with severe developmental delays and those who are medically fragile may be subtle or difficult to recognize. The limited motor control or involuntary movements of infants with cerebral palsy may interfere with the easy identification of which movements are true responses to sounds. And infants with autism may ignore sounds although they do not have hearing losses. These potential influences require careful, multiple, and systematic observations of infants with multiple disabilities and emphasize the need for these infants to receive audiological evaluations.

The questions in Sidebar 6.7 can be used to guide the early interventionist's observations of the infant's responses to sounds presented in structured situations. Figure 6.4 presents a sample completed form for recording observations in a structured situation.

1. What noisemakers or sound toys and voices were presented?
2. Were the sound stimuli familiar or novel?
3. How far away from the infant were the sound stimuli presented?
4. Were the sound stimuli presented randomly to the left and right sides of the infant's head?
5. Were the presentations short or long in duration?
6. How many times was each sound presented?
7. Was the infant drowsy, irritable, quiet, alert, or attentive?
8. Was the environment quiet and free of distractions?
9. What were the infant's reactions?
10. How long did it take to see the infant's responses to the sound toys and to a familiar voice?
11. Was the infant receiving any cues other than those provided by the sounds?
12. What is your impression of the infant's hearing? Does the infant respond better to some sounds than to others? Are his or her responses inconsistent or consistent?

**Figure 6.4 SAMPLE COMPLETED FORM
FOR RECORDING OBSERVATIONS TO SOUND
DURING A STRUCTURED OBSERVATION**

Structured Observation of Responses to Sound

Name: __Maria__   Date of Observations: __February 2, 1998__

Date of birth: __December 5, 1997__   __September 28, 1998__

Context: __2/22/98: Maria is sitting in her high chair. She is drinking her__
__bottle. She seems alert.__

__9/28/98: Maria is sitting on her father's lap on the sofa.__
__She seems sleepy.__

Participants: __9/22/98: Maria's mother, Mrs. Lopez.__

__9/28/98: Both Mr. and Mrs. Lopez__

Materials: __Selected sound toys from HEAR kit__

(continued on next page)

Figure 6.4 SAMPLE COMPLETED FORM FOR RECORDING OBSERVATIONS TO SOUND DURING A STRUCTURED OBSERVATION *(continued)*

Sound Stimuli	Distance (6 inches, 36 inches)	Location (right or left ear)	Date: 9/22/98 Responses	Date: 9/28/98 Responses
Egg rattle	36 inches	Lower right	No change in behavior observed	No change in behavior observed
Egg rattle	6 inches	Lower right	Short pause in sucking	Slight mouth movements
Bell	36 inches	Upper left	Moved right foot	Began to get sleepy and wanted to snuggle into father
Bell	36 inches	Upper right	Moved right foot	Began to fuss, so we stopped
Mother whispers "Maria, Maria"	36 inches	Left	No change in behavior observed	
Mother calls "Maria" in a normal voice twice	36 inches	Left	Removed bottle from mouth and smiled	
Maria calls "Mother" in a normal voice twice	36 inches	Right	Vocalized and turned head to the right	

**Sidebar 6.8   QUESTIONS TO GUIDE
THE IDENTIFICATION OF HIGH-RISK SIGNS**

1. Are the infant's face and ears typical in appearance?
2. What types of sounds elicit the infant's responses?
3. What responses to sound does the infant demonstrate? For example, do the responses indicate awareness-reflexive reaction, attention-alerting, localization, discrimination, recognition, or comprehension?
4. What types of vocalizations does the infant produce?

Signs of High-Risk for Hearing Loss

Observe the infant for indicators of possible hearing loss, as listed in Sidebar 6.4. Observe the infant's appearance, listening behaviors, and vocalizations. The questions listed in Sidebar 6.8 can be used to guide the early interventionist in identifying signs of high risk for possible hearing loss.

It is highly likely that early interventionists will need to conduct systematic and multiple observations of infants who have severe disabilities and visual impairments to feel confident about their impressions about the infants' hearing status. Infants vary in their cooperation with structured observations and may be irritable or drowsy during the observations. Some infants have subtle behavioral responses (slight changes in respiration, small body movements, or quieting) and may need more time (several seconds) to respond than others. Given infants' variable behaviors, subtle reactions, and response time, it may be difficult to obtain consistent responses to sound stimuli.

Analyze the Findings

The early interventionist should document and analyze the comprehensive information about an infant's hearing status collected from a careful review of the infant's medical reports, from extensive conversations with the family, and through structured observations. The findings should be used to determine whether the infant should be referred for an audiological evaluation. Observations and concerns should be discussed with available service providers, such as a nurse, speech and language therapist, and teacher who is certified in the field of deafness and hearing impairments. If an infant demonstrates high-risk indicators or signs of hearing loss, if the family has concerns, or if the infant's responses to sounds are questionable, then the early interventionist or service coordinator should assist the family in seeking a referral for an audiological evaluation, preferably from a pediatric audiologist who has expertise in evaluating infants, especially those with multiple disabilities.

Conduct a Follow-up

It is essential that the family receives follow-up services after the infant has received audiological evaluations that have been recommended. First, the family should receive support during this complicated, overwhelming, and confusing process. Second, the family and other members of the early intervention program team should discuss the test results and recommendations. Diagnoses and terminology may need to be explained. For example, the family and other team members may question the terms *deaf*, or *deaf-blind* if the infant reacts to some sounds and visual stimuli. Third, recommendations (such as for hearing aids or for alternative modes of communication) should be reviewed and decisions should be made regarding their implementation. If an infant has a hearing loss and hearing aids are recommended, it is important to follow up with the family to assist in the care of hearing aids, to encourage the infant to wear them consistently, to develop the infant's listening skills, and to observe the infant's auditory behaviors once he or she is wearing the hearing aids consistently.

WORKING WITH AN INFANT WHO HAS A HEARING LOSS

Developmental Progression in Responses to Sound

If an infant with a hearing loss has some available hearing, learning to listen takes time and must occur before the infant can listen to learn, particularly if the infant has other disabilities (Chen, 1997). It is important for the family and service providers to understand that there is a significant difference between the amount of hearing required to detect the presence of sound and the amount of hearing required to discriminate and comprehend sound. As the National Institutes of Health (1993) noted, an infant's response to the sound of hand clapping is not an effective measure of the infant's hearing. Because an infant with a moderate hearing loss will be alert to certain sounds, the caregiver or service providers may assume that the infant does not have a hearing loss, or if one has been identified, question the need for hearing aids that have been recommended. However, although the infant may be aware of the presence of sound and even turn to a parent's voice, without wearing hearing aids, the infant is probably not hearing well enough to discriminate between a range of sounds and to develop an understanding of spoken words, particularly if he or she is visually impaired and has additional disabilities.

Early interventionists serving infants whose multiple disabilities include both vision and hearing losses should work with families and teachers who are certified in the field of deafness and hearing impairments to identify the infant's level of response to sounds, as classified in Sidebar 6.9. Behaviors at any or all these levels do not indicate that an infant has normal hearing. Rather, this hierarchy provides a framework for understanding how the infant is processing sound and creating opportunities for the infant to develop listening skills, as appropriate.

Working with the Audiologist

An *audiologist* is a professional who is trained to administer and interpret clinical hearing evaluations and to prescribe hearing aids and assistive listening devices when appropriate (see Chapter 7). An audiologist has a master's or doctoral degree in audiology and professional certification (a state license or certificate of clinical competence from the American Speech-Language-Hearing Association; Early Education Unit, 1998; Flexer, 1994; Watkins, 1989). An early interventionist who serves an infant who has a hearing loss and the infant's family needs to work closely with an audiologist to provide appropriate interventions that address the infant's needs, such as the care of hearing aids, helping the infant wear and use hearing aids, and monitoring the infant's response to hearing aids. This close relationship occurs more frequently when the early interventionist has a background in hearing loss (a credential in teaching, nursing, or speech and language therapy) than when he or she does not. In the majority of cases, early interventionists serving infants with visual impairments and other disabilities do not have

SIDEBAR 6.9   HIERARCHY OF RESPONSES TO SOUND

Reflexive or awareness behaviors are observed in an infant's physical responses, such as body startle, a sudden jerk or slow movement of the arms or legs, facial movement, blinking the eyes, or changes in sucking behavior. These are reflexive reactions that are elicited at the lower brainstem level (Flexer, 1994; Northern & Downs, 1991). These behaviors do not indicate that the infant understands that sounds have meaning.

Attending or alerting behaviors are observed in an infant's orientation toward the source of sound, including looking, reaching, searching, or leaning; looking at the caregiver's face in anticipation; starting or stopping vocalization; widening the eyes; frowning; smiling; and quieting. These responses are the first indications that the infant is relating the sound to an object or person (Flexer, 1994, Northern & Downs, 1991) and provide a basis for engaging the infant's listening attention.

Localization behaviors are observed when the infant identifies what has made a sound by looking, turning, reaching, pointing, or moving toward the source. An infant who is totally blind will have difficulty localizing sound, especially if he or she also has a hearing loss. An infant who has both a visual impairment and a hearing loss needs to be given specific opportunities to learn to identify the location of the sources of sound. These opportunities will also increase the infant's orientation and mobility skills. Family members can develop calling games to gain the infant's attention and response, such as "come and find me," and searching games for noise-making toys and household sources of sound like a television or radio, vacuum cleaner, and washing machine.

Discrimination and recognition behaviors are observed when an infant responds differently to familiar and unfamiliar sounds; imitates vocalizations; responds to his or her name; and responds to simple directions, including "no" or "Give mama a kiss." These responses indicate that the infant is beginning to understand the meaning of sounds and words (Chen, 1990, 1997; Pollack, 1985). Games can be created to build on the infant's discrimination abilities, such as identifying which family member is speaking, the sounds of favorite toys, the source of environmental sounds, and animal sounds; imitating slow or fast, loud or soft rhythms made on a drum; and responding to directions of simple finger plays and action songs (Chen, 1996).

Comprehension behaviors are observed when an infant responds to questions and comments on activities. These language skills are supported by providing an appropriate language-learning environment with comprehensible language input—words that the infant can understand, supported by the context and experience; commenting on the infant's activities and interests; and involving the infant in conversational exchanges.

a background in hearing loss, so the collaboration with audiologists should be initiated for several reasons. First, the family members and the early interventionist should share their observations of how the infant responds to sound. The audiologist sees the infant in an unfamiliar and atypical setting and has limited interaction with and knowledge about the infant. The family's and early interventionist's perspectives contribute to a more comprehensive view of the infant's use of hearing. Second, because of his or her familiarity with the infant, the early interventionist can assist the audiologist in testing an infant with multiple disabilities in the following ways:

1. By suggesting adaptations for the infant's position, given his or her physical or other needs. For example, an infant may be more relaxed and attentive sitting in an infant seat, stroller, or adaptive chair than on the caregiver's lap. Furthermore, certain positions will allow the caregiver, test assistant, and audiologist to detect the infant's subtle responses.

2. By identifying the infant's idiosyncratic behaviors, such as changes in breathing, subtle movements of the arms or legs, or slight facial expressions.

3. By discussing the infant's response time. Many infants who have multiple disabilities need more time to respond than is usually expected by an audiologist. Whereas the normal response time may be 1–3 seconds, an infant with multiple disabilities may take 10–20 seconds to respond.

4. By identifying adaptations to the standard test procedures. For example, an infant who is blind or severely visually impaired will not respond to a visual reinforcement for responding to sound. A tactile, kinesthetic, or vibratory reinforcement such as tickle, fan, air puff, or vibrating toy, may be needed. In addition, an infant who is visually impaired may not turn toward a visual reinforcement but, rather, turn his or her body or lean toward the reinforcer.

When an infant receives an audiological evaluation, families and early interventionists should clarify the findings with the audiologist, as discussed earlier in the section on the functional hearing assessment and in Sidebar 6.5. See Chapter 7 for detailed information on hearing loss and audiological evaluations. In particular, they should ask about the tests that were used, the information that a particular test provided, what frequency range was tested, and what the results indicate about the status of the infant's hearing. They should also ask about recommendations for follow-up evaluations. If the evaluation indicates that an infant has a hearing loss, they should ask whether hearing aids are recommended and what they will do. If hearing aids are not recommended, they should ask why not.

Hearing Aids

Most infants who have hearing losses will benefit from amplification. The early interventionist who does not have a background in hearing loss should work with a teacher who is certified in the field of deafness and hearing impairments and an audiologist to assist the family with responsibilities related to the infant's hearing aid.

It is important for the infant to receive amplification as soon as possible for several reasons. First, the infant will have the advantage of early and consistent amplification, that is, more time to learn how to make sense of sounds and an opportunity to realize that hearing aids are helpful. Second, the infant is likely to keep the hearing aids on, since he or she does not have the motor abilities to remove them.

Daily Check

The audiologist or teacher who is certified in the field of deafness and hearing impairments can assist the family and the early interventionist with procedures for checking the hearing aids and for putting them on the infant. If this information is not clear, Sidebar 6.10 lists specific questions to ask the audiologist to clarify the use of hearing aids and how the infant can best be introduced to them. Hearing aids must always be in working condition and checked daily before being put on the infant, and the infant's earmolds should be clean and free of wax, to serve any purpose. The early interventionist or caregiver should test the batteries and then listen to the hearing aids in the following way: Using his or her own earmold or a hearing aid stethoscope, turn each aid on; hold it about 12 inches from the mouth; and say "ah," "oo," "ee," "sh," "s," and "m" while gradually turning the volume up. If the sounds are weak, intermittent, or distorted then the hearing aid is not working properly and needs to be sent to the audiologist or hearing aid dealer to be checked.

Sidebar 6.10   QUESTIONS FOR THE AUDIOLOGIST REGARDING HEARING AIDS

1. Where should the volume be set?

2. How long should the infant wear the hearing aid when it is first introduced?

3. What should be done if the hearing aid gets wet?

4. How can the hearing aids be secured on the infant's ears (such as with Huggie Aids, double-sided tape, ribbons, or eyeglass straps) if they keep falling off?

5. What can be done if the infant also wears eyeglasses and his or her ears are not big enough to accommodate both the hearing aids and the arms of the eyeglasses? Check also with the optometrist regarding the options for eyeglass frames.

6. What should be done if there is feedback when the infant is lying down, moving around, or has poor head control?

7. How long should the infant not wear the hearing aids when he or she has an ear infection?

8. How should the hearing aids be checked daily?

9. What should be done if the hearing aids make a squealing noise (feedback) when they are turned on and the infant is wearing them?

10. How should earmolds be cleaned?

11. How often should the infant get new earmolds?

Planned Introduction

When hearing aids are introduced to older infants who have multiple disabilities, the infants may pull off their hearing aids before they have the opportunity to learn how to use them. In these situations, it is helpful to schedule a time for using the hearing aids. A predictable routine is important for many aspects of an infant's early learning. Initially, the length of time that the infant wears the hearing aids will be short and then will be gradually increased as he or she accepts them. First, identify enjoyable activities for putting the hearing aids on the infant when he or she is attentive and interacting with a caregiver, such as during play, finger plays or songs, or mealtime. Other situations for encouraging the initial use of hearing aids should include the infant's interactions with the speech and language therapist, teacher who is certified in the field of deafness and hearing impairments, and other service providers who focus on listening skills. Try to put on and remove the hearing aids when the infant is in a good mood, rather than let the infant's irritable or unhappy behaviors dictate when the aids are removed. Be aware of when the infant has had enough of wearing the aids, so that putting on and removing the aids are associated with calm and positive interactions. The number of hours that the infant wears these aids (in working condition) is the period when the infant has the opportunity to develop listening skills (the infant's "listening time"). Monitor the environment for sounds that are loud (construction outside the building), distracting (music being played in the background), noisy (chairs being moved across an uncarpeted floor at a center-based program), and meaningless (sounds that are made randomly). The infant's initial listening experiences should be pleasant. Do not overstimulate the infant with meaningless sound stimulation, such as random environmental sounds and background noise. If an infant with multiple disabilities has unpleasant listening experiences, he or she is likely to become inattentive to auditory information, increase or display self-stimulatory behaviors (like rocking or hand waving), and refuse to wear the hearing aids. The purpose of amplification is to assist the infant in making sense of familiar sounds that will promote an understanding of speech, if appropriate.

Several publications offer suggestions for the use of hearing aids, daily checks on hearing-listening, and other care and maintenance issues (Flexer, 1994; Infant Hearing Resource, 1985; Northern & Downs, 1991; Watkins, 1989). The early interventionist and teacher trained in the field of blindness and visual impairments must collaborate with the teacher trained in the field of deafness and hearing impairments to understand the impact of hearing loss on the infant's ability to use auditory information; to address the infant's intervention needs; to become familiar with the care and use of hearing aids; and, when appropriate, to develop and plan appropriate ways for supporting the infant's development of listening skills.

Strategies to Support an Infant's Development of Listening Skills

There are simple strategies for enhancing opportunities for infants with multiple disabilities and hearing losses to develop listening skills, when appropriate (Chen, 1996). These strategies also apply to infants with visual impairments and other disabilities who do not have hearing losses, but require particular assistance in making sense of auditory information. The following are suggestions for interacting with infants at home:

- Imitate the infant's vocalizations. Infants are more likely to imitate behaviors that are within their own repertoire.
- Develop turn-taking and other vocal games, for example, by playing peek-a-boo and removing the scarf from the infant's face after saying "peek-a-boo," imitating the infant's sounds, rocking the infant to gentle vocalizations, or bouncing the infant in time to vocalizations. These early games provide opportunities for give and take and a foundation for later conversations.
- Speak naturally and close to an infant's ear. This proximity is a natural way to help the infant discriminate speech from environmental sounds, particularly if the infant has a slight hearing loss, middle ear infection, or other hearing problem and does not wear a hearing aid. Speaking closely to the infant's ear in a normal tone is a natural way of amplifying the sound (making it louder).
- Hold the infant on your chest and dance or sway in time to vocalizations.
- Use short phrases with repetitive words to allow the infant time to process and understand what is said, for example, "take a drink," "you're thirsty," "drink some juice," and "thirsty baby."
- Use "parentese," or an exaggerated intonation, such as "Hell-loo bay-bee," to engage the infant's attention.
- Add words to the infant's action to help the infant understand words and their meanings, for example, "Up, up, up" when picking the infant up.
- Identify environmental sounds that occur naturally to focus the infant's listening attention and help the infant to discriminate and localize sounds, as appropriate. For example, say "Listen, the telephone's ringing" and take the infant to the phone.
- Make sure the infant can see the speaker's face (in the visual field of an infant with low vision) and draw attention to the speaker's lips by making exaggerated lip movements during sound play or by wearing lipstick or having the infant touch the speaker's lips,

if appropriate. In this way, the infant will learn the source of vocalizations.

- Use animated facial expressions to engage the infant's attention, when possible; to support what is said; and to communicate in a natural way.
- Use natural gestures (if the infant has sufficient vision) to engage the infant's attention, to communicate the meaning of spoken words, and to model the use of gestures in communication; for instance, wave bye-bye when saying "bye-bye" and gesture when saying "come here." If the infant is blind, certain gestures, such as waving bye-bye, may be introduced physically by guiding the infant's hand (coactively).
- Reduce unnecessary noise. Turn off the television or radio and reduce other background sounds if you want the infant to pay attention to what is being said or other spoken information. The signal (speech) must be at least 30–40 dB louder than the background noise for a hearing infant to be able to attend to it, so background sounds will interfere with the ability to understand what is said.

In center-based settings, additional strategies for older infants include the following:

- Get the child's attention by calling his or her name before beginning to speak or giving directions; by standing still, rather than moving, while talking; and, when appropriate, by getting down to the child's physical level.
- Make sure that the child with low vision can see the speaker (avoid standing by a window or other situations that produce glare).
- Seat the child close to the source of sound (such as a speaker or audiotape player) so that the child can attend to and discriminate the target information from background sounds.
- Reduce unnecessary noise. Close your eyes and listen to the sounds of the classroom. Is the room filled with sounds of children and other noise? Can you hear the air conditioner, heater, traffic, or other noise that interferes with the child's listening attention? What can you do to reduce these sounds? As was discussed earlier, the signal-to-noise ratio is critical for a child to make sense of auditory information.

- Create a physical environment that supports the child's listening behavior. Evaluate the physical arrangement of the room. Is there carpeting or another type of floor covering? Are there centers for small-group activities and room dividers? Are there other ways to reduce the noise level in the room?
- Engage the child in communication and social interaction. Encourage the staff to listen and respond to interactions, to follow the child's interest and lead, to comment on the child's activities, and to initiate conversations.

CONCLUSION

Infants who have visual impairments in addition to other disabilities must receive hearing screenings and periodic audiological evaluations, as appropriate. Many of these infants are at a high risk of hearing losses. In addition to visual impairments, infants' hearing losses will severely complicate the usual process of early learning, social interaction, and communication. It is imperative that early interventionists and other service providers use a collaborative team model to work more effectively with families and to support the infants' access to meaningful sensory information and learning experiences that will promote early development.

REFERENCES

American Public Health Association & American Academy of Pediatrics. (1992). *Caring for our children: National health and safety performance standards: Guidelines for out-of-home child care programs.* Ann Arbor, MI: Edwards Brothers.

Berg, F. S. (1993). *Acoustics and sound systems in schools.* San Diego, CA: Singular Publishing Group.

Bluestone, C. D., & Klein, J. O. (1990a). Infratemporal complications and sequelae of otitis media. In C. D. Bluestone, S. E. Stool, & M. D. Scheetz (Eds.), *Pediatric otolaryngology* (pp. 487–545). Philadelphia: W. B. Saunders.

Bluestone, C. D., & Klein, J. O. (1990b). Otitis media, atelectasis and eustachian tube dysfunction. In C. D. Bluestone, S. E. Stool, & M. D. Scheetz (Eds.), *Pediatric otolaryngology* (pp. 320–400). Philadelphia: W. B. Saunders.

Bluestone, C. D., Stool, S. E., & Kenna, M. A. (1996). *Pediatric otolaryngology* (3rd ed.). Philadelphia: W. B. Saunders.

Chen, D. (1990). Functional hearing screening. In D. Chen, C. T. Friedman, & G. Calvello (Eds.). *Parents and visually impaired infants* (pp. 1–8). Louisville, KY: American Printing House for the Blind.

Chen, D. (1996). Parent-infant communication: Early intervention for very young children with visual impairment or hearing loss. *Infants and Young Children, 9*(1), 1–12.

Chen, D. (1997). *What can baby hear? Auditory tests and interventions for infants with multiple disabilities.* Baltimore, MD: Paul H. Brookes.

Downs, M. P. (1984). *The HEAR Kit System.* Englewood, CO: Bam World Markets.

Early Education Unit, Special Education Division. (1998). *Ear-resistible. Hearing test procedures for infants, toddlers, and preschoolers, birth through five years of age.* Sacramento: California Department of Education.

Elssmann, S. F., Matkin, N. D., & Sabo, M. (1987). Early identification of congenital sensorineural hearing impairment. *Hearing Journal, 40,* 13–17.

Fewell, R. R. (1983). Working with sensorily impaired children. In S. G. Garwood (Ed.), *Educating young handicapped children: A developmental approach* (2nd ed., pp. 235–280). Rockville, MD: Aspen Systems.

Flexer, C. (1994). *Facilitating hearing and listening in young children.* San Diego, CA: Singular Publishing Group.

Gatty, C. G. (1996). Early intervention and management of hearing in infants and toddlers. *Infants and Young Children, 9(1),* 1–13.

Hayes, D., & Northern, J. L. (1996). *Infants and hearing.* San Diego, CA: Singular Publishing Group.

Infant Hearing Resource. (1985). *Parent-infant communication. A program of clinical and home training for parents and hearing impaired infants* (3rd ed.). Portland, OR: Infant Hearing Resource, Good Samaritan Hospital and Medical Center.

Joint Committee on Infant Hearing. (1990). Position statement. *ASHA, 33,* 3–6.

Joint Committee on Infant Hearing. (1994). Position statement. *Audiology Today, 6*(6), 6–9.

Kramer, S. J., & Williams, D. R. (1993). The hearing-impaired infant and toddler: Identification, assessment, and intervention. *Infants and Young Children, 6(1),* 35–49.

Kile, J. E., & Beauchaine, K. L. (1991). Identification, assessment, and management of hearing impairment in infants and toddlers. *Infant-Toddler Intervention, 1,* 61–81.

Kile, J. E., Schaffmeyer, M. J., & Kuba, J. (1994). From assessment to management in infants and toddlers with unusual auditory behavior. *Infant-Toddler Intervention, 4,* 299–318.

Mahoney, T. M., & Eichwald, J. G. (1986). Model Program V: A high risk register by computerized search of birth certificates. In E. T. Swigart (Ed.). *Neonatal hearing testing* (pp. 223–240). San Diego, CA: College Hill Press.

National Institutes of Health. (1993). *Early identification of hearing loss in infants and young children: Consensus Development Conference on Early Identification of Hearing Loss in Infants and Young Children, 11*(1), 1–3.

Niswander, P. S. (1987). Audiometric assessment and management. In L. Goetz, D. Guess, & K. Stremel-Campell (Eds.), *Innovative program design for individuals with dual sensory impairments* (pp. 99–126). Baltimore, MD: Paul H. Brookes.

Northern, J. L., & Downs, M. P. (1991). *Hearing in children* (4th ed.). Baltimore, MD: Williams & Wilkins.

Nozza, R. J. (1994). The effects of mild hearing loss on infant auditory function. *Infant-Toddler Intervention, 4,* 285–298.

Pollack, D. (1985). *Educational audiology for the limited hearing infant and preschooler* (2nd ed.). Springfield, IL: Charles C Thomas.

Regenbogen, L. S., & Coscas, G. J. (1985). *Oculo-auditory syndromes.* New York: Masson.

Sobsey, D., & Wolf-Schein, E. G. (1991). Sensory impairments. In F. P. Orelove & D. Sobsey (Eds.). *Educating children with multiple disabilities: A transdisciplinary approach* (2nd ed.), (pp. 119–154). Baltimore, MD: Paul H. Brookes.

Steinberg, A. G., & Knightly, C. A. (1997). Hearing. Sounds and silences. In M. L. Batshaw (Ed.) *Children with disabilities* (4th ed., pp. 241–274). Baltimore, MD: Paul H. Brookes.

Trehub, A., Bull, D., & Schneider, B. (1981). Infants' detection of speech in noise. *Journal of Speech and Hearing Research, 24,* 202–206.

Watkins, S. (1989). *A model of home intervention for infant, toddler, and preschool aged multihandicapped sensory impaired children. The INSITE model.* Logan, UT: Hope.

Watt, M. R., Roberts, J. E., & Zeisel, S. A. (1993). Ear infections in young children: The role of the early childhood educator. *Young Children, 49,* 65–72.

7

Pediatric Audiology: Evaluating Infants

Caroline Abdala

Undetected and untreated hearing loss during childhood can be devastating to the emotional, social, and educational aspects of a child's and family's life. Recent evidence suggests that children with hearing losses that were identified before age 6 months have a better prognosis for developing language and speech and for progressing educationally than do children with similar hearing losses that are identified later (Yoshinaga-Itano, 1998). Thus, it is critical to identify hearing impairments and to give children with hearing loss appropriate support and aural rehabilitation as early in life as possible. This chapter describes the audiological procedures that are typically used to detect and evaluate hearing loss in children and introduces the reader to information that is important for understanding audiological concepts, techniques, results, and reports. For additional information on sound and hearing, see Chapter 6.

BASICS OF HEARING ASSESSMENT

The assessment of hearing and hearing loss is carried out by an audiologist, a hearing professional who records audiograms and conducts many other diagnostic and therapeutic procedures related to the auditory system. An audiologist must have a master's degree in communicative disorders or speech and hearing science and is required to complete a one-year supervised clinical fellowship before he or she can work independently.

Audiogram

An audiogram is the basic graph describing a person's hearing. It is a plot of a person's hearing threshold as a function of the *frequency* of a sound. The completed audiogram documents the individual's hearing threshold at each test frequency—that is, how loud a sound has to be at each test frequency before a person can reliably hear it. Figure 7.1 presents an example of an audiogram for an individual with normal hearing. The frequency in Hertz (Hz) is plotted on the horizontal axis of the audiogram, so that as one looks across the audiogram from left to right, the frequency goes from low to high. Generally, 250–2000 Hz are considered low frequencies, and 3000–8000 Hz are considered high frequencies. Frequency grossly refers to the pitch of the sound (high frequency is like a soprano flute, and low frequency is like a foghorn), but

Figure 7.1 PURE-TONE AUDIOGRAM: NORMAL HEARING

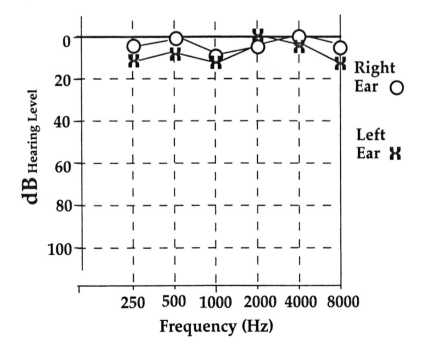

is defined in physical terms by the unit Hz, or vibrations per second. On the vertical axis of the audiogram, the level of the sound is plotted in decibels (dB). The decibel is the appropriate unit of measure for the *level* of sound, sometimes perceived as loudness.

As noted, to obtain a complete audiogram, hearing thresholds are determined for various frequencies. A hearing threshold is the lowest level of stimulus required to evoke a perception of sound by the listener. To generate an audiogram, *pure tones* (sounds that have energy at only one frequency) are presented, one at a time from 250 Hz to 8000 Hz. A pure-tone audiogram is completed using an *audiometer,* a calibrated instrument that presents tones of specified levels and frequencies through earphones or speakers. The audiologist is behind the audiometer in the test booth, and the patient is seated in the test booth, with a window usually between them. The test booth is a sound-treated room which significantly damps outside noise and maintains an ideal acoustic test environment. A pure tone is initially presented at a moderate-loud level, and the patient responds "I hear it" by raising his or her hand or pushing a button to let the audiologist know he or she can hear the sound. If the patient does not respond, the level of the tone is raised until it is audible to the patient. When the patient hears the tone, the threshold is *bracketed;* that is, the level of the tone is lowered again until he or she can no longer hear it and then increased slightly until the sound is barely audible. The standard technique for bracketing a person's response includes lowering the tone 10 dB and raising it 5 dB, although the techniques vary. The tone is presented around the threshold several times until the patient hears and responds to the tone about 50 percent of the time (the threshold level). Hearing thresholds are obtained for all the audiometric frequencies (250 Hz to 8000 Hz). Therefore, by recording an audiogram, the audiologist evaluates hearing in the low-, mid-, and high-frequency ranges.

As an example of how threshold is determined and graphed, if a person just hears a 1000 Hz sound 50 percent of the time at 5 dB hearing level (HL), the audiologist will find 1000 Hz along the horizontal axis and 5 dB along the vertical axis, then make an O (right ear) or an X (left ear) symbol where these two values intersect. The 0 dB value on the audiogram is not the absence of sound. It represents the average level at which young adults with the most normal hearing have thresholds at

the various audiometric frequencies (American National Standards In-
titute, 1969). Of course, the exact thresholds of people with normal
hearing vary; therefore 10 to 15 dB HL is usually considered normal.

In addition, with older children, *speech testing* is conducted when
possible. Speech testing, in which selected words, rather than pure
tones, are presented, can indicate the *level* at which speech is detected
(the *speech-reception* or *speech-awareness* thresholds). It can also
indicate how well speech is discriminated or perceived by generating
speech-discrimination scores.

It is important to recognize that the audiometric procedures and
the results described are conducted in the ideal test condition in which
a cooperative adult or child is able to indicate when a barely audible
sound is heard. This task requires concentration, a certain cognitive
level, motivation, physical integrity to press a button or raise a hand,
and the speech and language ability to say, "I hear it."

As the reader will see throughout this chapter, *pediatric* audiology
often involves less-than-ideal testing conditions and requires modified
techniques. Pediatric audiology with children who have multiple disabilities or pervasive developmental delays requires even more creative and
adaptive procedures than does standard pediatric audiology.

Assessing Hearing Loss

Regardless of the population tested, the goal of all audiometric testing
of infants and children is to identify a hearing loss early so as to initiate early intervention. Hearing loss present during the first 3 years of
life can be a severe obstacle to the acquisition of language and hence to
psychosocial and educational development (Menyuk, 1977; Osberger,
1986).

In children, a mild hearing loss is present when hearing thresholds
(plotted on an audiogram) are in the range of 15 to 30 or 35 dB HL; a
moderate loss is classified as 35 to 50 dB HL, and a moderate–severe
loss ranges from 55 to 70 dB HL. A severe hearing loss ranges from 70 to
85 or 90 dB HL, and a profound hearing loss is beyond 85 or 90 dB HL.
People who are called deaf typically have hearing thresholds at least in
the severe-to-profound range.

As was noted in Chapter 6, there are two basic types of hearing
loss: conductive and sensorineural. Conductive hearing loss involves

the pathway that conducts or transmits sound to the inner ear, such as the ear canal and middle ear. Sensorineural hearing loss involves damage to the inner ear, or nerve fibers of the auditory nerve. Conductive hearing loss can often be treated medically, whereas sensorineural hearing loss cannot be reversed, although rehabilitation with appropriate amplification is possible.

To determine whether a hearing loss is conductive or sensorineural, the audiologist obtains thresholds on the audiogram using two types of audiometric testing: air conduction and bone conduction. *Air-conduction* hearing thresholds are determined by presenting sound as acoustic energy through air waves. Air conduction testing is conducted through a transducer—a device that converts electrical energy into acoustic energy—in this case, either a conventional earphone or an insert earphone placed in the ear canal. Most people are familiar with earphones. An insert earphone is a newer device that is coupled to the ear with a tiny foam tip connected to a flexible tube and fits comfortably at the entrance of the ear canal. Many clinics have replaced their old, bulky earphones with insert phones. *Sound-field* testing, another way to present air-conducted sound, involves sounds presented through speakers inside the test booth. Since it stimulates both ears, it cannot provide information about ear-specific results.

Bone-conduction thresholds are determined by presenting sound through the physical vibration of a small object (called a bone vibrator) placed against the mastoid, the bone that protrudes slightly just behind the ear. Sound is actually transmitted from the bone vibrator through the vibration of skull bones, thus, the term, *bone conduction.* The results of air-conduction testing are influenced by conditions in the ear canal or middle ear. In contrast, bone-conduction testing bypasses the entire conductive pathway and directly stimulates the cochlea by vibrating the bones of the skull; this vibration stimulates the fluids in the cochlea and initiates the process of coding the sound so the brain can interpret it.

If hearing loss is present, and air- and bone-conduction thresholds are the same or within 5–10 dB of each other, the hearing loss is sensorineural and damage exists in the cochlea or nerve (see Figure 7.2). If the bone-conduction thresholds are better than the air-conduction thresholds, the loss is conductive (see Figure 7.3). For example, if air-

Figure 7.2   PURE-TONE AUDIOGRAM: MODERATE TO MODERATE-SEVERE SENSORINEURAL HEARING LOSS

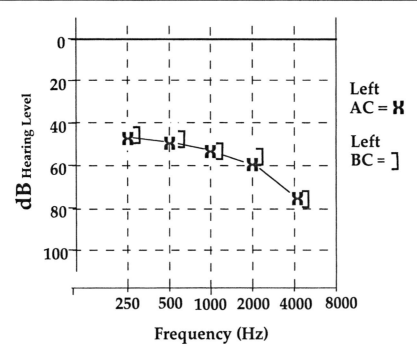

Left
AC = **X**

Left
BC = **]**

BC = bone conduction,
AC = air conduction

conduction thresholds indicate a mild level of hearing loss (45 dB HL) and bone-conduction thresholds appear normal (0 dB HL), the audiologist may surmise that something is wrong with the outer or middle ear, but that the cochlea is working perfectly well once sound gets through. Recall that detection of a conductive hearing loss indicates that something in the outer or middle ear is interfering with the transmission of sound into the inner ear.

Therefore, by obtaining audiogram thresholds by both air and bone conduction, it is possible to evaluate all three components of the ear to some extent: the outer ear (pinna and ear canal), the middle ear (tympanic membrane and middle ear bones, or *ossicles)* and the inner ear, or *cochlea.* A full audiological evaluation usually includes air- and bone-conduction thresholds.

Figure 7.3 PURE TONE AUDIOGRAM: MILD CONDUCTIVE HEARING LOSS

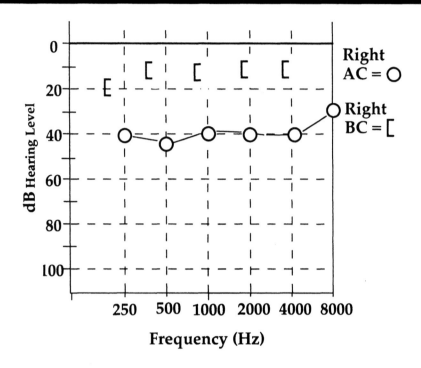

Immittance Tests

Immittance or impedance tests may be conducted, along with air- and bone-conduction thresholds to determine if a conductive loss is present. Impedance tests evaluate function of the middle ear system and include a *tympanogram*—a graph of how the tympanic membrane or ear drum moves as pressure is changed in the ear canal—and *acoustic reflexes*—contraction of tiny muscles in the middle ear that are sensitive to sound. A *type A* tympanogram is normal showing normal middle ear pressure. However, a tympanogram recorded from a dysfunctional middle ear is described as "flat" or "negative." Acoustic reflexes are absent when a hearing loss is of moderate degree or greater. Tympanograms and acoustic reflex thresholds, together with an air- and bone-conduction audiogram, aid in distinguishing a conductive from a sensorineural hearing loss.

PEDIATRIC AUDIOLOGY

Behavioral Observation Audiometry

An audiogram, such as the one described earlier and shown in Figure 7.1, can be recorded in ideal testing situations. It is not possible to obtain a full audiogram using conventional techniques, however, with young infants. Therefore, *behavioral observation audiometry* (BOA) is typically used with infants from birth to 5 or 6 months old. BOA involves the observation of auditory behavior in response to different sounds presented by the audiologist, with no conditioning, training, or reinforcement provided to the infant (Northern & Downs, 1991). Various sounds are presented, generally through a speaker, rather than an earphone, including bands of noise (like radio static); tones that change frequency slightly, or *warble;* and noisemakers, such as a rattle or bell. A variety of sounds are presented in an effort to assess both low- and high-frequency hearing. If the infant is a slow or poor responder, the audiologist may use the parent's voice or a favorite toy from home to elicit a response. Once the sound is presented, the audiologist watches for a time-locked response—a response within a given time after the sound is presented. If an infant began to suck a pacifier 30 seconds after the presentation of a sound, it would not be considered a response, but if he or she began to suck within 1 or 2 seconds of the sound, it may be considered a response.

Infants with multiple disabilities or any neurological impairment causing a generalized slowness of responding may need more time to respond. A slow response of this type can be detected by an astute audiologist in the first few moments of a test session. In addition, the parents or other caregivers can provide valuable information about an infant's typical response time and pattern to help the audiologist adapt the testing paradigm appropriately. Sidebar 7.1 presents more information about factors that affect audiometry with infants who have multiple disabilities.

Typical BOA responses include eye-widening, sucking or ceasing to suck if the infant was sucking before the sound was presented; startle response, with the entire body moving and the arms flung outward; crying or ceasing to cry; blinking; and arousal from sleep (Northern &

Sidebar 7.1 FACTORS TO CONSIDER WHEN CONDUCTING AUDIOMETRY FOR CHILDREN WITH MULTIPLE DISABILITIES

When an audiologist conducts behavioral observation audiometry (BOA) with very young children who have multiple disabilities, it is important for him or her to note that these children's responses to sound are likely to vary in latency from those of children who do not have disabilities. For example, a response from a child with multiple disabilities may be delayed beyond the typical response window. That is, normally, a child will show a behavioral response to sound within 1–2 seconds after hearing it, but if a child is neurologically impaired, large motor movement may be significantly slowed. Thus, an audiologist might increase the response window to include a 5-second time frame, for instance. The boundaries of this response window can be determined only by the audiologist at the time of the test on the basis of an individual child's pattern of response.

Children with multiple disabilities may have more subtle behavioral responses to sound than other children. One clue to identifying whether movement from a child with multiple disabilities is truly a response to sound is to look for consistency, for example, the child always responds with a slight head turn toward a sound and corresponding movement of the eyes after 4 seconds. It may be a subtle response, but the fact that it occurs the same way time after time is of value to the audiologist. This consistency gives the tester a clue that it is, in fact, a legitimate response to sound and may be the most robust response the child can give.

If the child has muscular dysfunction or related disabilities, the typical response behavior (such as a head turn or the placement of a block in a tub) may need to be modified to include a large motor activity that is appropriate for the child's particular ability. A child who cannot grasp a block because of fine motor difficulty or hypotonia may be instructed to touch a large character on an animated video monitor with any part of his or her hand or arm to indicate that he or she heard sound.

If a child has cognitive impairment that limits his or her ability to understand directions (such as "When you hear a sound, put a block into the box"), the instructions will need to be modified to ensure comprehension. Sometimes, simple imitation works well. The audiologist can act as the patient, listen for sound, present a high-level sound that all can hear, and then perform the desired behavior. A child will often mimic the behavior. It is critical, however, to be sure that the child understands that the response should be given *only* when the sound has been presented. It is important for the audiologist to "probe" the child's understanding prior to assuming that he or she is performing the task. This probing can be done by *not* presenting a tone during a given test interval and waiting to see if the child provides a response even in the absence of the test sound.

Downs, 1991). A speech-awareness threshold (SAT) is an important indicator of hearing. The SAT simply indicates that the infant responded (using any of the aforementioned behaviors) when the tester spoke to him or her through the speakers in the test booth. BOA is highly dependent on an audiologist's experience and skill in observing auditory behavior.

Even at the youngest ages, BOA can yield some valuable information about hearing. If the infant startles appropriately at 65 db HL, has a SAT of 40 dB HL, responds to both low- and high-frequency noisemakers at moderate levels of sound and the parent reports the infant's normal responding and interest in sound at home, it is likely that the infant has normal hearing in at least one ear (recall that no ear-specific testing is done by presenting sounds through speakers). Auditory thresholds and ear-specific information cannot be established with BOA. In addition, there is no way to differentiate between a conductive or sensorineural hearing loss with BOA because speakers, rather than a transducer (earphone or bone vibrator) on or around the ears present sound. Consequently, limited information is obtained. However, although follow-up testing with visual reinforcement audiometry (see the next section) when a child is older is still recommended, a normal, reliable BOA can rule out a profound hearing loss in both ears (deafness). This is critical information for both the audiologist and the parents. With a good BOA test, sufficient information may be obtained to guide decisions about managing the hearing loss, or to eliminate or confirm any urgency to continue diagnostic testing.

Although the general age guideline for BOA with normally developing infants is from birth to 6 months, if an infant is very delayed or unable to be conditioned for more advanced techniques, it may be necessary to perform an adaptation of BOA. A 1 year old or 18 month old, for example, may be observed for any response to sound. The reflexive behavior of the early months, such as a full-body startle, may be gone, but sounds can be presented and observations made to detect any response that is time locked to the sounds. This is a variation of BOA and may be used in the absence of a more appropriate technique.

If the results of BOA are abnormal or unreliable, further testing should be done. Whether further tests are performed immediately on the infant, or the audiologist decides to wait until the infant is old enough to perform a more complex and reliable test is unique to each situation and the many factors involved. For example, if the infant is not old enough for other behavioral tests, such as visual reinforcement audiometry, yet a parent or caregiver is concerned about the infant's hearing, a test of hearing that measures physiological responses to sound, such as the *auditory brainstem response* or *otoacoustic emissions,* should be considered. (These tests are discussed later in the chapter.) If BOA is ambiguous because of poor reliability, but neither parent nor caregiver is concerned about the infant's hearing and the infant shows normal auditory behavior, it may be decided to wait until the infant is old enough for conditioned audiometry. By age 6 months, most normally developing infants can be tested with conditioned visual reinforcement techniques.

The accompanying example of an audiological report describes a hearing test using BOA on an infant named Bobby Sanchez. In this case, BOA was used with and without hearing aids on to confirm the usefulness of Bobby's hearing aids. An audiological report such as this should present results clearly and give directions for further testing or observation. If any ambiguity is present, it is appropriate to call the audiologist and discuss the case further.

SAMPLE AUDIOLOGICAL REPORT USING
BEHAVIORAL OBSERVATION AUDIOMETRY

Audiological Report

Patient: Bobby Sanchez
Birthdate: 10-17-98
Age: 9 months

Background

Bobby is a 9-month-old boy who presents with a severe-to-profound hearing loss of unknown type at this time. He was referred by Ms. Gray at the Regional Center in Los Angeles and was originally seen at the Children's Auditory Research and Evaluation (CARE) Center of the House Ear Institute on 7-10-99 for an audiological evaluation. He currently wears binaural Phonak hearing aids he obtained at 6 months of age. He was seen today to confirm sound-field thresholds obtained on his initial visit.

Per the report, Bobby has Moebius syndrome, and had eye surgery for a visual impairment. An MRI revealed the lack of brainstem development. Bobby receives physical and occupational therapy twice a week at Casa Colina in Pomona. He is currently producing long vowels. His prenatal and birth histories were unremarkable. His mother reports that Bobby's twin sister does not have Moebius syndrome or any other medical conditions.

Audiological Evaluations

On 7-10-99, sound-field testing using behavioral observation audiometry (BOA) revealed a bilateral severe-to-profound hearing loss. The speech awareness threshold (SAT) was 65 dB HL. Eye widening and partial localization to sound were observed consistently in response to both low- and high-frequency bands of noise presented between 70 and 80 dB HL. Immittance testing revealed normal tympanograms in both ears and absent ipsilateral acoustic reflexes.

Bobby was fitted with hearing aids, and on 7-28-99 (today's test), aided sound-field testing using BOA was conducted. Aided BOA revealed responses at 55 dB HL with 500 Hz tones and 65 dB HL with 1000 Hz tones. Accepted responses included eye widening and attempts to localize sound with head turns in the sound field. Bobby became fatigued before more frequencies could be tested. The aided SAT was 40 to 45 dB HL.

Impressions and Recommendations

Bobby appears to receive good benefit from amplification. The exact extent of this benefit is difficult to assess owing to the lack of muscle tone in his head and neck and his inability to perform more specific and reliable audiometry tests, such as visual reinforcement audiometry. The following recommendations are made at this time:

1. gradually increase Bobby's use of the hearing aids with the ultimate goal of full-time use (two hours per day as a beginning target goal)

2. return in three months to obtain further audiological information

Please do not hesitate to contact us if you have any questions or if we could be of further assistance.

Visual Reinforcement Audiometry

Visual reinforcement audiometry (VRA) is conducted with normally developing infants ranging from age 6 months to approximately 2 years. (Thompson & Wilson, 1984; Thompson, Wilson, & Moore, 1979). Unlike BOA, which requires no conditioning or teaching, just observation, during VRA, a head-turn response is trained or conditioned to be a reliable indicator of whether an infant hears a sound. VRA is a much more reliable test than BOA.

With VRA, a high-level sound is initially presented through a speaker. The infant turns toward the sound, and a small animated animal in a plexiglas box under the speaker is turned on and marches or plays drums as a reward. At the beginning of the test, the infant may turn his or her head in response to the sound and have no idea that an animal will light up. However, once the infant reliably associates a head turn with the musical bunny or monkey, he or she is conditioned, or trained. The audiologist can then present a sound and withhold the animal reward until after the infant turns his or her head toward the sound.

As soon as the audiologist sees and reinforces several reliable head turns toward a loud sound, the level of the sound is lowered methodically to find the lowest sound at which the infant will reliably turn his or her head. This lowest sound is the infant's VRA threshold, however, not an ear-specific threshold. Because speakers are used, it will not be clear whether there is a unilateral (one ear only) hearing loss. If there is a difference in hearing between the ears, it is possible to determine hearing in the better ear only with sound-field VRA. In some cases, earphones are used to conduct VRA. It is important to read the notes on the audiogram to ascertain whether speakers or earphones were used. Speaker presentation is typically designated a sound-field response (SF) on a VRA audiogram.

VRA is conducted with tones of different frequency, with noise bands (staticlike sound made up of randomly presented acoustic energy) centered at certain frequencies, or even with voice or speech. The most interesting and complex sound is presented first to capture the infant's attention. At the University of Washington, where this technique was developed and refined, a noise band with frequencies centered on the speech frequencies (500 Hz–2000 Hz) is presented first (Thompson & Wilson, 1984). Thus, even if no other information is obtained, the audiologist gets an indication of hearing in a critical frequency range. Following this noise band, a high-frequency warble tone or noise band is presented. If a threshold is obtained at this frequency, the audiologist now has an indication of both low- to mid-frequency hearing and high-frequency hearing. Although this is not the same as having a pure-tone audiogram threshold from 250 Hz to 8000 Hz, it indicates hearing across the frequency range, so it is less likely that a high-frequency or low-frequency loss will be missed. Since the infant will give only a limited number of responses before he or she habituates to (loses interest in and stops responding to) VRA, hence it is critical to choose stimuli wisely. An average VRA procedure may last 1 hour with a "play" break in between. The two sample audiological reports of VRA with 2-year-old Fred Chan presented here represent two sequential attempts to obtain reliable results using VRA on a child who was difficult to test.

SAMPLE REPORTS OF VISUAL RESPONSE AUDIOMETRY (VRA) WITH A DIFFICULT-TO-TEST CHILD

Audiological Report

Patient: Fred Chan
Birthdate: 8-18-96
Age: 2 years
Test date: 7-15-98

Background

Fred was seen on 7-15-98 for an audiological evaluation. He was accompanied by his mother, who expressed concern about his speech and language development. She reported that Fred cannot follow directions and uses only the words, "no," "go," and "mama." Fred's medical history was unremarkable. Fred was the product of a full-term pregnancy and birth.

Audiological Evaluation

Fred was evaluated using visual reinforcement audiometry (VRA) in the sound field. Consistent head-turn responses were observed at a screening level of 20 dB HL from 250 Hz to 4000 Hz. Speech-detection responses were obtained at 10 dB HL. Tympanograms were within normal limits. Acoustic reflex thresholds could not be measured because of Fred's excessive movement.

Summary

The results are consistent with hearing sensitivity within the range of normal for at least the better ear. Fred's speech and language development should not be affected by his hearing ability.

Recommendations

1. Return for a speech and language evaluation
2. Return for an audiological evaluation in 6 months, when individual ear responses under earphones will be tested.

Test Date: 12-27-98

Background

Fred was seen on 12-27-98 for an audiological evaluation. He was accompanied by his mother. His previous audiological evaluation (7-15-98) was consistent with hearing sensitivity within normal limits at least in the better ear. No ear-specific results were obtained in the first evaluation. His mother stated that Fred has recently been diagnosed with autism. His medical history is significant for otitis media.

Audiological Evaluation

Fred was evaluated in the sound field using VRA techniques. He would not accept earphones. His responses to speech stimuli were within normal limits at least for the better ear. We were unable to assess fully Fred's responses to pure tones because Fred began to cry and cover his ears when the test stimuli were presented. Head-turn responses were seen at 50 dB HL for 500 Hz and 2000 Hz. Testing was discontinued because of Fred's distress.

Impressions

We could not rule out a hearing loss at this date; however, the previous audiological evaluation suggested hearing sensitivity within the range of normal in at least the better ear.

Recommendations

1. Fred's mother will practice listening to various sounds with Fred under earphones at home.

2. Fred should return in 6 months to attempt an audiological evaluation retest with earphones.

Most typically developing children are able to condition for VRA testing between 5 and 9 months of age. However, children who are delayed may not be able to turn their heads or understand the concept of pairing a sound with a reward. When an infant is unable to turn his or her head fully because of physical constraints, such as low muscle tone, cerebral palsy, or insufficient head control, adapted versions of VRA may be used. For example, if a partial head turn is consistent, it, too, can be trained as the appropriate response. Even consistent eye movement toward the source of sound can be conditioned. However, a *consistent* behavior must be associated with hearing to condition the response appropriately. If an eye movement is accepted during one trial and pulling at the ear is accepted during another trial, the test becomes similar to BOA, since the observation of any and all responses that are time-locked to the stimulus is accepted as an indication of hearing.

If an infant is visually impaired, the visual reinforcement task must be modified somewhat. Many infants with visual impairments are attracted to light, so a light may replace the animated toy as a reinforcer. If an infant does not perceive light, visual reinforcement provided with this technique is useless, and an alternative reinforcement must be found. The clinician may try a reward that is not visual, such as a tactile reward of some kind, to condition a response. For example, holding the child's hands and clapping together with him or her or simply patting the child on the arm. The keys to success with conventional VRA are that the animated, lighted animals motivate the infant as a reward and that the infant is physically able to turn his or her head toward the source of the sound. When either of these conditions is not present, VRA is not useful. In infants with multiple and severe disabilities that impair head turning or the perception of light it is probably most useful to consider a physiological test of hearing (discussed later in this chapter).

If an infant is physically able to spontaneously turn his or her head fully but cannot be reliability trained to do so, the VRA test is also inappropriate. For VRA to be successful, it is necessary for an infant who is severely cognitively delayed to pair the sound and the visual reward conceptually. Many children with cognitive delays will be able to do this task at a later chronological age then their typically developing peers; for instance, a child with Down syndrome may be 18 months old before he or she can do so. VRA may remain an appropriate test procedure for children with severe cognitive delays through age 8 or 9 years or throughout their lifetimes if they are unable to move on to a more advanced technique, such as *play audiometry* (discussed in the following section). Typically developing children become bored with the VRA task and reward between 2 and 3 years of age.

The results of VRA begin to resemble those of an audiogram if they are reliable and complete. That is, VRA thresholds are established at certain frequencies or within certain frequency ranges and can be plotted on an audiogram. It is essential to look closely at a VRA audiogram when interpreting it. If the VRA audiogram says sound-field (or SF), it means that the sounds were presented from a speaker and are not specific to any one ear. If it designates results for the right and left ears, earphones may have been used to obtain frequency-specific thresholds. An audiogram usually has a designated reliability rating as well. Poor and fair reliability ratings given by an audiologist should be suspect and are usually followed by recommendations for further testing. Good and excellent ratings suggest that the test was reliable and that the tester has confidence in his or her results. The accompanying report for Karen Garcia, a 16-month-old child with a hearing loss, describes a VRA hearing test that was conducted using insert earphones, rather than speakers, and produced reliable results. As with all audiological testing reports, VRA reports should be self-explanatory and give appropriate directions for future assessments.

SAMPLE REPORT OF VISUAL REINFORCEMENT AUDIOMETRY USING INSERT EARPHONES WITH A GIRL WHO HAS A PROFOUND HEARING LOSS

Audiological Report

Patient: Karen Garcia

Birthdate: 4-5-97

Age: 16 months

Background

Karen was referred to the CARE Center for audiological evaluation by California Hospital. She was recently diagnosed with significant hearing loss as determined by ABR results. Her mother reported that hearing loss was suspected by age 13 months and that ABR was first performed at that time, showing no response bilaterally, but Karen has a history of middle ear infection and had fluid in both ears when this test was performed. Karen had pressure equalization tubes inserted in both ears, and the ABR was then repeated by Lester Johnson on August 22. These results also indicated a profound level of hearing loss bilaterally.

Karen's parents reported no family history of hearing loss. Karen's motor development is delayed: at 16 months, she is now able to sit alone but does not stand alone. She is scheduled for an evaluation of her motoric function at the local regional center. Her parents report that she did babble for a period but stopped doing so at about 9 months and that she now communicates her needs by pointing and vocalizing.

Audiological Evaluation

Karen was tested behaviorally with insert ear phones using VRA. Clear head turns to voice and pure tone stimuli were consistent and reliable. In her left ear, responses to voice were seen at 100 dB HL. Questionable head turns were seen at 105 dB HL at 250 Hz and at 115 dB HL at 500 Hz, and a repeatable and reliable response was seen at 120 dB HL at 1000 Hz. In her right ear, responses to voice were seen at 85 dB HL, and response to tones ranged from 95 dB HL to 120 dB HL between 500 and 4000 Hz, with best thresholds being at 1000 Hz and 2000 Hz. There was no response at 250 Hz.

An otoscopic examination revealed the presence of PE tubes in both ears. An examination by a physician indicated that these tubes are open and functional bilaterally.

Impressions and Recommendations

Karen has a profound bilateral sensorineural hearing loss, with better thresholds in the right ear. There is no evidence of middle-ear dysfunction.

Karen should be fitted with hearing aids as soon as possible. Toward this end, ear impressions were taken, and the earmolds will be sent directly to the parents so they will have them for the hearing aid evaluation scheduled in September.

Information on various support facilities and educational facilities, including the John Tracy Clinic and TRIPOD, was given to Mr. and Ms. Garcia. Mr. and Ms. Garcia will contact their local school district regarding available early intervention programs.

Thank you for the opportunity to see this nice family. Please do not hesitate to contact us if you have any questions or if we can be of further assistance.

VROCA and TROCA

Finally, there are two alternative forms of testing for older infants and toddlers who are not yet mature enough for the more sophisticated play audiometry task (reviewed in the next section). These tests are used infrequently, but it is a good idea to be familiar with them in case they are mentioned in a hearing report. TROCA, or *tangible reinforcement operant conditioned audiometry*, and VROCA, or *visual reinforcement operant conditioned audiometry*, involve operant conditioning. They are typically lever-push paradigms in which a child ideally wears headphones and manipulates the reward himself or herself by pushing a button when the sound is heard and getting an edible treat or a visual toy reinforcer if the response is correct. More recently, a computer keyboard or mouse has been used to replace the lever, and the computer screen provides a visual reinforcement.

Play Audiometry

Between 18 months and 2 1/2 years is a transitional period during which children may either be able to give true audiometric thresholds through play activity or may require continued use of VRA or a combination of the two techniques, depending on their emotional, cognitive, and physical maturity. Typically developing 2 to 3 year olds are particularly challenging because they are often "between" techniques. Four and five year olds may be able to perform play audiometry, but maintaining their focus and attention on the task is challenging. Beyond about age 5 in typically developing children, the task of obtaining an audiogram becomes easier and can be comparable to testing adults.

Play audiometry involves a task, such as throwing a block in a tub, inserting a wooden peg in a pegboard, putting a piece in a puzzle, or moving a game piece, when a sound is heard. Whichever task is used, it must never be so interesting that the child loses interest in the real task of listening for a sound and begins to play the game without waiting for the sound. Play audiometry is conducted using earphones or insert earphones and thus yields ear-specific thresholds.

The task requires several skills that younger children do not possess. It is necessary to concentrate (to listen intently for very low-level near-threshold sounds), to be patient (to wait for the tone several seconds or more between presentations), to be motivated (to want to please the tester or parent), to cooperate (to be willing to accept earphones or insert phones for ear-specific information), and to be autonomous to some degree (to be able to accomplish a task independently without a parent's help or presence in some cases).

The play audiogram is filled out in the same way as a full adult audiogram; that is, a threshold is obtained at each frequency by varying the level of sounds up and down. The initial level of sound is high, so that the response is trained easily and the tester is certain that the initial sounds are heard. The child will need guidance at first and may need the audiologist or assistant (sometimes the parent will act as an assistant) to hold a block, for example, at the earphone until the sound is presented and then to guide it into the bucket. After several guided trials, the audiologist steps back and allows the child to perform the same task independently when the sound is heard. The audiologist gives praise for each correct response. It is critical to vary the time interval between trials to catch a child who plops the block in the bucket methodically every 5 seconds, sound or no sound. The sample audiometric report presented here from 2 1/2-year-old Billy Gee describes an audiogram obtained through play audiometry.

SAMPLE AUDIOLOGICAL REPORT
USING PLAY AUDIOMETRY

Audiological Report

Patient: Billy Gee

Birthdate: 10-16-96

Age: 2 years, 6 months

Background

Billy was seen on January 20, 1999, for an audiological evaluation. He was referred to the CARE Center by Children's Institute International because of a language delay. Children's Institute International is a foster care service center that places children with appropriate caregivers and houses children during transitional periods. Billy's developmental and medical histories were not available, although it was noted that he has a history of anemia.

Audiological Evaluation

Billy was tested with earphones and via a bone vibrator using play audiometry. He was conditioned to put a wooden block into a bucket each time he heard a sound. The reliability of the test was considered good. Billy gave consistent and reliable responses throughout the test session.

A speech-awareness threshold was obtained at 15 dB HL in the right ear and at 5 dB HL in the left ear. Air-conduction thresholds were present between 20 dB HL and 30 dB HL in the right ear and between 15 dB HL and 30 dB HL in the left ear for the frequencies of 500, 1000, 2000, and 4000 Hz. Bone-conduction testing revealed thresholds between 0 dB HL and 10 dB HL at these same frequencies for at least the better ear.

Tympanometry indicated abnormal middle ear function bilaterally, with flat tympanograms and absent acoustic reflexes.

Impressions and Recommendations

Air conduction results indicate a mild bilateral hearing loss. Bone conduction results, as well as tympanometry, indicate that the loss is conductive. It is recommended that Billy be seen by a physician for a medical evaluation to determine a proper course of treatment and that he return to the CARE center for a repeat audiological evaluation after treatment to see if the problem has been remediated. Because there is concern about Billy's language development, it is also recommended that he be evaluated by a speech-language therapist.

Please do not hesitate to contact us if you have any further questions or if we can be of further assistance.

Different children need different amounts of training for this task. Sometimes a child will attempt the task in one session and be unsuccessful because of poor concentration, anxiety, or another factor. The audiologist may notice the child's lack of success or anxiety quickly and use the remainder of the session for practice, making the test appear fun and self-motivating. The child may then be sent home with instructions for the parents to practice the "wait, listen, and put-the-block-in-the-bucket" task and then come back another time for continued testing.

Often, even if children learn the task the first day and provide reliable thresholds, they may not have sufficient attention spans for all the frequencies to be tested in both ears. Therefore, the audiologist must be wise in his or her choice of frequencies to test. For example, if a play audiogram has only 4000 Hz and 1000 Hz information in each ear, it may mean that the tester chose a low- and a high-frequency sound to present to each ear first before he or she sought detailed information from either ear. This partial audiogram is helpful but should always be followed up with a full hearing test at all frequencies when a child's attention and ability matures.

Age Appropriateness for Specific Tests

Although each test has a designated age range for typically developing children, a child who has multiple disabilities and a chronological age of 10 or 12 years old may not be able to perform standard audiometry. Such children often do well with play audiometry, VROCA, TROCA, or even VRA. Because these tasks are simple and entertaining, offer immediate reinforcement, and follow a simple conditioning paradigm, they may be much more effective in testing a 10-year-old child with Down syndrome, for instance, than may a conventional audiometric paradigm. Likewise, a child with attention deficit disorder may be more motivated by play audiometry than by conventional audiometry, even though his or her chronological age would suggest otherwise.

The key to successful pediatric audiology is to consider a child's developmental abilities, not just chronological age, before choosing a test technique. If an early interventionist is familiar with a child and his or her limitations and abilities and sees that the child is being tested with physical or cognitive tasks that are beyond these abilities, it is important to call the audiologist and discuss this concern. An audiologist has experience and knowledge of the auditory system and effective testing paradigms, whereas the early interventionist knows the child's cognitive and physical capacities. Consequently, a team approach for testing difficult-to-evaluate children with multiple disabilities is ideal.

The standard for audiological testing is a behavioral response to sound. Consequently, all the techniques described here may be utilized at various times to evaluate a child's auditory system appropriately. However, there are cases when a behavioral response cannot be obtained and more objective, physiological techniques to evaluate the auditory system must be used. The following section describes the two primary physiological tests of hearing.

PHYSIOLOGICAL TESTS OF HEARING

There are many reasons why an infant or young child may not be able to respond behaviorally to sound in a reliable manner. First, BOA can be a difficult test to interpret because it is simply observation and is highly dependent on the tester's experience. An infant may respond to sound but may not give responses that a particular audiologist considers consistent and reliable. BOA alone is not generally considered a highly reliable indicator of hearing, so some audiologists may not feel comfortable with the results, even if they are consistent. Therefore, if an infant is less than 6 months old, BOA is ambiguous or borderline normal, and the caregivers express a concern about the infant's hearing, physiological tests may be performed.

An older infant (more than 6 months) being tested with VRA may habituate to the sounds too quickly and stop turning his or her head, resulting in an incomplete test. A child who is visually impaired may be too old for BOA, unstimulated by VRA, and too young for play audiometry.

A child with cognitive delays may find the tasks too complex or demanding. There are many reasons why a newborn, young child, or child with multiple disabilities of any age may not be able to provide behavioral indications of hearing. In these cases, the audiologist uses objective physiological tests of hearing.

It is critical to understand that neither of the two tests described are actually "hearing" tests. Hearing is typically measured as a volitional response indicating that the sound has been detected. Neither the auditory brainstem response nor otoacoustic emissions involve volitional responses and so are not true measures of hearing. They are extremely useful, however, because they *correlate with hearing* in a systematic way and hence allow for predictive statements about hearing.

Auditory Brainstem Response

The auditory brainstem response (ABR) is a test of how the hearing nerve responds to sound as it exits the inner ear and how groups of nerve fibers in the auditory pathway above the cochlea respond to and conduct sound toward the brain. It does not involve any auditory structures beyond the brainstem, such as the cortex (brain). Other terms used for this same test are brainstem evoked response (BSER) or brainstem auditory evoked response (BAER). These terms are often used by physicians, but the accepted terminology in audiology and hearing science is ABR.

ABR Procedure

The ABR is used for either hearing or neurological evaluation. This section focuses on its application to hearing. An ABR can be done on a patient of any age and, including preparation time, may range from 1 to 2 hours in duration. To record the ABR, the patient must remain still, so it is nearly impossible to test most infants and children with the ABR unless they are sleeping. However, an adult or older, cooperative child may lie quietly and be tested while awake. Children aged 3 months to 4 or 5 years are usually given a mild sedative, such as chloral hydrate, to help them sleep. Beyond 4 or 5 years, the test is often conducted during natural, unsedated sleep. Especially when a child will not be sedated, the evaluation is scheduled for a time that coincides with naptime, and the parent is instructed to deprive the child of sleep the night before, to maximize the likelihood that the child will sleep while the test is being conducted and to prevent the need for repeated ABRs.

Often chloral hydrate is not successful as a sedative for children who are developmentally delayed or multiply disabled because it frequently causes hyperactivity, so the children do not sleep or even calm down enough for the test to be conducted. In addition, physicians may consider it too risky to administer sedatives to children with severe medical problems. There are some optional medications to induce sleep, and they should be discussed with the child's physicians before the test date. The reason sleep and/or stillness is so important for ABR testing is that the movement of muscles interferes greatly with the detection of the tiny neural responses being generated by the auditory system.

The ABR is recorded by applying noninvasive surface *electrodes* (measuring devices that detect neural activity below the skin, but they do not transmit any electrical activity *to* a child) on strategic spots on the head. Many clinics use disposable electrodes that are nothing more than stickers composed of the appropriate metal for detecting electrical energy and coated with a conductive gel, and others use "cup" electrodes (small, concave metal circles that are filled with a conductive gel and taped to the skin). Before either type of electrode is applied, the skin is cleaned with gauze and a special paste. This procedure is not painful and ensures good contact between the electrode and the skin, which is crucial because the neural activity that must be detected lies below the skin in the auditory nerve and brainstem pathways.

Once the electrodes are in place, an earphone is put over the ear or an insert phone is placed in the ear canal, and rapid clicklike sounds are presented. The electrodes detect, and the ABR equipment records, several thousands of the tiny neural firings of the auditory nerve and brainstem as they traverse the auditory pathway toward the brain. Although the ABR is typically evoked with air-conducted sound, it can also be recorded with bone-conduction stimulation. Fewer clinics perform bone-conduction ABR, although it provides valuable information when middle ear dysfunction is suspected.

The click sounds used to record an ABR do not offer frequency-specific information because they contain energy at a broad range of frequencies. They normally reflect hearing in the mid- and high-frequency areas (2000 Hz–6000 Hz). When an estimation of the audiogram must be made on the basis of the ABR alone, it is helpful to obtain frequency-specific information by using a low-frequency *tone burst* (a tone with a very short duration) instead of just a click. Typically a low-frequency tone burst (500 Hz), is used to obtain frequency-specific information after an ABR click threshold has been obtained. If an audiologist obtains a click ABR threshold and an ABR threshold for low-frequency tone bursts, he or she will have an indication of both low- and high-frequency hearing. This is useful information on which to base intervention strategies until behavioral responses can be obtained. In children with multiple disabilities, who will never be able to provide behavioral indications of hearing, the ABR is relied on heavily to fit hearing aids or other assistive listening devices. In these instances, it is especially important to obtain ABRs with both the click and low-frequency tones. Not all clinics are able to perform frequency-specific ABR tests, so it is important to review the need for these tests with an audiologist before an appointment is made at a specific clinic.

Analysis of the ABR

The ABR is displayed on a computer monitor as a series of waveforms that the audiologist can analyze and interpret. Figure 7.4 presents an example of ABR waveforms recorded from a child with normal hearing. ABR waveforms are judged in several ways, and the following terms are often included in ABR reports:

1. *ABR absence or presence:* If the cochlea is not functioning and the child is deaf, the clicks presented to elicit the ABR will not stimulate the cochlea. If the cochlea is not stimulated, the nerve fibers will not be stimulated, and an ABR will not be detected, even at high click levels. The failure to detect an ABR at high levels of sound is called a *flat* or *absent ABR.*

2. *ABR threshold:* The ABR threshold is to the lowest sound level at which an ABR is reliably detected. It gives an indication of the *degree* of hearing loss. Figure 7.5 shows the results of a child with ABR thresholds of 40 dB HL in each ear. In people with normal hearing, as in the example in Figure 7.4 the ABR click threshold is present at 0–20 dB HL.

3. *Latency:* Latency is the typical *time* between the presentation of a click and the appearance of the ABR waveform. *Delayed latency* may mean hearing loss or neurological problems.

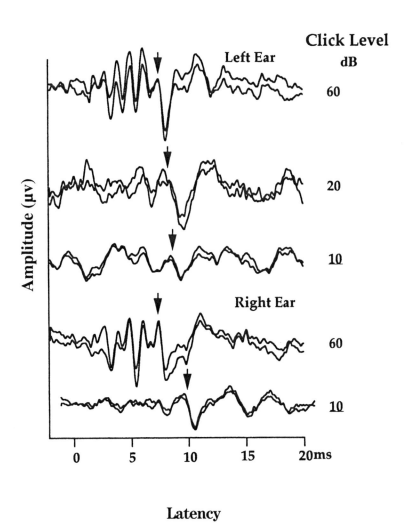

Figure 7.4 TYPICAL ABR WAVEFORMS FOR A CHILD WITH NORMAL HEARING

▼ = ABR Wave V

Click Level dB

Left Ear

60

20

10

Right Ear

60

10

Amplitude (μv)

0   5   10   15   20ms

Latency

ABR thresholds are 10 dB bilaterally. The arrows mark the most prominent ABR peak, wave I, down to threshold. Each peak represents a response from gross regions of the auditory brainstem pathway. The presence, amplitude, and latency of each peak determines whether the ABR is normal.

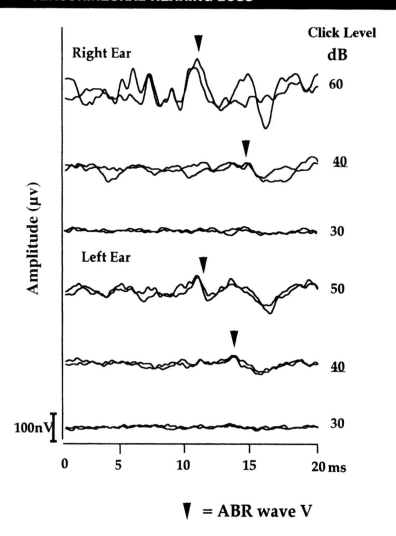

Figure 7.5 ABR WAVEFORMS WITH MILD SENSORINEURAL HEARING LOSS

Right Ear

Left Ear

Click Level dB

60

40

30

50

40

30

100nV

0   5   10   15   20 ms

Amplitude (µv)

▼ = ABR wave V

ABR thresholds are abnormally high; 40 dB bilaterally. The arrows mark the most prominent ABR peak, wave V, down to threshold. Each peak represents a neural response from gross regions of the auditory-brainstem pathway. The presence, amplitude, and latency of each peak determines whether the ABR is normal.

4. *Peak amplitude:* Amplitude refers to how *big* each waveform is. It is not used as commonly as latency to judge an ABR because it is variable.

5. *Morphology:* Morphology refers to the *shape* of a waveform and how normal the wave looks. Typically, two ABR waveforms are collected at the same click level to check how well they replicate one another. When an audiological report states, "Good morphology," it means that the waveforms replicate well, look typical, and are not contaminated by too much noise.

When evaluating an ABR test, the audiologist always uses age-appropriate standards or norms through approximately 18–24 months of age. These standards are used because the infant ABR is typically delayed and more poorly defined than the adult ABR. Beyond 2 years of age, ABR latency, morphology, and amplitude are adultlike (Salamy & McKean, 1976). The audiological evaluation for Susie O'Brian that is presented here is a typical ABR report for a 3-year-old child. This report also includes an otoacoustic emission evaluation, which is discussed in the following section. The formats of reports vary from clinic to clinic. Regardless of the format, a report should be clear and concise and contain a case history, results, diagnostic impressions, and recommendations. After reading an ABR report, an individual should understand the test results and what they mean and what the next course of action should be. If there is any ambiguity in the report, it is important to call the audiologist and ask for clarification.

SAMPLE REPORT OF A TYPICAL AUDITORY BRAINSTEM RESPONSE

Audiological Report

Patient: Susie O'Brian
Birthdate: 7-24-96
Test Date: 8-22-99

Brief History

Susie was referred for auditory brainstem response and otoacoustic emissions testing by the John Tracy Clinic. A sound-field audiogram performed at the John Tracy Clinic suggested normal hearing. However, Susie's mother reports that Susie is generally unresponsive to sound and, at age 3, she has no oral language. Susie points to objects she wants or directs her mother toward them. Ms. O'Brian began to be concerned about Susie's language development about eight months ago. Around that time, the family moved, and Susie suffered an apparently mild head injury; her mother stated that she had no concussion or fracture, according to the attending physician and that no X-rays were taken. A few months earlier, Susie was beginning to use a few words like "mama" and "bye-bye," but she stopped speaking about one year ago. She was seen recently by a developmental psychologist, who found her to have a severe communication delay.

Susie has a history of frequent ear infections during the winter months that have been treated with antibiotics. According to Ms. O'Brian, Susie's physical development has been normal. Ms. O'Brian also stated that Susie's behavior is becoming a problem; Susie bites when angry and bangs her head when frustrated.

Audiological Evaluation

Auditory Brainstem Response (ABR)

Susie was sedated with chloral hydrate and slept quietly throughout the test. Active electrodes were placed on the vertex, C7, and ipsilateral mastoid with a ground on the contralateral mastoid.

Click ABR: Activity was filtered from 100 Hz to 3000 Hz (12 dB/octave). Responses were elicited with 100 μs pulses sent to ER-3 insert earphones to produce rarefaction click stimuli presented at 25/sec. Averaging was performed on a Neuroscan evoked-potential computer system. Each response was averaged for 6,144 accepted sweeps or until the Fsp value (a statistical technique used to detect the presence of a true response) reached 2.25, corresponding to a 95 percent confidence level.

Tone-burst ABR: Activity was filtered from 30 Hz to 1000 Hz. Short-duration 500 Hz tones were presented at a rate of 25/sec with ipsilateral notched noise 20 dB below the signal level. Averaging was continued until noise reached 20 nv or until the response was visually detected by the clinician.

Otoacoustic Emissions: Transient otoacoustic emissions (TEOAE) were measured in response to click stimuli of 87 dB SPL. Distortion product otoacoustic emissions (DPOAE) were measured with 70 dB SPL equilevel stimuli.

Results

ABRs to click stimuli are clearly identifiable at 10 dB HL in both ears. Responses to 500 Hz tone-burst stimuli were present at 30 dB HL in both ears as well.

TEOAEs were present in the right ear, though not robust, but were absent in the left ear. DPOAEs were also present in the right and absent in the left ear. Emissions are expected to be absent in the presence of a hearing loss greater than 35 dB–45 dB, or when middle ear dysfunction is present, even if hearing is within normal limits.

Impedance testing revealed negative middle ear pressure in the left ear and normal pressure in the right ear. Acoustic reflexes were normal in the right and either absent or weak in the left ear.

Summary and Impressions

The results of today's evaluation are consistent with normal hearing sensitivity in both ears. There is no evidence of hearing loss that could be handicapping to speech and language development. The otoacoustic emission results in the left ear are consistent with negative middle ear pressure in this ear, as OAEs are often absent with middle ear dysfunction. Susie was referred to an otolaryngologist for treatment.

A speech-language evaluation was scheduled at the CARE center. Ms. O'Brian was referred back to the developmental psychologist for follow-up. A behavioral audiological evaluation should be scheduled following the speech-language evaluation, to determine frequency-specific thresholds and to observe Susie's responsiveness to auditory stimuli. Otoacoustic emission testing should be repeated when Susie's middle ear pressure is normal bilaterally.

Thank you for referring this patient to the Children's Auditory Research and Evaluation Center of the House Ear Institute. Please do not hesitate to contact me if you have any questions or if I can be of further assistance.

Hearing Screening and the ABR

The ABR has proved to be useful for screening the hearing of premature neonates and other neonates who are at risk of hearing loss (Folsom, 1990). An ABR screening test is much shorter than the full diagnostic test described earlier. If a newborn has "passed" an ABR screening at birth, this indicates that he or she had a present ABR with appropriate latency at either 30 or 40 dB HL (typical screening levels). By screening at these levels, the ABR identifies the great majority of hearing losses in neonates; the few losses that may slip by unidentified (false negatives) are mild sensorineural or conductive losses. In general, if an infant "passed" the ABR screening at birth, there is no high risk of hearing loss, and if the parent reports the infant's responsiveness to sound at home, then there may be no need to conduct a full diagnostic ABR at a later time. However, if an infant is at risk of a progressive hearing loss (one that gets worse over time) or shows inappropriate or absent responses to sound at home, it may be necessary to perform a full diagnostic ABR to search for hearing thresholds, even if the screening ABR at birth indicated a "pass."

Unfortunately, hearing screening of newborns is not routinely performed in all hospitals in the United States. If a hospital has a hearing screening program, it is often applied only to infants who are at a high risk for hearing loss ("Guidelines," 1989). High-risk factors include facial deformities, a family's history of hearing loss, and the administration of drugs that damage the ear (ototoxic drugs). An early interventionist should obtain the hospital's records of hearing screening, rather than rely only on a parent's report, since the parents are often not certain whether a hearing screening was done in the hospital before their newborn was discharged.

Infants and Children with Neurological Impairments

In infrequent cases when a child has multiple disabilities and has neurological dysfunction, the ABR may be difficult to obtain. If the neurological system is so impaired that many neural fibers of the hearing nerve cannot fire in a time-coordinated fashion, an ABR cannot be detected. Before assuming that hearing loss is present because of an absent ABR, the audiologist would need to take neurological dysfunction into consideration. Demyelination diseases, such as multiple sclerosis, may affect ABR morphology and latency adversely. Although abnormalities in latency and morphology are often indicative of hearing loss, in this case they would simply be consistent with multiple sclerosis. Consequently, it is critical to consider all of a child's problems when evaluating the abnormality or normalcy of the ABR, since some nonauditory problems that may affect the ABR negatively need to be taken into consideration before a hearing loss can be diagnosed on the basis of the results of this test.

The disadvantages of the ABR are minimal, especially in relation to the information gained. Administering sedation involves a small risk, and a few children have allergic reactions to the conductive gel or paste. There are no other known risks. Most audiological clinics routinely perform this test, but some clinics have staff audiologists with specific expertise in the ABR, and offer frequency-specific testing and bone-conduction ABR, if necessary. Also, some clinics specialize in pediatric assessments, so their audiologists have more experience and expertise with children who have multiple disabilities or are otherwise difficult to test. It is important to consider these factors when recommending an evaluation for an infant or young child.

Finally, although the ABR is an excellent auditory test, careful audiologists recommend follow-up behavioral testing even after normal results are found on an ABR and definitely after abnormal results are detected. It is important to remember that the gold-standard of hearing involves a behavioral response confirming that an infant or young child is hearing sounds. Even after an ABR has been obtained, it is important to strive for this goal. However, since this goal is impossible to achieve with some children with multiple disabilities, the ABR may be the only indicator of normal hearing or hearing loss. Thus, as was mentioned earlier, in these cases, the results of the ABR are relied on to fit hearing aids or other assistive listening devices.

In summary, the ABR is an important hearing assessment option for certain infants and young children because it requires no volitional response, yet gives an indication of hearing status in a noninvasive fashion by evaluating the conduction of sound through the hearing nerve and hearing pathways of the brainstem. Since its discovery and application in the early 1970s, the ABR has been an invaluable tool for estimating audiograms in cases where an estimation of hearing threshold is necessary, yet children are unable or unwilling to provide behavioral indexes of their hearing. It is a safe test and has been used clinically for over 20 years.

Otoacoustic Emissions

Otoacoustic emissions (OAEs) are sounds produced by a normally functioning inner ear, and measures of OAEs represent the most recently developed physiological test to assess hearing. Unlike the ABR, OAEs assess only cochlear or inner-ear function. The hearing nerve or brainstem are not involved in the testing.

To understand OAEs, it is important to understand a little bit about how the cochlea works. For many years, the cochlea was thought to be a passive system that received and coded sound and then sent it up the nervous system to the brain. It is now known that the cochlea is an active participant in the coding of sound. A signal comes in and vibrates the delicate *basilar membrane* in the cochlea; then the cochlea activates its own energy source and amplifies the movement of the basilar membrane. During this amplification, some of the energy that is generated escapes, like a leak. This escaped energy travels in reverse, back through the middle ear and toward the ear canal. The energy is called an otoacoustic emission (Kemp, 1978). If a sensitive microphone is put into the ear canal, this energy can be recorded. Inner ears that are functioning normally produce these sounds.

There are two types of clinically applied OAEs: *transient,* or *click-evoked, OAEs* (TEOAE), and *distortion product OAEs* (DPOAEs). Both types of OAEs tell something about the ear. They differ primarily because different types of sound are used to evoke them and they represent different frequencies. For example, a TEOAE is evoked with a click. The DPOAE is evoked with tones. Both types of OAEs reflect normal processes in the cochlea and can be thought of as "echoes" or energy that is leaking from the normally functioning cochlea.

OAE Analysis

Both TEOAEs and DPOAEs are related to hearing loss. When hearing loss exceeds about 35–45 dB (a mild loss), the cochlear amplifier is no longer functional, and OAEs are not present. Consequently, OAEs can be a reliable indicator of hearing loss only if the loss is greater than mild. A person can have a mild hearing loss and still have OAEs; however, they are usually smaller in amplitude and fairly sparse. Figures 7.6 and 7.7 display typical, normal TEOAE results. Figure 7.6 displays the "echo" from the ear as a function of time. Traces a and b are two simultaneously collected waveforms that should be highly replicable when the cochlea is normal. Figure 7.7 displays the same echo as a function of frequency. The noise is also displayed in Figure 7.7 so that the audiologist can clearly distinguish TEOAE energy from irrelevant energy. If the TEOAE energy rises sufficiently above the noise, the cochlea is functioning normally. Figure 7.8 displays normal DPOAE results and the DPOAE energy from the cochlea as a function of tone frequency. The important feature of this graph is the separation of the DPOAE (open circles) from the black region (noise). If the DPOAE is sufficiently greater than the noise, the cochlea is functioning normally. A report should always be included with these graphs to interpret the results.

At this point in audiology and hearing science, both TEOAEs and DPOAEs basically give present/absent categorical information only. When OAEs are present, hearing is either normal (from 0 to 15 dB HL on the

Figure 7.6   TEOAE TIME WAVEFORM

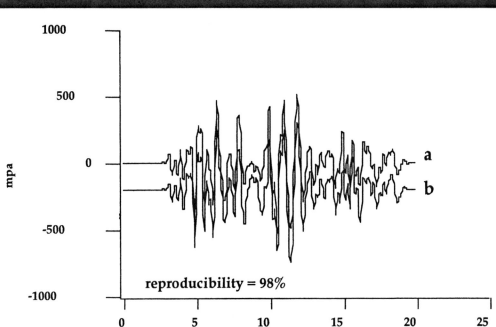

audiogram), or a mild hearing loss may be present (up to 40 dB HL on the audiogram). When OAEs are absent, a moderate to profound hearing loss may be present. OAEs do not discriminate among degrees of hearing loss or provide information about the configuration of hearing loss (such as high-frequency versus flat hearing loss). Consequently, if OAEs are absent, it simply indicates that hearing loss is present without yielding any information about the *degree* of hearing loss. Therefore, it is usually necessary to conduct an ABR as a follow-up or a behavioral test if the person is able to participate in it.

Because OAE results are categorical (evaluated as being absent or present), they cannot estimate thresholds as the ABR can. If a person is interested in getting threshold information on an infant or child who cannot cooperate with behavioral measures, an ABR, not OAEs, will provide this information. However, if the audiologist wants to rapidly rule out hearing loss or deafness, normal OAEs may provide this information quickly and effectively. A combination of ABR and OAEs provides

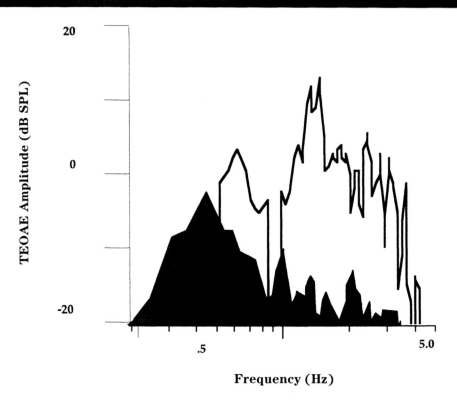

Figure 7.7   TEOAE NOISE (BLACK REGION) AND RESPONSE (WHITE OUTLINED IN BLACK) FOR A CHILD WITH NORMAL HEARING

the most comprehensive evaluation because the ABR focuses on hearing nerve and brainstem conduction and OAEs focus on cochlear function.

Advantages of OAE Testing

Although, as noted, there are many limitations to OAE results, there are some practical advantages as well. There are no electrodes to be applied, and the test itself may often be conducted in just 5–10 minutes. The speed of testing is a critical factor with babies in natural sleep or lightly sedated young children. Also, OAEs are completely noninvasive, require no skin preparation, and cause no discomfort.

OAEs are becoming a popular tool for screening the hearing of newborns in hospitals prior to discharge because of the factors just mentioned and the short time it takes to administer them. Furthermore,

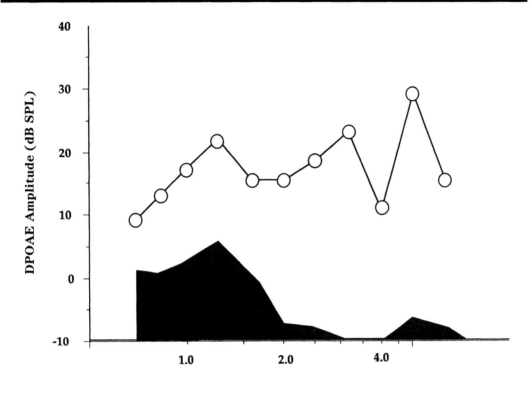

Figure 7.8   DP-GRAM-GENERATED FROM DISTORTION PRODUCT OTOACOUSTIC EMISSIONS FOR A CHILD WITH NORMAL HEARING

they can answer some preliminary questions about hearing and often eliminate the need for extensive testing. For example, if they are present, robust, and clearly normal, and a parent or early interventionist does not have a real concern about hearing and auditory function, it may not be necessary to perform an ABR.

Middle Ear Problems

One critical factor must be considered when an audiologist makes diagnostic decisions based on OAEs: The middle ear must be clear of fluid or infection for OAEs to be detected. Recall that the sound emitted from the ear travels backward from the inner ear, through the middle ear, and out into the ear canal. If the middle ear has an infection or fluid, the sound is often absorbed and becomes so soft that it is no longer detectable in the ear canal. Therefore, if an infant has a middle ear infection and OAEs are not present, it is impossible for an audiologist to know whether OAEs are being generated by the ear but cannot be detected because of the condition of the middle ear or are not generated by the inner ear because of a sensory hearing loss.

Because the condition of the middle ear is so important for OAE testing, an audiologist often conducts an otoscopic examination or a test of middle ear function called an *immittance test* (discussed earlier in this chapter) to evaluate the status of this portion of the auditory system before he or she conducts an OAE test. If the audiologist suspects a middle ear problem, he or she will make the appropriate medical referral. The sample report of Susie O'Brian, presented earlier in this chapter, contains results of OAE testing. In this case, the results together with impedance testing, suggested abnormal middle-ear pressure, and Susie was referred to an otolaryngologist.

Auditory Neuropathy

A rare auditory condition, called an *auditory neuropathy* (Sininger, Hood, Starr, Berlin, & Picton, 1995) is an exception to some of the general statements made here. In infrequent cases, children or infants have apparently normal inner ear function, so that OAEs are present and appear normal, yet the children have abnormal hearing nerve function so that the ABR is absent. This condition is termed *auditory neuropathy* because some kind of pathology of the auditory nerve fibers is interfering with the detection and transmission of sound. Auditory neuropathy may be more prevalent in infants and young children with multiple disabilities. The presence of OAEs, with no further information, would lead the clinician to believe that the ear was "hearing" and processing sound normally. However, once the ABR is done and deemed "absent," it is evident that there is some kind of neural dysfunction in the auditory system.

In most cases of auditory neuropathy, the parents or early interventionists complain that the children are not functioning well in school, do not hear or pay attention, or sometimes hear better than at other times. If an audiogram has been obtained, the hearing thresholds often fluctuate over time, and speech-discrimination scores are much poorer than one would expect on the basis of the audiogram thresholds. Auditory neuropathy indicates that a person is neurally deaf. Even if the cochlea receives sound input normally, the brainstem or nerve cannot send the information upward to the brain effectively so it can interpret it as speech or other meaningful sound. Children with auditory neuropathy are deaf in a different way from other deaf children. This combination of findings is being seen more and more as clinics are obtaining OAE equipment and conducting both ABRs and OAEs on the same patients. Research is currently being conducted on its etiology and on rehabilitation for individuals who have these symptoms.

CONCLUSION

In conclusion, the ideal tool for defining hearing at all relevant frequencies is the audiogram. However, in young children, the audiogram or approximations of the audiogram must be obtained with creative behavioral techniques, ranging from BOA to play audiometry. In many cases, even these techniques do not produce reliable results, so more objective physiological tests, such as the ABR and OAEs, must be used to assess auditory function. The ABR can estimate hearing thresholds at various frequencies, whereas OAEs can rule out significant hearing loss when they are present but do not yield information on thresholds. Audiologists must be versatile and creative in conducting the appropriate battery of tests for individual children. As children mature, the long-term goal is always to obtain an accurate behavioral reflection of their hearing. In this way, audiologists and others on a child's early intervention team will be able to tackle the goal of aural rehabilitation and education in the most precise and appropriate manner.

REFERENCES

American National Standards Institute. (1969). *American National Standard Specifications for Audiometers* (ANSI S3.6–1969). New York.

American Speech Language and Hearing Association Guidelines: Audiologic screening of newborn infants who are at risk for hearing impairment, *ASHA,* Rockville Pike, MD *31,* 89–92.

Folsom, R. (1990). Identification of hearing loss in infants using auditory brainstem response: Strategies and program choices. *Seminars in Hearing, 11,* 333–341.

Kemp, D. (1978). Stimulated acoustic emissions from within the human auditory system. *Journal of the Acoustical Society America, 64,* 1386–1391.

Menyuk, P. (1977). Cognition and language. *Volta Review, 78,* 250–257.

Northern, J., & Downs, M. (1991). *Hearing in Children.* Baltimore, M.D.: Williams & Wilkins.

Osberger, M. (1986). Language and learning skills of hearing-impaired students. *American Speech, Language and Hearing Association Monograph,* Rockville Pike, MD 23.

Salamy, A., & McKean, C. (1976). Postnatal development of human brain stem potentials during the first year of life. *Electroencephalography and Clinical Neurophysiology, 40,* 418–426.

Sininger, Y., Hood, L., Starr, A., Berlin, C., & Picton, T. (1995). Hearing loss due to auditory neuropathy. *Audiology Today, 7,* 10–13,

Thompson, G., & Wilson, W. (1984). Application of VRA. *Seminars in Hearing, 5,* 85–99.

Thompson, G., Wilson, W., & Moore, J. (1979). Application of visual reinforcement audiometry (VRA) to low-functioning children. *Journal of Speech and Hearing Disorders, 44,* 80–90.

Yoshinaga-Itano, C. (1998, June 4–7). *Educational systems and achievement levels of deaf children without cochlear implants.* Paper presented at the seventh Symposium on Cochlear Implants in Children, Iowa City.

PART III

Developing Learning Strategies

Undertaking effective early intervention is a complex process involving acute observation, sensitivity, and the skillful application of well-thought-out strategies. All this effort is rewarded by the promotion of the optimal development of the child. The chapters that follow provide information on how to develop intervention activities that benefit the child and the family and lead to the child's successful participation in his or her family, school, and wider areas of life.

8

Developing Meaningful Interventions

Jamie Dote-Kwan and Deborah Chen

The goal of early intervention services is to promote an infant's early development. However, providing high-quality early intervention services is not a simple matter. First, services should meet the family's concerns about the infant's development, some of which may not be clearly identified or may involve different priorities from those of the service providers. Second, infant-centered activities should be developmentally appropriate and individualized to address each infant's abilities and disabilities. There is great variation not only in the developmental levels and skills of infants with multiple disabilities, but in the intervention needs of younger and older infants. Therefore, to serve these infants and their families, early interventionists need to have specific knowledge and skills about intervention strategies and strong interpersonal skills and to understand the complexity of families.

Early interventionists need specific procedures for gathering information, identifying family concerns, and implementing meaningful interventions to facilitate the inclusion of infants with multiple disabilities in family routines and community activities. In general, they also should facilitate collaboration among service providers from different disciplines in developing and implementing early intervention programs. However, the appropriateness of a specific strategy depends on where early intervention services are delivered (that is, whether they are home based, center based, or a combination of the two); the nature and extent of an infant's multiple disabilities; and the values and practices of the family. To assist early interventionists in their work, Figure 8.1 presents a flowchart for implementing the procedures and strategies that are introduced in this chapter, along with the vision and hearing assessment procedures discussed in Chapters 4, 5, 6, and 7. This chapter describes strategies for gathering information about an infant, analyzing the caregiving environment, and developing interventions that are meaningful and motivating for infants and are valued by their families through the following procedures, each of which is explained in this chapter:

1. Conducting an interview to obtain the family's perspective and to identify the family's priorities and concerns about the infant's development.
2. Conducting systematic observations of the characteristics of the infant's interactions with caregivers at home and in center-based environments.
3. Establishing priorities among intervention outcomes to identify the most critical skills to encourage and for the infant to practice.
4. Developing meaningful intervention outcomes that are child directed, easily integrated within the family routine, and functional.
5. Developing an analysis of the routines involved in various activities to identify appropriate activities for which essential skills can be encouraged or reinforced.
6. Creating an Objectives-Within-Routines matrix to identify specific routines within the daily schedule of activities in which specific objectives for the infant can be integrated at home or in the center.

GATHERING INFORMATION

Family Interview

In interviews with family members, an early interventionist obtains the family's perspective on the infant's development and identifies the family's priorities and concerns. Interviews conducted in the family's home also give the early interventionist an opportunity to interact with the family and infant in a natural and familiar setting. The early interventionist should be skilled in conducting family interviews and use

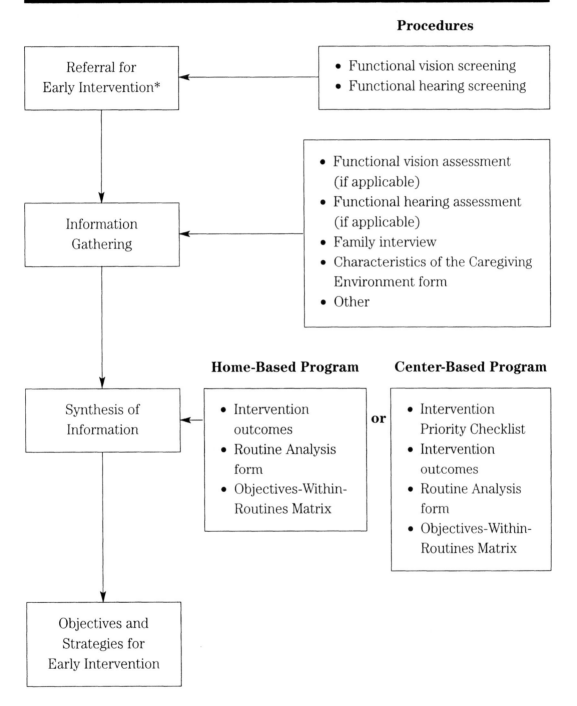

Figure 8.1 A PROCESS FOR DEVELOPING MEANINGFUL EARLY INTERVENTION OUTCOMES

Procedures

Referral for Early Intervention*

- Functional vision screening
- Functional hearing screening

Information Gathering

- Functional vision assessment (if applicable)
- Functional hearing assessment (if applicable)
- Family interview
- Characteristics of the Caregiving Environment form
- Other

Home-Based Program

Center-Based Program

Synthesis of Information

- Intervention outcomes
- Routine Analysis form
- Objectives-Within-Routines Matrix

or

- Intervention Priority Checklist
- Intervention outcomes
- Routine Analysis form
- Objectives-Within-Routines Matrix

Objectives and Strategies for Early Intervention

* Referral based on (1) identified significant developmental delay, (2) established disability condition, or (3) at-risk for (1) or (2).

active listening skills, such as paraphrasing, clarifying, reflecting, and summarizing, to facilitate the interview process. He or she should also be aware of nonverbal messages, body language, facial expressions, and tones of voice.

Before an early interventionist interviews a family from a cultural or linguistic background that varies from his or her own, it is essential to obtain information from "cultural interpreters" or otherwise find out about differences in verbal and nonverbal communication and the language and literacy level of the family, as well as to plan enough time for the interview with the family (Chen, Chan, & Brekken, in press; Dennis & Giangreco, 1996). Information must be obtained in a respectful and culturally sensitive manner. There are likely to be differences between the family's and early interventionist's values, perspectives, and practices that need to be considered. Additional tips for conducting interviews with families of different cultural or linguistic backgrounds appear in Sidebar 8.1.

Sidebar 8.1   INTERVIEWING FAMILIES FROM DIFFERENT BACKGROUNDS

Early interventionists frequently work with families from different backgrounds. They may find the following suggestions helpful when interviewing a family whose language or culture is different from their own:

• Work with a trained interpreter who can interpret both the language spoken and the nonverbal cues provided by the family members. Plan the interview with the interpreter so that terminology and other explanations can be identified in advance.

• Generally, interview the family members at home, where they will be the most comfortable. If they are uncomfortable having visitors in their home, hold the interview in a neutral setting (such as a community center or coffee shop).

• Schedule the interview for a time when the significant family members can be present. Although the father or grandfather may not be the primary care provider, he may be the primary decision maker in the family and should participate in the interview. Likewise, an older sibling or grandparent may have major care-providing responsibilities and thus should be included in the interview.

The following steps have been identified as helpful in conducting family interviews in general (Bennett, Lingerfelt, & Nelson, 1990; Dunst, Trivette, & Deal, 1988; Lowenthal, 1993):

1. Contact the parent and schedule the interview. Explain the purpose of the visit, for example, "I need to meet with you to find out more about Joey and what you want for him." Ask the parent who should be at the interview and what time would be convenient for the family.
2. Select a meeting place that is convenient for the family. Some families may prefer to have the interview held in their home, whereas others may not.
3. Begin the interview by thanking the family members for being present and by identifying each person's relationship in the family. Assure the family that the discussion is confidential. Then restate the purpose of the meeting, for instance, "I know you have questions about Joey's vision and his development. I want to get to know him better and to find out what you want for him."
4. Use open-ended questions, for example, "Tell me about Joey" or "What is Joey's day like?" Note each family member's concerns, interests, strengths, and goals.
5. Assist the family in identifying their priorities by asking, for example, "What do you think is most important to work on first?" "What would make a big difference?" "What would you like Joey to learn in the next six months?"
6. End the interview by restating the infant's strengths, the family's concerns, and priorities for services that were discussed and agreed to. Thank the family, reassure them about confidentiality, and let them know what will happen next, for example, "Next week I will bring some toys for Joey to play with, and we will see what he does and what toys he likes."

Other questions (Able-Boone, Sandall, Loughry, & Frederick, 1990; Chen, Friedman, & Calvello, 1990) that may be used to gather more information about caregiving roles and family activities are these:

1. What activities do you enjoy doing with your infant?
2. What are some tasks that you do for your infant? Who helps with these tasks?
3. What kinds of activities do your family enjoy together?

Once the early interventionist has gathered information from family members about their concerns about and priorities for the infant, then he or she should develop a more complete understanding of the infant's abilities and learning needs. For subsequent discussions with family members, the early interventionist can select as appropriate, from questions regarding specific disabilities listed in Chapter 3, from questions about vision and hearing abilities listed in Chapters 5 and 6, and from questions about communication abilities listed in Chapter 9.

Initially, gather information only in areas that the family members identified as priorities and concerns. Ask the family to describe a typical day for their infant: the usual activities and how he or she participates in them. This typical daily routine is the family's Monday-through-Friday schedule. If the infant goes to day care for part of the day, focus on activities from the time the infant wakes up in the morning until he or she goes to day care and the activities from the time the infant arrives home until he or she goes to bed. For example, ask, "What is Stevie's typical day like?" or "How does Stevie get up in the morning?" The purpose of these questions is to obtain information about the infant's activities, the approximate length of time that a specific caregiving activity may take, how the infant participates in the specific activity, and how the infant communicates preferences and needs to the caregiver during the activity. For example, if Stevie's father feeds him breakfast in the morning, the early interventionist may follow up with these suggested questions:

- Tell me about breakfast. Where does Stevie have his breakfast?
- How does Stevie tell you he is hungry?
- How does he drink his juice?
- How does he eat his breakfast?
- What are his favorite things to eat for breakfast?

By asking a series of probing, open-ended questions, the early interventionist obtains information not only about what Stevie does, but, more important, how the activity occurs within the cultural context of his family. The following example of a dialogue between the early interventionist and Stevie's father illustrates this process:

Early Interventionist: How does Stevie drink his juice?

Father: From his cup.

> **Early Interventionist:** What type of cup does he drink from?
> **Father:** A sippy cup.
> **Early Interventionist:** How does he find his cup on the tray?
> **Father:** I tap it on the tray and he reaches for it.
> **Early Interventionist:** How does he hold his cup? With one hand? With two hands? With help?
> **Father:** With both hands—I sometimes help.
> **Early Interventionist:** How does he drink his juice? All at once? A little at a time? At the beginning? At the end? Throughout breakfast?
> **Father:** I give him his juice when he is finished eating. He drinks it all down.
> **Early Interventionist:** What are his favorite drinks?
> **Father:** Apple juice and grape juice
> **Early Interventionist:** Do you give Stevie a choice of juice in the morning?
> **Father:** He gets what is in the refrigerator.
> **Early Interventionist:** How does he tell you what juice he wants?
> **Father:** I know he likes apple juice and grape juice.

By asking these types of questions, the early interventionist can learn about Stevie's preferences for foods, how the foods are presented, Stevie's ability to locate items on the tray, and whether Stevie has opportunities to make choices within his family contexts (rules or rituals regarding mealtimes). For example, in Stevie's family, the children receive drinks at the end of meals.

During the interview, the early interventionist should also find out whether the family has certain activities that they would like Stevie to learn or participate in more fully. This information helps establish some of the family's priorities and possible preferences for intervention activities within the scope of the daily routine. All this information can be recorded on the Family Interview of Daily Activities form. A completed example of this form is provided in Figure 8.2 in the accompanying case study of Bobby (a blank form is provided in the Appendix).

BOBBY

Part I

Bobby is a 9 month old with a severe-to-profound hearing loss. He lives with his parents, Robert and Sandra Sanchez; two older brothers; and a twin sister, Monica. Bobby has Moebius syndrome, a congenital facial diplegia that has weakened his head and neck muscles, and a visual impairment. His twin sister, Monica does not have Moebius syndrome or any other medical conditions. Bobby receives in-home infant intervention services once a week. He also receives physical and occupational therapy twice a week at Casa Colina in Pomona, California.

Bobby and his family receive home-based services, so his Individual Family Service Plan required the following:

- a clinical hearing examination
- a functional vision assessment
- a family interview, which produced a schedule of his daily activities at home,
- an observation-interview of the characteristics of the caregiving environment conducted at the mother's request

Bobby was given binaural Phonak hearing aids at 6 months of age, and his current audiological evaluation stated that he appears to benefit from amplification. (Bobby's audiologcal report is presented in Chapter 7.) Using a Behavioral Observation Audiometry (BOA) with hearing aids, Bobby was able to respond to tones at 55 dB HL at 500 Hz and 65 dB HL at 1000 Hz. In addition to a three-month follow-up evaluation, it was recommended that Bobby's use of hearing aids should be increased, beginning with two hours a day and gradually extended to full-time usage.

When asked about Bobby's vision, Mrs. Sanchez reported that she thought that Bobby did see brightly colored toys and objects. She stated that Bobby swipes at and reaches for preferred objects, stares at his hands as he waves them in front of his face, and loses interest in objects beyond 12 inches. Bobby primarily responds by widening his eyes, turning his head to the source of a sound, and reaching for desired objects.

A family interview was conducted with Bobby's parents in their home. At that time, Mrs. Sanchez thought she had more time to devote to Bobby during the day, since her husband and her older children are not at home. Therefore, the schedule of daily activities identified during the family interview (see Figure 8.2) identifies only those activities that occur during the day. The following is Mrs. Sanchez's account of Bobby's day, and Figure 8.3 shows how it would be recorded on the Daily Activities form.

- Each morning Mrs. Sanchez wakes up Bobby and his sister and changes their diapers and clothes. She wakes Monica up first, since Bobby cries when he is left unattended.
- During breakfast, Bobby sits in a slightly reclined infant seat when his mother feeds him his cereal. While she is feeding Monica, Mrs. Sanchez gives Bobby a bottle.
- After breakfast, Bobby and Monica are placed on a quilt in the living room while Mrs. Sanchez does the breakfast dishes and cleans up the kitchen.
- Next, Mrs. Sanchez plays with both Bobby and Monica on the quilt with some toys.

Figure 8.2 SAMPLE FAMILY INTERVIEW OF DAILY ACTIVITIES FORM COMPLETED FOR BOBBY

Daily Activities

Child: __Bobby__   Date: __August 3, 1999__

Parent-Caregiver: __Mrs. Sanchez, mother__   Interviewer: _____

Other Family Members Present: __Mr. Sanchez, father; Bobby's two older__
__brothers; and Bobby's twin sister__

Weekday: __xx__   Weekend: _____

Time of Day	Activity	What the Child Does	How the Child Communicates	Family Priority (Yes/no)
7:30 A.M.	Wake up	Cooperates while his diaper and clothes are changed.	Moves his arms and legs to cooperate with changing.	No
	Breakfast	Sits in the reclined infant seat, needs assistance to open his mouth, drinks from a propped bottle.	Pushes the food out of his mouth, cries.	Yes
	Clean up	Lies on the floor and sometimes finishes his bottle; waves his hands in front of his face.	Smiles and laughs when happy; cries when distressed.	No
	Playtime	Plays with toys briefly by reaching for or touching them.	Smiles, laughs, vocalizes, and turns his head toward sound	Yes
11:00 A.M.	Preparing lunch	Cooperates while his diaper is changed; enjoys being carried.	Moves his arms and legs during diaper change, smiles, vocalizes.	No

(continued on next page)

Figure 8.2   SAMPLE FAMILY INTERVIEW OF DAILY ACTIVITIES FORM COMPLETED FOR BOBBY *(continued)*

Time of Day	Activity	What the Child Does	How the Child Communicates	Family Priority (Yes/no)
	Lunchtime	Sits in the reclined infant seat, needs assistance to open mouth, drinks from a propped bottle.	Pushes the food out of his mouth, cries.	Yes
1:00 P.M.	Naptime	Cooperates while his diaper is changed and naps.	Moves his legs during diaper change.	No
2:30 P.M.	Walk outside	Looks and smiles at different things; sits calmly in the stroller.	Smiles, laughs, and vocalizes.	No
4:00 P.M.	Preparing dinner	Cooperates while his diaper is changed and lies on the floor; waves his hands in front of his face	Smiles and laughs when happy; cries when distressed.	Yes

- After playtime, Mrs. Sanchez changes the babies' diapers and starts preparing lunch. During this time, Mrs. Sanchez carries Bobby and places Monica in an infant walker in the kitchen.
- At lunchtime, Mrs. Sanchez feeds Bobby first and then Monica in the same manner as breakfast.
- After lunch, Mrs. Sanchez puts both babies down for their naps while she does some housekeeping chores.
- In the afternoon, Bobby and Monica are placed in a double stroller and are taken for a walk around the neighborhood.
- When they return, Mrs. Sanchez places Bobby and Monica on the quilt in the living room while she prepares dinner.

When the discussion of the typical daily activities for a weekday is completed, the process may be repeated, if appropriate, by asking the family to describe typical weekend or weekly activities. In this way, activities may be identified that do not occur daily, but that do occur at least once a week, such as grocery shopping, going to the park, going to church, going to a play group, or visiting neighbors or grandparents. This schedule of the infant's and family's daily activities provides the framework for identifying, organizing, and individualizing daily routines for possible intervention. If the infant participates in a day care or center-based program, then the schedule of daily activities should be obtained from the child care staff or teachers using a similar interview process as conducted with the family (see the case study of Jessica later in this chapter).

Examining the Characteristics of the Caregiving Environments

During the first years of life, interactions between the caregiver and infant are perhaps the most important aspect of a family's daily routine with an infant. These early interactions also influence the infant's development of emotional, communicative, social, and cognitive competence (Barnard & Kelly, 1990). (The significance of interactions between caregivers and infants as a focus for early intervention is discussed in Chapter 2.) Although research has not focused specifically on infants with visual impairments and additional disabilities, the data suggest that caregivers of these infants have more difficulty responding to and engaging them in mutually satisfying interactions without assistance (Chen et al., 1990; Fraiberg, 1974; Rogow, 1984; Rowland, 1984).

The early interventionist should help the caregivers identify the characteristics of the infant's interactions with the social environment that may facilitate development and positive outcomes. These interactions should naturally include the home environment, but if the infant is in a center-based program, his or her interactions within that environment should also be examined. The early interventionist needs to be sure that the characteristics that are identified are meaningful and important to the specific family (McCollum & McBride, 1997). This should not be a judgmental process but an opportunity for the early interventionist and family members to discuss the infant's characteristics and for the family members to examine their interactions with the infant. The early interventionist can sensitively observe these interactions and routines, identify the family members' expectations for interactions with the infant, and ask the parents to interpret the meaning and intent of their and their infant's behavior during interactions. In this way, appropriate outcomes for intervention to enhance these interactions will be developed (McCollum & McBride, 1997). Interviewing family members and observing their interactions with the infant using the questions on the Characteristics of the Caregiving Environment form, is likely to assist the early intervention team in identifying the specific strengths of the home or center-based program, as well as areas of concern. The early interventionist should interview relevant family members who will provide a comprehensive picture of the infant's caregiving environment. For example, the mother might identify the grandfather or older brother as spending a significant amount of time playing with the infant. Using this process, the early interventionist will obtain information about everyone who is a significant caregiver for that young child. (A completed example of this form appears in Figure 8.3 in the second part of Bobby's story; a blank form is provided in the Appendix.) The form covers such areas as how the caregiver attempts to engage the infant, how the infant responds to the caregiver (and vice versa), and the physical characteristics of the environment that may affect the infant's ability to learn new skills. Through this process, the early intervention team can identify which characteristics of the caregiver should be encouraged, reinforced, and possibly shared with other caregivers, as well as the characteristics of the environment that can be modified to facilitate the infant's learning or that are promoting the infant's development and should be continued and encouraged.

For example, if a grandfather is particularly skillful in engaging and maintaining his granddaughter's attention, for example, by his tone of voice, then identifying his particular actions or characteristics can be helpful to other caregivers. On the other hand, an infant who is blind may seem to be overwhelmed by the hustle and bustle of a day care center and is often inattentive and drowsy. In this situation, the staff should examine the auditory environment and seek ways to eliminate meaningless background noise, for instance, by turning off background music and adding carpets.

BOBBY
Part II

After the family interview, the early interventionist and Mrs. Sanchez discussed the need to conduct an inventory of the characteristics of the caregiving environment. Mrs. Sanchez expressed a concern that sometimes she may not be meeting all Bobby's needs, since she has to take care of both Bobby and Monica at the same time. She also would like some assistance in how to help Bobby. The early interventionist completed the Characteristics of the Caregiving Environment form (Figure 8.3) with Mrs. Sanchez.

Figure 8.3   SAMPLE CHARACTERISTICS OF THE CAREGIVING ENVIRONMENT FORM COMPLETED FOR BOBBY

Characteristics of the Caregiving Environment

Child: ___Bobby___   Date: ___August 10, 1999___

Environment: ___Home___   Respondent: ___Mrs. Sanchez, mother___

Directions: Have the family and/or early intervention staff complete the inventory.

Question	Response
How does the child receive physical contact (for example, hugs, touches, being held)?	I hug and kiss him. I try to carry him when possible.
How is the child encouraged to move and explore his surroundings?	I place Bobby on a quilt with his toys or carry him.
How does the caregiver get the child's attention before interacting with the child (for instance, says the child's name, touches the child, taps the object)?	I say his name and touch his hand.
How does the caregiver provide opportunities for exploring objects (such as by pausing or giving prompts to encourage the child to explore)?	When we play in the morning, I place his favorite toys or objects within his reach.

(continued on next page)

Question	Response
How does the caregiver engage the child to keep the child's attention and interest (for example, by pacing)?	I repeat the name of the object and put the object in his hands.
How does the caregiver facilitate the child's participation in activities (for instance, by rearranging materials, the child's position, or his or her own position)?	I place objects within his reach and carry him when possible.
How does the caregiver identify and interpret the child's nonverbal cues (such as quieting means "I'm interested" or turning the head away means "I don't like it")?	If he pushes the food out of his mouth, I assume he doesn't like it. If he smiles or laughs, I assume he likes the thing.
How does the caregiver indicate the child's turn (for instance, by pausing, waiting, or touching the child)?	I wait for Bobby to respond, but he often does not.
How are the child's requests for objects or assistance acknowledged (complied with, ignored, or denied)?	He doesn't make requests.
How are the child's communicative intents and behaviors acknowledged and/or expanded (such as exaggerated vocalization, touch cues, object cues, or adapted manual signs)?	Bobby's limited vocalizations are usually praised.
How are augmentative communication methods used, if necessary?	I speak loudly to Bobby.
What activities are mutually enjoyable for the child and caregiver (like bathing, feeding, playtime)?	Playtime and walks outside.
How is the child included in ongoing activities-daily routines (for example, placing the child near the adult or providing him or her with toys)?	I give Bobby toys when he's on the quilt and carry him when possible.

(continued on next page)

Figure 8.3 SAMPLE CHARACTERISTICS OF THE CAREGIVING ENVIRONMENT FORM COMPLETED FOR BOBBY *(continued)*

Question	Response
How is the environment organized to encourage movement and exploration (uncluttered, specific places for toys or objects, adaptations)?	All his toys are placed in a basket, and a quilt is used when he plays on the floor.
How is the environment organized to encourage the use of vision, if applicable (for instance, proper lighting, high contrast, glare-free)?	I bring things closer to him so he can see them.
How is the environment organized to encourage listening skills, if applicable (such as reduced background noise, floors carpeted)?	We keep the radio or television off when we play with Bobby.

The interview with Mrs. Sanchez revealed several positive aspects of Bobby's caregiving environment such as:

- she is very responsive to his nonverbal communicative intents and interprets behaviors meaningfully,
- she is affectionate and interacts with him physically through hugs and kisses, and
- she is making accommodations for Bobby's hearing loss and visual impairment by reducing background noise and bringing objects within his visual range.

The early intervention team met to develop desired outcomes of intervention for Bobby. The team members included Bobby's early interventionist, a teacher certified in the field of visual impairments, a teacher certified in the field of hearing impairments, a physical therapist, and Mrs. Sanchez. These objectives were as follows:

1. Bobby will open his mouth in anticipation of being fed.

2. Bobby will reach for and explore preferred toys with help from an adult.
3. Bobby will communicate preferences by looking or pointing at an object or person.
4. Bobby will wear his hearing aids for two hours a day.

As a result of the early intervention team meeting, several routine analyses were conducted to facilitate the integration of these outcomes within specific routines in Bobby's home. The purpose is to integrate specific objectives from each discipline into the activity. The routine analysis for playtime is presented in Figure 8.4 as an example. (A blank form is provided in the Appendix.)

Next, the team developed an Objectives-Within-Routines Matrix (Figure 8.5) to identify which activities in Bobby's daily schedule can be used to implement each objective. The specific strategies identified in the matrix can be implemented by both service providers and caregivers within the daily home routine. (A blank form is provided in the Appendix.)

Figure 8.4 SAMPLE COMPLETED ROUTINE ANALYSIS OF BOBBY'S PLAYTIME

Routine Analysis

Name: Bobby   Date: August 17, 1999   Activity: Playtime

Steps in Routine	Natural Cues	Behaviors to Encourage	Input and Adaptive Strategies	Area (Discipline)*
Getting ready for playtime	Mother puts quilt on the floor Mother gets the toy basket	Looks at quilt area Smiles Leaves hearing aids alone when wearing them	"Playtime." "Hearing aid on" Provide an object cue: a favorite ball with bell inside. Provide good contrast between toys and the quilt; use brightly colored toys that produce sound	HI VI
Peek-a-boo with mother	(Early interventionist) Monica on quilt Picked up Placed on quilt	Looks at mother Says "boo"	"Are you ready?" Peek-a-boo with exaggerated vocalization Crawl fingers up child's body to chin, then say "boo." "Are you ready?	EI
Playing with toys	Monica takes toys out of basket Preferred noise-making toys	Looks at toy Says "boo" Swipes or reaches for toy Holds and looks at toy	Touch toy to child's hand Peek-a-boo with exaggerated vocalization Move toy up child's body to chin, say "boo," and then hold toy within child's reach. Limit toys to two or three preferred ones.	VI HI PT
Clean up	Monica and mother put toys in basket	Reaches for toy Places toy in basket with assistance	"Time to clean up." "All done." Provide an object cue: an empty basket.	HI EI PT VI

Figure 8.5. SAMPLE OBJECTIVES-WITHIN-ROUTINES MATRIX COMPLETED FOR BOBBY

Objectives-Within-Routines Matrix

Name: Bobby

Date: August 17, 1999

Daily Routines

Objectives	Breakfast	Playtime	Lunch	Walk Outside
1. Bobby will open his mouth in anticipation of being fed.	Hold the spoonful of food within 12 inches of Bobby's face and wait 3–4 seconds. Touch the spoon to Bobby's lips and wait until he responds.		Hold the spoonful of food within 12 inches of Bobby's face and wait 3–4 seconds. Touch the spoon to Bobby's lips and wait until he responds.	
2. Bobby will reach for and explore preferred toys with facilitation by an adult.		Provide brightly colored toys and objects within 12 inches of Bobby's face. Provide toys that make a sound when acted upon.		Hang brightly colored toys on the stroller within 12 inches of Bobby's face.
3. Bobby will communicate preferences by looking or pointing at an object or person.	Provide high-contrast black-and-white striped bottle. Present bottle within 12 inches of Bobby's face and wait until he responds.	Provide high contrast between the toys and background. Provide only 2–3 toys at a time and wait until he responds.	Provide high contrast between his choices of food (such as peas or potatoes). Bring the plate or bowl within 12 inches of Bobby's face.	
4. Bobby will wear his hearing aids for two hours a day.	Encourage Bobby to wear the hearing aids even for 10 minutes while he is being fed and an adult is interacting with him.	Add short intervals of 10 minutes' "wear time" during sound play with caregivers. Reduce background noise.	Encourage Bobby to wear the hearing aids even for 10 minutes while being fed and an adult is interacting with him.	

DEVELOPING OUTCOMES AND OBJECTIVES FOR INTERVENTION

Choosing Skills to Develop

Once the early interventionist has documented a family's routines and identified the strengths and weaknesses of the caretaker and the environment, he or she can begin, with the early intervention team, to identify which skills should be the focus of intervention with this particular infant. The team can then develop outcomes and objectives for teaching these skills. To develop objectives that reflect outcomes for the infant that are relevant to the family, several questions need to be addressed:

- Is the identified skill a priority for the family and a preferred activity for the infant?
- Does the identified skill assist the infant to participate more actively in the family's daily routine?
- Can the skill be easily generalized to meaningful activities?
- Can the skill be practiced frequently and easily within the family's daily routine?
- Is the skill developmentally appropriate for the infant?

Priorities and Preferences

Identifying priorities for intervention includes examining the preferences of the family and individual infant. Once the family's priorities have been identified, it is essential to establish the infant's preference for each activity for which the skill is required. If the infant likes a particular activity, he or she will probably be motivated to learn the skills needed to perform it, but if the infant dislikes a particular activity, he or she may exhibit negative reactions or refuse to engage in it. For example, an infant who enjoys eating may be more motivated to pick up a piece of banana than an infant who is orally defensive or tactilely sensitive and dislikes different textures in his or her mouth or hands.

Functionality

The early interventionist needs to address two components of functionality. First, does the skill increase the infant's interactions with people and objects in everyday activities? Second, if the infant does not learn the identified developmentally appropriate skill, will it have to be done for him or her? (Dote-Kwan, 1995; Notari-Syverson & Shuster, 1995). For example, if an infant is unable to hold a cracker, then someone will have to hold it for him or her. Having someone hold the cracker limits the infant's interaction with it, since someone else will decide how much and how often the cracker is brought to the infant's mouth. In contrast, if the same infant is unable to stack rings on a tower, someone will not need to do it for him or her in order to promote participation in everyday activities.

Generality

Generality refers to whether a skill can be applied across a variety of activities and environments and occurs frequently enough to ensure multiple opportunities to practice and learn the skill. Looking at a preferred object by shifting the gaze to facilitate choice making is an example of a skill that can be encouraged and reinforced frequently in the course of a day and in a variety of environments. An infant can use shift of gaze to select a bottle versus a graham cracker at breakfast, a favorite toy at playtime, a favorite stuffed animal or blanket at nap time, and so forth. Furthermore, using shift of gaze to facilitate choice making can occur at home, at a local family restaurant, and at the park.

Ease of Integration

The ease of integrating a skill within the context of the family and its daily routine is essential for meaningful and culturally relevant intervention (Notari-Syverson & Shuster, 1995). Skills should be encouraged and reinforced in a way that reflects how the specific skill is required during the daily routine and should be easily elicited within those routines. For example, the skill of fixating on an illuminated black-and-white shape requires an artificial educational environment in which the early interventionist brings in a light box and black-and-white shapes. In contrast, fixating on the caregiver's face can be practiced and reinforced using naturalistic intervention strategies that provide the family with many meaningful opportunities to integrate the skill within the daily routine and take advantage of naturally occurring situations. Furthermore, an infant's recognition of a caregiver's face has a powerful effect on the relationship between them.

Developmentally Appropriate

Although family priorities are the focus of the intervention process, the early interventionist needs to exercise his or her professional judgment when determining objectives for a particular infant, including whether the infant can acquire the skills, given the amount of time available. The early interventionist also needs to match the characteristics of the tasks and the skills needed to complete them to the infant's strengths and desires. For example, the parents of an infant who is totally blind may want her to recognize significant family members by their voices. However, this infant also has a severe hearing loss and although she is aware of sound, she cannot discriminate among voices. Therefore, it is the responsibility of the intervention team to identify the infant's strengths and needs to determine whether auditory recognition of family members is a reasonable expectation at this time and to establish alternative strategies. It may be that a tactile cue needs to be paired with each family member as he or she speaks to the infant. That is, the father can take the infant's hand and touch his beard or the mother can have the infant touch her long hair when she first speaks to the infant.

Completing the Intervention Priority Checklist can help the early intervention team identify critical skills to be encouraged and reinforced. (A completed sample of this form is included in Figure 8.8 in the case study of Jessica; a blank form is provided in the Appendix.) Each skill that has been identified as a possible focus for early intervention is listed in the columns at the top and scored on the various criteria that have been explained in this section based on a 4-point Likert scale (in which 3 = strongly agree, 2 = agree, 1 = somewhat agree, and 0 = disagree). The skills with the highest total scores should be included when the early intervention team develops the infant's intervention program. Using this method, Jessica's early intervention team took eight possible outcomes and selected five priorities: moving to a preferred activity, making choices, communicating desires and needs, playing with toys, and eating with his fingers. When they transformed these priorities into specific objectives, the team members made sure that these goals would make sense to Jessica and her family, encourage Jessica to be active, and be easily integrated into the family's daily routines, as discussed in the following section.

JESSICA

Jessica, aged 2 years, 9 months, has cerebral palsy and cortical visual impairment caused by birth asphyxia and brain trauma at age 5 months. At 3 months of age, she moved in with her grandparents, and her grandmother, Mrs. James, is her primary caregiver. Jessica is nonverbal and nonambulatory. She is able to lift her head and push up on her arms when placed in a prone position. Jessica is usually happy and always smiling. She cries only when she has one of her frequent stomachaches, for which she is given Pepto Bismol.

For the past two months, Jessica has attended a center-based program for infants with and without disabilities. Of the 12 children in her class aged 24 to 36 months, 4 have disabilities. Jessica is the only nonambulatory child in the room and is placed in an adaptive wheelchair. She receives speech therapy one day a week for 30 minutes and physical therapy two days a week for a total of 60 minutes. However, in three months, she will be leaving this center-based program because she will be 3 years old. Jessica and her grandparents have been through many changes recently. First, she moved in with her grandparents, then she began to attend the infant center-based program, and soon she will be leaving that program and going to a new one. Jessica's early intervention team is composed of her classroom teacher, a physical therapist, and a teacher who is certified in the field of visual impairments, as well as her grandparents. Even though Jessica will be in the early intervention program only for a short time, it is important to determine how to support her participation in home and center activities and to obtain information that will promote an individualized program in her future setting. Her grandparents would like her to attend the community child development preschool that is in their neighborhood. Chapter 10 provides strategies for inclusive preschool settings.

In preparation for her clinical visual evaluation, her grandmother answered questions about Jessica's vision (see the questions for family members in Chapter 5). She thinks that Jessica sees lights, can track her fingers when she moves them, and responds when she speaks to her. An examination by an optometrist (see Chapter 4) revealed that Jessica has moderate hyperopic refractive error with significant astigmatism and cortical visual impairment. Eyeglasses were prescribed, although the optometrist was not sure that Jessica would benefit from them, given her severe visual impairment. Jessica was unable to fixate consistently and had an alternating outward eye turn. It was recommended that her pictures and toys should be large, with high contrast and primary colors. Objects should be at least 4 inches in size at 1 foot and 8 inches in size at 2 feet. A family interview was conducted with Jessica's grandparents in their home. The interview revealed the following daily routine (see Figure 8.6):

- Each morning, Mrs. James wakes up Jessica and changes her diaper and clothes. She brushes her teeth and washes her hands and face.
- During breakfast, Jessica sits in an infant seat while her grandmother feeds her cereal.

Figure 8.6 SAMPLE DAILY ACTIVITIES FORM COMPLETED FOR JESSICA

Daily Activities

Child: __Jessica__   Date: __January 26, 1999__

Parent-caregiver: __Mrs. James, grandmother__   Interviewer: __Jane Chang, teacher__

Other family members present: __Mr. James, grandfather__

Weekday: __XX__   Weekend: _____

Time of Day	Activity	What the Child Does	How the Child Communicates	Family Priority (Yes/no)
7:00 A.M.	Wake up	Cooperates while her diaper and clothes are changed.	Moves her arms and legs to be changed.	No
	Grooming	Gives each hand to be washed; opens her mouth when her teeth are being brushed.	Moves her hands and mouth to cooperate with activity.	No
	Breakfast	Opens her mouth when being fed; drinks from a held cup with minimal spillage.	Turns her head away when she does not want something.	Yes
8:30 A.M.	Going to center-based program	Cooperates while her jacket is being put on by moving her arms.	Smiles on seeing and hearing her teacher.	No
1:00 P.M.	Going home	Cooperates with being transferred from her adaptive wheelchair to the car.	Smiles on seeing and hearing her grandmother.	No
1:30 P.M.	Arrival home Nap time	Cooperates while her diaper is changed and her jacket and shoes are removed; naps.	Moves her arms and legs to cooperate with changing.	No

(continued on next page)

Figure 8.6 SAMPLE DAILY ACTIVITIES FORM COMPLETED FOR JESSICA *(continued)*

Time of Day	Activity	What the Child Does	How the Child Communicates	Family Priority (Yes/no)
3:00 P.M.	Snack time	Attempts to feed herself small pieces of graham crackers or bananas with her fingers; drinks from a held cup with minimal spillage.	Picks up crackers, reaches for the juice cup.	Yes
	Playtime	Momentarily looks at different toys, reaches for different toys, brings the toys to her mouth.	Reaches for desired toys; pushes away unwanted toys.	Yes
4:30 P.M.	Dinner preparation	Lies in the play pen; sometimes will roll back and forth; reaches for different toys.	Reaches for desired toys; cries if distressed.	No
5:30 P.M.	Dinner	Sits in an adaptive highchair at the table; opens her mouth when being fed; drinks from a held cup with minimal spillage.	Reaches for desired foods; turns her head away from disliked foods.	Yes
6:30 P.M.	Bath time	Splashes in water; cooperates while being undressed and dressed.	Moves her arms and legs to cooperate, laughs, splashes.	No
7:00 P.M.	Bedtime	Sometimes vocalizes with the song.	Rocks back and forth; vocalizes.	No

- After breakfast, Mrs. James gets ready to drive Jessica to her center-based program.
- Upon their arrival at the center-based program, Mr. Preston, Jessica's teacher, meets her with her adaptive wheelchair. He removes Jessica from the car, places her in her wheelchair, and wheels her to the classroom.
- In the afternoon, Mrs. James arrives to drive her home. Mr. Preston wheels Jessica to her grandmother's car and places her in the car.
- When they get home, Mrs. James carries Jessica into the house, removes her jacket and shoes, changes her diaper, and puts her down for her afternoon nap.
- After about an hour, Mrs. James wakes Jessica; changes her diaper; and feeds her a snack, usually some juice and a graham cracker or banana. Then they play together on the rug with some toys for a brief period.
- Mrs. James places Jessica in a playpen while she prepares dinner.
- After Mr. James arrives home from work, they all sit down and have dinner together. Jessica is placed in a special adaptive highchair during dinner.
- After dinner, Mr. James bathes Jessica and puts on her pajamas.
- At bedtime, Mrs. James changes Jessica's diaper and then sings to Jessica and rocks her in a rocking chair until she falls asleep.

In the family interview, Jessica's grandparents identified what they would like her to learn: drinking from a cup, feeding herself with a spoon, feeding herself more independently with her fingers, playing with toys, communicating what she wants, crawling or moving independently, and making choices.

Since Jessica attends the center-based program from 9:00 A.M. to 1:00 P.M. each day, the early interventionist interviewed the center staff to obtain Jessica's schedule of daily activities during this time. Using a similar interview process as with Jessica's grandparents, she added to the family's Daily Activities form with input from Jessica's teacher, Mr. Preston (see Figure 8.7).

After these interviews, the early interventionist, program staff, and Mrs. James discussed the need to complete a Characteristics of the Caregiving Environment form. Mrs. James felt confident about her interactions with Jessica, and the early interventionist agreed with her, so it was not necessary to complete this form for the home environment. However, everyone expressed concerns about Jessica's limited involvement in the center-based program, so the program staff decided to use the Characteristics of the Caregiving Environment inventory (see Figure 8.8).

Together, Mrs. James, Mr. Preston, and the early interventionist identified the following possible outcomes of intervention:

- drinking from a cup
- eating with a spoon
- establishing a toileting schedule
- crawling or moving to a preferred activity
- making choices
- communicating desires and needs
- playing with toys
- feeding himself with her fingers

Then they completed the Intervention Priority Checklist (see Figure 8.9) based on those possible goals. This process identified the following priorities for intervention:

Daily Activities

Name: __Jessica__   Date: __February 1, 1999__

Parent-Caregiver: __Mr. Preston, Teacher, Duffy Preschool__

Interviewer: __Jane Chang, Teacher__

Other Family Members Present: __—__

Weekday: __XX__   Weekend: _____

Time of Day	Activity	What the Child Does	How the Child Communicates	Staff Priority (Yes/no)
9:00 A.M.	Arrival	Cooperates with being transferred from the car to her adaptive wheelchair; cooperates while her diaper is changed and her jacket is removed.	Smiles upon seeing and hearing her teacher; moves her arms and legs to cooperate.	No
9:30 A.M.	Circle time	Moves her body in response to the song; occasionally looks at the child whose name has been called.	Smiles on seeing and hearing each child; moves her body.	No
10:00 A.M.	Center activity (varies)	Attempts to reach for and manipulate objects; occasionally looks at objects involved in the activity.	Reaches for or looks at objects.	Yes
10:45 A.M.	Snack time	Attempts to feed herself with her fingers; drinks from a held cup with minimal spillage.	Picks up crackers; reaches for the juice cup.	Yes

(continued on next page)

Figure 8.7 INTERVIEW WITH CENTER STAFF REGARDING JESSICA'S DAILY ACTIVITIES (continued)

Time of Day	Activity	What the Child Does	How the Child Communicates	Staff Priority (Yes/no)
11:00 A.M.	Outside playtime	Attempts to select a desired toy (such as a swing, scooter); reaches for objects in sand or water table.	Reaches for desired toys; pushes away unwanted toys.	Yes
11:45 A.M.	Clean-up	Gives each hand to be washed; cooperates while her diaper is changed.	Moves her hands and legs to cooperate with diaper change.	Yes
12:00	Lunch	Sits in the adaptive highchair at the table; opens her mouth when being fed; drinks from a held cup with minimal spillage.	Reaches for desired foods; turns head away from disliked foods.	Yes
1:00 P.M.	Going home	Cooperates while being transferred from her adaptive wheelchair to the car.	Smiles on seeing and hearing her grandmother.	No

Figure 8.8 SAMPLE CHARACTERISTICS OF THE CAREGIVING ENVIRONMENT FORM COMPLETED FOR JESSICA

Characteristics of the Caregiving Environment

Child: __Jessica__   Date: __February 2, 1999__

Environment: __Duffy Preschool__

Directions: Have the family and/or early intervention staff complete the inventory.

Questions	Response
How does the child receive physical contact (for example, hugs, touches, being held)?	We touch her hands or shoulders.

(continued on next page)

Figure 8.8 SAMPLE CHARACTERISTICS OF THE CAREGIVING ENVIRONMENT FORM COMPLETED FOR JESSICA *(continued)*

Questions	Response
How is the child encouraged to move and explore his surroundings?	Jessica sits in a wheelchair most of the day, except when her phy-therapist works with her.
How does the caregiver get the child's attention before interacting with the child (for instance, says the child's name, touches the child, taps the object)?	We say her name.
How does the caregiver provide opportunities for exploring objects (such as by pausing or giving prompts to encourage the child to explore)?	We place preferred toys or objects within her reach.
How does the caregiver engage the child to keep the child's attention and interest (for example, by pacing)?	We repeat her name, tap the object, or bend down to her eye level.
How does the caregiver facilitate the child's participation in activities (for instance, by rearranging materials, child's position, or his or her own position)?	We place objects within her reach and place her wheelchair as close as possible.
How does the caregiver identify and interpret the child's nonverbal cues (such as quieting means "I'm interested" or turning the head away means "I don't like it")?	If Jessica pushes something away or turns her head, that's a no. If she smiles or laughs, we assume she likes the thing.
How does the caregiver indicate the child's turn (for instance, by pausing, waiting, or touching the child)?	We wait for Jessica to respond, but she often does not.
How are the child's requests for objects or assistance acknowledged (complied or denied)?	If Jessica reaches for an object, we give it to her.
Are the child's communicative intents and behaviors acknowledged and/or expanded?	Jessica's limited vocalizations are repeated and praised.
How are augmentative communication methods (such as exaggerated vocalization, touch cues, object cues or adapted manual signs) used, if necessary?	None is currently being used.

(continued on next page)

Figure 8.8   SAMPLE CHARACTERISTICS OF THE CAREGIVING ENVIRONMENT FORM COMPLETED FOR JESSICA *(continued)*

Questions	Response
Which activities are mutually enjoyable for the child and caregiver (like bathing, feeding, playtime)?	Circle time and outside playtime.
How is the child included in ongoing activities-daily routines (for example, placing the child near the adult or providing him or her with toys)?	Jessica is placed as close as possible to the activities.
How is the environment organized to encourage movement and exploration (uncluttered, specific places for toys or objects, adaptations)?	Toys, objects, and supplies are placed in consistent places.
How is the environment organized to encourage the use of vision, if applicable (for instance, proper lighting, high contrast, glare-free)?	We bring things to her to see them.
How is the environment organized to encourage the use of listening skills, if applicable (for example, reduced background noise, floors carpeted)?	Not applicable.

- moving to a preferred activity
- making choices
- communicating desires and needs
- playing with toys
- feeding herself with her fingers

After these priorities were established, the early intervention team met to develop specific objectives for intervention with Jessica. The team members included Jessica's classroom teacher, Mr. Preston, who has a background in severe disabilities; the early interventionist (a teacher who is certified in the field of visual impairments and early intervention); a speech and language therapist; a physical therapist; Jessica's grandmother, Mrs. James; the early childhood special education inclusion facilitator from the community child development preschool; and the preschool teacher. They specified the following objectives:

1. Jessica will move to a preferred activity with minimal assistance.

Figure 8.9 SAMPLE INTERVENTION PRIORITY CHECKLIST COMPLETED FOR JESSICA

Intervention Priority Checklist

Name: Jessica Date: February 3, 1999

Completed by: Mr. and Mrs. James, grandparents; Mr. Preston and Ms. Chang, Teachers

Directions: List each skill or objective in the spaces across the top. Answer each question for each skill or objective listed.

Ratings: 3 = Strongly agree 2 = Agree 1 = Somewhat agree 0 = Disagree

	Activity							
Criteria	Cup Drinking	Using a Spoon	Toilet Skills	Move to activity	Make Choices	Communi-cation	Play with Toys	Finger feeding
Learning this skill is a family priority.	3	3	0	3	3	3	3	2
The activity or activities in which the skill is required are preferred by the child.	2	2	1	2	2	3	3	3
The skill increases the child's ability to interact with people and objects during daily activities.	3	3	1	3	3	3	3	3
If this skill is not learned by the child, someone else will be required to do the task for him or her.	3	3	3	3	3	3	1	3
This skill can be applied across a variety of activities and/or environments.	3	3	3	3	3	3	3	3
This skill occurs frequently enough to ensure multiple opportunities to practice and learn it.	3	3	2	3	3	3	3	3
This skill can be encouraged and reinforced in a natural and meaningful way during daily activities.	3	3	2	3	3	3	3	3
This skill can be easily elicited during different activities.	3	3	2	3	3	3	3	3
The child can acquire the skills in the designated period.	2	1	2	3	3	3	3	2
The skill and characteristics of the task match the child's strengths and desires.	1	1	2	2	3	3	3	2
Total score (Possible total score = 30)	26	25	18	28	29	30	28	27

2. Given small bite-size pieces of food, Jessica will feed herself with her fingers.
3. Jessica will first use shift of gaze and then look at a specific object to make choices.
4. Jessica will manipulate and explore preferred toys with assistance from an adult or classmate.
5. Jessica will communicate preferences using conventional gestures (nodding to indicate yes and shaking her head to indicate no).

As a result of the team meeting, several routine analyses were conducted to facilitate the integration of the objectives within specific routines in Jessica's home and classroom environment. The completed Routine Analysis for Jessica's circle time is presented in Figure 8.10 as an example.

Finally, an Objectives-Within-Routines Matrix was used to identify when during Jessica's day each priority for intervention could be addressed. The matrix in Figure 8.11 provides an overview of Jessica's daily schedule of activities at the center-based program, the specific opportunities during Jessica's day when each of the objectives can be encouraged and practiced, and strategies for addressing specific objectives in the identified activities. Although Jessica will be leaving the infant program in three months, the team thought that this planning process enabled them to provide a more appropriate program while she is at the center. The procedures that were used for planning and implementing his infant program will be helpful when she enters the preschool program as well.

Developing Meaningful Intervention Outcomes

Once the early intervention team has identified the skills to be developed, they must develop intervention outcomes that are meaningful to the infant and family. That is, the goals and objectives must be child directed, easily integrated within the family routine, and functional. Child-directed objectives mean that the infant's lead is followed by focusing on the infant's strengths and interests and that the infant is actively engaged in doing something, rather than encouraged to do nothing. In other words, the objective should identify what the infant *is* to do, not what he or she is *not* to do.

> **Example 1:** "Gaby will stop flapping her hands in front of her eyes." *This example requires the child to do nothing.*

> **Example 2:** "Gaby will clap her hands to music." *This example requires the child to do something.*

Figure 8.10 SAMPLE COMPLETED ROUTINE ANALYSIS FOR JESSICA'S CIRCLE TIME

Routine Analysis

Name: Jessica   Date: February 19, 1999   Activity: Circle Time

Steps in Routine	Natural Cues	Behaviors to Encourage	Input and Adaptive Strategies	Area (Discipline)*
Getting ready for circle time	Children arriving. Carpet squares placed on the rug.	Communicate her desire to move to the rug area. Move to rug area.	"Circle Time!" "Everyone sits down on a carpet square." Place Jessica on the rug near the circle area.	ST
Greeting song, "Good morning"	Children sitting on carpet squares. Tape recorder playing "Good morning" song. Teacher and children singing the song and clapping their hands	Vocalize along with the song. Move her body with the music. Clap with the song.	Let's sing our "Good Morning" song. "Good morning, good morning, good morning to you . . ." Secure a tambourine on Jessica's lap or one arm of her wheelchair.	PT
"Who's Here Today?"	Children's name are called. Children individually stand up.	Look at each child as his or her name is called. Raise her hand when her name is called.	"Who's Here Today? _____ [Jessica]" Pause until everyone is looking at the identified child. Wave hand above the identified child's head. "Look at _____ [Jessica]." "Raise your hand."	VI
Announcing the day's activity	Teacher holds up the object representing the activity. Center area set up for the activity.	Look at the object. Look at the center area.	"Today, we are going to _____." Wave the object to attract Jessica's attention. Walk over to the center. "Look at the center, we are going to _____."	VI
Clean up Transition to centers	Children stand up. Carpet squares put away.	Communicate her desire to move to the center area.	"Pick up your carpet square and put it away." "Go to the center."	ST

ST = speech therapy, PT = physical therapy, VI = visual impairment.

Figure 8.11 SAMPLE OBJECTIVES-WITHIN-ROUTINES MATRIX COMPLETED FOR JESSICA

Objectives-Within-Routines Matrix

Name: Jessica

Date: February 22, 1999

	Daily Routines			
Objectives	**Circle Time**	**Center Activity**	**Snack Time**	**Outside Playtime**
1. Jessica will move to a preferred activity with minimal assistance.	Place Jessica on the rug near the circle activity.			Place Jessica on a scooter board.
2. Given small bite-size pieces of food, Jessica will feed herself with her fingers.			Provide Jessica with bite-size pieces of her preferred foods. Provide good contrast between the foods and the plate. Use a nonskid mat under the plate.	
3. Jessica will first use shift of gaze and then look at a specific object to make choices.	Encourage Jessica to look at the specific child named. Teacher waves hand over the child's head. Teacher says, "Look at Sara."		Provide Jessica with a choice between juice or water and wait until she responds. Teacher gently waves each choice, one at a time.	Provide Jessica with a choice between two activities or objects and wait until she responds.
4. Jessica will manipulate and explore preferred toys with the facilitation of an adult or peer.		Provide large objects in primary colors with interesting textures and shapes. Provide only 2–3 objects at a time.		Provide large objects in primary colors with interesting textures and shapes. Have another child hand the object to Jessica.
5. Jessica will communicate preferences using conventional gestures (nods to indicate yes and shaking her head to indicate no).	Ask yes–no-format questions (such as "Is Lisa here today?")	Ask yes–no-format questions (such as "Do you want the blue crayon?" "Do you want to sit next to Rob?").		Ask yes–no-format questions (such as "Do you want to play with the sand?").

Objectives that are infused within the family's everyday activities are more easily integrated into the family's routine. Therefore, the behaviors or skills that are identified in the objectives can be elicited naturally and reinforced with natural consequences. If an infant sees her bottle (antecedent) and requests the bottle by reaching for it (response), then the natural consequence is to drink the milk from the bottle.

> **Example 1:** "James will look at an optokinetic drum." *This example requires the use of clinical and unnatural visual stimuli, since the optokinetic drum is a black-and-white vertically striped drum that is used by eye specialists during clinical examinations.*

> **Example 2:** "James will look at his caregiver's face when he is held." *This example is easily incorporated into the family's routine and involves a meaningful visual stimulus.*

Finally, objectives for infants who have severe multiple disabilities must address functional behaviors or skills. Functional behaviors increase an infant's level of participation by reducing dependence on others. Meaningful behaviors or skills are those performed within the context of the family's daily routines.

> **Example 1:** "Erin will reach for a shiny pom-pom presented to her at a distance of 12 inches." *This example is not functional.*

> **Example 2:** "Erin will find her spoon on the tray during mealtime." *This example is functional.*

> **Example 3**: "Erin will wave bye-bye when requested by an adult." *This example is functional but not necessarily performed in a meaningful context.*

> **Example 4:** "Erin will wave bye-bye when a family member leaves the house." *This is a functional skill and is used in a meaningful context.*

Meaningful Ways to Encourage Visual Attention

When infants have low vision and multiple disabilities, they may be subjected to visual stimulation programs using artificial and meaningless stimuli, such as, lights, pom-poms, and black-and-white patterns (Chen & Haney, 1995). However, as discussed earlier in Chapter 3, meaningless and noncontingent stimulation only decreases an infant's motivation and ability to learn. Chapter 5 emphasizes the need to encourage the infant to look in everyday activities and selected ways to engage the infant's visual attention to objects and people. Initially, even with environmental modifications (such as lighting, high contrast marking on the object), some infants with multiple disabilities may not respond to natural visual stimuli (such as bottle, caregiver's face); but they will look at shiny objects or lights; so some early intervention programs tend to focus solely on these artificial stimuli.

When it is difficult to encourage a child's participation in an activity, the system of least prompts strategy can be used to provide a gradual increase in the amount of assistance that the child needs (Doyle, Wolery, Ault, & Gast, 1988). This strategy can be adapted to encourage an infant's use of functional vision by selecting specific cues or prompts based on the nature of the object, the distance of the object from the infant, the placement of the object in the infant's visual field, and the lighting situation. First, the visual characteristics of the object can be accentuated by providing highly contrasting materials, enlarging the materials, or illuminating the object with a flashlight or penlight to elicit visual attention (Tavernier, 1993). Second, auditory referencing, or pairing an auditory cue with the object (i.e., tapping the bottle on the table) can be used to encourage the desired visual behavior (Downing & Bailey, 1990). Third, the distance of the object from the infant can be altered by moving either the child or the object to decrease the distance between them. Initially, the object should be positioned optimally to allow the infant to look at it, based on the infant's visual field. For example, some infants with cortical visual impairment are more likely to attend visually if an object is first presented in their peripheral field and then moved more centrally. Whenever possible, lighting should be glare-free; natural or normal indoor lighting and individualized for an infant's needs. For example, an infant with albinism may be light sensitive while an infant with myopia and very thick glasses may require high levels of illumination. The use of darkened rooms to view illuminated or lighted objects should be used only if all other less intrusive prompts have been employed to encourage the infant's visual attention.

The hierarchy of least prompts is illustrated in Figure 8.12 to show the progression for engaging an infant's visual attention. The desired visual behavior is to have the baby look at his or her mother's face. The natural cues are the mother's face at a distance of 14–16 inches from the baby's face under normal indoor lighting conditions. If these natural cues do not elicit a visual response from the baby, then the mother may choose to accentuate her face with bright lipstick or by wearing a brightly colored scarf on her head (additional cues/prompts). If this prompt does not elicit a response, then the mother should alter the distance by moving closer to her infant (additional cue/prompt). If the infant still does not look, then the mother should try positioning her face in various sections of the infant's peripheral field starting with the left field, then right, top, and bottom (additional cue/prompt). If there is still no response, then the mother could illuminate her face with a flashlight to engage the infant's visual attention (additional cue/prompt). The last cue/prompt (provides the most amount of assistance) would be to darken the room, while the mother's face is illuminated.

Routine Analysis

Once meaningful outcomes of interventions have been identified, the next step is to identify and select daily caregiving or play routines in which to integrate interventions that are enjoyable for the family and the infant. A focus on daily routines encourages instruction during natural situations and facilitates the infant's understanding of and response to significant natural cues. Natural cues, such as the objects used in an activity, the individuals who are present, the infant's position and location in the room, and the time of day, are natural occurrences that inform the infant what is about to occur (Downing & Eichinger, 1990). Infants with severe visual impairments may be unaware of the numerous natural cues that signal the beginning or end of an activity, so it is essential for their caregivers to use consistent cues or signals to prepare and involve them. For example, a sighted infant can see his mother putting on her coat, picking up her purse, and searching for her car keys. Over time these naturally occurring visual cues prepare the infant for

Figure 8.12 HIERARCHY OF LEAST PROMPTS FOR ENCOURAGING VISUAL ATTENTION

(Rule: **If** no response after several attempts, **then** move to next prompt ⟶)

Newborn

Object: Caregiver's face ⟶ **Accentuate** caregiver's face with exaggerated facial expressions or bright lipstick or contrasting cap ⟶ **Illuminate** the caregiver's face with a flashlight or penlight

Distance: Close to infant's face ⟶ Move caregiver's face closer to infant

Placement: Central field ⟶ Identify optimum position for viewing based on infant's central and peripheral fields

Lighting: Natural or normal indoor lighting ⟶ **Darken** room

3 Months

Object: Bottle or favorite toy ⟶ **Accentuate** object (e.g., black-and-white strips) or provide contrasting background ⟶ **Move** the object slowly and continuously or **pair with an auditory cue** (e.g., tapping bottle on table) ⟶ **Illuminate** the object with a flashlight or penlight

Distance: Close to infant's face ⟶ Move object closer to infant

Placement: Central field ⟶ Identify optimum position for viewing based on infant's central and peripheral fields ⟶ Present object in the infant's peripheral field

Lighting: Natural or normal indoor lighting ⟶ **Darken** room

the mother's departure. These sequences of events increase the infant's ability to participate actively by providing predictability, which, in turn, promotes a sense of control over events.

Families' daily routines differ in the steps in activities and perhaps the sequences of the steps. For example, the meal routine in one family may be to serve all the children first and then the father; the mother will sit down to eat only after everyone has been served. In another family, everyone eats together. Some families put the food in serving bowls and place them on the table, while others put individual portions on plates and then place the plates on the table. Each family's practices should be incorporated into the analysis of routines. Early interventionists should work with the families to design and implement appropriate interventions that fit the families' priorities, culture, and practices (Lynch & Hanson, 1998).

A routine should be analyzed to identify the beginning of, the steps in, and the end of the routine; the natural cues that are involved in the activity; and the infant's behaviors that are to be encouraged or practiced. Through careful observations, the early interventionist can also identify what the infant can do independently, as well as possible strategies and materials that may be effective for motivating the infant's active participation. These observations can be recorded on a Routine Analysis form, as demonstrated in the Routine Analysis of Bobby's playtime at home (see Figure 8.4) and Jessica's circle time at the center (see Figure 8.10).

For example, a breakfast routine may include the following steps: placing the infant in the high chair, putting a bib on the infant, bringing a bowl of cereal to the tray, feeding the infant, and so forth. The natural cues that let the infant recognize that breakfast is about to be served, include the time of day (morning), actions (being carried into the kitchen), objects (high chair, bib, cereal bowl, and spoon), odors (smell of food), and sounds (the whistle of the kettle or the bell of the microwave). Within the breakfast routine, there are natural opportunities for encouraging an infant with low vision to look at her mother's face when her mother has the spoon, look at the bowl of cereal or spoon, and open her mouth to take a bite when she sees the spoon. Similarly, an infant who is blind may be encouraged to search for the bowl or spoon, to reach for and touch his mother, and to open his mouth when his mother says "take a bite."

In the example of Bobby's playtime, the Routine Analysis (Figure 8.4) shows how specific objectives from each discipline are integrated into the playtime routine. The form indicates specific strategies that Mrs. Sanchez can use to encourage Bobby to perform specific behaviors, such as looking, reaching, speaking, and smiling. Similarly, the analysis for Jessica's circle time (Figure 8.10) targeted specific behaviors for her teacher to encourage and specific strategies to use.

Understanding Family Rituals

Early interventionists need to gather information about family rituals. Family rituals are highly valued social activities that occur frequently and repeatedly during family interactions. They reflect the family's core culture and vary considerably among families. There are three types of family rituals: (1) daily rituals, such as dinnertime customs, bathtime rituals, and bedtime practices; (2) family traditions; and (3) family celebrations (Schuck & Bucy, 1997). For example, a bedtime routine for a toddler and her mother may include the following activities:

- getting ready for bed by picking up and putting toys away together
- changing her diaper
- putting on her pajamas
- placing her in her bed.

These activities are completed before the toddler is put to bed each night. The rituals associated with these activities may include a mother singing the "Itsy, Bitsy Spider" and moving her fingers slowly up her daughter's leg as she changes her daughter's clothes, or a mother softly singing a lullaby and rubbing the infant's back until he falls asleep. These rituals are not necessary activities, but special procedures that the mother wants to engage in during a daily routine.

The early interventionist must be aware of and attend to the family's rituals when developing interventions (Schuck & Bucy, 1997). For example, suggesting that the mother should encourage the infant to take off her clothes by herself may disrupt the existing natural interaction of the mother's ritual of singing and playing with her daughter. Furthermore, the family may not see the need to encourage a child who is under 3 years old to learn to dress and undress independently.

Expectations for toddlers regarding feeding, sleeping, toilet training, and discipline vary across cultural groups and may differ from those of the early interventionist or mainstream culture; these differences must be recognized and respected (Lynch, 1998). Early intervention and child care programs tend to emphasize schedules for caregiving activities and encourage toddler's development of independent eating, toileting, and other adaptive skills (Gonzalez-Mena, 1993). For example, an early interventionist may be concerned that a child who is almost 3 years old is still drinking from a bottle and sleeping with his parents, whereas his family may depend on the infant's own natural biological rhythms and think it is natural for 3 year olds to drink from a bottle and unnatural to sleep alone. These differential expectations may be based on the infant's disabilities, as well as cultural values.

It is essential for an early interventionist to listen carefully to the family's expressed concerns about the infant's development and to provide suggestions that will fit the family's situation. Family members will not follow through on suggestions that conflict with their practices (Anderson, 1989). For example, if they do not see the importance of helping an infant to drink from a cup, they will continue to use a bottle. Similarly, family members may not want to put the infant on the floor to provide experiences for motor development or to allow the infant to put objects in his or her mouth for exploration because they think it is unhealthy to do so (Alvarez, 1998; Lieberman, 1990). In such instances, the early interventionist needs to explain why it may be important to encourage an infant with visual impairments and other disabilities to drink from a cup, roll around or crawl on the floor, and explore objects with his or her mouth while respecting the family's values and concerns. The early interventionist may explain for example, that whereas a sighted infant may see other people using cups and be motivated to imitate them, an infant with severe visual impairments and other disabilities may not have access to these models. Furthermore, this infant may need additional opportunities, time, and assistance to develop motor skills and concepts of objects. To alleviate some of a family's concerns about cleanliness, an early intervention program can provide opportunities for an infant to be on the floor in a clean carpeted area where shoes are not allowed and the infant can be encouraged to play on a blanket with toys that have been washed thoroughly. The carpet and blanket also provide helpful landmarks for an infant who is visually impaired. Thus, activities are implemented in such a way as both to meet the infant's learning needs and to fit with the family's values.

Objectives-Within-Routines Matrix

Developing a matrix to show where the infant's objectives and interventions can be integrated within the daily schedule of activities is a helpful practice for families and service providers (Cripe & Venn, 1997). Infusion of objectives within the daily routine makes various interventions easier to implement and facilitates a transdisciplinary approach because it provides a systematic format for addressing all the identified objectives and provides multiple opportunities for the infant to work on these identified areas throughout the day with a variety of individuals. Most important, a focus on the daily routine supports the infant's participation and interaction in natural social contexts and physical settings. This emphasis on context is a distinguishing characteristic of a naturalistic curriculum model in which the content of the curriculum is derived from the requirements of activities in typical situations (Noonan & McCormick, 1992).

The Objectives-Within-Routines Matrix is a convenient format for identifying the specific activities in which an infant has the opportunity to focus on particular skill areas. The first step in developing such a matrix is to list the infant's intervention objectives down the left-hand column. Then, the daily activities in which there is sufficient time and flexibility to allow for intervention strategies are listed across the top row. Finally, for each objective, the specific activity or activities are selected that can best accommodate strategies to support that objective. For each activity that is selected, one or more strategies are specified to encourage the infant's participation in the activity toward achievement of the identified objective.

This format is most appropriate for a center-based program, as shown in the matrix for Jessica (Figure 8.11). However, if a family chooses to use this procedure, the list of daily activities need not encompass every waking moment of the child. For example, Bobby's mother, Mrs. Sanchez, does not have time to focus on Bobby until her other children and husband are at school or work. By identifying activities between midmorning and early afternoon, on Bobby's matrix (Figure 8.5), Mrs. Sanchez will be better able to focus her attention on Bobby and the selected interventions.

Infusing objectives within the daily routine provides the infant with multiple opportunities to engage in the desired behaviors and to practice skills with a variety of people throughout the day, rather than only during limited times with a specific service provider. For example, Jessica's third objective, using shift of gaze to look at objects and make choices, can be encouraged at circle time by the physical therapist, during snack time by the early interventionist and at recess time by the orientation and mobility instructor, instead of only when the teacher who is certified in the field of visual impairments is present. Thus, in addition to providing multiple learning opportunities for the infant, the Objectives-Within-Routines Matrix facilitates a transdisciplinary approach to the implementation of interventions, since each service provider implements a variety of intervention objectives with the infant.

The final case study of Mindy again illustrates the process through which the early intervention team can develop meaningful intervention outcomes for an infant whose multiple disabilities include visual impairment, using the procedures and instructional strategies discussed in this chapter. It is important to emphasize that when gathering information, the early intervention team needs to determine which procedures will be necessary and appropriate to use. For example, as was previously noted, the Characteristics of the Caregiving Environment form is appropriate only if the family has shared a concern in this area. The selection and use of procedures also depend on whether the infant is involved in a home-based or center-based program (or both). For example, since Bobby is cared for at home and his mother was concerned about adequately meeting his needs, given her circumstances at home, the early interventionist assessed the caregiving environment of the home. On the other hand, Jessica and Mindy both attend center-based programs, and no concern was expressed about their home environments, so the team assessed the caregiving environments of only those programs.

It is also instructive to compare the planning done to create appropriate interventions for Jessica and Mindy, both in a center-based environment. For example, a Routine Analysis of circle time is presented for both Jessica and Mindy. The steps in the activity and nearly all the natural cues are the same. However, some of the behaviors to be encouraged and the adaptive strategies to be used are different because of the two infants' different abilities and needs.

In Mindy's situation, because she was uncomfortable handling new objects and hated being forced to touch things, special strategies were needed to introduce new objects and to encourage her to explore them. These specific strategies are explained in detail in Mindy's case study.

MINDY

Mindy, aged 32 months, is in a center-based infant program and will be making the transition to a preschool program for children without disabilities. She was born three months premature and is totally blind because of retinopathy of prematurity. Mindy is developmentally delayed and has seizures. She is just beginning to talk, although she tends to repeat what her mother says. She walked at 9 months adjusted age and has advanced mobility skills. However, she dislikes handling and exploring objects with her hands. In her new preschool with sighted peers, Mindy will receive services from a teacher, who is certified in the field of visual impairments, an orientation and mobility instructor, and a speech and language therapist. In this case, the following information-gathering procedures have already been conducted:

- a family interview, which produced a schedule of her daily activities at home
- an interview with the staff at the center, which produced a schedule of Mindy's daily activities at the center
- an observation-interview of the center-based program's caregiving environment.

This information identified the most critical intervention outcomes for Mindy as

1. developing her communication skills
2. using her hands to examine objects
3. interacting with other children
4. developing early literacy skills
5. expanding her orientation and mobility skills.

On the basis of the identified priorities, the staff developed several routine analyses of Mindy's various activities. As an example, Figure 8.13 shows the routine analysis for circle time. Then the staff was able to create an Objectives-Within-Routine matrix (Figure 8.14) to plan how to integrate her intervention objectives within the routines of her center-based program.

In addition, specific strategies were discussed to encourage Mindy to explore and handle objects. Like other young children with severe visual impairments, Mindy cannot examine objects visually; she must tactilely explore and manipulate them to recognize and become familiar with them. Objects are constantly being placed in her hands to facilitate this process. Mindy dislikes having objects put in her hands or having her hands manipulated to handle objects and tends to drop the objects and become irritable. Since this practice does not allow her to have control over

Figure 8.13 SAMPLE COMPLETED ROUTINE ANALYSIS OF MINDY'S CIRCLE TIME

Routine Analysis

Name: ___Mindy___   Date: ___January 25, 1999___   Activity: ___Circle Time___

Steps in Routine	Natural Cues	Behaviors to Encourage	Input and Adaptive Strategies	Area (Discipline)*
Getting ready for circle time	Children arriving. Carpet squares placed on the rug.	Communicate her desire to move to the rug area. Move to the rug area.	"Circle Time!" "Everyone sits down on a carpet square." Use the sighted guide technique to assist Mindy to find the rug near circle area.	ST O&M
Greeting song, "Good morning"	Children sitting on carpet squares. Tape recorder playing "Good morning" song. Teacher and children singing the song and clapping their hands.	Vocalize along with the song. Move her body with the music. Clap with the song.	Let's sing our "Good Morning" song. "Good morning, good morning, good morning to you. . . ." Encourage Mindy to participate with hand-under-hand assistance.	ST VI
"Who's Here Today?"	Children's names are called. Children raise their hands.	Listen to each name called. Raise her hand when her name is called.	"Who's Here Today? _____ [Mindy]" "_____ [Mindy] Hands up" Pause until the identified child raises her hand and says "Me," if appropriate. "_____ [Mindy] is here today."	ST
Announcing the day's activities	Teacher holds up the object representing the activity. Center area set up for the activity.	Handle the object	"Today, we are going to _____ [read stories and play with sand]." Give object [book, pail] to Mindy to examine. Walk over to each center. "At the _____ [book corner], we are going to _____ [read stories]."	VI
Clean up Transition to centers	Children stand up. Carpet squares put away.	Put carpet square on the shelf. Communicate the choice of activity by saying the word.	"Pick up your carpet and put it away." "Do you want to read a book or play play with sand?" [show the objects]	O&M ST

ST = speech therapy, O&M = orientation and mobility instruction, VI = visual impairment.

Figure 8.14   SAMPLE OBJECTIVES-WITHIN-ROUTINES MATRIX COMPLETED FOR MINDY

Objectives-Within-Routines Matrix

Date: _February 3, 1999_

Name: _Mindy_

| | | **Daily Routines** | | |
Objectives	**Breakfast**	**Center Activity**	**Snack Time**	**Outside Playtime**
1. Mindy will use sighted guide, trailing, and other orientation and mobility skills without assistance.	Call Mindy to the rug area for the circle activity.	Ask a peer to use the sighted guide technique to help Mindy locate the center that she chooses.	After washing her hands at the sink, encourage Mindy to locate the snack table by trailing along the counters to the table.	The orientation and mobility instructor will work with Mindy on using the cane to go outside to the playground and to return to the classroom. He will also assist Mindy in developing her skills in locating and playing on playground equipment with peers.
2. Given toys and other objects, Mindy will examine them tactilely.	Introduce toys and other objects related to the circle-time activity. Use hand-under-hand strategies, when possible, and fade assistance.	Introduce toys and other objects related to the circle-time activity. Use hand-under-hand strategies, when possible, and fade assistance.	Encourage Mindy to drink from a cup and eat finger foods at snack time.	
3. Mindy will listen to stories and scan braille sentences in a Twin Vision book.	During the group story time encourage Mindy to examine a book with tactile symbols, braille, or objects related to the story, as appropriate.	When Mindy chooses the book center, use hand-over-hand strategies and then fade to hand-under-hand strategies to encourage her to examine the braille book.		
4. Mindy will interact with peers by sharing toys, taking turns, and responding to them.	Encourage Mindy and peers to interact with each other, by touching each other to get attention and responding to questions.	Encourage Mindy and peers to share toys and materials in the center activities and to talk about what they are doing.		Encourage Mindy and peers to play together on outdoor equipment, for example, take turns on the slide.

how much and when she wishes to handle a particular object her reactions are quite understandable.

A better strategy for presenting an object, especially an unfamiliar one, would be for the presenter to hold the object in the palm of his or her hand and then place the back of his or her hand under Mindy's hand. This strategy would give Mindy the opportunity to interact with the object at her own level of comfort. For example, Mindy may want to touch the object initially only with her fingertips and eventually hold more of the object. Thus, using the preferred strategy, the presenter first offers Mindy a familiar and safe object (a warm, soft, and familiar hand), rather than an unfamiliar and potentially tactilely offensive object. The following procedure is an alternative method for introducing objects that will provide Mindy with a sense of comfort and control:

1. Hold the object in your hand and place the back of your hand under Mindy's (see Figure 8.15A). This way Mindy is comfortable and secure in having physical contact with another's hand. She is familiar with the feel of another's hand and will hold an adult's hand.

2. With Mindy's hand on yours, slowly turn your hand around until Mindy can feel the object being held in your hand—in this case, a hairbrush (see Figures 8.15B

Figure 8.15   OFFERING AN OBJECT FOR EXPLORATION

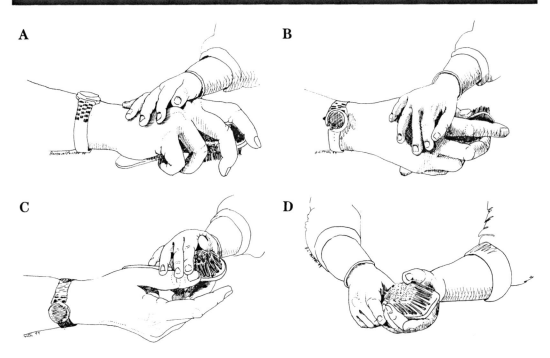

A   B

C   D

Illustration: Barbara Porter

and C). This slow introduction allows Mindy to become more comfortable with the new or less familiar tactile input of the object. She can also adjust her hand position to increase or decrease the amount of contact with the object.

3. Finally, encourage Mindy to handle and explore the object with both hands so she

can examine the object carefully and completely (see Figure 8.15D).

Another possible strategy: hand-over-hand assistance. Mindy's new preschool program stresses early literacy experiences and reading stories. The teachers want to introduce books with braille to Mindy but are not sure how to do so. As discussed in Chapter 3,

Figure 8.16   INTRODUCING BRAILLE USING HAND-OVER-HAND ASSISTANCE

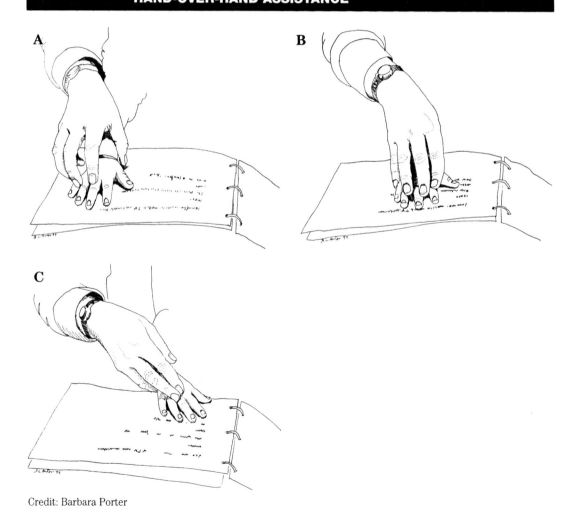

Credit: Barbara Porter

hand-over-hand assistance should be used carefully and decreased as soon as possible. While reading aloud to Mindy, the adult can provide hand-over-hand assistance, if necessary, to help her learn that braille dots have meaning.

1. Have Mindy place her hand on the page, then physically guide her to reposition it to the top left corner Figure 8.16A shows the adult in the process of repositioning the child's hand.

2. With your hand on hers, help Mindy to move her hand from left to right across the line of braille, as shown in Figure 8.16B.

3. Gradually decrease the amount of assistance that your hand provides while

Figure 8.17   READING A BRAILLE BOOK USING HAND-UNDER-HAND ASSISTANCE

A

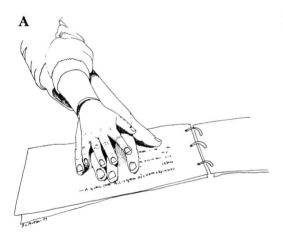

B

C

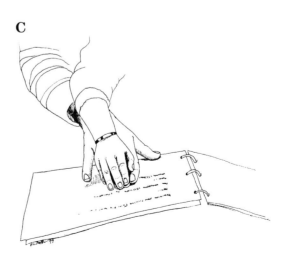

Credit: Barbara Porter

guiding Mindy to move her hand from right to left across each line and down the lines of braille on the book, as shown in Figure 8.16C.

When possible, if Mindy is motivated to engage in this reading activity, hand-under-hand assistance may be used in the following steps:

1. Place your hand on the book and encourage Mindy to place her hand on yours, as shown in Figure 8.17A. This procedure allows Mindy to locate your hand on the book and to imitate its placement.

2. Move your fingers from left to right along each line of braille, as shown in Figure 8.17B. This process allows Mindy to experience the hand movements that are required for the reading activity.

3. Slowly pull your hand back from under Mindy's hand so she will feel the lines of braille and move her hand with minimal physical guidance of your hand under hers, as shown in Figure 8.17C. This gradual fading of assistance encourages Mindy to "read" braille on her own.

CONCLUSION

Infants vary in their strengths, interests, and needs. Families differ in their priorities, concerns, and practices. Service providers differ in their philosophies and approaches to early intervention. Despite these differences, however, early intervention services need to meet the family members' concerns about their infant's development, address the infant's abilities and disabilities, and provide support for the infant's participation in everyday activities. To fulfill these professional responsibilities, therefore, an early interventionist needs specific strategies for gathering information about the infant and from the family, knowledge of and skills in conducting specific intervention strategies, and ways to provide coordinated intervention services with other members of the infant's intervention team. This chapter provides a starting place for service providers to meet their professional responsibilities by obtaining specific strategies and expanding on their professional skills.

REFERENCES

Able-Boone, H., Sandall, S. R., Loughry, A., & Frederick, L. L. (1990). An informed, family-centered approach to Public Law 99–457: Parental views. *Topics in Early Childhood Special Education, 10,* 100–111.

Alvarez, L. I. G. (1998). A short course in sensitivity training. Working with Hispanic families of children with disabilities. *Teaching Exceptional Children, 31,* 73–77.

Anderson, P. P. (1989). Issues in serving culturally diverse families of young children with disabilities. *Early Child Development and Care, 50,* 167–188.

Barnard, K. E., & Kelly, J. F. (1990). Assessment of parent-child interaction. In S. J. Meisels & J. P. Shonkoff (Eds.), *Handbook of early childhood intervention* (pp. 278–302). Cambridge, England: Cambridge University Press.

Bennett, T., Lingerfelt, B. V., & Nelson, D. E. (1990). *Developing individualized family support plans.* Cambridge, MA: Brookline Books.

Chen, D., Chan, S., & Brekken, L. (in press). Conversations for three: Communicating through interpreters [Booklet & video]. Baltimore, MD: Paul H. Brookes.

Chen, D., Friedman, C. T., & Calvello, G. (1990). *Parents and visually impaired infants.* Louisville, KY: American Printing House for the Blind.

Chen, D., & Haney, M. (1995). An early intervention model for infants who are deaf-blind. *Journal of Visual Impairments & Blindness, 89,* 213–221.

Cripe, J. W., & Venn, M. L. (1997). Family-guided routines for early intervention services. *Young Exceptional Children, 1,* 18–26.

Dennis, R. E., & Giangreco, M. (1996). Creating conversation: Reflections on cultural sensitivity in family interviewing. *Exceptional Children, 63,* 103–116.

Dote-Kwan, J. (1995). Essential steps for getting started. In D. Chen & J. Dote-Kwan, *Starting points: Instructional practices for young children whose multiple disabilities include visual impairment* (pp. 29–42). Los Angeles: Blind Childrens Center.

Downing, J., & Bailey, B. (1990). Developing vision use within functional daily activities for students with visual and multiple disabilities. *RE:view, 21,* 209–219.

Downing, J., & Eichinger, J. (1990). Instructional strategies for learners with dual sensory impairments in integrated settings. *Journal of the Association for Persons with Sever Handicaps, 15,* 98–105.

Doyle, P. M., Wolery, M., Ault, M. J. & Gast, D. L. (1988). System of least prompts: A literature review of procedural parameters. *Journal for The Association for Person with Severe Handicaps, 13,* 28–49.

Dunst, C. J., Trivette, C. M., & Deal, A. G. (1988). *Enabling and empowering families: Principles and guidelines for practice.* Cambridge, MA: Brookline Books.

Fraiberg, S. (1974). Blind infants and their mothers: An examination of the sign system. In M. Lewis & L. S. Rosenblum (Eds.), *The effect of the infant on its caregiver* (pp. 215–232). New York: John Wiley & Sons.

Gonzalez-Mena, J. (1993). *Multicultural issues in child care.* Mountain View, CA: Mayfield.

Lieberman, A. F. (1990). Culturally sensitive intervention with children and families. *Child and Adolescent Social Work, 7,* 101–120.

Lowenthal, B. (1993). The family interview: A technique of early childhood assessment. *Infant-Toddler Intervention, 3,* 101–108.

Lynch, E. W. (1998). Developing cross-cultural competence. In E. W. Lynch & M. J. Hanson, *Developing cross-cultural competence: A guide for working with young children and their families* (2nd ed., pp. 47–89). Baltimore, MD: Paul H. Brookes.

Lynch, E. W., & Hanson, M. J. (1998). Steps in the right direction: Implications for interventionists. In E. W. Lynch & M. J. Hanson, *Developing cross-cultural competence: A guide for working with young children and their families* (2nd ed., pp. 491–512). Baltimore, MD: Paul H. Brookes.

McCollum, J. A., & McBride, S. I. (1997). Ratings of parent-infant interaction: Raising questions of cultural validity. *Topics in Early Childhood Special Education, 17,* 494–519.

Noonan, M. J., & McCormick, L. (1992). A naturalistic curriculum model for early intervention. *Infant Toddler Intervention, 2,* 147–159.

Notari-Syverson, A. R., & Shuster, S. L. (1995). Putting real-life skills into IEP/IFSPs for infants and young children. *Teaching Exceptional Children, 27,* 29–32.

Rogow, S. M. (1984). The uses of social routines to facilitate communication in visually impaired and multihandicapped children. *Topics in Early Childhood Special Education, 3,* 64–70.

Rowland, C. (1984). Preverbal communication of blind infants and their mothers. *Journal of Visual Impairment & Blindness, 78,* 297–302.

Schuck, L. A., & Bucy, J. E. (1997). Family rituals: Implications for early intervention. *Topics in Early Childhood Special Education, 17,* 477–493.

Tavernier, G. G. F. (1993). The improvement of vision by vision stimulation and training: A review of the literature. *Journal of Visual Impairment & Blindness, 87,* 143–148.

9

Beginning Communication with Infants

Deborah Chen

Communication is fundamental to all social interactions and learning experiences. Therefore, enhancing the development of communication is a primary focus of many early intervention programs. When infants have visual impairments and additional disabilities, particular attention is often needed to encourage their communication with parents and other significant caregivers. Daily activities provide an important context for infants to engage in early social interaction and communication. It is through responses from caregivers in everyday routines that all infants learn that their behaviors have meaning. This chapter explains the developmental process of early communication, identifies how infants communicate before they use words, describes the potential effects of visual impairment and additional disabilities on early communication, and suggests strategies for supporting and increasing infants' early communicative behavior within the context of daily activities with their families.

THE DEVELOPMENT OF EARLY COMMUNICATION

Early communication develops through a caregiver's interpretation of and response to an infant's behaviors (Dunst, 1978). Through early interactions, infants and caregivers develop preverbal conversations, or "pseudo-dialogues," that form the basis for later conversations. Developmental psychologists have observed that at about 3 months, infants begin to participate in early "games" or face-to-face play with their caregivers. Between 3 and 9 months, the time that infants and their mothers spend in these interactions increases, and the games expand to include objects (Tronick, 1980). All communication, even with infants, involves two participants, a topic of conversation, and a method of communication that is mutually understood. When infants are visually impaired and have additional disabilities, the early communication process may be severely affected.

First, they may have subtle or atypical behaviors that are difficult to recognize and interpret. For example, infants who are blind may use hand movements to indicate interest and to make requests that are difficult to identify (Fraiberg, 1977). Infants who also have cerebral palsy may display involuntary facial and limb movements that interfere with an easy interpretation of purposeful initiations or responses. Similarly, infants with other disabilities in addition to visual impairments may have limited repertoires of early communicative behaviors. For instance, infants who are medically fragile may lack the stamina to be interactive.

Second, the infants may not respond to their caregivers. Depending on the type and severity of their visual impairment, they may not have access to visual stimuli that elicit early responses. Thus, whereas, sighted infants usually display clear and positive responses to caregivers' animated facial expressions, infants with severe visual impairments and developmental delays may need more time to discriminate their caregivers' faces, and their responses may be muted. Infants without disabilities demonstrate easily recognized responses to familiar voices, but the responses of visually impaired infants who are developmentally delayed, have hearing losses, or are autistic to their caregivers' voices may be limited. When infants are visually impaired and have additional disabilities, early intervention strategies are needed to help caregivers recognize, interpret, and respond to their signals and to assist infants in recognizing and responding to their caregivers' initiations.

HOW INFANTS COMMUNICATE

Long before they develop words, all infants communicate through cries, emotional expressions, hand movements, and gestures. First, they display *preintentional communication* through a number of behaviors (fussing, smiling, and looking) that caregivers can interpret as having meaning. Next, they show the *beginning of intentional communication* through signals and gestures (pointing, reaching, and body movements) that clearly have meaning. Finally, they develop *intentional communication* through vocalizations, gestures, and words (Bates, 1979). Studies of infants without disabilities (Bruner, 1981; Dore, 1974) have classified these early communicative behaviors as having the following main functions:

- *behavior regulation*   to get someone to stop or start doing something by protesting, refusing, or rejecting or requesting objects or actions
- *social interaction*   to get someone's attention by greeting, seeking attention, or requesting social routines or comfort
- *joint attention*   to call attention to something by commenting on objects or actions or information.

A form for recording observations of such behaviors is discussed in conjuction with the case studies of Maria and Huey, presented later in this chapter.

These classifications have been used to examine the communicative behaviors of young children with disabilities (Coggins & Carpenter, 1981; Rowland, 1990), and studies have found that many of these children do not demonstrate a range of communication functions. Young children with severe disabilities communicate mainly to protest, refuse, reject, and request objects or actions (Wetherby, Yonclas, & Bryan, 1989). Similarly, the early communication of young children with visual impairments and additional disabilities tends to be limited to behavioral regulation purposes and to familiar social routines, such as finger plays and action songs (Evans & Johnson, 1988; Rogow, 1982). Infants with developmental delays and other disabilities are at risk for delays and difficulties in communication and require intervention to support the development of their communication (Rossetti, 1996). Thus, a primary focus of early intervention should be to assist infants to expand their repertoire of communication and range of communicative purposes.

ENCOURAGING COMMUNICATION

Most of us are more communicative in situations that are familiar, with people we like, and on topics that are interesting to us. This simple observation can be applied to interventions with infants who have multiple disabilities. To motivate communication, caregivers should first recognize when infants are attempting to communicate or are displaying behaviors that may be interpreted as communicative. Next, they should respond contingently to these behaviors and, when appropriate, expand on these communicative behaviors. Moreover, all communication occurs within a context, so intervention strategies must include identifying situations that motivate the infants' interactions (such as turn-taking routines) to provide the context for early communication. At the same time, communication requires a mode that is understood by the participants, so intervention strategies must include identifying the most effective means for individual infants to send and receive messages by selecting options for increasing receptive and expressive communication.

Understanding Communication Behaviors

The first strategy for encouraging early communication is to determine how individual infants communicate and what they are communicating about. Information about the infants' communicative behaviors should be gathered by interviewing caregivers about their observations and then by making careful observations to recognize the infants' behaviors and patterns of responses.

Interviews with Caregivers

Caregivers are usually familiar with how the infants react to certain situations, what the infants like and dislike, and when the infant seems alert and attentive. Ask them about how the infants communicate; what the infant's favorite objects, people, and activities are; and when the infants seem most communicative. These discussions will reveal early behaviors that the caregivers identify as communicative; situations that are familiar, people who are liked, and topics that are interesting to the infants; and when the infants are engaged in interaction. This information provides the basis for developing meaningful and motivating interventions that will encourage the infants to interact.

Guidelines for Observation

In addition to interviewing caregivers, early interventionists should observe the infant in a variety of natural and structured situations. By doing so, they can not only assist the caregivers in making systematic observations of the infants, but can obtain additional information about the infants' communicative behaviors and engage in a more informed discussion with the caregivers about the particular infants. Observations should reveal how the infants express interest or disinterest and preferences or dislikes, when they seem ready for interaction, and when they need to take a break. Systematic observations will assist early interventionists and caregivers in recognizing early behaviors that have communicative potential and identifying situations that will motivate the infants to interact. For example, some infants may indicate their interest in their caregivers by quieting, whereas others may become more active. Some infants prefer active play, whereas others prefer gentle movement games. The first goal is to identify highly motivating situations that will engage the infants. The following questions may be used both to gather information from caregivers and to guide observations of particular infants' communicative behaviors. (A blank questionnaire appears in the Appendix for the reader's use.)

1. What are your infant's favorite objects, activities, and people?

The answer to this question will identify the most motivating objects, activities, and people that can be used to elicit communicative behaviors in the infant. For example, these situations may be used to elicit awareness, discrimination, recognition, or request behaviors from the infant.

2. What are your infant's most disliked objects, activities, and people?

Observations of these naturally occuring situations will reveal how the infant protests about or rejects these situations.

3. How does your infant communicate with you? What is he or she usually trying to tell you?

Discussion of the family's observations will identify behaviors of the infant that the family interprets as meaningful and provide information on the infant's communication repertoire.

4. In what situations is your infant the most communicative?

This discussion will assist the early interventionist and caregivers in identifying optimal times of the day when and situations in which the infant can be engaged. For example, an infant may be the most vocal in the afternoon when a brother is playing with her. This would be an optimal time to observe the interaction and identify what the brother is doing to elicit the infant's vocalizations and, perhaps, to add strategies that will encourage vocal imitation and vocalizations for other communicative purposes.

5. Have you found any special ways that help you communicate with your infant?

This discussion encourages caregivers to think about what they are doing and what else they could be doing to promote their infant's communication development. For example, a parent may have a special greeting for the baby who is blind and has medical problems, such as stroking the infant's cheek, by which the infant learns to recognize that parent.

Create Opportunities for Communication

Information from interviews with the caregivers and observations should be used to determine how the infant communicates and for what purposes. This information can be recorded on the Functions of Early Communicative Behaviors form, which is discussed later in this chapter in Maria's case study. (A blank copy of this form also appears in the Appendix for the reader's use.) On the basis of this information, intervention strategies can be implemented to expand the infant's communicative repertoire by creating opportunities.

As was noted earlier, communication begins when an infant is able to participate in nonverbal interactions, that is, to send and receive messages through nonverbal behaviors. Through nonverbal signals, infants learn to communicate their preferences, requests, and early comments. These early communicative functions of language in early childhood have their roots in nonverbal behaviors in infancy. Thus, communication interventions should begin when infants are at the nonverbal level, and strategies to elicit verbal communication should be based on the infants' nonverbal communication skills (Mahoney & Weller, 1980). For example, if an infant can communicate dislike for an activity by fussing or desire for an activity through body movement, then verbal or symbolic communication (speech and/or sign) can be mapped onto these nonverbal behaviors to promote the infant's development of verbal communication.

Research and practice with infants who have disabilities have identified a number of strategies for promoting their early communication, including responding contingently to the infant's behaviors, creating early conversations through turn-taking routines, providing slight expansions of the infants' communicative behaviors, and gradually increasing requirements for communicative behaviors (Chen, 1996; MacDonald, 1982; MacDonald & Gillette, 1986; Manolson, 1984).

Respond Contingently to Infants' Behaviors
As was discussed in Chapter 2, contingent responsiveness to infants' behaviors is a significant influence on early learning. To respond contingently, caregivers and early interventionists must recognize and interpret the infants' behaviors and then respond in a way that the infants can perceive. For example, if an infant who is visually impaired and has a hearing loss becomes fussy while sitting in an infant seat, to respond contingently, the caregiver should not only respond verbally, but should interact physically, such as by patting the baby or laying him or her down for a nap. The importance of identifying ways for providing accessible input for communication with infants who are visually impaired and have additional disabilities is discussed in a later section on Selecting Communication Options.

Develop Turn-taking Routines
Turn-taking simply requires caregivers and early interventionists to respond in some way (that the infants can perceive) to the infants' behaviors and then supporting another response from the infants. These opportunities for early exchanges provide the basis for developing conversation. Through these interactions, infants realize that their behaviors elicit responses and that caregivers expect them to respond as

well. There are many natural opportunities for turn-taking games in daily caregiving situations, such as, playing tickle games, peek-a-boo, and imitating the infants' sounds or movements while dressing, feeding, and bathing the babies (Chen & Haney, 1995). Research on infants with visual impairments and those with hearing losses revealed that parents modify turn-taking routines to fit the infants' sensory abilities and developmental levels by using game-based, imitation-based, action-based, or reference-based exchanges (Chen, 1996).

Imitation-based routines involve repeating an infant's sounds or actions on objects. When the infant is making sounds (such as "bah, bah, bah") or movements (like patting the high chair tray), wait for a break in the vocalization or action and imitate the sounds and/or actions to encourage turn taking. Once the infant is making the sound or action consistently, change the sound slightly (for example, from saying "bah, bah, bah" to "baaahhh" or from patting the high chair tray to patting a toy on the tray). Objects may be used with vocal imitation routines to add interest and structure to the game (for instance, saying "bah, bah, bah" while banging on a drum).

Game-based routines involve predictable tactile or movement games that an infant likes (such as blow-on-tummy or blanket swing). Once the infant recognizes the game, delay the next step (for example, blow on the infant's tummy and then stop), wait for the infant to react in some way, and then respond to the infant's vocalizations or movements by blowing on the tummy again). When the infant realizes that he or she can get you to play the game, show the infant how to say "let's play" (for example, by pulling up on his or her shirt to request blow-on-tummy, clapping his or her hands for pat-a-cake, or raising the arms for "So big"). The bouncing game described later is an example of interrupting a routine.

Imitation-based and game-based routines are helpful for engaging an unresponsive infant. Imitating the baby's sounds and actions should be changed slowly to include different sounds, actions, objects, and words to fit the infant's development. Object play in imitation-based and game-based routines helps to differentiate between the infant's and caregiver's turns and supports a transition to action-based routines.

Action-based routines involve turn-taking and joint attention to specific objects. Simple activities, such as pouring water out of a cup at bathtime, taking toys out of a basket, and putting blocks into a container, invite an infant to act on an object. Use gestural prompts (pointing, showing, or tapping an object or modeling an action) to support the infant's response. The caregiver should take turns in different ways that support the infant's actions, such as by filling the cup for the infant to pour or pouring some water on the infant's stomach and then filling the cup for the infant, by commenting or acting on the toys the infant takes out of the basket, or by giving the infant a block to put in the container or by putting a block in the container. Simple language and related sounds should mark the actions in these routines, by saying, for example, "On your tummy" or "ooohh" when pouring water, "all gone" when the infant empties the cup, "block" when handing the infant a block for the tub, or "Ah boom" when the infant puts a block in the tub.

Reference-based routines involve turn taking, joint attention to specific topics, a focus on symbolic language, and encouragement of a verbal response from the infant. The caregiver provides labels to help the infant develop specific language concepts for a variety of objects, for instance, identifying body parts or toys, looking at books, and playing with dolls and other symbolic toys. An infant's focus is engaged when the adult uses exaggerated intonation (if an infant has some hearing), makes the manual sign on the object (if an infant has low vision and a hearing loss), or makes the manual sign on the baby's body, (if the infant is blind or severely visually impaired and has a hearing loss). Considerations for using manual signs with infants who are both visually impaired and deaf or hard of hearing are discussed later in this chapter. Adaptations for showing objects and "reading" a book to an infant who is totally blind are described in Chapter 8. Progressively matched turn-taking (MacDonald & Gillette, 1986) and similar interventions (Manolson, 1984) with infants who have a variety of communicative needs support the importance of developing early turn-taking routines as a critical intervention strategy. In progressively matched turn-taking, the adult engages the infant in turn-taking by imitating what the infant does and then adding a bit more:

1. If the infant does not communicate intentionally, then imitate his or her sounds and actions. For example, if the infant vocalizes "Mama-ma" or pats the table, the adult does the same when the infant pauses and then waits for the infant to vocalize or pat the table again.

2. If the infant uses gestures and sounds that represent words, the adult imitates the infant's behaviors and provides the words. For example, if an infant reaches toward a caregiver or vocalizes "uh," the caregiver then reaches toward (and touches, if necessary) the infant and says, "Up, up you go" and picks the infant up.

3. If the infant uses words, then the adult provides the standard form of the word and adds a bit more information. For example, if the infant says or signs "Dada," the caregiver responds by saying (and signing, if appropriate) "Daddy's outside. Let's find him" or "Daddy's at work."

Interrupting a Routine

Once an infant's preferred activities have been identified; then particular movement activities can be selected to elicit requests from the infant by interrupting the usual routine of the activity. Using the following steps, a favorite activity can be interrupted after it has begun:

1. Select a favorite activity and do about three movements; for example, begin bouncing the infant on your lap for three bounces.

2. Create a need for the infant to communicate by stopping the movement and keeping still.

3. Wait quietly (count silently to 10 or 15, depending on the infant's response time) and observe what the infant does, such as, wiggling his or her body.

4. If the infant responds, interpret the infant's behavior as communicative, for example, wiggling means "I want more bouncing." Add words to the infant's behaviors; for instance, say or sign, if appropriate, "More bouncing," and respond to the infant's communication by continuing the activity as requested; that is, bounce the infant on your lap.

5. If the infant does not demonstrate an observable response, prompt him or her through the desired response; for example, wiggle the infant's arms or legs and immediately continue the activity. Repeat this prompting two more times, so the infant has three direct instruction experiences. Then repeat the procedure from Step 3: Interrupt the activity and wait quietly for the infant's response.

Once an in fant responds to an interruption in an activity, and indicates a request for more, the activity can be interrupted or delayed before it is begun.

1. Set up the situation for a favorite activity but do not begin the activity; for instance, sit the infant in a swing or sit the infant on your lap and keep still.

2. Wait quietly (count silently to 15, if necessary) for the infant to initiate a request for the activity, such as by wiggling his or her body in anticipation.

3. If the infant displays any anticipatory behaviors, respond immediately by putting words to the infant's behaviors and beginning the activity, for example, saying (and signing, when necessary) "Swing, let's swing" and pushing the infant in the swing or "Bounce, let's bounce" and bouncing the infant on your lap.

4. If the infant does not display any anticipatory behaviors, such as by wiggling his or her arms or legs, prompt the infant to do so and then begin the activity.

5. Repeat this procedure the next time the activity is introduced.

The strategies of progressively matched turn-taking and interrupting and delaying a routine involve prompting, modeling, or requiring communicative behaviors that are within the infant's abilities. For example, an infant wiggles in excitement in anticipation of being swung. The wiggling behavior can be used to encourage him or her to request more swinging. Once the infant is consistently wiggling his or her body to signal a request for more swinging, then a symbolic form (speech and/ or sign) can be encouraged by modeling the words ("More swing"). In this way, an infant uses behaviors that are within his or her repertoire for new communicative purposes and is encouraged to develop new means of communication as appropriate.

Jan van Dijk's Framework for Developing Early Communication

Another way to encourage communication is through van Dijk's movement-based strategies. On the basis of the developmental theory of Werner and Kaplan (1963), van Dijk (1965) developed a framework for early communication strategies for supporting the development of communication in young children who are deaf-blind. His framework is composed of five main phases that occur before the child develops expressive language: nurturance, resonance, coactive movement, nonrepresentational reference, and natural gestures.

These phases illustrate an increase in the physical distance between the child and teacher and in the use of less concrete and more symbolic forms of communication. *Nurturance* is the development of an emotional tie between the child and teacher through affection and positive interactions. *Resonance* involves proximity or close physical contact between teacher and child that allows the teacher to imitate the child's movements or actions and to develop turn taking through these interactions. In *coactive movement,* the teacher extends resonance strategies to help the child learn to imitate the teacher's actions during specific activities (such as, making a sandwich or completing an obstacle course). In *nonrepresentational reference,* the child and teacher both attend to an object or person by pointing to, looking at, or handling this referent without using words to name the object or person. Next, the child develops *natural gestures* to represent how he or she uses an object (such as making a patting motion to ask for a "drum") and his or her participation in activities. Teachers should respond to and use the child's natural gestures to promote communication. Over time, the teacher can shape the child's natural gestures to approximate a more conventional gesture or manual sign. At this point, the child will demonstrate symbolic communication through words (Jurgens, 1977; MacFarland, 1995; van Dijk, 1967). Although van Dijk's model has been implemented primarily with preschoolers and older children who are deaf-blind and with students with severe and multiple disabilities (Alvares & Sternberg, 1994), the strategies may be adapted to be developmentally appropriate for infants who have multiple disabilities as follows:

1. *Nurturance* should be developed through loving and pleasurable interactions between infants and caregivers, thus establishing a trusting relationship.

2. *Resonance* can be achieved through nonverbal interactions, such as by imitating the infant's behaviors and rocking with the infant.

3. *Coactive movements* should be used to provide a model to help the infant perform motor (crawling or walking) and functional activities (such as playing in a sand box, putting a block in a tub, taking a bite of a cracker). The caregiver or another child can provide a model by performing the action beside the infant.

4. *Nonrepresentational reference* can be used to build the infant's skills in imitation, body image, and communication by having the infant imitate the positions of a person or a doll, for example, by touching his or her head in imitation of the caregiver's model.

5. *Natural gestures* should be developed on the basis of the caregiver's observations of the infant's motor experiences in activities. For instance, to an infant who bounces in a swing, a bouncing motion is a natural gesture for "I want to swing." The caregiver should assist the infant in making the connection that the gesture refers to the object by first introducing the gesture with the object present—in this instance, the swing—so the infant sees and/or touches it. After the infant recognizes that the gesture refers to the object, the caregiver should use the gesture without the object present to encourage the infant to make a request. Once the infant understands gestures and uses them for expressive communication, he or she is more likely to make the association between other symbols (spoken words or signs) and their referents and to use symbolic language.

Expanding Communication Behaviors

As infants progress in their development of communication and develop verbal behaviors, the meanings of messages are supported by the contexts of the interactions and nonverbal cues, such as gestures. At this stage, a caregiver may up the ante, that is, increase the requirements for the infant's communication behaviors. For example, the caregiver may "play dumb" by ignoring the infant's generalized body movement or reaching to indicate a desire for a cookie. Although the cookie jar is on the table, the caregiver may look perplexed, point, and ask, "What do you want?" to encourage the infant to vocalize or make a more specific gesture. The caregiver may say, "Want cookie?" to encourage the infant to nod yes or say "cookie." Or the caregiver may allow the infant to experience "little problems" to elicit expanded communication from the infant. For example, by "forgetting" to provide needed objects in routine situations (such as a cup for juice or a favorite toy in the car), the caregiver can encourage the infant to ask for familiar objects. These strategies should be used with a responsive conversational attitude. Care should be taken not to frustrate the infant, but to provide supports for the infant to participate in interactions and expand his or her communicative behaviors.

SELECTING OPTIONS FOR COMMUNICATION

Many early interventionists and families wonder how to begin to encourage communication with infants who have multiple disabilities. Many of these infants benefit from a specific focus on communication input, rather than bombardment with every possible communication method at one time. Close your eyes and consider how confused you would be if someone spoke to you in an unfamiliar language while he or she held your hands and moved them and then put an unfamiliar object in your hand. Imagine the experience of an infant who is exposed to a haphazard approach to communicative input. There are many alternative methods for communicating with infants who are visually impaired and have additional disabilities; these methods include touch cues, object cues, tangible symbols, pictures, and signs (Chen, 1995a, b; Rowland, Schweigert, & Prickett, 1995). The following section will assist early interventionists and caregivers in selecting specific communication modes to fit the needs and abilities of individual infants.

Communication Input and Output

When infants have visual impairments and additional disabilities, it is essential to differentiate between the means of providing communicative input to them and the means of communicative output from them. From the infants' perspective, *input* is *receptive communication,* or understanding what another person is conveying to them, whereas *output* is *expressive communication,* or what they want to communicate. The modes or means used for input and output may need to be different, depending on the infants' understanding and abilities. The following outlines of input and output methods are intended to assist early interventionists and families in determining (1) the method of communication input that individual infants are *most likely to understand* and (2) the communication output that the infants will *produce the most easily.* These modes of communication are not mutually exclusive; more than one mode can be used for one message, and a variety of modes may be used for different messages. The process is not meant to restrict the communicative options for a particular infant, but to emphasize the systematic and consistent use of selected methods that are the most likely to produce results.

Communication Input

Communication input involves ways to send messages to the infant—in other words—receptive communication. The following methods are different ways for others to attempt to communicate with an infant who has multiple disabilities. The choice of communication method for a particular infant depends on the infant's abilities and preferences.

Touch cues (tactile signals), such as touching the infant's lips before offering a bottle or tugging on the infant's diaper before changing it. For touch cues to be meaningful, the infant must be aware of and attend to the tactile input. Touch cues should be used selectively and systematically. An infant will not be able to discriminate the meaning of a touch cue if other tactile input is simultaneously being given or if he or she does not like being touched. For example, touching the infant's lips while patting his or her hand is confusing if the message is "Here's your bottle." Similarly, touching the infant's lips sometimes, stroking the infant's cheek at other times, and tapping the infant's chin at still another time will not help the infant easily decipher the meaning of the touch cue for "Here's your bottle."

Object cues, objects or parts of objects that are used in an activity or associated with a person, for example, touching the bottle to the infant's hand to signal, "Here's your bottle." To obtain information from object cues, the infant must be aware of tactile input and, when possible, be helped to handle the object.

Gestures or natural body movements, for instance, waving "bye-bye" to indicate that the caregiver is leaving the infant. To receive information from gestures, the infant must be aware of tactile and kinesthetic input. An infant will receive more information if he or she has some vision.

Vocalizations (vocal sounds), such as making sounds to movements or saying "uh oh" when something falls out of reach of the infant or "yum-yum" when the infant eats a favorite food. The infant must have some hearing and be aware of sounds to discriminate, recognize, and then associate them with meaning.

Three-dimensional tangible symbols (objects or parts of objects that represent activities and may be used on communication boards), including a spoon to represent meals or a piece of a blanket to represent a blanket swing. For these symbols to have meaning, the infant must have made an association between the three-dimensional referent and what it represents. The infant will receive more information if he or she can discriminate the object through visual or tactile examination.

Pictures (two-dimensional forms of tangible symbols that may be used on communication boards), such as a picture of a banana to represent a preferred snack. The infant must be able to make an association between the two-dimensional illustration and what it represents, so he or she needs visual discrimination. Some infants are able to discriminate simple and colorful line drawings before they are able to recognize photographs of objects.

Manual signs, like the sign of *SWING* or *EAT* before the infant is swung or fed. To understand the meaning of signs, the infant must be able to make an association between the movements of a sign and what it represents. This association will be made more easily if the infant discriminates a sign by seeing it or "feeling" the sign movements while he or she is physically guided through the sign. Many infants with multiple disabilities benefit from key word signs which are selected signs adapted for the infant's learning needs. Using key word signs is not the same as using the simultaneous method (spoken English together with a manual sign system based on English) or using American Sign Language (ASL) which has its own grammar and visual-spatial rules and is a different language than English. Initially, a key word sign is really a prompt or cue to engage the infant's attention and to build an understanding of the meaning of a word and what it represents. For example, the sign EAT made either by the adult touching the infant's lips with "a flat O handshape" or by assisting the infant to touch his own lips is really a touch cue or gesture rather than a sign.

Speech, for example, saying "Let's swing" or "Want to eat?" to introduce an activity. To understand spoken words, the infant must make an association between how the word sounds and what it represents. This association requires the infant to have some hearing and the ability to attend to and discriminate between sounds. Depending on the degree of the infant's hearing loss, certain words will be more easily discriminated than others. For instance, "All done" provides more auditory information than "Finished" to an infant who has a high-frequency hearing loss. Whether the infant has normal hearing or a hearing loss, spoken input must have the characteristics of "parentese" or "caregiver's speech" to attract and maintain the infant's attention. These characteristics include simple, short, clear, and fluent repetitive phrases; exaggerated intonation; and words related specifically to the experiences of the infant as they occur (Snow, 1972), accompanied by gestures and animated facial expressions. Prolonged descriptions of everything in the environment and everything that is going on will not be meaningful to an infant who is just developing language.

Communication input is enhanced when an infant can make use of his or her available senses through amplification, corrective lenses, magnification, and other sensory cues that provide pertinent information. Moreover, it must be comprehensible; that is, (1) it must match the infant's abilities, (2) the infant should be able to differentiate it from the background noise and visual clutter of the environment, and (3) the infant must be able to associate it with the message it conveys.

Communication Output

Communication output describes the ways the infant sends messages, or expressive communication. The methods listed here include a variety of options. Again, the method of expressive communication the infant may be encouraged to use depends on the infant's abilities and preferences. *Body movements (generalized movements or actions),* like wiggling the arms to indicate a request to be swung. To use body movements to express requests and desires, the infant must be able to make some movements. At first, movements may be unintentional communicative behaviors (such as leaning toward an object to indicate a preference or turning away to indicate dislike) that can be shaped into gestures (such as reaching for a desired object and pushing away a disliked one). If an infant has a severe physical disability, such as spastic cerebral palsy, the quantity and quality of his or her movements will be affected. In this case, the caregiver and early interventionist need to identify the infant's movements that could be interpreted as communicative. For example, the infant may become excited when a preferred object is introduced and display uncontrollable arm movements.

Object cues (objects or parts of objects that are used in an activity or are associated with a person), including a spoon, piece of a blanket, or bag to represent mealtime, a blanket swing, or play time with the early interventionist, respectively. To obtain meaning from object cues, the infant must recognize objects and associate them with specific activities or people. This association is facilitated by repeated experiences connecting the objects with the person or activity. If the infant has some vision, then an association can be made visually. Otherwise, the infant needs to discriminate and recognize the object by examining it tactilely.

Gestures (natural body movements that have specific meanings), for example, waving "bye-bye" as a request to leave; rocking back and forth to ask to play "row, row, row, your boat"; or clapping hands to request pat-a-cake. To use gestures to express desires and requests, the infant must have had experiences with activities, be able to associate certain body movements with particular activities or situations, and must have some voluntary movements. Infants will develop a larger repertoire of gestures (such as reaching, pointing, and imitating other people's gestures) if they have some vision.

Vocalizations (vocal sounds), such as saying "da" to request an object. To use vocalizations to communicate, the infant must have some hearing and be aware of sounds.

Three-dimensional tangible symbols (objects or parts of objects that represent activities; may be used on communication boards). For example, a spoon may be used to represent meals or a piece of a blanket to represent swinging. To communicate desires and requests through three-dimensional tangible symbols, an infant must have made an association between the three-dimensional referent and what it represents. This association is more easily made if the infant has some vision or can examine the three-dimensional tangible symbol by touching and manipulating it.

Pictures (two-dimensional forms of tangible symbols), like a picture of a cookie to indicate a snack. To use pictures as a means for expressive communication, the infant must be able to make visual discriminations to associate the two-dimensional illustration with what it represents. As was noted in the discussion on modes of communication input, the picture should be easy to discriminate.

Manual signs, such as using the sign *COOKIE* to initiate a request for a cookie. To use signs as expressive communication, the infant must have adequate motor abilities to produce signs and be able to make an association between the movements of the sign and what the sign represents. This association is made more quickly if the infant has some vision or has had repeated opportunities in making the sign movements by being guided through them.

Speech, for example, saying "cookie." To use speech for expressive communication, the infant must have adequate oral-motor skills to produce speech and sufficient hearing to recognize words and to make an association between how the word sounds and what it represents.

An infant's communication output is promoted when he or she receives comprehensible communication input and necessary adaptations are made to motivate the infant to communicate expressively. An infant with multiple disabilities is more likely to initiate and respond to communication when

- situations are familiar, meaningful, and preferred
- there is an expectation for the infant to communicate
- the infant's behaviors receive contingent responses

Examples of completed forms that can be used to identify the communication input is likely to be most accessible to two infants and the output they will produce easily appear in the accompanying case study of Maria. (Blank copies of the Functions of Early Communicative Behaviors form and the Communication Options worksheet are provided in the Appendix.)

MARIA

Maria Leon, aged 15 months, has been diagnosed with retinopathy of prematurity, hypotonia, and a moderate hearing loss caused by bilateral atresia. She has just received bone-conduction aids but pulls them off. Maria is totally blind. She makes some babbling sounds, drinks from a bottle on her own, and is beginning to scoot around on the floor. Her father plays a vigorous airplane game that makes her laugh. Maria begins to move her arms and legs and makes sounds when her father picks her up. She is quiet when her mother sits and holds her in a rocking chair for a lullaby before a nap and bedtime.

HOMEWORK FOR THE HOME VISIT

Maria's family told the early interventionist that they are concerned about Maria's development of communication. In preparation for a home visit, the early interventionist reviews the Functions of Early Communicative Behaviors worksheet (Figure 9.1) and the Communication Options worksheet (Figure 9.2) based on her familiarity with Maria. She believes that Maria is showing purposeful behaviors that can be developed into more conventional communication. She notes that signs will need to be adapted because Maria is totally blind and that Maria has functional

Figure 9.1   SAMPLE COMPLETED FORM FOR RECORDING THE FUNCTIONS OF EARLY COMMUNICATIVE BEHAVIORS

Functions of Early Communicative Behaviors

Name: _Maria_   Date: _Febuary 9, 1999_

Date of Birth: _December 8, 1997_   Age: _15 months_

Informant: _Mrs. Leon_   Interviewer: _Patsy Miller_

Function of communication	How does the infant communicate?	Situations that elicit these behaviors
Behavioral regulation		
Protest, refusal, or rejection	Cries, pushes away, fusses	New foods; loud active people
Request for object	Pats the tray	Meals
Request for action	Gets excited and wiggles	Playing with Dad
Social interaction		
Greet	Not yet	
Seek attention	Fusses to get attention	Sometimes in the morning when she wakes up
Request social routines	Gets excited and wiggles	Airplane game
Request comfort	Will lean into me	Visits to physicians and loud people
Joint attention		
Comment on object	Not yet	
Comment on action		
Request information		

hearing, although encouraging her to wear her bone conduction aids will require some effort. She decides to complete the Functions of Early Communicative Behavior worksheet with the family. She plans to discuss the communication options of using speech, adapted signs, and object cues to provide communication input and to encourage Maria to communicate through vocalizations, object cues, and gestures or signs.

WORKING TOGETHER

During the home visit, the early interventionist discusses the communication functions worksheet with Mrs. Leon. They agree that Maria is clearly demonstrating the behavioral regulation functions of protesting or rejecting and requesting objects and activities. She also uses the social interaction functions of seeking attention, requesting social routines, and requesting comfort.

The early interventionist suggests that signs be introduced to Maria, as indicated on the Communication Options worksheet (Figure 9.2) to encourage her to communicate for the purposes of behavioral regulation and social interaction. This way, she will develop a new form of communication that is based on familiar functions. In addition, the early interventionist has observed that Maria recognizes her parents' voices and seems to discriminate between familiar and unfamiliar people on the basis of voice and odor. For example, Maria seems to like people who smoke, perhaps because her father smokes and she associates the tobacco odor with him. Given Maria's strengths and interests, it seems likely that she will benefit from input that includes speech, the use of signs (with tactile adapta-

tions), and touch and object cues. Initially, Maria may need hand-over-hand or coactive assistance to make signs. She will also be encouraged to communicate through gestures and adapted signs, vocalization, and showing objects.

Patsy Miller has noticed that Maria loves both rough-and-tumble games with her father and lullaby time in the rocking chair with her mother. She asks whether Maria wears her hearing aids during those activities. Maria's parents indicate that she fusses and pulls them off. The early interventionist suggests that the lullaby–rocking chair activity may be a motivating time for Maria to wear her hearing aids. Maria's mother says she will put them on when they sit in the rocking chair and take them off when she puts Maria in her crib. The early interventionist explains the interrupted routine strategy to the parents. Together they develop the following strategy for the lullaby–rocking chair time:

1. Sing "Row, row, row your boat gently down the stream, merrily . . . " and pause. Stop singing and rocking.
2. Wait and watch for Maria's response.
3. Verbalize her response. For example, if she makes a movement or sound, say "You want more singing, more rocking" and help her to make the sign for MORE).
4. Continue the song.

They develop another strategy for the airplane game. Maria's father lies on the floor and holds her parallel over his body. He moves her up and down and side to side while he makes funny noises. He agrees to add the words *up,* and *down* with exaggerated intonation to coincide with those movements when he plays this game. He will pause when he holds her up, wait for a reaction, and respond to her sounds

Figure 9.2 SAMPLE COMPLETED COMMUNICATION OPTIONS WORKSHEET FOR MARIA

Communications Options Worksheet

Name: Maria

Age: 18 months

Date: February 1, 1999

Child's Strengths and Needs

Area	Observations
Vision	Totally blind
Hearing	Moderate hearing loss, unaided
Motor	Low tone, rolls, sits, moves arms and legs, bangs, holds bottle, removes hearing aid
Tactile	Now tolerates holding
Responses to movement	Loves movement games
Cognitive level	
Awareness	
Discrimination	Discriminates familiar from unfamiliar people and toys
Recognition	Recognizes parents' voices

Communication Options

Input	Output
Adapted signs	Signs
Vocal	Vocalizations
Interactive and coactive signs, objects	Objects
Touch cues	Body movements, Gestures

objects, people, activities

Selected options to discuss with family

Input	Output
Adapted signs	Vocalizations
Speech	Signs/gestures
Objects	Objects

and movements as communication by continuing the movement game. Before she leaves, the early interventionist checks Maria's bone-conduction aids to make sure they are working and to see that the headband fits Maria comfortably. When she returns the next week, she will bring some videotapes of signs that the family can borrow and learn to use with Maria.

The Functions of Early Communicative Behaviors form (Figure 9.1) may be completed by the early interventionist, with or without the caregiver, to record the different ways in which the infant already communicates his or her needs, likes and dislikes, and desires prior to intervention. In Maria's case, for example, these ways included getting excited and wiggling when she wanted an action or routine from someone and crying, fussing, and pushing away when she disliked something. After observing such a behavior, the early interventionist classifies it according to the function it serves for the infant using the classification of communicative behaviors into behavioral regulation, social interaction, or joint attention that appear on the form (and were outlined earlier in this chapter). This interventionist also records situations in which each identified behavior occurs. Completing this form helps the early interventionist to identify the infant's existing ability to communicate and to see which behaviors can best be emphasized or expanded on.

The early interventionist reviews this form with the infant's caregiver or family—as she did with Mrs. Leon, Maria's mother—usually together with the Communications Options Worksheet that includes broad observations about the infant's abilities in each of several areas. On the basis of each observation, methods of communication that may be feasible for the infant are listed. When reviewed together, these two forms help the early interventionist and family decide which options for and strategies of communication to focus on. In Maria's case, the options included adapted signs, vocalization, and showing objects. The parents agreed to introduce the interrupted-routine strategy during several routines that Maria enjoyed to encourage her expressive communication.

Strategies for Using Selected Options for Beginning Communication

As an infant such as Maria continues to progress in her communication skills, the early interventionist needs to supply additional strategies to refine and expand her use of object cues and adapted signs. This section discusses specific strategies for implementing a variety of the communication options that have been discussed for infants whose multiple disabilities include visual impairment.

Touch Cues

Touch cues, as was discussed earlier, are tactile signals made on an infant's body that are used to communicate a specific message during everyday situations. They are particularly useful for communicating with infants with multiple disabilities who do not seem to understand signs or speech. For example, tugging on the infant's diaper means "I'm going to change your diaper." Touch cues should be paired with specific words to support the infant's attention to and understanding of the spoken word. They must be presented consistently and systematically on a specific part of the infant's body if they are to become meaningful. For instance, the infant will not begin to anticipate "getting diaper changed" if she sometimes receives a pat on the bottom and at other times feels a tug on her diaper. Moreover, the infant's preference for and response to particular types of tactile stimulation must be considered. Infants are more likely to prefer a touch cue that is a firm touch or deep pressure than a light feathery stroke. Certain types of touch on specific areas of the body may trigger aversive or reflexive movements in infants who are medically fragile or neurologically impaired. For example, as a result of having many blood samples drawn from the heel, an infant's feet may be very sensitive (Chen, 1995a). It is important to collaborate with the infant's family and other team members, including the physical or occupational therapist, to determine the most appropriate type and placement of touch cues for a particular baby.

Touch cues have the following specific forms and functions:

Form
- specific signals on the infant's body
- consistent and systematic
- individualized

Input Functions
- Provide information to the infant. For example, grasping under both arms of the baby means "Up we go!"

- Provide comfort. For instance, stroking the baby's back means "There, there, tired baby."
- Offer praise. For example, patting the baby's chest means "Yeaa! Big boy!"
- Request an action. For instance, touching the baby's mouth means "Take a bite."

The early interventionist and caregiver should begin by identifying daily situations in which a few touch cues would help the infant understand what is about to happen and that can be used easily. Discuss these cues with all people who interact with the baby, so they can be used consistently in familiar and unfamiliar activities.

Object Cues

An object cue is an actual object that is used in an activity with the infant that informs the baby about what is to happen next; for example, a bottle indicates mealtime. However, the baby must use the object during the activity, such as drink from the bottle, to understand what the object cue represents. Once the infant associates certain objects with particular activities, object cues may be used to offer a choice. Initially, the infant will indicate a choice through interest or disinterest when one object is offered. When the infant recognizes more than one object cue, he or she can be given a choice between two objects. Begin with a preferred object (like a bottle) and a disliked one (such as an apple slice) to develop an understanding of choice making.

Object cues should be selected and presented from the baby's perspective and experience. For example, placing a bottle in the baby's hand may not elicit recognition of this object if the infant does not hold his or her bottle, but the infant may respond to the feel of the nipple on his or her lips. Similarly, a cup should not be used as an object cue for "Have a drink" if the infant drinks from a bottle. Once the infant associates the actual object with the activity (for example, a blanket means a blanket swing), a part of the object may be paired with the actual object as a cue. In this way, the actual object may be faded gradually, and the smaller object cue (such as a piece of a blanket) may be used instead. Object cues should be presented consistently in natural situations and familiar activities for them to become meaningful. The cues have the following specific forms and functions:

Form
- a real object
- part of a real object
- a miniature of an object (not meaningful to most infants with multiple disabilities or who are blind)

Input Functions
- Provides information to the infant; for example, giving the infant a diaper means "Let's change your diaper."
- Provides the infant with a choice; for instance, giving the infant a piece of a blanket or a bottle means "Want to swing or want a drink?"

Output Functions
- The infant can indicate a preference by, for example, grabbing a blanket that the adult offers to indicate "I wanna swing."
- The infant can make requests such as giving an empty bottle to the adult to indicate "I wanna drink."

Object cues can be used to help infants recognize familiar people. Infants who have multiple disabilities may discriminate people by obvious distinctive characteristics (like long hair, a a beard, eyeglasses, or a ring) and how they smell. It is important to recognize that infants will associate certain smells with comfort and preferred people and other smells with disliked situations or people. For example, an infant may alert and brighten because her father (who just finished a cigarette) walks into the room. Conversely, an infant may become upset when the nurse approaches her because she associates the smell of antiseptic with discomfort. These observations provide information about infants' development and may be used to add touch or object identification cues, such as helping an infant touch his or her father's mustache or the nurse's eyeglasses to recognize the person.

Encouraging Gestures

A baby's movements in an activity or action on an object can be used to develop gestures. For instance, an infant with both a visual impairment and a hearing loss will not readily understand the spoken or signed word for *swing*. However, the infant's natural action of bouncing his or her upper body while on a swing may be used as a gesture that the infant will recognize more easily. The gesture must be based on the infant's perspective; for example, the infant would not as easily understand a pushing gesture with the hands. This strategy encourages gestures and the infant's active participation in everyday activities as essential learning experiences. Moreover, conventional gestures should be used as appropriate, that is, to indicate agreement (nodding the head), disagreement or refusal (shaking the head), or directing attention or making a request (pointing or tapping an object).

Adapting Signs

When an infant has both a hearing and a vision loss, manual signs need to be made so the infant can receive them. If the infant has low vision, signs must be produced within his or her visual field, at an optimal viewing distance, and at an appropriate pace. It is also important for the signer to wear clothing that provides a high contrast and solid background for the signs to be seen easily, such as a shirt in a solid color that provides a strong contrast with the the skin color of the signer's hands. Depending on the infant's developmental level and other learning needs, the rate of signing may need to be slowed down, the number of words may need to be limited, and the hand movements may need to be made smaller to allow the infant time to process the visual input. When the infant is totally blind, other adaptations of signs are required—coactive and interactive signing (Watkins, 1985). This infant will need physical guidance to make the sign (coactive signing) and should be encouraged to feel the signer's movements (interactive signing). For an infant, coactive signing should be used to prompt the infant to communicate (output). Care must be taken to help the infant distinguish between when someone is communicating with him or her (input) and when someone is asking him or her to communicate (output). The infant may be confused by the variety of "transition" movements that accompany taking and positioning his or her hands for coactive signing. Thus, the same transition movements should be used consistently (such as touching the backs of the infant's hands and then grasping them), and the sign movements should be made distinctly (Chen, 1995a).

Observations of deaf parents and their infants have revealed a number of strategies for engaging an infant's attention to signs (Maestas y

Moores & Moores, 1980). These strategies include making signs on the infant's body, physically guiding the infant through a sequence of signs, making signs smaller and close to the infant's face, using a variety of modes (lip movements, fingerspelling, voice) with signs, and orienting the infant's attention to a signer by touching the infant's face or body. A number of these strategies may be used to introduce signs to infants with visual impairments and additional disabilities (Chen, 1995a; Watkins, 1985):

1. Make the sign on the infant's body for communication input. For example, the signer will touch the infant's lips to sign *eat* to let the infant know it is time for lunch.

2. Use physical guidance to help the infant make the sign (also called coactive signing) for communication output. For instance, if it is clear that the infant wants more to eat, take the infant's hand and touch it to his or her mouth to sign EAT, to make a request for more food.

3. Help the infant make the sign on your body for communication output, for example, when you want to demonstrate taking a bite of food.

4. If the infant has low vision, make the sign movements smaller and within the infant's visual field.

5. If the infant is blind, use tactile modeling by placing the baby's hands on yours to feel the sign movements (also called interactive signing) for communication input.

6. Make the sign on the object for communication input; for example, sign BOTTLE on an infant's bottle or SHOE on the infant's shoe while the baby is looking at or handling the object.

7. Match the number of movements of the sign with the number of syllables in the word when providing communication input; for instance MAMA is two movements. This way, the infant with adequate hearing may associate the sound of the word with the movements of the sign.

Additional considerations for adapting signs, depending on the infant's vision, are presented in Sidebar 9.1.

To decide which signs should be taught first, ask the family to make a list of words that are the most important for communicating with their baby. Review the list with the family and other team members, de-

Sidebar 9.1   CONSIDERATIONS FOR ADAPTING SIGNS

Signs will be presented and taught differently, depending on whether the infant is totally blind or has low vision.

If the infant has low vision

1. Identify how close the signs need to be made to the infant for the infant to see them (the infant's viewing distance for signs).

2. Consider whether the rate or speed of signs and the size or number of movements need to be adjusted so the infant can attend to them visually. Some infants with multiple disabilities and visual impairments may have difficulty attending to a sequence of signs made at a normal speed and rate. They may respond better to one- or two-word signed phrases that are repeated.

3. Notice whether the position and placement of the signer's hands are easy for the infant to discriminate—that they are within the infant's visual field and viewing distance and are easily seen against the signer's clothing.

If the infant is blind

1. Identify how to provide tactile signs to the infant, either by having the infant place his or her hand on the signer's hand or by guiding the infant's hands through the sign movements.

2. Consider whether the rate or speed of signs and the size or number of movements need to be adjusted so the infant can attend to them tactilely. Tactile signs may need to be introduced one at a time so the infant can make an association between the sign and its referent.

3. Notice whether the movements of the sign are easy for the infant to discriminate from other movements—that the signer stops all other movements and tactile stimulation of the infant before making the sign. For example, if the sign EAT (touching the infant's lips) is used during meals, the signer stops all other movements (such as wiping the infant's lips or hands with a napkin), signs EAT by touching the infant's lips, and then gives the infant a spoonful of food.

cide on the signs to be used for these words, identify any adaptations that are needed, and use selected signs consistently across activities. The more exposure and repetition the infant has to selected signs (communication input), the more likely the infant will be to understand their meaning. For communication output, however, infants with multiple disabilities are more likely to produce signs that represent preferred objects (BLANKET), favorite activities (BOUNCING, or EAT), and familiar people (MAMA); that are used for daily routines (EAT and BATH); that are easy to produce, touch the body, and have symmetrical movements (MORE, EAT, and MAMA); and that look or feel like what they represent (EAT, WASH, and DOWN). The more of these criteria that the first signs meet, the more likely the infant will be to produce them. Thus, selecting first signs that meet all four of these criteria will provide the infant with a quick understanding of the power of communication (Chen, Friedman, & Calvello, 1990).

IMPLEMENTING INTERVENTIONS

Once early interventionists are familiar with the different ways that infants with visual impairments and other disabilites may be encouraged to understand communication from others and to express their needs, desires, and interests, as well as a variety of strategies for encouraging the infants to begin using them, they still need to know how to build on the infants' abilities and interests to develop communication interventions that fit into the families' routines and preferred activities. The case of Maria, presented earlier in this chapter, is an example of how an early interventionist planned strategies to implement specific interventions. One way to begin such planning is to use the forms introduced in this chapter (including Functions of Early Communicative Behaviors, Communication Options Worksheet, and Routine Analysis) to gather and organize information about individual infants' strengths, needs, and abilities; existing methods of communication; and home environments. These forms help early interventionists to develop strategies for encouraging further communication. Early interventionists should be familiar with the key components contained on each form to guide their observations of infants and discussions with caregivers. Not all forms should be used with every infant and family, however. Rather, early interventionists should select the forms that will be helpful to specific families. For example, a form to examine an infant's communication behavior is sometimes unnecessary because the infant's behaviors are just beginning to be interpreted as communicative. A routine analysis at a family's home is necessary only when the caregiver wants to examine each step of a particular activity for developing specific strategies (as shown in the example of Huey's bathtime in the accompanying case study).

HUEY

Huey, aged 24 months, has been diagnosed with cortical visual impairment and severe developmental delays and is nonambulatory because of spastic cerebral palsy. Several months ago, his mother, who was a single parent, was killed in a traffic accident and there were no extended family members to assume his care. Consequently, Huey has been in foster placement for the past six months with the Woo family and is now receiving home visits from an early interventionist and has begun to make a transition to center-based services. He prefers to be left alone and does not like to be held or touched. His foster mother reports that he eats pureed foods and drinks from a bottle. She is concerned about his self-injurious behaviors (biting his hand in the calloused area) and his fussing and crying episodes.

HOMEWORK
FOR THE HOME VISIT

From her own initial observations of Huey and information gathered from Mrs. Woo, the early interventionist decides to review the Communication Options worksheet (Figure 9.3) and the Functions of Early Communicative Behavior worksheet (Figure 9.4). She discussed the forms with the speech and language therapist at the center for which she works to determine where to begin with Huey's communication. Huey does not have any words and does not seem to understand any speech. He had an audiological evaluation a year ago that indicated that his responses were "within normal limits." The early interventionist made a note to discuss this evaluation with Mrs. Woo and to observe Huey's responses to sounds and speech. Although Huey may learn signs, his present sensitivity to touch, level of visual attention, and motor ability do not support a sole focus on signs to supplement speech input. The early interventionist decides to discuss both forms with Mrs. Woo, to gather more information about Huey's communication behaviors, to explain the systematic use of object and touch cues as communication input for Huey, and to suggest the use of object cues for his expressive communication.

WORKING TOGETHER

During the next home visit the early interventionist introduces the worksheets and asks Mrs. Woo about Huey's communicative behaviors. Mrs. Woo says that she knows when Huey dislikes something because he fusses or bites his hand, but she cannot really identify any other behaviors as communication. She is excited to learn about object and touch cues. She had wondered about Huey's communication, since he did not make any sounds except for fussing and crying. She tries to speak to him in English, although the rest of the family speaks Mandarin at home. Over the next few weeks, both the early interventionist and Mrs. Woo observe Huey during the daily routine. They discover that he expresses interest by breathing noisily and seems to enjoy being in the bath. Mrs. Woo says he is cooperative during bathtime and that she tends to wash him slowly because she feels this is "their special time." She observes that he fusses and cries when she

Figure 9.3 SAMPLE COMPLETED COMMUNICATION OPTIONS WORKSHEET FOR HUEY

Communications Options Worksheet

Name: __Huey__   Age: __24 months__   Date: __January 20, 1999__

	Child's Strengths and Needs		Communication Options	
Area	**Observations**	**Input**	**Output**	
Vision	Low vision	Sign possible Object cues Pictures	Picture communication board—adapted Objects that are easy to discriminate visually	
Hearing	Normal limits, ear infections	Speech	Nonvocal	
Motor	Nonambulatory, fluctuating muscle tone, not sitting independently, arm movement/ moves arm	Limit coactive signing	Generalized body movements to read and shape to gestures Orientation to people and objects	
Tactile	Does not like to touch anything but hard objects Does not like to be held	Limit coactive signing Object cues possible Tactile cues possible	Objects that are solid (such as a spoon versus a teddy bear)	
Responses to movement	Screams when picked up and bites hand	Does not use movement as gestures		
Cognitive level				
Awareness		Pictures: not yet		
Recognition		Object cues: beginning		
Discrimination				
Selected options to discuss with family		Object cues	Body language	
		Tactile cues	Objects	
		Speech		

Figure 9.4   SAMPLE COMPLETED FORM FOR RECORDING THE FUNCTIONS OF EARLY COMMUNICATIVE BEHAVIORS

Functions of Early Communicative Behaviors

Name: _Huey_   Date: _Febuary 4, 1999_

Date of Birth: _January 5, 1997_   Age: _24 months_

Informant: _Mrs. Woo_   Interviewer: _Martha Jones_

Function of communication	How does the infant communicate?	Situations that elicit these behaviors
Behavior regulation		
Protest, refusal, or rejection	Fusses, cries, bites own hand	When I picked him up suddenly. When I need to dress or bathe him quickly.
Request for object		
Request for action	Noisy breathing	When I bathe him slowly
Social interaction		
Greet	Not yet	
Seek attention		
Request social routines		
Request comfort		
Joint attention		
Comment on object	Not yet	
Comment on action		
Request information		

picks him up quickly or must complete a caregiving task rapidly. She wonders whether he is startled or confused by quick movements and rapid interactions and is becoming concerned about his hand-biting behavior.

When she returns to her office, the early interventionist discusses Mrs. Woo's concern about Huey's behavior with the program's psychologist. The psychologist suggests using the Motivation Assessment Scale (Durand &

Figure 9.5 ROUTINE ANALYSIS OF HUEY'S BATHTIME

Routine Analysis

Name: __Huey__

Date: __February 4, 1999__

Activity: __Bathtime__

Steps in Routine	Natural Cues	Behaviors to Encourage	Input or Adaptive Strategies
1. Going to the bathroom	After dinner Being in the bathroom Smell and feel of air	Put hand in washcloth mitt	Object cue: washcloth mitt
2. Getting undressed	Change of temperature Skin contact with air On towel or rug	Relaxed, not fighting Move limbs out of clothes	Touch cue: for removing clothing
3. Getting into the tub	Water and temperature Foam cutout that supports head and body Feeling of tub	Cooperate	Sign: *WASH* (on body) Object cue: tub
4. Washing	Soap Washcloth mitt Pouring water	Rub hands together Coactively rub body with mitt Play tickle game	Object cue: liquid soap in hand Object cue: pour water over leg or hand
5. Rinsing	Pouring water	Playful anticipation	Object cue: pour water over leg or hand
6. Getting out of the tub	Picked up and out of tub	Keep head erect	Touch cue: for pick up
7. Drying off	Towel Lotion on limbs Desitin on bottom	Cooperate Reaching for lotion/hand Touch lotion	Object cue: towel, lotion bottle
8. Getting dressed	Diaper Pajamas on	Cooperate Push hand and foot through clothes	Object cue: diaper Coactive sign: ALL DONE

Crimmins, 1992) to identify the function of Huey's hand-biting behavior. During the next home visit, Mrs. Woo and the early interventionist complete the Motivation Assessment Scale. They discover that Huey bites his hand when he is left alone, that he seems fairly calm, and seems to like biting on his hand. They decide to decrease the time that Huey spends alone, to increase opportunities for Huey to interact with different family members, to identify other sensory activities that he seems to enjoy, and to pick him up and move him slowly, so he has time to adjust to the change. They also plan to consult with the occupational therapist at the program regarding activities that will motivate Huey to use his hands in other stimulating ways.

The following week, the early interventionist introduces the Routine Analysis form (see Figure 9.5) to analyze the bath routine and to build opportunities for intervention objectives. She asks Mrs. Woo about the bath routine—where and when each step takes place. They brainstorm on the variety of input that Huey may accept. Through the process, Mrs. Woo discovers that Huey anticipates bathtime because of all the natural cues associated with the activity. She agrees to encourage Huey to use his hands in a variety of ways and to provide communication input when possible. The early interventionist demonstrates each of the cues that they selected and offers to make a late home visit during Huey's bathtime to help Mrs. Woo with this goal. She stresses that Mrs. Woo should try the Routine Analysis for bathtime with Huey and settle on a sequence of input that is natural and comfortable for them both. She emphasizes that it may not be possible to use all the identified object cues, touch cues, and signs during every bath. In addition, she encourages Mrs. Woo to continue to talk to Huey in Mandarin (the language that he will hear at home and in which Mrs. Woo feels the most comfortable) while she uses the selected options for communication.

In addition, early interventionists must do their homework in preparation for home visits. They have a professional responsibility to develop the skills and competencies necessary to make professional recommendations and to balance these recommendations with priorities, values, and concerns of a particular family.

As noted, Huey's situation requires different types of analyses than Maria's did. The Routine Analysis worksheet (see Figure 9.5) helps the interventionist and caregiver break a daily routine into its component steps and discover both natural cues for the activity and cues that can be introduced as receptive communication.

Predictable Routines

Huey's bath routine illustrates a critical component of creating opportunities for communication—developing predictable routines. Every activity has a beginning, a middle, and an end. These are natural steps in preparing the baby for the activity, beginning the activity, supporting the infant's participation in the activity, and ending the activity. All infants learn to recognize daily activities by the cues naturally associated with the routine. Infants with multiple disabilities may need additional cues to develop an understanding of daily activities. (Routine analysis was discussed in greater detail in Chapter 8; a blank form is provided in the Appendix.)

In Huey's case, bathtime demonstrates a sequence, natural cues, and opportunities to provide additional cues, if needed. Consistent sequences such as this provide infants with predictability, promote their sense of control over events, and support their participation. Moreover, the use of daily routines

- enhances the family's involvement in intervention strategies
- promotes the infant's understanding of and response to significant natural cues
- provides frequent and repetitive opportunities for the infant to engage in interaction

Culturally Responsive Interventions

Huey's situation also illustrates the need for the early interventionist to be sensitive to families' cultures and to plan interventions that are responsive to these cultures. The United States is one of the most culturally and linguistically diverse countries in the world. Therefore, it is likely that families who receive early intervention services will represent a variety of cultures, languages, socioeconomic backgrounds, values, and beliefs that will influence their child-rearing practices, beliefs about disability, and interactions with service providers. In many cases, the cultural backgrounds, languages, and values of early interventionists differ from those of the families they serve, as was the case with Huey and Mrs. Woo, whose home language was Mandarin. The early interventionist in this situation was aware that sometimes speaking English to Huey and sometimes Mandarin would make his development of communication even more difficult, so she recommended that Mrs. Woo should speak only Mandarin to Huey.

Working with the family, the early interventionist should endeavor to develop and implement intervention activities that will enhance the infant's communication skills. This process begins by asking a family about their typical activities, concerns, and priorities for their infant's development of communication through such questions as these:

1. What activities do you enjoy doing with your infant?
2. What songs or baby games do you play in your family?
3. What words do you use a lot in everyday activities with your baby?
4. What do you say when your baby does something that you like or makes you feel proud?
5. When is a good time to or what is a good activity in which to talk with your baby?
6. What words would you like your baby to learn first?

On the basis of the family's responses to these questions, the early interventionist can provide specific suggestions for ways to develop opportunities for communication that fit into the family's routine, values, and culture. For example, if it is not usual for families of certain cultural backgrounds to engage in social interactions and conversation during meals, then suggesting that a caregiver emphasize opportunities for communication while feeding the baby may not be feasible. Similarly, suggesting that the family use certain signs or words with an infant may be inappropriate if the family never uses these words. For example, saying "good boy" may not be a natural way for a family to praise a child; some families may say "bravo" instead. In Hawaii, saying "*pau*" may be more typical than saying "finished" or "all done." In some cases, explaining a sign based on the initial letter of a word in English by saying "It will be easy for you to remember the sign for SHOE because it is made by tapping S together" may be disrespectful to a non-English speaking family for several reasons. First, this explanation implies that the early interventionist assumes that the family knows the English word "shoe." The family may not be familiar with this word in English. If they are not, then the explanation may give them the impression that the early interventionist believes that they should be speaking English to their child. Most likely, the family is using their first language at home. Third, it indicates that an English-speaking early interventionist has not taken the time to find out how to communicate in a way that the family would understand. This lack of planning suggests that the early interventionist views this discussion as not important. Fourth, a direct translation of the early interventionist's comment by an inexperienced interpreter will not make any sense if the word for "shoe" in the family's language does not begin with an "s," such as "zapata" in Spanish. The family might be confused if the interpreter does not use both English and Spanish words to communicate the meaning of the early interventionist's explanation. Furthermore, some signs may even be offensive to some families. For example, the *T* hand shape used to indicate TOILET is a vulgar sign in some cultures (Chen, Chan, & Brekken, in press). Additional tips for working with families who have different languages and cultures are presented in Chapter 8.

Sidebar 9.2 summarizes the key strategies for developing communication in infants who have multiple disabilities that have been presented in this chapter.

Sidebar 9.2   KEY STRATEGIES FOR DEVELOPING COMMUNICATION IN INFANTS WITH MULTIPLE DISABILITIES

- Interpret the infant's cues, identify communicative behaviors, and respond to them in ways that the infant can perceive.
- Encourage the infant's use of functional vision, if appropriate (see Chapter 5, "Functional Vision Assessment and Early Intervention").
- Encourage the infant's use of available hearing, if appropriate (see Chapter 6, Understanding Hearing Loss: Implications for Early Intervention").
- Develop predictable routines and opportunities for repetitive input and for the infant to anticipate or request what will happen next.
- Identify motivating situations that create a need for the infant to communicate (such as the use of the interrupted routine or delay strategies, create "problems," or "up the ante").
- Use short, repetitive phrases with intonation to focus the infant's attention to speech.
- Talk about what the infant is experiencing (for instance, "up, you go" while picking up the infant).
- Provide selected information on what the infant cannot see (for example, "Mama's getting your milk from the refrigerator").
- Select options for communication (like touch cues, object cues, and adapted signs) for infants who need additional methods beside speech.
- Develop enjoyable turn-taking games (such as action-based, game-based, imitation-based, or reference-based routines and progressive-matched turn-taking strategies) within the context of everyday situations.
- Make communication fun.

CONCLUSION

Enhancing the early communication of infants with visual impairments and additional disabilities should be the primary focus of all early intervention programs that serve these infants and their families. Because all infants discover the power of communication through daily interactions with caregivers and other family members, early interventionists must work with families to develop and implement methods and strategies for communication that fit a family's routine and culture. In addition, the complexity of communication input should fit the infant's developmental and cognitive levels. Communication about what the infant is doing should coincide with the infant's actions and focus on the most critical aspects of the activity. Providing too much or too complicated input will result in a decrease in interaction by the infant. On the other hand, providing too little input will not engage the infant. Similarly, expecting communication output that far exceeds the infant's current ability will limit the infant's immediate possibilities for independent expressive communication, whereas expecting too little communication from the infant will not encourage the development of communication. There is a fine and delicate balance in creating the most appropriate beginning communication interventions for each infant who is visually impaired and has additional disabilities.

REFERENCES

Alvares, R., & Sternberg, L. (1994). Communication and language development. In L. Sternberg (Ed.), *Individuals with profound disabilities: Instructional and assistive strategies* (3rd ed., pp. 193–229).

Bates, E. (1979). On the evolution and development of symbols. In E. Bates (Ed.), *The emergence of symbols. Cognition and communication in infancy* (pp. 3–32). New York: Academic Press.

Bruner, J. (1981). The social context of language acquisition. *Language and Communication, 1,* 155–178.

Chen, D. (1995a). The beginnings of communication: Early childhood. In K. M. Huebner, J. G. Prickett, T. Rafalowski Welsh, & E. Joffee (Eds.), *Hand in hand: Essentials of communication and orientation and mobility for your students who are deaf-blind* (pp. 185–218). New York: AFB Press.

Chen, D. (1995b). Understanding and developing communication. In D. Chen & J. Dote-Kwan (Eds.), *Starting points: Instructional practices for young children whose disabilities include visual impairment* (pp. 57–72). Los Angeles: Blind Childrens Center.

Chen, D. (1996). Parent-infant communication: Early intervention for very young children with visual impairment or hearing loss. *Infants and Young Children, 9*(2), 1–12.

Chen, D., Chan, S., & Brekken, L. (in press). *Conversations for three: Communicating through interpreters* [Booklet & video]. Baltimore, MD: Paul H. Brookes.

Chen, D., Friedman, C. T., & Calvello, G. (1990). *Learning together: A guide to socially-based routines for visually impaired infants.* Louisville, KY: American Printing House for the Blind.

Chen, D., & Haney, M. (1995). An early intervention model for infants who are deaf-blind. *Journal of Visual Impairment & Blindness, 89,* 213–221.

Coggins, T. E., & Carpenter, R. L. (1981). The Communication Intention Inventory: A system for observing and coding children's early intentional communication. *Applied Psycholinguistics, 2,* 235–251.

Dore, J. (1974). A pragmatic description of early language development. *Journal of Psycholinguistic Research, 4,* 343–351.

Durand, V. M., & Crimmins, D. (1992). *Motivation Assessment Scale.* Topeka, KS: Monaco Associates.

Dunst, C. (1978). A cognitive-social approach for assessment of early nonverbal behavior. *Journal of Childhood Communication Disorders, 2,* 110–123.

Evans, C. J., & Johnson, C. J. (1988). Training pragmatic language skills through alternate strategies with a blind multihandicapped child. *Journal of Visual Impairment & Blindness, 82,* 109–112.

Fraiberg, S. (1977). *Insights from the blind.* New York: Basic Books.

Jurgens, M. R. (1977). *Confrontation between the young deaf-blind child and the outer world: How to make the world surveyable by organized structure.* Amsterdam, The Netherlands: Swets & Zeitlinger.

MacDonald, J. D. (1982). Communication strategies for language intervention. In D. P. McClowry, A. M. Guilford, & S. O. Richardson (Eds.), *Infant communication: Development, assessment and intervention.* New York: Grune & Stratton.

MacDonald, J. D., & Gilette, Y. (1986). Communicating with persons with severe handicaps: Roles of parents and professionals. *Journal of the Association for Persons with Severe Handicaps, 11,* 255–265.

MacFarland, S. Z. C. (1995). Teaching strategies of the van Dijk curricular approach. *Journal of Visual Impairment & Blindness, 89,* 222–228.

Maestas y Moores, J., & Moores, D. F. (1980). Language training with the young deaf child. *New Directions for Exceptional Children, 2,* 49–61.

Mahoney G., & Weller, E. L. (1980). An ecological approach to language intervention. *New Directions for Exceptional Children, 2,* 17–32.

Manolson, A. (1984). *It takes two to talk.* Toronto, Ont., Canada: Hanen Early Language Resource Centre.

Rogow, S. (1982). Rhythms and rhymes: Developing communication in very young blind and multihandicapped children. *Child: Care, Health and Development, 8,* 249–260.

Rossetti, L. M. (1996). *Communication intervention: Birth to three.* San Diego, CA: Singular Publishing.

Rowland, C. (1990). *Communication matrix.* Portland, OR: Center on Self-Determination, Oregon Health Sciences University.

Rowland, C., Schweigert, P. D., & Prickett, J. G. (1995). Communication systems, devices, and modes. In K. M. Huebner, J. G. Prickett, T. Rafalowski Welsh, & E. Joffee (Eds.), *Hand in hand: Essentials of communication and orientation and mobility for your students who are deaf-blind* (pp. 219–260). New York: AFB Press.

Snow, C. (1972). Mothers' speech to children learning language. *Child Development, 43,* 1–22.

Tronick, E. (1980). Infant communicative intent. In A. P. Reilly (Ed.), *The communication game: Perspectives on the development of speech, language and non-verbal communication skills* (pp. 4–9). Skillman, NJ: Johnson & Johnson Baby Products.

van Dijk, J. (1965). The first steps of the deaf-blind child towards language. In *Proceedings of the Conference on the Deaf-Blind,* Refsnes, Denmark (pp. 47–50). Boston: Perkins School for the Blind.

van Dijk, J. (1967). The non-verbal deaf-blind child and his world: His outgrowth toward the world of symbols. *Proceedings of the Jaarverslag Instituut voor Doven, 1964–1967* (pp. 73–110). Sint Michielsgestel, The Netherlands: Instituut voor Doven.

Watkins, S. (1985). *Developing sign communication with the multi-handicapped sensory impaired child.* Logan, UT: SKI*HI Institute.

Werner, H., & Kaplan, B. (1963). *Symbol formation.* New York: John Wiley.

Wetherby, A., Yonclas, D., & Bryan, A. (1989). Communication profiles of handicapped preschool children: Implications for early identification. *Journal of Speech and Hearing Disorders, 54,* 148–158.

10

Critical Transitions: Educating Young Children in a Typical Preschool

June Downing

Children typically learn a great deal by watching, listening to, and interacting with their siblings and other children they play with. They learn to play, share, interact, gain attention, request assistance when needed, and express themselves. Children who have severe and multiple disabilities (especially visual impairment) are at a distinct disadvantage when it comes to vicarious learning (McInnes & Treffry, 1982). They may not be able to obtain information from a distance or act on that information if they are physically disabled or talk about what they experience if they have communication difficulties. When these children are placed in separate classes apart from nondisabled youngsters, their disabilities may be exacerbated and learning may be more difficult because they lack appropriate role models and interactive playmates. They have much fewer interactions with effective communication partners and various objects if they cannot see or hear well or move easily. Opportunities to learn from one another may be greatly reduced if everyone has the same disability (Heller, Alberto, & Bowdin, 1995).

Bringing young children of diverse strengths and abilities together creates many opportunities for all children to grow and develop. Children learn at a young age that everyone is different and has unique qualities, that all children are to be valued and respected, and that they need not be afraid of differences. They also learn to interact in ways that are most effective for different individuals. Early interactions with young children of different races, genders, cultural backgrounds, and abilities help lay a solid, positive foundation for later life experiences. These benefits have been clearly documented (see Buysse, 1993; Demchak & Drinkwater, 1992; Diamond, Hestenes, Carpenter, & Innes, 1997).

Parents and other family members who want their children with disabilities to be educated with children without disabilities may find support for their decision from the legal mandates of the Individuals with Disabilities Education Act (see Chapter 1). The decision about any educational placement should be based on the family's preferences and the child's needs, and every program should be individually tailored to address these needs. If parents choose an inclusive program for their child, specific accommodations have to be made because educating all children together does not mean that individual needs and differences are ignored. Since all children learn differently, the teaching staff need information on each child's learning style and needs so that adaptations can be made to ensure that each child receives as much information as possible and uses it effectively. Accommodations may involve related services (such as occupational therapy and vision services), adapted materials and equipment, and specialized instructional strategies. Given the appropriate supports, all children can benefit from learning together.

This chapter discusses some of the unique learning needs of young children with severe and multiple disabilities in inclusive preschools, as well as different strategies to meet those needs. It is intended to help preschool teachers, teaching assistants, related service providers, and parents in their efforts to educate children together despite different abilities. Sections in this chapter target physical and sensory accommodations that need to be considered for these children. Although much of the information is relevant for children with only one disability (a severe visual impairment or a physical impairment), this chapter focuses on children with multiple disabilities. First, some general information is provided for parents to consider when selecting a preschool program for their child. Then different sections target various considerations for working in the classroom with a child who has multiple disabilities, including environmental considerations, social considerations, adaptations of materials, instructional strategies, partial participation, and what outcomes can be expected. The chapter concludes with information related to the sometimes unconventional behaviors that these young children may exhibit, why these behaviors may exist, and how to interpret them in a positive way.

CHOOSING AN APPROPRIATE PRESCHOOL PROGRAM

Although the majority of preschool programs that are specifically designed to accommodate young children with disabilities are housed in separate facilities (Cavallaro, Ballard-Rosa, & Lynch, 1998; Odom, McConnell, & Chandler, 1993; Peck, Furman, & Helmstetter, 1993), the needs of children with even severe disabilities can be met in typical preschools, just as they are met at home (Cavallaro & Haney, 1999; Odom & McLean, 1996; Peck, Odom, & Bricker, 1993). That is, the necessary special support is provided to the children wherever they are rather than taking the children to receive special support in a special place.

When they are deciding on a preschool program (for any child), parents need to take certain factors into consideration. The list of indicators of a high-quality preschool is presented in Sidebar 10.1.

When looking for an appropriate inclusive preschool program for their child with severe and multiple disabilities, parents may want to start with high-quality preschool programs close to their home or work. Preschools with fully credentialed staff and that are recommended by friends, neighbors, or coworkers for having several of the aforementioned qualities may be the best starting points in identifying a potential program.

Parents may be able to locate appropriate inclusive preschool programs by contacting university programs that train early childhood special educators in inclusive educational practices. These universities may offer their own inclusive preschool programs that serve as training sites for future teachers. Federally funded programs, such as University-Affiliated Programs at universities may also provide valuable information on high-quality inclusive preschool programs, especially if they have federally funded projects in this area. Other sources of information for parents may include state agencies for individuals with developmental

Sidebar 10.1   INDICATORS OF HIGH-QUALITY PROGRAMS FOR YOUNG CHILDREN WITH DISABILITIES

The following are factors that parents will want to consider when looking for an appropriate preschool program for a child with severe or multiple disabilities. All indicators need not be present, and other factors may also be important, but these guidelines will give parents a place to begin when evaluating preschool programs for their child.

- a stated program philosophy that all children are to be valued and respected for what they bring to school
- a stated program philosophy on the positive ways children will be treated
- a stated program philosophy of active family involvement in all aspects of the program
- an open, warm, nurturing, flexible, and qualified staff
- an effective staff training program
- a staff-to-pupil ratio that supports all students and permits the objectives of the Individual Family Service Plan (IFSP) or the Individual Education Program (IEP) to be met
- a majority of students who do not have disabilities
- an emphasis on play as a major avenue for learning
- a structure that is apparent, with both specific routines and rules and flexibility evident, and children encouraged to make individual choices
- toys that are accessible to encourage independence
- an environment that is clean, safe, and fun and that has sufficient age-appropriate, multisensory materials to stimulate learning and facilitate interactions
- children encouraged to interact
- collaborative teaming in evidence
- support services (such as orientation and mobility, speech and language, and physical therapy) available as needed
- equipment to facilitate participation in activities
- transition planning to prepare children for future learning environments

disabilities, advocacy organizations, and resource centers for families. (An extensive list of resource agencies can be found in the *AFB Directory of Services for Blind and Visually Impaired Persons in the United States and Canada,* 1997.)

BEGINNING STEPS

Once a high-quality program has been found and the decision is made to include the young child with severe and multiple disabilities, certain initial steps can help ease the transition.

Introduce the Child to the Staff

Parents play a critical role in helping their child get a good start in a new preschool program. Instead of focusing on their child's disabilities, they can help the staff understand their child's strengths, abilities, likes, and dislikes. By highlighting how their child is like other children without disabilities, the parents can help the staff feel less hesitant and more confident in their abilities to meet the child's needs (see Mattheis, 1996). The parents can inform the teachers how the child learns best and communicates most effectively and what motivates the child to learn. Sharing such critical information with the teachers not only helps them be effective with a given child, but reduces the need to elaborate on the areas in which the child has limitations. For example, when the parents inform a teacher that their 3 year old communicates by smiling, reaching for objects, making "happy" sounds, crying, grimacing, and grinding teeth, the teacher does not need to hear about all the communication skills that the child has *not* mastered. The focus is on what the child *can* do, not on the child's limitations.

Identify Basic Needs

If the child has significant disabilities, it is important for the preschool staff to obtain specific information to ensure the child's safety, health, and learning potential. The parents should provide information on the child's medical needs (allergies, medications, and respiration) and basic physical needs (nutritional intake, toileting schedule, and physical positioning) just as they would with any other provider of care. They are in the best position to show the staff how to lift, carry, and position their child, although this information should be reinforced by physical and occupational therapists. Information about the child could be written out and kept in various places in the preschool (for example, in a journal that goes back and forth with the child each day and is written in by both the parents and teachers, with the child's IEP, on the refrigerator where meals are kept, and in the bathroom) to remind the staff of necessary precautions.

Besides basic information to ensure physical comfort and safety, the parents and other family members can tell the staff what they would like the child to learn and how he or she will learn it. Parents know best how their child learns and should share this information with teachers and other service providers; doing so saves time and keeps the child from becoming frustrated. Parents also have dreams for their child's future education at the elementary school level. Listening carefully to these dreams can help the teaching staff to focus educational interventions and lead to desired outcomes.

Help Peers Understand

Research on inclusive educational practices for young children with disabilities has found that just physical placement with nondisabled peers is insufficient if inclusion is truly the goal (Guralnick & Groom, 1987, 1988; Hill & Rabe, 1992). Young children with no disabilities need encouragement and sometimes specific instruction on ways to interact with their classmates who have disabilities. When a child cannot see or hear, move efficiently, or speak, his or her classmates may have concerns and questions that need to be addressed. Both the parents and teachers can explain to the classmates what a particular child likes and does not like to do, what the family is like, if the family has a pet, and so forth. The focus is on the similarities, not the differences, among children. Person-first language is always used to help the children focus on the person, not the disability (e.g., "the little girl who doesn't see," rather than "the blind child").

During introductory sessions of this nature, the classmates can be encouraged to recognize how all children are alike. Any questions they may have are answered matter-of-factly and at a level that young children can understand. Since young children (aged 3–5) do notice differences among individuals and may use these differences to avoid classmates, preferring to play with those who are similar to them (Diamond, 1994), they should be encouraged to discuss openly any differences they may perceive (such as clear physical differences in size or ability, unusual mannerisms, or lack of speech). The teachers and parents of the child with disabilities can facilitate the discussion by presenting the differences factually, highlighting how everyone is different from everyone else in some ways, and how important those differences are. Rab and Wood (1995, pp. 140–141) presented the following excellent guidelines for helping teachers deal with children's' comments or reactions to a child with disabilities in the classroom:

- Always respond to a child's question even if it is embarrassing.
- Always respond in a positive and practical way (for example, to the question "What's wrong with him?" answer "Nothing is wrong; he just can't use his eyes, so he uses his hands and ears instead").
- Provide information in small, easily understood amounts (do not go into too much detail).
- Use descriptive words that relate to the children's own experiences (for instance, "When you wear mittens, it's very hard to pick up things. That's what it's like for Jenny without mittens").
- Watch how a child acts around a child with disabilities and be ready to intercede (for example, "Does it bother you that Jason waves his arms a lot and makes that sound? It's not what you do, is it? Maybe Jason is trying to tell us something. What could it be?").
- In addition it is important to let all the children explore any special equipment, materials, and toys for the child who is disabled so they can feel comfortable with certain adaptations.

Besides learning how they are like the child who has a disability, the classmates also need to learn how to interact with him or her, particularly when the child has a sensory and/or physical impairment that can interfere with interactions. The classmates need specific guidance and encouragement for their efforts to interact (Fad, Ross, & Boston, 1995; Strain & Odom, 1986). They need to learn simple ways of greeting the child and saying good-bye, asking the child questions, and understanding his or her responses. They also need to be able to interpret the child's unique sounds, body language, facial expressions, and movements in such a way that makes sense and that they can relate to their own means of communication. In addition, they need to be shown how to use their voices (especially with children who cannot see), use touch cues, and use objects to interact. Gaining experience using a child's augmentative and alternative communication device is necessary to help the classmates feel comfortable interacting with the child and to make them aware that the child can communicate effectively, albeit not through speech.

Finally, the classmates need to understand what it means when a child cannot hear, see, move, or speak well. They do not need to know technical terms, just what to expect from the child, so they can adjust their interactions accordingly. For instance, they need to learn to put objects (such as, toys and bowls) in the hands of a child who is blind or physically disabled, rather than hold the objects at a distance. They need to learn to tell a child who is blind when they are leaving and going elsewhere and to talk to him or her while they are playing. They also need to learn to gain the visual attention of a child who is deaf or has a severe hearing impairment before they try to share information. Learning these skills occurs over time and as children are encouraged to learn and play together. Information can be provided when the children either express the interest or demonstrate a need to improve their interaction skills.

EDUCATING EVERYONE TOGETHER: ADAPTATIONS

To ensure that everyone is benefiting from an inclusive preschool program, the teachers must make adaptations to accommodate unique learning styles and needs (Downing, 1996; Gee, 1995). Modifications for children with severe and multiple disabilities in typical preschools can involve the following:

- environmental adaptations (both physical and social)
- participation adaptations
- material adaptations
- instructional adaptations
- outcome adaptations.

Each general type of adaptation is described in greater detail for children who have severe and multiple disabilities and divided into sections according to whether the children also have visual or hearing impairments and physical disabilities. Sidebar 10.2 summarizes the key points that are discussed about each of these groups regarding each type of adaptation.

Sidebar 10.2   KEY POINTS TO REMEMBER ABOUT ADAPTATIONS FOR EDUCATING CHILDREN WITH SEVERE AND MULTIPLE DISABILITIES IN TYPICAL PRESCHOOL SETTINGS

Children with Severe and Multiple Disabilities Who Are Visually Impaired or Blind

Access to toys that are colorful, interesting to touch, and have sound and/or vibration

Close physical proximity to others (teachers and classmates)

A safe, predictable environment in which to explore

A structured environment and routines

Sufficient lighting on task or play areas

Clear, verbal directions and physical prompts as needed

Tactile materials to replace visual activities (such as textured collages rather than drawings)

Emphasis on active and interactive play

Good contrast when providing visual information (for example, the foreground information is clear from the background)

Concrete, real items to introduce concepts

Exposure to braille and/or large print (for instance, labels on items in the room, including books)

Increased time to understand concepts

Children With Severe and Multiple Disabilities Who Are Hearing Impaired or Deaf

Lots of visually interesting stimulation

Close proximity to others

(continued on next page)

Sidebar 10.2   KEY POINTS TO REMEMBER ABOUT ADAPTATIONS FOR EDUCATING CHILDREN WITH SEVERE AND MULTIPLE DISABILITIES IN TYPICAL PRESCHOOL SETTINGS (continued)

Acoustically sound environments—acoustic tile, acoustic dividers, carpeting

Emphasis on active and interactive play

Easy visual access to persons who are speaking

Use of FM systems and auditory trainers as appropriate

Access to multiple modes of communication (such as manual signs, pictorial books, gestures, and facial expressions)

Highly structured activities and routines

Children with Severe and Multiple Disabilities Who Are Physically Impaired

Safe, accessible environment

Adaptations to allow the easy manipulation of toys and other items (such as elongated, widened handles; magnetic boards; and nonslip mats)

Positioning equipment to facilitate participation in activities

Close proximity to others

Support (from both adults and classmates) to participate partially in activities

Emphasis on the communicative aspects of an activity (making decisions and choices)

Emphasis on active and interactive play

Increased time to demonstrate skills

Although a child with multiple disabilities may have two or more of these learning needs, services providers need information about specific adaptations for each need separately to decide what combination of adaptations will best support the child. In this way, individual adaptations can be tailor made for each child. The overall intent of adaptations is to help make learning together as effective and efficient as possible (Rosenberg, Clark, Filer, Hupp, & Finkler, 1992). Of course, the necessary adaptations will be determined by the individual student's strengths and needs, as illustrated by the case studies of Angelina and Robbie at the end of this chapter.

Adaptations to the Physical Environment

Children with Visual Impairments and Other Disabilities

For children with visual impairments, perhaps the most important adaptation of the physical environment is the *lighting*. Depending on the visual impairment, a child will need solid lighting on the work or play area, but not light that creates a glare or shines in his or her eyes. Therefore, not only is the type of light important, but the child's position with regard to that source of light.

A child with severe and multiple disabilities and a visual impairment may need to wear eyeglasses to correct his or her acuity problem. The ophthalmologist or teacher credentialed in visual impairment can assist the teaching staff to understand the child's need for the eyeglasses, their benefits, and how to care for them. Such information is usually no more complex or different from that for any young child who wears eyeglasses, who has no visual impairment when corrected. However, teachers need to understand whether the eyeglasses are correcting for near or distant vision. A child may try to take off the eyeglasses when he or she is looking at things up close if his or her near vision is functional without eyeglasses. Thus, forcing the child to keep the eyeglasses on for all activities may be unnecessary and frustrate him or her.

When a child has limited or no vision, the environment must be structured so that it is easy and safe to move around in and encourages the child to explore. The child needs to be taught specific routes to get to frequented places; the orientation and mobility instructor can provide direct instruction, as well as teach the staff ways to help the child practice these skills. In addition, items (such as toys, books, and tapes) should be kept in specific places to accommodate the child's ability to follow directions and obtain desired items. Shelves and drawers can be color coded and tactilely coded to assist the child to find certain items (like his or her personal cubby and coat hook). The tactile markers can be the braille word, braille child's name, a design made by dried glue dots or puff paints, or textures (velvet or foam rubber). The only real restrictions are that the tactile cue should be something that the child feels comfortable touching and can easily discriminate from other tactile cues.

Children Whose Severe and Multiple Disabilities Include a Hearing Loss

The physical environment for a young child with some functional hearing needs to accommodate the remaining hearing. The acoustics of an environment need to be checked to ensure that everything has been done to enhance the transmission of sound (Prickett & Welch, 1995). Curtains and rugs can be placed on bare walls and floors to absorb extraneous sounds and keep the noise level down, and dividers can be used to create quiet areas for all children when needed. Ambient sounds, such as from air conditioners, fans, or radios, should be monitored so they do not distract the child or make it more difficult for the child to hear the teacher or classmates. As with a child with a visual impairment, the position of the child with a hearing impairment may be critical. The child needs to be close to the teacher and classmates, so he or she can receive verbal information and has close visual contact to help him or her understand the information.

Equipment may be needed that will increase and highlight auditory information. An FM (frequency-modulated) system may be used to block background noise and increase the volume of the teacher's voice. Most children with hearing impairments benefit from amplification devices, such as hearing aids, to improve their reception of auditory information. The audiologist or hearing specialist can provide valuable information on hearing aids, their use, settings, and care. As with eyeglasses, this information is not complex and can be readily acquired. The audiologist or teacher who is certified in the field of hearing impairments can also explain how amplification devices work, what they can and cannot do, and what the child may and may not be hearing. For example, hearing aids may amplify sounds to bring them into the child's range of hearing, but if the child has a sensorineural hearing loss (one in which clarity of sound is affected), what the child hears may be loud enough but distorted and extremely unclear. Therefore, the child may indicate that he or she has heard a sound but will be unable to make sense of it. Service providers need to be aware that just detecting a sound does not equate with understanding the sound or what to do as a result. This concept is particularly important for children who have severe and multiple disabilities and are struggling to make sense of their world because of cognitive limitations.

Children Whose Severe and Multiple Disabilities Include a Physical Impairment

The child with severe physical disabilities has a difficult time maneuvering in space, so the best environmental adaptations should address the need for accessibility. Ramps must be used to bypass steps, bathrooms must accommodate a child in a wheelchair or one who needs to have diapers changed, and there must be sufficient space to encourage a child to move around using a wheelchair or walker. Items need to be easily accessible so that the child can either obtain them independently or partially participate in obtaining them. The child with difficulty controlling his or her movements should have sufficient room to play with toys without having to worry about knocking things over. In general, the learning environment should be laid out so it is safe for the child to move as freely as possible.

Often a child with physical disabilities will be unable to engage in activities without the aid of positioning equipment that puts him or her in a comfortable and functional position and provides passive therapy by maintaining proper posture and position of the body (Campbell, 1993). Positioning equipment enhances participation by supporting the child in various positions that resemble those of other young children. In other words, if the classmates are sitting on the floor, the child with a physical disability also needs to be on the floor and physically supported so that his or her arms and hands are free to engage in the activity. When the classmates stand to paint or sing, the child may need to be positioned in a standing table or a prone or supine stander. The positioning equipment that is needed depends on the activity, how others engage in the activity, and the child's physical abilities and needs. A physical therapist can recommend appropriate equipment, either commercially available or handmade, and can teach the preschool staff to use and care for it.

Resources for Physical Accommodations

Initially the physical accommodations required for a child with a physical disability may seem overwhelming to a typical preschool program. Since the Individuals with Disabilities Education Act and the American with Disabilities Act legally require accommodations to be made for an individual child, a preschool that offers a program for a child can receive some financial assistance through the state department of education. In addition, nonprofit advocacy organizations, such as United Cerebral Palsy, Easter Seals, March of Dimes, Lions Foundation, and the American Foundation for the Blind (see the Resources Section), can provide some equipment and materials for the child to use and may provide training in the use of the equipment.

Social Environment

All young children, whether or not they have disabilites, need help to learn the social skills for engaging in cooperative play and making friends (Hoffman & Undram, 1984; Martin, Brady, & Williams, 1991; Wolf & Fine, 1995). Teachers can facilitate interactions by encouraging children to play together; by ensuring that toys are interactive, not solitary; and that children are given toys to share. Instead of having children spend the majority of their time playing individually with puzzles, painting at easels, or looking at books, teachers can make sure that the children spend substantial time in imaginative play with dolls, dollhouses, toy cars, building materials, and sand or water tables. Opportunities to target social interactive skills are much more prevalent in these types of activities than in those in which children play alone.

Children with disabilities need to be positioned physically close to their classmates without disabilities, especially if they have physical disabilities and are unable to move easily on their own. Teachers should be alert to the physical positions of the children in the class and ensure that the child with the disability is supported in a similar position. They also need to make certain that in their efforts to support the children, they avoid physically interfering with child-to-child interactions (Giangreco, Edelman, Luiselli, & MacFarland, 1997). For instance, if during circle time, a child with physical and multiple disabilities is positioned on the floor at one end of the circle with a teaching assistant sitting between the child and his or her classmates, the child's access to classmates is automatically blocked and he or she is prevented from observing their behavior.

As was discussed earlier, the other children in class need specific and practical information on how best to interact with the child with disabilites. Throughout the day, the teacher can do a great deal to encourage the children to share toys, food, and art materials; ask each other questions; show each other what they are doing; help each other; look out for each other; and say nice things to each other. For a child who cannot speak, the teacher must make sure that the classmates can understand and can adequately interpret his or her facial expressions, body language, vocalizations, and use of alternative and augmentative communication systems. Although the teacher may initially suggest ways in which the children can interact, the goal will be slowly to fade support so that the children naturally respond to one another (Luetke-Stahlman, 1994), as in the following example:

> During block play, the teacher encourages Christopher to pick up and hand blocks to Jeremy so he can build a tower. Christopher is 3 years old and has severe physical disabilities, a cognitive impairment, a visual impairment, and a profound hearing impairment. He is learning to hold his head up, look at people when they touch him or visually obtain his attention, and handle items. Although Jeremy could build a tower on his own, depending on Christopher to supply him with the blocks creates a social interaction that is of value to both children. At present, the teacher must provide considerable support for Christopher to respond to Jeremy's physical and gestural request to get a block, grab a block, and extend it to Jeremy. The goal is to fade this support as Christopher develops the necessary skills.

Material Adaptations

Children Whose Severe and Multiple Disabilities Include Visual Impairment

Since most teachers use visual information while teaching, especially at the preschool level, adaptations of teaching materials will be most obvious for children with visual impairments. Children who have functional vision need to be encouraged to use it by enhancing the visual characteristics of materials (Bailey & Downing, 1994). Considerable information is available on this subject (Downing & Bailey, 1990; Jan &

Groenveldt, 1993; Levack, 1994). In general, bright colors (especially yellow, orange, and red) can be added to items (if they are not already on the toys). Reflective tape can be added, as well, to draw the child's attention to such objects as cassette tapes, spoons, cups, cubbies, and shoes. Using a flashlight or penlight to highlight items to draw the child's visual attention and encourage both looking and reaching is another option, but a flashlight should *not* be shined in a child's eyes. Maintaining high contrast between the information (whether a picture or an object) and background information is critical. Keeping a solid color as the background behind relevant information can help the child discern the appropriate item or picture. Once the child can be helped to see that something is there, then instruction can concentrate on teaching the child *what* he or she is seeing. Just because children can indicate that they recognize something is visually in front of them does not mean that they know what it is or what they are to do as a result. That connection has to be taught, especially if a child has severe intellectual impairments as well.

For a child with insufficient vision to detect things visually, the use of objects for tactile exploration is recommended. The objects should be used in whatever activity they represent and should be the actual items, not miniatures (Downing & Eichinger, 1990). For instance, a 3-inch plastic toy tree should not be used to represent a real tree. It would be more meaningful to let the child tactilely explore and smell a real tree or a branch from a real tree, so the child can obtain accurate information about its size, shape, texture, and scent and, if pertinent, any auditory information. For items that are too large to bring to a child, the teacher needs to determine what parts of the item would provide the most relevant and meaningful information. For example, since it would be difficult for a child to see or handle a live eagle, obtaining a taxidermist's recreation of an eagle or showing the child an eagle's feathers and nest and playing a tape of an eagle's cry would be appropriate. Even when a child has some functional vision, it is important to make use of other sources of information, such as hearing, touch, and smell.

Adaptations that keep materials close to the child and within easy reach are easy to make and helpful to the child. For a toy that rolls or moves around (such as a ball and a toy car), the teacher can attach a string to it so the child does not lose control over where it has gone. A tray can be used to contain a child's toys (like marbles, blocks, and small plastic dolls) so they will be easy to find and manipulate during play.

One critical activity that may pose some difficulty for a child with sensory impairments is reading. At this age, young children typically sit around their teacher and listen to a story being told and look at colorful pictures that add to the information and interest of the story. Having a severe visual impairment that interferes with the ability to perceive pictures can diminish the child's enjoyment of the story. In response, the child (especially if he or she has other disabilities as well) may resort to self-stimulatory behaviors, such as rocking or hand flapping. To reduce the need for such behaviors and to increase his or her understanding of the story, the child needs to handle and explore real items that are directly related to the story (if possible). For some stories, such as a story about a balloon, the items are easy to obtain, but for others, such as a story about bears they cannot be obtained. When real or related items cannot be obtained, the child may need to handle an unrelated small item (like a piece of onyx or leather or a rubber band) to provide some form of additional stimulation while listening. Of course, telling stories that particularly relate to a child's life experiences (for example, a trip to Disneyland, a visit to the beach, or pets) will help maintain the child's attention and promote greater understanding, especially when the child is encouarged to handle an item directly related to the experience.

Finally, when activities (coloring, drawing, or painting), require the child to create what is typically a visual product, adaptations must be used to make them meaningful for the child with no vision. A child can create tactile designs by using a pointed (but not sharp) instrument (such as the tip of a ballpoint pen) on a piece of paper placed over a plastic mesh screen to produce raised lines. The child does not have to create the same image as his or her sighted peers, but should be encouraged to experiment with this art form instead. Using colors (as in crayoning and painting) to create designs could be bypassed by using different textures and materials (like cotton, felt, sandpaper, pipe-cleaners, feathers, and pieces of rubber) and gluing them in a creative manner to a heavy piece of paper. These adaptations allow the child to participate fully, although the final product may look different.

Children Whose Severe and Multiple Disabilities Include a Hearing Loss

Materials may not need to be adapted as much for a child who can see but has limited functional hearing because this child will rely on visual information to a large extent. However, when the activity (such as singing and listening to music), involves sound, special adaptations may have to be made. One simple adaptation is to add light to replace sound. For example, if the game of musical chairs is being played, a light can be turned on when the music goes on and turned off when the music stops. For music, the child can feel the vibrations of certain instruments (guitar, piano, drum), play a rhythm instrument, or clap his or her hands with the teacher as a model. The teacher may wish to increase the volume or increase the bass to help the child either feel the vibrations or actually hear the music.

Children Whose Severe and Multiple Disabilities Include a Physical Impairment

A child with a severe physical disability could require certain adaptations to gain access to materials he or she can see and hear. If the child also has visual or auditory impairments, then the adaptations mentioned previously are relevant as well. The child may need help grasping crayons, paintbrushes, and glue bottles or holding any object. To make an item easier to grasp and handle requires enlarging the area that the child is to grasp. Although commercial devices can be obtained to aid a child's ability to grasp, simple and inexpensive aids can be made with common materials. The occupational therapist on the educational team can help the teacher or aide with adaptations, such as wrapping tape, cloth, or Play-Doh around a crayon, paintbrush or felt-tip marker or placing a pencil grip or sponge curlers on a thin handle. If a child is hypotonic (has low muscle tone) and does not have the strength to maintain a grasp, he or she can wear a special mitt or mitten with a Velcro strap on the wrist to hold items. Utensils that glide on paper are easier for the child to handle than those that require a more specific grasp. Stamp-pad designs can be on rollers and pushed, rather than grasped and stamped. Wide roller pens may be easier to use than crayons; scissors (available from craft and sewing stores) that can be pushed across paper to cut it, rather than scissors that require the traditional open and close movements, are also recommended.

Dowels can be added to items that are hard to handle (such as small toy cars, paper dolls, and miniatures of farm animals), so the child can manipulate them more easily during play. If turning the pages of a book is difficult, "page fluffers" with a small piece of foam rubber glued to them (tongue depressors that extend out from each page and separate the pages) can be glued to each page as a permanent adaptation or paper clipped to each page as it is being read. Book pages can also be turned by using a wide-handle dowel or mouthpiece with a substance like HandiTak® at the end that adheres slightly to each page, making it easier to push over.

A slant board (a board placed on a desk or table to elevate material at various angles) can be used to bring material closer to a child with a physical impairment and at a more accessible angle; it is also helpful for a child with low vision. Magnetic boards also can be helpful for children with physical disabilities and visual impairments. Papers can be kept from bunching or slipping away by taping them down or placing Dycem (or another nonslip material) under them.

Various forms of assistive technology have been helpful in increasing the level of participation of children with physical disabilities (Flippo, Inge, & Barcus, 1995). Simple switch devices allow children to turn on toys, lights, and music—essentially, anything that is either electrical or battery operated—by using whatever movement is under the greatest control (of the head, arm, knee, foot, or chin) to activate the switches. For example, when children are listening to music that tells them what action to engage in, a child with severe physical disabilities who cannot perform the various movements can still participate by turning the music on and off as directed by the teacher. A physical therapist can help the teaching staff acquire the necessary equipment, can help determine the movements that allow the child the greatest control, and can teach the child to make use of the equipment. The teacher needs to determine the number of opportunities within each activity that can be used to include a child in activities that could be difficult without switch adaptations.

As young children gain greater access to computers and software programs for learning and play, high-tech adaptations allow a child with a limited use of his or her hands to participate as well. There are many adaptations that bypass the traditional keyboard on a computer and hence make access to software programs much easier by the use of simple movements to activate programs. For example, touch windows allow a child more direct access to information on the screen; joysticks make it easier to move the cursor; and adapted keyboards (such as IntelliKeys, Muppet Keyboard, and Key Largo) eliminate the need to understand traditional keyboard commands. In addition, software programs with colorful characters and unique sounds and that make interesting movements on the screen promote fun ways of learning cause and effect; control; and a variety of other skills, such as identifying colors, matching, and number concepts. Learning how to use a computer with such adaptations helps a child with severe physical disabilities develop a firm foundation for later computer use, which can have a significant and positive impact on him or her as an adult.

Augmentative communication devices (both simple and complex) allow a child who is unable to speak to communicate with others. Considerable information exists on the development and use of augmentative communication devices (see, for example, Baumgart, Johnson, & Helmstetter, 1990; Beukelman & Mirenda, 1998; Downing, 1999; Mirenda & Mathy-Laikko, 1989; Tanchak & Sawyer, 1995; Van Tatenhove, 1993). A speech and language therapist, in collaboration with other members of the early intervention team, especially the parents, can help develop and obtain the appropriate devices for a particular child. As the child develops and his or her needs for communication change, augmentative and alternative communication strategies and devices will also change. Therefore, ensuring that children have access to appropriate alternative and augmentative communication supports should be a dynamic concept.

Sidebar 10.3 presents a checklist of adaptations that have been discussed so far that teachers can use to assess the physical and social environoments and the adaptations provided for children with severe and multiple disabilities in the classroom.

Sidebar 10.3   CHECKLIST OF MODIFICATIONS TO ENHANCE THE LEARNING ENVIRONMENT OF TYPICAL PRESCHOOL SETTINGS FOR YOUNG CHILDREN WITH SEVERE AND MULTIPLE DISABILITIES

Physical Environment

☐ Play items are easily accessible—in view and within reach.

☐ The area is safe and accessible, making it easy to get around.

☐ The lighting is sufficient and adjustable to accommodate individual needs. Glare is reduced.

☐ Excessive sound is absorbed through the use of carpets, rugs, curtains, acoustic tile, and sound-absorbent room dividers.

☐ Toys are brightly colored and interesting; have sound, vibration, and movement; and are easy to handle.

☐ Toys encourage interactive play.

☐ Areas are organized for different lessons with clear demarcations and landmarks.

☐ Furniture can be adapted to meet the individual needs of children (such as the proper height of a table with feet on the floor).

☐ Cubbies are accessible to each child and labeled (color coded, brailled, textured, or written in large print) so that each child can find his or her name.

Social Environment

☐ Toys such as blocks and toy animals are used that encourage interactive play.

☐ The children are encouraged to sit together and play together.

☐ The children are *not* grouped by ability.

☐ The adults facilitate and support interactions, but do not interrupt or interfere.

☐ Social interaction skills are specifically taught.

☐ The children with no disabilities are taught how to communicate with the child who has a disability and how to interpret that child's communication modes.

☐ The staff are positive, supportive, and follow the lead of the child, when possible.

(continued on next page)

Sidebar 10.3   CHECKLIST OF MODIFICATIONS TO ENHANCE THE LEARNING ENVIRONMENT OF TYPICAL PRESCHOOL SETTINGS FOR YOUNG CHILDREN WITH SEVERE AND MULTIPLE DISABILITIES *(continued)*

Personal Adaptations

☐ Individual children have the optical and/or auditory aids (such as eyeglasses and hearing aids) that they need, and the staff know how to help the child make the best use of these aids.

☐ Individual children have the positioning equipment they need to participate in different activities, and the staff know how and when to use this equipment.

☐ Materials are adapted for individual use (for example, switches or dowels are added, as are tactile materials for art projects).

☐ Augmentative communication devices are available at all times for the children who need them.

☐ The staff know communicative methods (such as sign, object symbols, gestures) that are appropriate for each child.

☐ The staff know how to recognize, interpret, and respond to each child's communicative attempts and how to encourage communicative interactions.

Instructional Adaptations

Children Whose Severe and Multiple Disabilities Include a Visual Impairment

With limited or no visual information to rely on, young children with visual impairments need to learn some adaptive instructional techniques. In general, a teacher needs to be verbally specific and to use language that has meaning for the child (both at the child's level of understanding and that relates to the child's experiential background). Vague directions like pointing and saying, "Go over there" or "Start at Center 1 by the red sign" will not suffice. Rather, such directions as "Go to the carpet area where we listen to stories" provide the child with much more concrete and usable information.

The teacher also needs to make sure that the child has information that can be seen or felt that adds to the verbal information being given. Often teachers use visual demonstration and (ask the children to "look at" them or "watch" what they are doing and to do the same thing). For a child who is visually impaired, the teacher will need to accommodate for the inability to obtain information visually by providing tactile demonstrations (modeling under the child's hands), so the child can follow directions for a given project tactilely and actively make use of his or her hands, which is vital for present and future learning. For a child with some visual function, the teacher needs to demonstrate the upcoming task close to the child. Finally, the teacher has to allow sufficient time for the child to acquire, process, and act on the available information, whether visual, verbal, or tactile, because he or she will have to piece together bits of information and formulate them into a meaningful whole—a difficult and time-consuming process. The teacher should be aware of how much quicker and easier it is to take the whole and disassemble it into its various pieces than to take individual pieces and try to assemble them into a whole. The difficulty of this task becomes even more apparent when the final product cannot be visualized. When a child has severe and multiple disabilities, the need for additional time to process information and act on it is exacerbated.

Reinforcing a child's efforts to learn is one obvious element of teaching at any age. The child with a severe visual impairment may be hesitant to try new things for fear of encountering an unfamiliar and uncomfortable environment and may seem afraid to touch things or to move toward them because he or she has not had the opportunity to learn from natural exploration and watching others do things. Therefore, the child needs to explore using his remaining modes of obtaining information (hearing, touch, and kinesthesia).

The current emphasis in early childhood is to provide programs of intervention that are child centered, play based, and active (Tompkins, 1991). In such a program, the teacher needs to make the learning environment as safe and stimulating as possible, while praising all the child's efforts to engage in active learning. Alerting the child verbally to what he or she is about to come in contact with helps the child anticipate encountering a certain texture, temperature, or size. Whereas vision prepares the child at a distance for upcoming contact and provides myriad cues that help him or her anticipate what is to be touched, the lack of vision greatly reduces this anticipation. Since the inability to give oneself some advance warning before things enter one's personal space can contribute to a child's reluctance to engage in exploration, the use of verbal cues that give some information and make an item sound interesting can encourage the child to explore. For example, when students are looking at a seashell and passing it around, the teacher can prepare the child with limited or no vision by saying, "Doesn't the shell feel cool?" "Do you feel where the shell has some smooth spots and some rougher ones?" "Can you put your finger in the hole?" These verbal cues take the fear out of touching something new, while giving the child some cues as to what to expect and do with the shell when he or she gets a chance to hold it. The case study of Angelina at the end of this chapter provides several examples of how instruction can be adapted for a young child with severe disabilities that include a visual impairment.

Children Whose Severe and Multiple Disabilities Include a Hearing Loss

Instructional strategies for children with hearing impairments rely on the sense of vision. However, the teacher also needs be fluent in and to interact with the child using the child's natural language, such as American Sign Language (ASL) for a child who is deaf. In such a situation, a teacher who does not know ASL could team teach with a teacher who is fluent in ASL, so all students could benefit. The teacher who does not know ASL could still interact with the child who is hearing impaired by being more visually expressive—ensuring he or she has the child's visual attention by getting close to the child and using facial expressions, natural gestures, pointing, and touch cues, when appropriate, as well as using objects, pictures, and any acquired signs. Visually modeling what is expected several times before having the child perform the activity helps with understanding. If the child also has a visual impairment, it is essential to model the activity within the child's visual range.

For a child who has some hearing, every effort should be made to use sound as a source of information. The child can learn to respond to the tone of words that are spoken even if he or she cannot clearly perceive the actual words and can be encouraged to use his or her voice in different ways to gain others' attention. The child's attention can be directed to environmental sounds that add information, such as music being played, the loud squeak of playground equipment, and the sound of a dropped object. The child also needs to learn what creates a sound (such as a fire alarm) and how to use that information in a purposeful way, since each distinct sound can require a unique response. The teacher should use words that refer to hearing and listening (for example, "Listen, Heather is making sounds like a lion"). This type of verbal prompt, paired with a gestural cue (such as pointing to the ear), can help cue the child to listen (Flexer, 1994). In general, children with severe and multiple disabilities need to be taught how to understand what they are hearing and what they are expected to do as a result. Consistency in teaching and engaging in structured routines can help them make these associations.

Children Whose Severe and Multiple Disabilities Include a Physical Impairment

Instructional strategies for children who have difficulty moving their bodies and handling objects require more time than usual to allow a child to demonstrate the desired behavior. If a child also has sensory impairments, the strategies suggested earlier should also be considered. When the child is unable to learn by doing (performing all steps of an activity), then he or she must obtain information from other sources (visual, auditory, and tactile). To check a child's comprehension, the teacher has to find an alternative way for the child to respond. For example, when a child cannot point to or say the correct color, the teacher can offer choices of color and ask the child to look at the correct color. Without such ongoing opportunities to demonstrate learning throughout each day, the child may become passive and uninvolved.

Making sure the child is in the most comfortable and appropriate physical position for a given activity is a prerequisite before any instruction can begin. The physical therapist can monitor the child's position and suggest changes that will most benefit the child functionally and socially. For instance, it may be appropriate for the child to use a prone stander when the other children in the class are standing.

As is true for all children, it is critical to make activities fun and interesting for children with severe and multiple disabilities. At the preschool level, learning should occur naturally during typical play activities rather than through overly structured and teacher-directed drills (Carta, 1995). The importance of play to a child's development, especially when a child has intellectual disabilities, has been well documented (Greenspan, 1992; Linder, 1993; Rogers, 1988). Play is young children's work and provides many opportunities for all children to learn valuable life-long skills. Therefore, teachers and other service providers should carefully examine play activities to ensure that they facilitate communication skills; interactions with peers; and social skills, such as sharing toys and helping.

Adaptations for Participation

Children Whose Severe and Multiple Disabilities Include a Visual Impairment

How children with visual impairments participate in activities, as well as their level of participation, depends on a number of factors, including the adaptations that were previously discussed and whether certain rules and expectations for each activity can be modified. For example, during a game of Duck, Duck, Goose, a child with no vision and no speech can be helped by a classmate to walk around the circle of children and be expected to tap the head of each child ("duck") once and the head of the chosen child ("goose") two or three times instead of just saying the usual words. In addition, the child can be allowed to keep in constant contact with the chairs during musical chairs, while the music is playing; be asked simple yes–no questions following a story, rather than to come up with a specific answer to a question; and "sign" his or her name to artwork by peeling off a self-adhesive braille name label. Since children with visual impairments cannot be expected to know colors, but rather the object a color pertains to, instead of asking the child to identify the color of an apple, the teacher can ask him or her to find the apple from other common objects and then tell the child the color. The emphasis in all participatory accommodations is to minimize the reliance on visual information and encourage active involvement via other sensory modes.

Children Whose Severe and Multiple Disabilities Include a Hearing Loss

How the child with limited or no hearing participates in activities depends on the teacher finding creative and alternative ways to accommodate the hearing impairment. Although the child may not be expected to respond to verbal information, he or she can respond to visual information. For example, instead of following the actions required by a song, the child can imitate his or her classmates or teacher. For self-expression, the child will be expected to point to pictures; shake or nod the head to no-and-yes questions; produce some signs, when appropriate, to make requests or comments; use natural gestures; and show the teacher or classmates what others would normally express in words. The case study of Robbie at the end of this chapter provides several examples of adaptations used throughout the day to allow for his greater participation and learning.

Children Whose Severe and Multiple Disabilities Include a Physical Impairment

Children with severe physical disabilities should be expected to participate to the maximum extent possible using many of the adapted materials and assistive technological adaptations previously mentioned. When a child cannot physically perform the steps of an activity (such as coloring), then the child should be expected to communicate to the teacher or teaching assistant what color he or she would like, where that color should go, and what size coloring instrument should be used. The child should be expected to make choices and decisions and thus take control of a situation, just as the other students are doing. The main difference is that the actual physical steps are completed by someone else. A child should also be given every opportunity to engage in the physical properties of the activity, for example, by slightly squeezing clay or Play-Doh even though he or she cannot actually form an object out of clay. Allowing children to play the most active role possible despite their severe limitations facilitates learning and may increase their strength and endurance. The vignettes of both Angelina and Robbie at the end of this chapter indicate how accommodations can be made to allow for active participation despite the presence of a severe physical disability.

Outcome Adaptations

Children Whose Severe and Multiple Disabilities Include a Visual Impairment

When a child has a visual impairment, it may be particularly important not to expect his or her performance or outcome to be the same as that of the sighted classmates. Children need to perform in a manner that is most meaningful and efficient with or without visual abilities. Accomplishing certain tasks is likely to take longer than it would for children who have normal vision, as in Carla's situation.

> Carla, who has multiple disabilities, including a severe visual impairment, can find her own cubby, but because she does not walk, it takes her longer than her classmates to reach her cubby (by crawling) and to search tactilely for her name on the textured label. In this case, the outcome is the same, but the manner of reaching the outcome is slightly different.

The child may not have the same understanding of visual concepts, such as colors, sunsets, drawings, shadows, enormous objects (like airplanes and elephants) and tiny items (such as patterns on spider webs and mosquitoes). Children who are visually impaired develop nonvisual concepts of such things, which are just as important and far more meaningful. Although a child may learn that a banana is yellow, what is more important is that the child recognizes the feel and taste of a banana, learns how to request and peel one, and decides if he or she likes to eat it. The child may associate a spider with a tickling feeling on the arm and stickiness (the web), rather than the actual insect with eight legs.

Although much of what is done in preschool results in visual outcomes (such as art projects), allowance must be made for a child with a visual impairment because he or she cannot be expected to make the same final product. Instead, the emphasis should be placed on the child's involvement and creative expression in whatever form, as occurred with Maria.

> Maria's preschool classmates are coloring pictures of pumpkins to decorate the classroom for Halloween. However, Maria, who has both a severe cognitive impairment and limited functional vision, dislikes coloring. Rather, she likes puffed stickers, especially those with scents, and uses a variety of them to decorate her picture of the pumpkin. Since the other children also like these stickers, they all get to ask Maria for one to put on their pictures. In

this way, all the children contribute to the activity of decorating the room, and Maria is given numerous opportunities to interact with her classmates.

Children Whose Severe and Multiple Disabilities Include a Hearing Loss

Perhaps the most obvious difference in the expected outcomes for children who are hearing impaired, compared to children who can hear, is the use of spoken language. Children who are hearing impaired and can speak may not articulate words clearly, demonstrate expected tonal qualities, or make themselves clearly understood, but all their efforts to produce speech should be rewarded and accepted as desired outcomes. Children with no speech can demonstrate their knowledge by using signs or gestures, recognizing pictures, physically demonstrating the skill or activity, and drawing or painting pictures. Their outcomes will be primarily visual (or tactile if they have no functional vision).

Children Whose Severe and Multiple Disabilities Include a Physical Impairment

A child with a physical disability may not be able to demonstrate acquired skills in exactly the same way as children with no physical disability. Expected outcomes for this child could involve increased strength and control to be able to participate in activities and the demonstration of acquired knowledge via augmentative communication systems and assistive technology. For instance, the child may not be able to interact verbally with others, but should be able to communicate requests and comments by looking at, reaching toward, or grasping a chosen picture or object. He or she may master the ability to make decisions and communicate the decisions to others, but not in the same form (such as speech) that others may. Outcomes reflect what the child wants or desires, not necessarily what the child has created independently. The physical adaptations mentioned previously may give the child greater independence.

UNDERSTANDING UNCONVENTIONAL BEHAVIOR

When children have multiple impairments, especially when the impairments involve sensory losses, they often develop unique behaviors that meet certain needs. All children (and adults) engage in a number of unique behaviors for a variety of different reasons, but typically to alleviate boredom or to relax. If the behaviors that children with severe and multiple disabilities engage in do not approximate the behaviors of children without disabilities, it may be because they lack appropriate models to observe or hear or have a greatly reduced ability to engage in the physical aspects of the behaviors. However, they still have the need to stimulate or calm themselves and in fact, the need may be even greater for them. Therefore, they engage in whatever behaviors address these needs.

A teacher may initially target the behaviors that seem to be aberrant in an effort to reduce or eliminate them. Unfortunately, attending to them may actually increase some behaviors (particularly if they are intended to draw an adult's attention), take valuable time away from teaching the child other skills, and create a punitive tone to interactions between the child and teacher. Therefore, the critical point for teachers (and parents) to remember is that these behaviors meet normal needs and thus should never be punished. The following paragraphs present descriptions and interpretations of these possible behaviors and ways to address them.

Self-stimulatory Behavior

Young children with severe and multiple disabilities may exhibit some unique behaviors to alleviate boredom and keep themselves amused. Because of limitations to stimulation through vision, hearing, or moving and handling items, these behaviors may look different from those of their classmates who do not have disabilities. For example, without visual stimulation to perceive, children who are blind may resort to rocking back and forth, flicking their fingers against different parts of their bodies, turning around in circles, pressing their hands against their eyelids, and making interesting noises. Children who cannot hear may make interesting noises that create internal vibrations, and children with severe physical disabilities may exhibit unique sounds and movements.

Although unique self-stimulatory behaviors should *not* be punished, if they draw negative attention to a child or prevent the child from interacting with people or materials, the teacher may want to redirect the child to engage in a behavior that serves the same purpose and provides similar stimulation (visual, auditory, vibratory, tactile, or kinesthetic) but in a way that is more accepted and conventional (Durand, 1993). For example, a child who pats her face with her hands may be directed to squeeze a small Koosh ball or small piece of Play-Doh. It is the teacher's responsibility (with specific input from the parents) to recognize the need that the child has to engage in certain behaviors, decide if the behavior could draw negative attention from others, and then provide the child with another and more acceptable means of meeting the same basic needs.

Recognizing that all children normally engage in certain self-stimulatory behaviors, such as twirling their hair, doodling, fiddling with items, and playing with different parts of their bodies (like picking scabs and rubbing their heads), will help the teacher see past the initial determination of the unconventionality of a behavior. Even when they are actively engaged in an appropriate activity (which is the first thing to ensure), children with severe and multiple disabilities need ways to engage in conventional or accepted self-stimulatory behaviors. Acceptable forms of self-stimulation for a preschool child may include holding a small vibrating toy, rocking in a rocking chair, scribbling with a bright-colored pen, rubbing a smooth item (such as a stone), or squeezing a rubbery object. The acceptability of a behavior depends on the parents' approval and on the situation (for example, quiet activities require quiet self-stimulatory behavior). The example of Michael illustrates how self-stimulatory behavior can be modified without punishing it.

> Michael often placed the back of his hand against his forehead and repeatedly tapped himself. Since he has severely limited hearing and vision, he appeared to enjoy feeling this form of tactile and proprioceptive stimulation. This behavior usually occurred when Michael was waiting for an activity or was bored with the activity in which he was engaged. Since it made Michael look different from the other children, he needed another behavior to engage in when he is bored. Therefore, the teacher placed a wide covered elastic band on his wrist and taught Michael to replace tapping his forehead with pulling on or twisting the elastic band. Since pulling

on or twisting the elastic band is also tactile, Michael receives similar stimulation from it as he did from tapping his forehead. However, this behavior more closely resembles the same kind of nervous activity demonstrated by his classmates and thus is much more acceptable.

Of course, if Michael engages in this new behavior to the exclusion of other activities, then his program must be modified to make it more meaningful and stimulating.

Aggressive or Noncompliant Behavior

All children may engage in undesired behavior that conveys their unwillingness to participate in a given activity, even when they thoroughly understand what is expected of them and can easily express their preferences. Children who do not fully understand an activity or what is expected and who cannot communicate their preference for another activity or the reason for their irritation display behaviors that signal their frustration, such as crying, screaming, hitting, refusing to move, spitting, and scratching. As in dealing with the self-stimulatory behavior, the teacher needs to recognize that a child who behaves this way is attempting to convey his or her feelings about an activity or some aspect of it or something else entirely, and it is imperative to treat the behavior as an attempt to communicate, rather than punish the child in an effort to eliminate the behavior (Carr et al., 1994; Lovett, 1996; Reichle & Wacker, 1993). Punishing the child's efforts will have the impact of reducing the child's attempts to communicate. Every effort should be made to understand what the child is trying to say and to teach the child an alternative and more acceptable way to convey the same meaning (Carr & Durand, 1985; Durand, 1993; Reichle & Wacker, 1993).

The teacher should not ignore the unconventional and undesired behavior, but recognizes the need to replace this way of communicating with a more conventional and acceptable means, as demonstrated in the following example:

> Juan often scratches to indicate when he is unhappy with an activity and wants it to end. This behavior has been successful in the past because when he scratches, the person assisting him with

the activity stops, and he does not have to continue. Since Juan is labeled deaf and blind and has no formal communication system, he may have learned that scratching is an appropriate way to communicate the desire to stop an activity and be left alone. To help Juan learn an alternative, more appropriate and equally effective way to convey the same message, Juan's teacher closely watches Juan for signs of irritation (facial expressions) that precede the scratching. When she thinks he is about to scratch or when he starts to scratch, she quickly shows him how to push the items in the activity away. She then offers him choices of other activities to do using representative items. By consistently pairing this preferred behavior with his desire to finish an activity, Juan no longer needs to scratch. Of course the teacher has to be highly responsive to Juan's wishes so he understands that this is another way to get what he needs.

In sum, teachers (and parents) need to view the sometimes unconventional behavior exhibited by children with severe and multiple disabilities not as something bizarre and aberrant that needs to be eliminated, but as a unique means of communication. When service providers and nondisabled classmates understand such behaviors and gain skill at interpreting them, the strengths and determination of the child can be recognized and encouraged.

CONCLUSION

Young children with multiple disabilities, including sensory impairments, require a high-quality preschool program just as nondisabled children do. They need a safe, nurturing, enriched, and supportive environment in which to learn. They do not need a separate facility that keeps them apart from other young children. Rather, they need a program that will meet their unique needs while allowing them to grow and develop with other children. In this environment they will learn from their peers while their peers learn from them.

ANGELINA

Angelina, is a 3-year-old Hispanic girl who lives with her mother, grandmother, and two older brothers, is an active member of her close family and well known in her neighborhood. She likes to make a variety of interesting sounds, listen to music, play with her brothers, and especially eat pudding. When she wears a hearing aid, Angelina can hear most sounds, but normal speech is not clear. She communicates by smiling, making various sounds, reaching for things, moving toward things, crying, and resisting. She can stand, and is learning to walk when holding onto a hand or using a walker. She has no functional vision and thus could be labeled deaf-blind.

Angelina attends a preschool located near her mother's place of employment. Angelina is one of five children with a disability in the class; the majority of children who attend this preschool do not have disabilities. Teaching assistants (TA) and parent volunteers assist the teachers. The following chart shows the schedule of the preschool and the adaptations or accommodations that help Angelina participate in each activity:

Preschool Schedule	Adaptations/Accommodations
Arrival. Put personal items in cubby. Greet teacher.	Angelina's mother helps her into the room and to the cubby, which is tactilely marked for her to recognize. The teacher and TAs greet Angelina by holding her hands and saying "hi" and giving positive feedback if Angelina smiles or makes a sound.
Good Morning Circle. Calendar. Theme for the week. Movement to songs.	Angelina is assisted to the circle area where she is encouraged to feel the rug as a landmark for this activity. She sits close to the other children with extra support (provided from behind) when needed. When the children are shown their names and asked to respond by taking the name cards and putting them on the attendance board, Angelina is shown two cards (one in print and one in braille). She is to feel both, grab the braille card, and help to get it on the board. (She is not learning to read braille, but to recognize differences tactilely. Through the songs, she is encouraged to wear her hearing aid and to try the movements of the songs while given tactile cues. The directions from the songs are repeated more clearly and close to her by the teacher or TA.
Activity centers: dress up, blocks, water table, listening to taped stories, clay.	Choices are given to Angelina every 10 minutes by handing her the objects (two at a time) that represent each center, telling her what her choices are, and encouraging her to grab

the one she wants. Angelina is given sighted guide assistance to the centers, where she sits close to the other children (so she can feel them). She is learning certain routes to where daily activities occur. The teacher or TA provide guidance only when necessary to encourage exploration. They offer her many choices in each center, and facilitate her interactions with the other children.

Outside play

Choices are given to Angelina by showing her objects or parts of objects representing different outside play activities (such as a sand toy for sandbox play, a chain for swinging, and a wood handle for the seesaw). Angelina is paired with other children who want to play in the same activity. She works on her walking while going outside.

Snack

The TA makes sure that Angelina is sitting close to the other children, offers support from behind (for example, reminds her to keep her hands on the food or spoon while bringing it to her mouth). Her snack is on a small tray so she can easily find it.

Group storytime on theme for the week (color, animal, family)

Angelina sits close to the teacher and, when possible, gets to hold and explore an item related to the story's theme. Key words are emphasized for language comprehension and speech production.

Free play

The teacher gives Angelina two choices at a time for each activity using objects or parts of objects that represent the activities. She facilitates Angelina's interactions with the other children by encouraging her to reach toward them and by having them share items with her.

Art projects on theme for the week

The teacher makes sure that Angelina is sitting close to a classmate and has access to a variety of different materials she can manipulate (on a tray). The TA shows Angelina a sample of a finished tactile project (a collage) and then offers her three choices of materials for her to start with. She asks Angelina where she wants each piece glued to the cardboard using speech, gestural cues, and pauses. Then she helps Angelina to use the glue appropriately.

Closing circle. Getting personal items to go home

Angelina walks to the circle with support after being shown the carpet square that she sits on. She is encouraged to wear her hearing aids and move to the music of the good-bye song. She is being taught to wave good-bye to her teacher with physical prompts. She is helped to walk to where her backpack is kept and to find it tactilely.

ROBBIE

Robbie is a 3 1/2-year-old Caucasian boy who lives with his mother and father and a large dog. He has a terrific smile, enjoys being with people, has strong preferences, and tries hard to please. Robbie is unable to hear, even with a hearing aid. He has cortical visual impairment, but does respond to some visual information, such as bright colors, lights, and movement. Robbie also has a severe medical condition and seizures, eats through a tube, and is nonambulatory. He can move his body, but has limited fine motor skills. Robbie makes his needs known by making happy-contented sounds, crying, using a variety of facial expressions and body movements, and touching objects.

Robbie attends a preschool in his neighborhood. Although a few children with disabilities also attend this school, Robbie has the most significant impairments. The teacher has additional supports from a teaching assistant (TA), practicum students from a university early childhood teacher preparation program, and parent volunteers. The following is the schedule of the preschool and description of the adaptations and accommodations that allow Robbie to participate in each activity. In addition, Robbie uses objects and parts of objects to anticipate what the activities will be throughout the day and when they will occur. These items are placed in several sequentially arranged boxes that are convenient to the adults in the room. After every activity, Robbie is assisted to return the representative item to its container (box) and then tactilely explores the next box in the sequence to find the item that signals the next activity.

Preschool Schedule
Arrival. Greet teachers and classmates. Put things away.

Adaptations/Accommodations
His father or mother helps Robbie into the room and pushes him in the wheelchair to the cubby area. His cubby is the first one and is outlined in bright orange reflective tape. His parent waits until Robbie makes a movement with his arms toward his cubby. Then he or she helps him put his things in. The teacher greets Robbie by touching his hand and guiding it to a ring she always wears. She waits for him to smile, wave his hands a bit, or make a sound as his greeting.

Good Morning Circle, Calendar, Songs.	The teacher makes sure that Robbie is positioned close to her on the floor. When the teacher calls the children's names for attendance, the TA shows Robbie his tactile name card that he is learning to grasp and recognize as belonging to him. Robbie uses a vibrating touch switch to activate the music on the cassette recorder when he is cued tactilely by his teacher. The TA helps Robbie move to the music and works physical therapy (stretching, range of motion) into this activity.
Cooking project	Robbie is seated close to his classmates, so they can easily touch him and he can touch them. He is learning to grasp different utensils, hang on to them while stirring or scooping, and pass them to a classmate. He can also turn on a blender using the vibrating touch switch. He is encouraged to smell and taste different ingredients with the other children. Even though Robbie cannot eat most of the goodies made, he can taste the different food items and in so doing learn to distinguish differences, develop preferences, and gradually take in more food orally over time.
Outdoor play	Robbie chooses activities he enjoys doing outside. Two choices are offered (one preferred and one not preferred). Both are presented to him tactilely using parts of the objects that represent each choice (for example, a piece of plastic rope for the swing and a toy car and ramp for car play). Robbie chooses by reaching for one or hitting at it. He has an adapted swing seat that provides sufficient support. Robbie also likes to ride on the merry-go-round, to play in sand and water, and to go for very fast "stop–start walks" in his wheelchair.
Story time	Robbie is positioned in a chair on the floor close to the teacher and other children. Since he cannot hear the story and has difficulty seeing the pictures, he is allowed to fiddle with a small inflated balloon attached to the side of his chair. He also receives some physical and occupational therapy from specialists or the TA while sitting with the children. If the story is about something that Robbie can activate with his vibrating tactile switch (such as battery-operated toy animals, cars, train), he will do so when prompted.

Activity centers (music, measuring, magnets, finger painting)	Robbie is offered choices of activity centers by giving him objects or parts of objects that represent the centers that he expores tactilely. He is given two choices (preferred and non-preferred). Once he chooses an activity, he is helped to get to that center. Adaptations, such as built-up handles on the toys used for measuring in the rice table, allow him to participate. Robbie is taught to share with the other children by having him respond to their tactile cues on his shoulder, turning toward the classmate who tapped him, and relinquishing his toy if the classmate taps on it. He is also encouraged to explore with his hands to find out what the other children are doing.
Snack	Robbie joins his classmates at the snack table and sits in his wheelchair close to them. Although he cannot eat a snack orally, he takes in nutrition through his tube. However, he is also encouraged to taste things like yogurt, applesauce, and a fruit smoothie to indicate his preferences, enjoy the taste of food, and gradually to begin eating orally. Robbie's facial expressions and movements toward or away from the food offered are accepted as his means of expressing his preferences and dislikes.
Goodbye circle and departure	Robbie sits on the floor with support from either the TA or the teacher. He is encouraged to move to the music as previously described. He also starts the music using his vibrating tactile switch. When the children leave for the day, each touches Robbie on his arms, hands, or shoulders in farewell. One classmate brings him his backpack that goes on his wheelchair.

REFERENCES

AFB directory of services for blind and visually impaired persons in the United States and Canada (25th ed.). (1997). New York: AFB Press.

Bailey, B., & Downing, J. (1994). Using visual accents to enhance attending to communication symbols for students with severe multiple disabilities. *RE:vew, 26,* 101–118.

Baumgart, D., Johnson, J., & Helmstetter, E. (1990). *Augmentative and alternative communication systems for persons with moderate and severe disabilities.* Baltimore, MD: Paul H. Brookes.

Beukelman, D., & Mirenda, P. (1998). *Augmentative and alternative communication: Management of severe communication disorders in children and adults* (2nd ed.). Baltimore, MD: Paul H. Brookes.

Buysse, V. (1993). Friendships of preschoolers with disabilities in community-based child care settings. *Journal of Early Intervention, 17,* 380–395.

Campbell, P. (1993). Physical management and handling procedures. In M. E. Snell (Ed.), *Instruction of students with severe disabilities* (4th ed. pp. 248–263). New York: Macmillan.

Carr, E. G., & Durand, V. M. (1985). Reducing behavior problems through functional communication training. *Journal of Applied Behavior Analysis, 18,* 111–126.

Carr, E. G., Levin, L., McConnachie, G., Carlson, J. E., Kemp, D. C., & Smith, C. E. (1994). *Communication-based intervention for problem behavior: A user's guide for producing positive change.* Baltimore, MD: Paul H. Brookes.

Carta, J. J. (1995). Developmentally appropriate practice: A critical analysis as applied to young children with disabilities. *Focus on Exceptional Children, 27*(8), 1–14.

Cavallaro, C. C., Ballard-Rosa, M., & Lynch, E. W. (1998). A preliminary study of inclusive special education services for infants, toddlers, and preschool-age children in California. *Topics in Early Childhood Special Education, 18,* 169–182.

Cavallaro, C. C., & Haney, M. (1999). *Preschool inclusion.* Baltimore, MD: Paul H. Brookes.

Demchak, M., & Drinkwater, S. (1992). Preschoolers with severe disabilities: The case against segregation. *Topics in Early Childhood Special Education, 11,* 70–83.

Diamond, K. E. (1994). Evaluating preschool children's sensitivity to developmental differences in their peers. *Topics in Early Childhood Special Education, 14,* 49–62.

Diamond, K. E., Hestenes, L. L., Carpenter, E. S., & Innes, F. K. (1997). Relationships between enrollment in an inclusive class and preschool children's ideas about people with disabilities. *Topics in Early Childhood Special Education, 17,* 520–536.

Downing, J. E. (1996). *Including students with severe and multiple disabilities in typical classrooms: Practical strategies for teachers.* Baltimore, MD: Paul H. Brookes.

Downing, J. E. (1999). *Teaching communication skills to students with severe disabilites.* Baltimore, MD: Paul H. Brookes.

Downing, J., & Bailey, B. (1990). Developing vision use within functional daily activities for studies with visual and multiple disabilities. *RE:view, 21,* 209–220.

Downing, J., & Eichinger, J. (1990). Instructional strategies for learners with dual sensory impairments in integrated settings. *Journal of the Association for Persons with Severe Handicaps, 15,* 98–105.

Durand, V. M. (1993). Functional communication training for challenging behaviors. *Clinics in Communication Disorders, 3*(2), 59–70.

Fad, K. S., Ross, M., & Boston, J. (1995). We're better together: Using cooperative learning to teach social skills to young children. *Teaching Exceptional Children, 27*(4), 28–34.

Flexer, C. (1994). *Facilitating hearing and listening in young children.* San Diego, CA: Singular Publishing Group.

Flippo, K. F., Inge, K. J., & Barcus, J. M. (1995). *Assistive technology: A resource for school, work, and community.* Baltimore, MD: Paul H. Brookes.

Gee, K. (1995). Facilitating active and informed learning and participation in inclusive school settings. In N. G. Haring & L. T. Romer (Eds.), *Welcoming students who are deaf-blind into typical classrooms: Facilitating school participation, learning, and friendships* (pp. 369–404). Baltimore, MD: Paul H. Brookes.

Giangreco, M. F., Edelman, S. W., Luiselli, T. E., & MacFarland, S. Z. C. (1997). Helping or hovering? Effects of instructional assistant proximity on students with disabilities. *Exceptional Children, 64,* 7–17.

Greenspan, S. I. (1992). *Infancy and early childhood: The practice of clinical assessment and intervention with emotional and developmental challenges.* Madison, WI: International Universities Press.

Guralnick, M. J., & Groom, J. M. (1987). The peer relations of mildly delayed and nonhandicapped preschool children in mainstreamed playgroups. *Child Development, 58,* 1556–1577.

Guralnick, M. J., & Groom, J. M. (1988). Peer interactions in mainstreamed and specialized classrooms: A comparative analysis. *Exceptional Children, 54,* 415–425.

Heller, K. W., Alberto, P. A., & Bowdin, J. (1995). Interactions of communication partners and students who are deaf-blind: A Model. *Journal of Visual Impairment & Blindness, 89,* 391–401.

Hill, A., & Rabe, T. (1992). Preschool mainstreaming: Ideals and reality. *Issues in Special Education and Rehabilitation, 7*(2), 25–39.

Hoffman, S., & Wundram, B. (1984). Sharing is . . . Views from 3-year-olds and thoughts from teachers. *Childhood Education, 60,* 261–265.

Jan, J. E., & Groenveld, M. (1993). Visual behaviors and adaptations associated with cortical and ocular impairment in children. *Journal of Visual Impairment & Blindness, 87,* 101–105.

Lueke-Stahlman, B. (1994). Procedures for socially integrating preschoolers who are hearing, deaf, and hard-of-hearing. *Topics in Early Childhood Special Education, 14,* 472–487.

Levack, N. (1994). *Low vision: A resource guide with adaptations for students with visual impairments* (2nd ed.). Austin: Texas School for the Blind and Visually Impaired.

Linder, T. W. (1993). *Transdisciplinary play-based assessment: A functional approach to working with young children.* (rev. ed.). Baltimore, MD: Paul H. Brookes.

Lovett, H. (1996). *Learning to listen: Positive approaches and people with difficult behavior.* Baltimore, MD: Paul H. Brookes.

Martin, S. S., Brady, M. P., & Williams, R. E. (1991). Effects of toys on the social behavior of preschool children in integrated and nonintegrated groups: Investigation of a setting event. *Journal of Early Intervention, 15,* 153–161.

Mattheis, M. G. (1996). The Mac Book: Highlighting the person in the I.E.P. *Disability Solutions, 1*(3), 1–9.

McInnes, J. M., & Treffry, J. H. (1982). *Deaf-blind infants and children: A developmental guide.* Toronto: University of Toronto Press.

Mirenda, P., & Mathy-Laikko, P. (1989). Augmentative and alternative communication applications for persons with severe congenital communication disorders: An introduction. *Augmentative and Alternative Communication, 5,* 3–13.

Odom, S. L., McConnell, S. R., & Chandler, L. K. (1993). Acceptability and feasibility of classroom-based social interaction interventions for young children with disabilities. *Exceptional Children, 60,* 226–236.

Odom, S. L. & McLean, M. E. (Eds.) (1996). *Early intervention/early childhood special education: Recommended practices.* Austin, TX: Pro-Ed.

Peck, C. A., Furman, G. C., & Helmstetter, E. (1993). Integrated early childhood programs: Research on the implementation of change in organizational contexts. In C. A. Peck, S. L. Odom, & D. D. Bricker (Eds.), *Integrating young children with disabilities into community programs: Ecological perspectives on research and implementation* (pp. 187–205). Baltimore, MD: Paul H. Brookes.

Peck, C. A., Odom, S. L., & Brickes, D. D. (1993). *Integrating young children with disabilities into community programs: Ecological perspectives on research and implementation.* Baltimore, MD: Paul H. Brookes.

Prickett, J. G., & Welch, T. R. (1995). Adapting environments to support the inclusion of students who are deaf-blind. In N. G. Haring & T. L. Romer (Eds.), *Welcoming students who are deaf-blind into typical classrooms: Facilitating school participation, learning, and friendships* (pp. 171–194). Baltimore, MD: Paul H. Brookes.

Rab, V. Y., & Wood, K. T. (1995). *Child care and the ADA: A handbook for inclusive programs.* Baltimore, MD: Paul H. Brookes.

Reichle, J., & Wacker, D. P. (1993). *Communicative alternatives to challenging behavior: Integrating functional assessment and intervention strategies.* Baltimore, MD: Paul H. Brookes.

Rogers, S. (1988). Review of methods for assessing young children's play: A review. *Journal of the Division for Early Childhood, 12,* 161–168.

Rosenberg, S., Clark, M., Filer, J., Hupp, S., & Finkler, D. (1992). Facilitated active learner participation. *Journal of Early Intervention, 16,* 262–274.

Strain, P. S., & Odom, S. L. (1986). Peer social initiations: Effective intervention for social skills development of exceptional children. *Exceptional Children, 52,* 543–551.

Tanchak, T. L., & Sawyer, C. (1995). Augmentative communication. In K. F. Flippo, K. J. Inge, & J. M. Barcus (Eds.), *Assistive technology: A resource for school, work, and community* (pp. 57–86). Baltimore, MD: Paul H. Brookes.

Tompkins, M. (1991). Active learning: Making it happen in your program. In N. A. Brickman & L. S. Taylor (Eds.), *Supporting young learners: Ideas for preschool and day care providers* (pp. 5–13). Ypsilanti, MI: High/Scope Press.

Van Tatenhove, G. M. (1993). *What is augmentative and alternative communication (AAC)?* Wooster, OH: Prentke-Romich Co.

Wolf, A., & Fine, E. (1996). The sharing tree: Preschoolers learn to share. *Teaching Exceptional Children, 28*(3), 76–77.

Selected Resources

This section presents sources of further information for early interventionists and the families they work with. The first part lists a selected group of organizations that provide information, publications, and assistance for professionals as well as families. The second part is a bibliography, categorized by subject area and type of publication, listing books, journals, videos, and additional materials for professionals. There is also a section for material directed specifically to families. These Resource listings are not intended to be exhaustive; readers can contact the sources listed for additional information in various areas.

SOURCES OF INFORMATION AND ASSISTANCE

Most of the organizations listed in this section provide information and further referrals in their specified area of expertise. Many also produce books, journals, videos, and informational pamphlets. A number are membership organizations for parents and/or professionals, and some provide direct support and advocacy for parents and their children.

American Council of the Blind
1155 15th Street, N.W., Suite 720
Washington, DC 20005
(202) 467-5081 or (800) 424-8666
fax: (202) 467-5085
E-mail: info@acb.org
URL: http://www.acb.org
Promotes the effective participation of blind people in all aspects of society. Provides information and referral, legal assistance, scholarships, advocacy, consultation, and assistance with program development.

Interest groups include the Deaf-Blind Committee and the Council of Citizens with Low Vision International. Publishes the *Braille Forum.*

American Foundation for the Blind
11 Penn Plaza, Suite 300
New York, NY 10001
(212) 502-7600 or (800) 232-5463
TDD: (212) 502-7662
fax: (212) 502-7777
E-mail: afbinfo@afb.net
URL: http://www.afb.org
Provides services to and acts as an information clearinghouse for people who are blind or visually impaired and their families, professionals, organizations, schools, and corporations. Stimulates research and mounts program initiatives to improve services to visually impaired persons, including the National Initiative on Literacy; advocates for services and legislation; maintains the M. C. Migel Library and Information Center and the Helen Keller Archives; provides information and referral services; operates the National Technology Center and the Career and Technology Information Bank; produces videos; and publishes books, pamphlets, the *Directory of Services for Blind and Visually Impaired Persons in the United States and Canada,* and the *Journal of Visual Impairment & Blindness.*

American Printing House for the Blind
1839 Frankfort Avenue, P.O. Box 6085
Louisville, KY 40206
(502) 895-2405 or (800) 223-1839
URL: http://www.aph.org
Publishes books and manufactures educational tools and materials related to individuals of all ages who are blind or visually impaired.

Association for the Education and Rehabilitation of the Blind and Visually Impaired (AER)
4600 Duke Street, Suite 430
Alexandria, VA 22304
(703) 823-9690
E-mail: aernet@laser.net

A professional organization for practitioners serving infants, children, youths, and adults who are blind or visually impaired. Publishes the journal *RE:view*. Has a division that addresses the educational needs of infants and preschoolers and another that focuses on the needs of students with multiple disabilities. Holds a national conference every two years and publishes the newsletter *AER Report*. Has state or regional AER chapters.

Association for Persons with Severe Handicaps (TASH)
29 West Susquehanna Avenue, Suite 210
Baltimore, MD 21204
(410) 828-8274
URL: http://www.tash.org
An advocacy organization for professionals who work with infants, children, and youths who have severe disabilities and their families. Holds an annual national conference and publishes the *Journal of the Association for Persons with Severe Handicaps* and the *TASH Newsletter*. Has a committee on early childhood that meets at the annual conference. There are state or regional TASH chapters.

Council for Exceptional Children (CEC)
1920 Association Drive
Reston, VA 22091-1589
(703) 620-3660 or (888) 232-7733
URL: http://www.cec.sped.org
Division of Early Childhood
URL: http://www.dec-sped.org
A professional organization for practitioners serving infants, children, and youths who have disabilities. Holds an annual national conference and publishes two journals: *Exceptional Children,* which contains research and scholarly articles; and *Teaching Exceptional Children,* which contains articles on strategies and practices. The Division for the Visually Handicapped (DVH) publishes the newsletter *DVH Quarterly* and has a stand in the annual national CEC conference. The Division of Early Childhood (DEC) has a separate annual conference, state DEC chapters, and publishes two journals: *Journal of Early Intervention,* which contains scholarly articles; and *Exceptional Young Children,*

which contains articles on early childhood special education strategies and practices.

DB-LINK (The National Information Clearinghouse on Children Who Are Deaf-Blind)

345 North Monmouth Avenue
Monmouth, OR 97361
(800) 438-9376
URL: http://www.tr.wou.edu/dblink
E-mail: dblink@tr.wou.edu
Serves as a federally funded clearinghouse that provides information and copies of written materials related to infants, children, and youths who have both visual and hearing impairments. Publishes the newsletter *Deaf-Blind Perspectives*.

Federation for Children with Special Needs

1135 Tremont Street, Suite 420
Boston, MA 02120
TTY/TDD: (617) 236-7210
fax: (617) 517-2094
Supports organized parent-to-parent efforts to enable parents to work more effectively with professionals in educating children with disabilities. Serves the Parent Training and Information centers funded under the Individuals with Disabilities Education Act.

National Association for Parents of the Visually Impaired

P.O. Box 317
Watertown, MA 02471
(617) 972-7441 or (800) 562-6265
A national organization for parents of children who are blind or visually impaired. Publishes the newsletter *Awareness*. Has chapters in many regions or states.

National Federation of the Blind, Parents Division

c/o National Federation of the Blind
1800 Johnson Street
Baltimore, MD 21230
(410) 659-9314

fax: (410) 685-5653

URL: http://www.nfb.org

Strives to improve social and economic conditions of people who are blind, evaluates and assists in establishing programs, and provides public education and scholarships. Publishes the *Braille Monitor* and *Future Reflections.*

National Information Center for Children and Youth with Disabilities

P.O. Box 1492

Washington, DC 20013-1492

voice/TTY/TDD: (800) 695-0285

fax: (202) 884-8441

URL: http://www.nichcy.org

Serves as a national information clearinghouse on subjects related to children and youths with disabilities. Provides information and referral to national, state, and local resources. Disseminates numerous free publications.

National Organization for Rare Disorders

100 Route 37, P.O. Box 8923

New Fairfield, CT 06812-8923

(203) 746-6518 or (800) 999-6673

TTY/TDD: (203) 746-6927

fax: (203) 746-6481

E-mail: orphan@rarediseases.org

URL: http://www.rarediseases.org

Serves as an information clearinghouse on thousands of rare disorders. Brings together families with similar disorders for mutual support. Promotes research, accumulates and disseminates information about special drugs and devices, and maintains a database on rare diseases.

NTAC (National Technical Assistance Consortium for Children and Young Adults Who Are Deaf-Blind

Western Oregon University Teaching Research

345 North Monmouth Avenue

Monmouth, OR 97361

(503) 838-8391; TTY/TDD: (503) 838-8821

fax: (503) 838-8150

URL: http://www.ntac@wou.edu

http://www.tr.wou.edu/ntac

Provides technical assistance to families and agencies serving children and young adults who are deaf-blind. NTAC is a federally funded consortium project of Teaching Research and The Helen Keller National Center.

BIBLIOGRAPHY

The publications and materials in this Bibliography are listed first by subject area and then by type of material. Materials specifically addressed to families are at the end of the Bibliography. Addresses of the publishers are listed in the section following the Bibliography.

PUBLICATIONS ON INFANTS AND YOUNG CHILDREN WITH DISABILITIES

Assessment

Meisels, S. J., & Fenichel, E. (1996). *New visions for the developmental assessment of infants and young children.* Washington, DC: Zero to Three: Clinical Center for Infants, Toddlers, and Families.

Rossetti, L. M. (1990). *Infant-toddler assessment. An interdisciplinary approach.* Austin, TX: Pro-Ed.

Communication

Casey-Harvey, D. G. (1995). *Early communication games. Routine-based play for the first two years.* Tucson, AZ: Communication Skill Builders.

Klein, M. D., Chen, D., & Haney, M. (in press). *Promoting learning through active interaction: An early communication curriculum.* Baltimore, MD: Paul H. Brookes.

Manolson, A. (1984). *It takes two to talk. A Hanen early language parent guide book.* Toronto: Hanen Early Language Resource Centre.

Rossetti, L. M. (1996). *Communication intervention. Birth to three.* San Diego, CA: Singular Publishing Group.

Rowland, C. (1996). *Communication matrix. A communication skill assessment for individuals at the earliest stages of communication development.* Portland: Center on Self-Determination, Oregon Health Sciences University.

Cultural and Linguistic Diversity

Chang, H. N. L., Muckelroy, A., & Pulido-Tobiassen, D. (1996). *Looking in, looking out. Redefining child care and early education in a diverse society.* San Francisco: California Tomorrow.

Gonzalez-Mena, J. (1993). *Multicultural issues in child care.* Mountain View, CA: Mayfield.

Lynch, E. W., & Hanson, M. J. (1998). *Developing cross-cultural competence* (2nd ed.). Baltimore, MD: Paul H. Brookes.

Rothenberg, B. A. (1995). *Understanding and working with parents and children from rural Mexico.* Menlo Park, CA: CHC Center for Child and Family Development Press.

Deaf-Blindness

Freeman, P. (1985). *The deaf-blind baby: A programme of care.* London: William Heinemann Medical Books.

Huebner, K. M., Prickett, J. D., Welch, T. R., & Joffee, E. (Eds.). (1975). Hand in hand: Essentials of communication and orientation and mobility for your infants who are deaf-blind. New York: AFB Press.

McGinnes, J. M., & Treffry, J. A. (1982). *Deaf-blind infants and children: A developmental guide.* Toronto: University of Toronto Press.

Regenbogen, L. S., & Coscas, G. J. (1985). *Oculo-auditory syndromes.* Chicago: Year Book Medical Publishers.

SKI-HI Institute. (1993). *A resource manual for understanding and interacting with infants, toddlers, and preschool age children with deaf-blindness.* Logan, UT: Hope.

Watkins, S. (1989). *A model of home intervention for infant, toddler, and preschool aged multihandicapped sensory impaired children. The INSITE model.* Logan, UT: Hope.

Developmental Assessments and Curricula

Anderson, S., Boigon, S., & Davis, K. (1986). *The Oregon project for visually impaired and blind preschool children* (5th ed). Medford, OR: Jackson Education Service District.

Bricker, D. (1993). *Assessment, evaluation, and programming system (AEPS) for infants and children.* Baltimore, MD: Paul H. Brookes.

Bricker, D., Pretti-Frontczak, K., & McComas, N. (1998). *An activity-based approach to early intervention* (2nd. ed.). Baltimore, MD: Paul H. Brookes.

Bricker, D., Squires, J., & Mounts, L. (1999). *Ages and stages questionnaires (ASQ)—A parent-completed child-monitoring system* (2nd ed). Baltimore, MD: Paul H. Brookes.

Browne, B. C., Jarrett, M. H., Hovey-Lewis, C. J., & Freund, M. B. (1995). *Developmental playgroup guide.* Tucson, AZ: Communication Skill Builders.

Cavallaro, C. C., & Hanley, M. (1999). *Preschool inclusion.* Baltimore, MD: Paul H. Brookes.

Cook, R. E., Tessier, A., & Klein, M. D. (1999). *Adapting early childhood curricula for children with special needs* (5th ed.). Upper Saddle River, NJ: Merrill/Prentice Hall.

Dunst, C. (1980). *A clinical and educational manual for use with the Uzgiris and Hunt scales of infant psychological development.* Baltimore, MD: University Park Press.

Dunst, C. J. (1981). *Infant learning. A cognitive-linguistic intervention strategy.* Hingham, MA: Teaching Resources.

Fewell, R., & Langley, M. B. (1984). *DASI-II Developmental activities screening inventory.* Austin, TX: Pro-Ed.

Furuno, S., Inatsuka, T. T., O'Reilly, K. A., Hosaka, C. M., Zeisloft-Falbey, B., & Allman, T. (1985). *Hawaii early learning profile (HELP) activity guide.* Palo Alto, CA: VORT Corporation.

Furuno, S., O'Reilly, K. A., Inatsuka, T. T., Hosaka, C. M., & Falbey, B. Z. (1993). *Helping babies learn. Developmental profiles and activities for infants and toddlers.* Tucson, AZ: Communication Skill Builders.

Ireton, H., & Thwing, E. (1980). *Minnesota infant development inventory.* Minneapolis, MN: Behavior Science Systems.

Johnson-Martin, N. M., Jens, K. G., Attermier, S. M., & Hacker, B. J. (1991). *The Carolina curriculum for infants and toddlers with special needs* (2nd ed.). Baltimore, MD: Paul H. Brookes.

Klein, M. D. (1988). *Pre-sign language motor skills.* Tucson, AZ: Communication Skill Builders.

Morgan, E., & Watkins, S. (1989). *Assessment of developmental skills for young multihandicapped sensory impaired children.* Logan, UT: Hope.

Newborg, J., Stock, J. R., Wnek, L., Guidubaldi, J., & Svinicki, J. (1984). *Batelle developmental inventory.* Allen, TX: DLM Teaching Resources.

Parks, S. (1986). *Make every step count: Birth to 1 year. Developmental parenting guide.* Palo Alto, CA: VORT Corporation.

Hearing Loss

Flexer, C. (1994). *Facilitating hearing and listening in young children.* San Diego, CA: Singular Publishing Group.

Gorlin, R. J., Toriello, H. V., & Cohen, M. M. (1995). *Hereditary hearing loss and its syndromes.* New York: Oxford University Press.

Hayes, D., & Northern, J. L. (1996). *Infants and hearing.* San Diego, CA: Singular Publishing Group.

Infant Hearing Resource Staff. (1985). *Parent-infant communication. A program of clinical and home training for parents and hearing-impaired infants* (3rd ed.). Portland, OR: Infant Hearing Resource, Good Samaritan Hospital and Medical Center.

Northern, J. L. & Downs, M. P. (1991). *Hearing in children* (4th ed.). Baltimore, MD: Williams & Wilkins.

Roberts, J. E., Wallace, I. F., & Henderson, F. W. (1997). *Otitis media in young children. Medical, developmental, and educational considerations.* Baltimore, MD: Paul H. Brookes.

Roush, J., & Matkin, N. D. (1994). *Infants and toddlers with hearing loss: Family-centered assessment and intervention.* Timonium, MD: York Press.

Watkins, S., & Clark, T. C. (1992). *The SKI*HI model: A resource manual for family-centered, home-based programming for infants, toddlers, and preschool-aged children with hearing impairment.* Logan, UT: Hope.

Infant Mental Health

Brazelton, T. B. (1992). *Touchpoints. The essential reference. Your child's emotional and behavioral development.* Menlo Park, CA: Addison-Wesley Longman.

Carey, W. B., & McDevitt, S. C. (1995). *Coping with children's temperament. A guide for professionals.* New York: Basic Books.

Greenspan, S., & Greenspan, N. T. (1985). *First feelings: Milestones in the emotional development of your baby and child.* New York: Penguin Books.

Klaus, M. H., Kennell, J. H., & Klaus, P. H. (1995). *Bonding: Building the foundations of secure attachment and independence.* Menlo Park, CA: Addison-Wesley Longman.

Sroufe, L. A. (1996). *Emotional development: The organization of emotional life in the early years.* New York: Cambridge University Press.

Zeanah, C. H., Jr. (1993). *Handbook of infant mental health.* New York: Guilford Press.

Visual Impairment

Chen, D., & Dote-Kwan, J. (1995). *Starting points: Instructional practices for young children whose multiple disabilities include visual impairment.* Los Angeles: Blind Childrens Center.

Chen, D., Friedman, C. T., & Calvello, G. (1990). *Parents and visually impaired infants.* Louisville, KY: American Printing House for the Blind.

Ferrell, K. A. (1985). *Reach out and teach. Meeting the training needs of parents of visually and multiply handicapped young children.* New York: AFB Press.

Hanson, M. (1988). *Beyond tracking: Enhancing vision development from birth to one year of life.* Bridgeview, IL: Vision Unlimited.

Harrell, L., & Akeson, H. (1987). *Preschool vision stimulation: It's more than a flashlight!* New York: AFB Press.

Hyvarinen, L. (1988). *Vision in children: Normal and abnormal.* Orlando, FL: Vision Associates.

Lueck, A. H., Chen, D., & Kekelis, L. (1997). *Developmental guidelines for infants with visual impairment: A manual for early intervention.* Louisville, KY: American Printing House for the Blind.

Morgan, E. C. (Ed.). (1994). *Resources for family centered intervention for infants, toddlers and preschoolers who are visually impaired: VIISA Project* (2nd ed.). Logan, UT: Hope.

Nielsen, L. (1992a). *Educational approaches for visually impaired children.* Orlando, FL: Vision Associates.

Nielsen, L. (1992b). *Space and self: Active learning by means of the Little Room.* Orlando, FL: Vision Associates.

Nielsen, L. (1993). *Early learning step by step: Children with vision impairment and multiple disabilities.* Orlando, FL: Vision Associates.

Pogrund, R. L., Fazzi, D. L., & Lampert, J. S. (Eds.) (1992). *Early focus: Working with young blind and visually impaired children and their families.* New York: AFB Press.

Warren, D. H. (1994). *Blindness and children: An individual differences approach.* New York: Cambridge University Press.

Other Resources

Alexander, R., Boehme, R., & Cupps, B. (1993). *Normal development of functional motor skills: The first year of life.* Tucson, AZ: Communication Skill Builders.

Batshaw, M. L. (Ed.) (1997). *Children with disabilities* (4th ed.). Baltimore, MD: Paul H. Brookes.

Bredekamp, S., & Copple, C. (Eds.). (1997). *Developmentally appropriate practice in early childhood programs* (rev. ed.). Washington, DC: National Association for the Education of Young Children.

Capute, A. J. & Accardo, P. L. (Eds.) (1996). *Developmental disabilities in infancy and childhood. Volume 2. The spectrum of developmental disabilities* (2nd ed.). Baltimore, MD: Paul H. Brookes.

Coling, M. C. (1991). *Developing integrated programs: A transdisciplinary approach for early intervention.* Tucson, AZ: Communication Skill Builders.

DEC Task Force on Recommended Practices. (1993). *DEC recommended practices: Indicators of quality in programs for infants and young children with special needs and their families.* Pittsburgh, PA: DEC Executive Office.

Hanson, M. J., & Lynch, E. W. (1995). *Early intervention: Implementing child and family services for infants and toddlers who are at risk or disabled* (2nd ed.). Austin, TX: Pro-Ed.

Klass, C. S. (1996). *Home visiting: Promoting healthy parent and child development.* Baltimore, MD: Paul H. Brookes.

Meisels, S. J., & Shonkoff, J. P. (1990). *Handbook of early childhood intervention.* New York: University of Cambridge Press.

VandenBerg, K. A., & Hanson, M. J. (1993). *Homecoming for babies after the neonatal intensive care nursery: A guide for professionals in supporting families and their infants' early development.* Austin, TX: Pro-Ed.

OTHER TYPES OF MATERIALS

Assessment Tools

Vision

Baby screen kit. Orlando, FL: Vision Associates.

Early Education Unit, Special Education Division, California Department of Education. (1997). *First look: Vision evaluation and assessment for infants, toddlers, and preschoolers, birth through five years of age.* Sacramento, CA: Publications Division, California Department of Education.

Exsted, R., Lastine, D., & Paul, B. (1996). *Individualized, comprehensive, evaluation of functional use of vision in early childhood (I-CEE). An evaluation protocol.* Fairbault, MN: Minnesota Resource Center for Blind and Visually Impaired Students.

McDowell Vision Kit. Los Angeles: Western Psychological Services.

Hearing

Early Education Unit, Special Education Division, California Department of Education. (1998). *Ear-restible: Hearing test procedures for infants, toddlers, and preschoolers, birth through five years of age.* Sacramento, CA: Publications Division, California Department of Education.

HEAR KIT. Denver, CO: HearScreen Systems.

Dictionaries

Accardo, P. J., Whitman, B. Y. (1996). *Dictionary of developmental disabilities terminology.* Baltimore, MD: Paul H. Brookes, Box 10624, Baltimore, MD 21285-0624.

Berkow, R., & Fletcher, A. J. (Eds.) (1992). *The Merck manual of diagnosis and therapy* (16th ed.). Rahway, NJ: Merck Publishing Group, Merck & Co.

Cassin, B., Solomon, S., & Rubin, M. (Eds.) (1990). *Dictionary of eye terminology.* Gainesville, FL: Triad Publishing.

Coleman, J. G. (1993). *The early intervention dictionary. A multidisciplinary guide to terminology.* Bethesda, MD: Woodbine House.

McDonough, J. T. (Ed.) (1994). *Stedman's concise medical dictionary* (2nd ed.). Baltimore, MD: Williams & Wilkins.

Stach, B. A (1997). *Comprehensive dictionary of audiology, illustrated.* Baltimore, MD: Williams & Wilkins.

Professional Journals

Infant-Toddler Intervention: A Transdisciplinary Journal. San Diego, CA: Singular Publishing Group.

Infants and Young Children: An Interdisciplinary Journal of Special Care Practices. Frederick, MD: Aspen.

Journal of Early Intervention. Reston, VA: Division of Early Childhood, Council for Exceptional Children.

Topics in Early Childhood Special Education. Austin, TX: Pro-Ed.

Young Exceptional Children. Denver, CO: Division of Early Childhood.

Zero to Three Bulletin. Washington, DC: Zero to Three National Center for Infants, Toddlers, and Families.

Videos

Can Do video series. Louisville, KY: Visually Impaired Preschool Services.

Helping your child learn video series. Verona, WI: BVD Promo Services.

Chen, D., Klein, M. D., & Haney, M. (in press). *Promoting learning through active interaction. Supporting early communication with infants who have multiple disabilities* [video & booklet]. Baltimore, MD: Paul H. Brookes.

Chen, D. (1997). *What can baby hear? Auditory tests and interventions for infants with multiple disabilities* [video & booklet]. Baltimore, MD: Paul H. Brookes.

Chen, D. (1998). *What can baby see? Vision tests and interventions for infants with multiple disabilities* [video & booklet]. New York: AFB Press.

Chen, D., & Orel-Bixler, D. (1997). *Vision tests for infants.* [video & booklet]. New York: AFB Press.

Chen, D, & Schachter, P. H. (1997). *Making the most of early communication: Strategies for supporting communication with infants, toddlers, and preschoolers whose multiple disabilities include vision and hearing loss* [video & booklet]. New York: AFB Press.

Fish, M. E. (1990). *Getting there: A look at the early mobility skills of four young blind children.* San Francisco: Blind Babies Foundation.

Heart to heart: Conversations with parents of blind children. (1986). Los Angeles: Blind Childrens Center.

Let's eat: Feeding a child with visual impairment. (1994). Los Angeles: Blind Childrens Center.

Books and Booklets for Families

Brody, J., & Webber, L. (1994). *Let's eat:. Feeding a child with visual impairment.* Los Angeles: Blind Childrens Center.

Charkins, H. (1996). *Children with facial difference: A parents' guide.* Bethesda, MD: Woodbine House.

CHARGE Accounts [a quarterly newsletter for parents of children with CHARGE syndrome/association]. Columbia, MO: Quota Club.

Chen, D., & McCann, M. E. (1993). *Selecting a program: A guide for parents of infants and preschoolers with visual impairment.* Los Angeles: Blind Childrens Center.

Chernus-Mansfield, N., Hayashi, D., Horn, M., & Kekelis, L. (1986). *Heart to heart. Parents of children who are blind and visually impaired talk about their feelings.* Los Angeles: Blind Childrens Center.

Chernus-Mansfield, N., Hayashi, D., & Kekelis, L. (1985.) *Talk to me II: Common concerns.* Los Angeles: Blind Childrens Center.

Child development [correspondence course]. Winnetka, IL: Hadley School for the Blind.

Ferrell, K. A. (1984). *Parenting preschoolers: Suggestions for raising young blind and visually impaired children.* New York: AFB Press.

Geralis E. (Ed.). (1998). *Children with cerebral palsy: A parents' guide.* Bethesda, MD: Woodbine House.

Harrell, L. (1984). *Touch the baby: Blind and visually impaired children as patients: Helping them respond to care.* New York: AFB Press.

Hefner, M. A., Thelin, J. W., Davenport, S. L. H., & Mitchell, J. A. (1988). *CHARGE syndrome: A booklet for families.* Columbia, MO: Quota Club.

Holbrook, M. C. (Ed.). (1996). *Children with visual impairments. A parent's guide.* Bethesda, MD: Woodbine House.

Hug, D., Chernus-Mansfield, N., & Hayashi, D. (1987). *Move with me: A parents' guide to movement development for visually impaired babies.* Los Angeles: Blind Childrens Center.

Kekelis, L., & Chernus-Mansfield, N. (1984). *Talk to me. A language guide for parents of children who are visually impaired.* Los Angeles: Blind Childrens Center.

La-Prelle, L. L. (1996). *Standing on my own two feet.* Los Angeles: Blind Childrens Center.

Learning, play, and toys [correspondence course]. Winnetka, IL: Hadley School for the Blind.

Meyers, L., & Lansky, P. (1991). *Dancing cheek to cheek: Beginning social, play, and language interactions.* Los Angeles: Blind Childrens Center.

Moore, S. (1985). *Beginnings: A practical guide for parents and teachers of visually impaired babies.* Louisville, KY: American Printing House for the Blind.

Off to a Good Start: Access to the World for Infants and Toddlers with Visual Impairments (1999). San Francisco: Blind Babies Foundation.

O'Mara, B. (1989). *Pathways to independence: Orientation and mobility skills for your infant and toddler.* New York: The Lighthouse.

Overbrook School for the Blind, Parent Early Childhood Education Series. Louisville, KY: American Printing House for the Blind.

Pediatric visual diagnosis fact sheets. (1998). San Francisco: Blind Babies Foundation.

Recchia, S. (1987). *Learning to play: Presenting play activities to the preschool child who is visually impaired.* Los Angeles: Blind Childrens Center.

Schmitt, P., & Armenta-Schmitt, F. (1999). *Fathers. A common ground.* Los Angeles: Blind Childrens Center.

Schwartz, S. (Ed.). (1996). *Choices in deafness: A parents' guide to communication options* (2nd ed.). Bethesda, MD: Woodbine House.

Simmons, S. S., & Maida, S. O. (1992). *Reaching crawling walking . . . Let's get moving.* Orientation and mobility for preschool children. Los Angeles: Blind Childrens Center.

Understanding retinopathy of prematurity. (1996). Mountain View, CA: IRIS Medical Instruments.

PUBLISHERS

Addison-Wesley Longman
2725 Sand Hill Road
Menlo Park, CA 94025

AFB Press
11 Penn Plaza, Suite 300
New York, NY 10001

American Printing House for the Blind
Box 6085
Louisville, KY 40206-0085

Aspen Publications
7201 McKinney Circle
Frederick, MD 21701

Basic Books
10 East 53rd Street
New York, NY 10022-5299

Behavior Science Systems
Box 1108
Minneapolis, MN 55440

Blind Babies Foundation
1200 Gough Street
San Francisco, CA 94109

Blind Childrens Center
4120 Marathon Street
Los Angeles, CA 90029

Paul H. Brookes
Box 10624
Baltimore, MD 21285-0624

BVD Promo Services
P.O. Box 9303182
Verona, WI 53593-0182

California Department of Education
Publications Sales Office
Box 271
Sacramento, CA 95812-0271

California Tomorrow
Fort Mason Center, Building B
San Francisco, CA 94123

Cambridge University Press
40 West 20th Street
New York, NY 10011-4211

Center on Self-Determination
Oregon Health Sciences University
3608 S.E. Powell Boulevard
Portland, OR 97202

CHC Center for Child and Family Development Press
Box 7326
Menlo Park, CA 94026

Council for Exceptional Children
Division of Early Childhood
1920 Association Drive
Reston, VA 20191-1589

Communication Skill Builders
3830 East Bellevue, Box 42050
Tucson, AZ 85733

DEC Executive Office
320 East North Avenue
Pittsburgh, PA 15212

Division of Early Childhood
1444 Wazee Street, Suite 230
Denver, CO 80222

DLM Teaching Resources
1 DLM Park
Allen, TX 75002

Guilford Press
72 Spring Street
New York, NY 10012

Hadley School for the Blind
P.O. Box 299
Winnetka, IL 60093-0299

Hanen Early Language Resource Centre
48 Roxborough Street West
Toronto, Ont. M5R 1T8, Canada

HearScreen Systems
P.O. Box 100735
Denver, CO 802590

William Heinemann Medical Books
23 Bedford Square
London, WCIB 3NN, England

Hope
55 East 100 North, Suite 203
Logan, UT 84321

Infant Hearing Resource
Good Samaritan Hospital and Medical Center
1015 N.W. 22nd Avenue
Portland, OR 97219

IRIS Medical Instruments
340 Pioneer Way
Mountain View, CA 94041-1506

Jackson Education Service District
101 North Grape Street
Medford, OR 97501

The Lighthouse International
111 East 59th Street
New York, NY 10022

Mayfield Publishing Company
1240 Villa Street
Mountain View, CA 94041

Merck Publishing Group
Merck & Company
P.O. Box 2000
Rahway, NJ 07065

Merrill-Prentice Hall
Upper Saddle River, NJ 07458

**Minnesota Resource Center for Blind
and Visually Impaired Students**
615 Olof Hanson Drive, Box 308
Fairbault, MN 55021-0308

National Association for the Education of Young Children
1509 16th Street, N.W.
Washington, DC 20036-1426

Oxford University Press
198 Madison Avenue
New York, NY 10016-4314

Penguin Books
375 Hudson Street
New York, NY 10014

Pro-Ed
8700 Shoal Creek Boulevard
Austin, TX 78757

Quota Club
2004 Parkade Boulevard
Columbia, MO 65202

Singular Publishing Group
401 West A Street, Suite 325
San Diego, CA 92101-7904

Teaching Resources
50 Pond Park Road
Hingham, MA 02043

Triad Publishing
Box 13355
Gainesville, FL 32604

University of Toronto Press
5201 Dufferin
North York, Ont. M3H 5T8, Canada

University Park Press
233 East Redwood Street
Baltimore, MD 21202

Vision Associates
2512 Dr. Philips Boulevard, No. 50-316
Orlando, FL 32819

Vision Unlimited
P.O. Box 1591
Bridgeview, IL 60455

Visually Impaired Preschool Services
1229 Garvin Place
Louisville, KY 40203

VORT Corporation
Box 60132
Palo Alto, CA 94306

Western Pyschological Services
12031 Wilshire Boulevard
Los Angeles, CA 90025-1251

Williams & Wilkins
428 East Preston Street
Baltimore, MD 21202-2436

Woodbine House
6510 Bells Mill Road
Bethesda, MD 20817

Year Book Medical Publishers
35 East Wacker Drive
Chicago, IL 60601

York Press
Box 504
Timonium, MD 21094

**Zero to Three: Clinical Centers
for Infants, Toddlers, and Famlies**
734 15th Street, N.W., Suite 1000
Washington, DC 20005-1013

GLOSSARY

This Glossary presents definitions of the technical terms used in this book. There are many helpful dictionaries that serve as more comprehensive sources for explaining terms that are frequently used in early intervention services with infants and young children who have multiple disabilities and their families. A list of these sources appears in the section on Selected Resources.

Accommodation: The ability of the eye to maintain a clear focus as objects are moved closer to it by changing the shape of the lens.

Accommodative esotropia: The frequent turning of an eye toward the nose to maintain a clear focus. Is found in infants as young as 6 months and young children, usually those who are hyperopic (farsighted). Eyeglasses to correct for the farsightedness relax accommodation and help keep the eyes aligned.

Achromatopsia: The inability to see colors from birth caused by the lack of or defects in the cone photoreceptors of the eyes. Accompanied by decreased visual acuity, nystagmus, and photophobia.

Acuity card procedure: A test of visual acuity using cards with black-and-white stripes of various widths to determine whether and how consistently infants and nonverbal children look at these grating targets.

Adapted signs: Modified manual signs that facilitate an infant's ability to receive or to produce them. For example, the movement of a sign may be made more slowly, the hand may be positioned in the infant's field of vision, or the sign may be made on the object to which it refers.

Air conduction: The process by which sound is conducted to the inner ear through the air in the external auditory canal.

Albinism: The absence of pigment in the eyes, hair, and skin. A congenital condition generally accompanied by decreased visual acuity, nystagmus, and photophobia.

Alternative communication: Any form of communication (including pictorial, gestural, and manual sign) used by a person who is unable to rely solely on speech or sounds.

Amblyopia: Reduced vision without observable changes in or damage to the structure of the eye, caused by eyes that are not straight (strabismus) or by a difference in the refractive error of the two eyes; sometimes called "lazy eye"; not correctable with eyeglasses or contact lenses.

American Sign Language: The formal and abstract language of people who are deaf in the United States. A visual-spatial language of hand shapes, positions, and movements, with its own unique syntax, semantics, and pragmatic functions.

Amplification: An increase in the intensity (loudness) of sound. May be used to refer to a hearing aid or assistive listening device.

Anisometropia: Different refractive errors in each eye of at least 1 diopter difference.

Anterior: Near or on the front.

Apgar score: The sum of numerical values given to five criteria—heart rate, response to stimuli, muscle tone, respiratory effort, and skin color—assigned to a newborn 1 minute after birth to indicate his or her physical status. The best possible total score is 10.

Aphakia: The absence of the lens, usually the result of the removal of a cataract.

Astigmatism: A refractive error caused by a spherocylindrical curvature of the cornea; corrected with a cylindrical lens.

Asymmetrical tonic neck reflex (ATNR): Normal reflex in infants to about 6 months. Simulates a fencer's pose because turning the head to one side causes the arm and leg to stiffen (extend) toward the same side as the head is turned, and the arm and leg on the other side to bend or flex.

Audiogram: A graph showing the hearing threshold level as a function of frequency.

Audiologist: A professional with at least a master's degree, trained in the measurement and evaluation of hearing and in techniques for the aural rehabilitation of people with hearing impairments. Also has extensive knowledge of the normal anatomy and function of the hearing mechanism.

Augmentative communication device: Any aid that supplements existing vocal or verbal communication (may be simple and inexpensive or highly technological).

Augmentative visual cue: An object, such as a light, that highlights another object to draw attention to it.

Autism: A developmental disorder that is diagnosed by age 36 months and is characterized by problems in social interaction and communication, hyperactivity, repetitive, self-stimulatory or stereotypical behaviors, resistance to change, and sensitivities to textures.

Base-out prism: A triangle-shaped glass that moves the image of an object inward when it is put in front of an eye with its widest edge placed on the outside toward the ear. Used to measure or treat esotropia.

Binocular indirect ophthalmoscope (BIO): An instrument, consisting of a bright source of light worn on the head, that gives the tester three-dimensional views of the interior of the eye, especially the fundus, retina, optic disc, macula, and blood vessels.

Binocular vision: The vision of both eyes that forms a fused image in the brain and results in three-dimensional vision.

Bone conduction: The process by which sound is conducted to the internal ear through vibration of the cranial bones.

Biomicroscope (slit lamp): A microscope of different magnifying powers that projects a beam of light whose size, shape, and focus can be altered. Used on a table or held in the hand to examine in detail each structure of the eye (including the lens, cornea, fluids, and membranes).

Bronchopulmonary dysplasia: A chronic lung disorder that occurs in severely ill infants who have received high concentrations of oxygen for long periods and prolonged support on respiratory ventilators for the treatment of respiratory distress syndrome usually associated with prematurity.

B-wave: The electrical signal recorded on an electroretinogram from the front surface of the eyeball in response to stimulation by light.

Cataract: An opacity of the lens that inhibits vision.

Central auditory processing disorder: Difficulty understanding sound or recognizing speech despite a normal audiogram. Similar to central deafness or cortical deafness.

Cerebral palsy: A nonprogressive disorder of movement, posture, and delayed motor development caused by a neurological problem. Usually diagnosed during the second year of life. Associated with other disabilities including mental retardation, seizures, visual impairment, and hearing loss.

CHARGE association: A diagnostic label for a pattern of congenital anomalies—*c*oloboma, *h*eart defect, choneal *a*tresia, *r*etarded growth and development and abnormalities of the central nervous system, *g*enital hypoplasia, and anomalies or malformation of the *e*ars and hearing impairment.

Choneal atresia: Congenital absence or closing of the choanae (the opening between the nasal cavity and the back of the throat); results in breathing difficulties.

Chorioretinitis: An inflammation of the choroid and retina.

Choroid: The vascular layer of the eye, between the sclera and retina, that nourishes the retina.

Ciliary body: Tissue inside the eye, composed of the ciliary processes and ciliary muscle; the former secretes aqueous, and the latter controls the shape of the lens.

Click: A brief (transient) sound with almost instantaneous onset and duration and including a broad range of frequencies.

Clinical vision assessment: An eye examination that includes tests conducted in an eye care specialist's office.

Coactive signing: Physically guiding a child to produce sign movements by taking the child's hands and moving them so the child's hands are under the adult's hand. This technique should be used to help the child convey a message.

Cochlea (inner ear): A spirally coiled, tapered bony tube of about 2 3/4 turns located in the inner ear that contains the sensory organ for hearing.

Coloboma: A congenital cleft, gap, or hole in some portion of the eye caused by the improper fusion of tissue during gestation (the optic nerve, ciliary body, choroid, iris, lens, or eyelid); sometimes seen as a keyhole pupil. Retinal coloboma is the most common form.

Color vision: The perception of color as a result of the stimulation of specialized cone receptors in the retina.

Communication board (picture board): A flat surface with a set of pictures or tangible symbols. A child conveys a specific message by touching or pointing to a representative picture or symbol. The board may contain a single picture or symbol representing a preferred activity.

Communication input: The method by which a message is received (receptive communication).

Communication output: The method by which a message is sent (expressive communication).

Communication systems (symbolic communication systems): The two main types of communication systems are aided systems that require equipment, such as a computerized device or objects, photographs, and picture or symbol cards or boards, and unaided systems, in which hand or body movements, such as gestures and sign language, are used for communication.

Computerized axial tomography (CAT): A diagnostic test that generates a computer analysis of multiplex rays pinpointed to yield precise, detailed images of the orbit, oculomotor nerves and muscles, and the central nervous system.

Conductive hearing loss: A hearing impairment caused by an interruption in the transmission of sound through an abnormal outer or middle ear.

Cones: Photoreceptor cells of the retina that are sensitive to light and provide keen visual acuity and color discrimination.

Confrontation test: A test of vision in which the tester observes a person's eyes using objective measures of fixation and alignment and movement of the eyes. Frequently the first battery of tests conducted to establish rapport with infants and young children.

Confrontation visual field: A method of detecting gross defects in the visual field in which the examiner uses his or her eyes as a point of fixation and a moving target (such as a finger or penlight toy) as peripheral targets.

Congenital: Present at birth; caused by hereditary factors or those that occurred during gestation.

Congenital stationary night blindness: A stable, inherited visual disorder, generally caused by a defect in the retinal rods, that causes extremely lower vision in dim light owing to difficulty adapting to the dark.

Conjunctiva: The thin, clear mucous membranes that cover the inner parts of the eyelids and outer part of the eyeball except the cornea.

Consensual illumination (also called consensual light reflex or response): The constriction of the pupil of one eye caused by shining a light in the other eye.

Contingency experiences: Experiences that are dependent on a person's behavior. For example, when a baby swats a musical mobile, the mobile moves and makes a sound; the sound and music are contingent on the infant's action. A windup mobile is an example of a non-contingent experience because its movement and sound are not dependent on an infant's actions.

Contrast luminance contrast: The difference in brightness between a foreground (what a person is looking at) and a background, such as when a black object is placed on a yellow background to create high contrast. Light-dark contrast is the amount of light reflected off different areas of a surface that makes one side or area brighter than another.

Contrast sensitivity: The ability to detect differences in grayness and background. Because more of the retina is used in discriminating contrast, it may be a better test of visual function, since it uses more than central visual acuity.

Convergence: The inward movement of both eyes toward each other in an effort to maintain the fusion of separate images when looking at an approaching object.

Cornea: The transparent tissue at the front of the eye that is curved to provide most of the eye's refractive power.

Cortical blindness: The absence of or minimal functional vision caused by damage to the occipital lobe and/or posterior visual pathway (behind the lateral geniculate body); detectable through magnetic resonance imaging (MRI) scans.

Cortical visual impairment (CVI): A temporary or permanent visual impairment (from severe to total blindness) as a result of the disturbance of the posterior visual pathways and/or the occipital lobes of the brain.

Cover test (cover-uncover test): A test used to diagnose strabismus or the tendency for the eyes to misalign in which a person looks at a fixation target with one eye covered and the other eye observed for movement. Then the cover is taken off and the movement of both eyes is observed.

Cue: Any sound, smell, sight, or temperature sensation that gives a person information about an ongoing activity or what will happen next.

Cycloplegia: A condition in which the ciliary muscles in the eye accommodation are paralyzed.

Cytomegalovirus (CMV): A common maternal infection ranging in severity and may include hepatitis that can cause a range of disabilities in a newborn. Its effects on vision include chorioretinitis and microcephaly.

Deaf-blind: The co-occurrence of visual impairment and hearing impairment that may require specialized instruction and special methods of communication.

Deafness: The general term for the inability to hear. A deaf person typically has a severe-to-profound degree of hearing loss.

Decibel (dB): A unit of the intensity or level of sound (perceived as loudness). The decibel is calculated as the logarithm of a sound–pressure ratio.

Delayed visual maturation: A condition in which visual development is delayed so a child will seem to be visually impaired. Nystagmus may be present and the delay may be related to abnormalities in the anterior visual pathway. Visual function generally develops at 6–24 months and continues to improve until 2–3 years.

Depth perception: The ability to detect the relative spatial location of objects, some of which are nearer the observer than are others.

Diplopia (double vision): Seeing two images from one object.

Diopter: A unit of measurement of the refractive power of the lenses of eyeglasses and of the extent to which light converges or diverges. Equal to the reciprocal of the focal length of a lens (in meters).

Down syndrome (Trisomy 21): A condition caused by an extra chromosome 21 resulting in distinct physical characteristics: moderate to severe developmental delays, possible cardiac abnormalities, hearing impairment, and various visual impairments (including high refractive errors, strabismus, nystagmus, esotropia, cataracts, and keratoconus).

Duane's syndrome: A congenital disorder that affects the muscles that move the eye and hamper the eye's horizontal movement outward past the midline. Results in esotropia and retraction of the eye into the orbit (the cavity in the skull that holds the eyeball). The eyelid opening narrows when the eye attempts to move toward the nose.

Dysplasia: The abnormal development of tissue.

Eccentric fixation: A visual defect in which an area of the retina other than the fovea is used for visual fixation. Sometimes is an adaptation by people who have amblyopia or whose fovea has been destroyed by a pathological condition.

Ecological inventory: An analysis of the environment in which a child participates to identify the types of activities that occur, who participates in them, the skills required to participate in them, and the supports needed by the child to participate actively.

Educational assessment of vision: See functional vision assessment.

Ear canal: Part of the external ear that is lined with skin and encased by cartilage or bone that ends at the eardrum or tympanic membrane. Receives sound from the environment and carries it toward the eardrum.

Electroretinogram (ERG): An electrophysiological test of retinal function; the waveforms show the function of rods, cones, and bipolar cells.

Esotropia: A condition in which the eyes are misaligned; one eye moves toward the nose and the other looks straight ahead.

Exotropia: A condition in which the eyes are misaligned; one eye moves away from the nose and the other looks straight ahead.

Eye–hand coordination: The ability to use the eyes and hands together to locate, reach out to, touch, or pick up an object.

Familial exudative vitreoretinopathy: An inherited slow-growing disease of the eyes characterized by detachment of the posterior vitreous, vitreous membranes, or retina; abnormal placement of the macula, the development of new blood vessels, and recurrent bleeding. May sometimes be confused with retinopathy of prematurity.

Farsightedness (hyperopia): A refractive error caused by an eyeball that is too short; corrected with a plus (convex) lens.

Field loss: The inability to see part of an area of view when looking straight ahead, measured in degrees from the fixation point.

Figure-ground discrimination: The ability to sort out single features (of a picture, person, event, or object) from a background and elements of a scene that exist at different distances from the eye.

Fixating: Looking at an image by coordinating eye movements to enable the image to focus on the fovea.

FM (frequency-modulated) system: A wireless amplification system that uses a frequency-modulated radio signal to broadcast sound from a transmitting device (speaker) to the receiving unit (listener). Enables a person with a hearing impairment to hear and understand a speaker more clearly with less interference from background noise.

Forced-choice preferential looking test: A means of testing the vision of nonverbal or preverbal children in which patterned stimuli are presented to the right or left, and the movement of the individual's eyes is noted.

Fovea: The central depression in the macula that contains only cone photoreceptors and affords the sharpest vision.

Fragile X syndrome: An X chromosome located near the end of the long arm of the X chromosome. Is frequently related to X-linked mental retardation.

Frequency (referring to acoustic energy): The number of vibrations or oscillations per unit time. Often denoted in hertz (Hz; cycles per second). Frequency is typically associated with the perceptual value of pitch; the higher the frequency, the higher the pitch of a sound.

Full-spectrum lighting: Lighting that most closely simulates the wavelength of natural light.

Functional behavior: A behavior or skill that a child should learn to do, or another person will have to do it for him or her.

Functional hearing screening: A set of procedures involving the review of medical records, interviews with caregivers, and observations of an infant in typical and structured activities to determine how the infant is using his or her hearing and responds to sounds and whether the infant should be referred for an audiological evaluation.

Functional vision assessment: An evaluation of how an individual uses vision in a variety of tasks and settings, including measures of near and distance vision; visual fields; eye movements; and responses to specific environmental characteristics, such as light and color. The assessment report includes recommendations for instructional procedures, modifications-adaptations, and additional tests.

Fundus: The inside part of the eyeball that includes the retina, optic disc, macula, and posterior pole and is examined with an ophthalmoscope.

Fusion: The blending of two separate images, one from each eye, into one image that is maintained as the eyes converge or diverge.

Gavage tube: A tube inserted through the mouth (orogastric), nose (nasogastric), or stomach (gastrostomy) that goes straight to the stomach and is used for feeding.

Geniculostriate pathway: The occular neural pathway located between the lateral geniculate body and the occipital visual cortex.

Gesture: A body movement that conveys a message, such as waving to indicate "bye-bye" or turning away to indicate "I don't like this."

Glaucoma: A disorder characterized by increased intraocular pressure, associated with a buildup of aqueous fluid, which, if left untreated, may cause damage to the nerves of the retina and the optic nerve and eventual visual field defects.

Goldenhar syndrome: A congenital disorder characterized by atypical facial features, small ears, atresia of the ear canal, hearing impairment, and abnormalities of the eyes.

Grating acuity test: A resolution acuity test in which an infant or child detects the presence of parallel lines of decreasing width. When a striped pattern is presented in front of an infant simultaneously with a gray surface of the same size and luminance, the infant is likely to look at the striped pattern, which is more interesting visually than the gray surface.

Grating target: Alternating black-and-white stripes that are used as the target for the assessment of visual acuity in infants and nonverbal children.

Hand-over-hand technique: An instructional strategy in which an adult takes a child's hand to guide the child to explore an object or to demonstrate a certain action.

Hand-under-hand technique: An instructional strategy in which a child puts his or her hand over an adult's hand and is able to feel the movements or action.

Hemianopsia: A defect in the right or the left half of the visual field.

Herpes: Blisterlike skin lesions on the face and sometimes an inflammation of the cornea, sclera, ciliary body, and optic nerve. Affects the first division ophthalmic nerve of the fifth (trigeminal) cranial nerve. In most cases, the disorder (mild to severe) is transmitted at the time of delivery to an infant from an infected mother with active genital lesions.

Hertz (Hz): Cycles per second used to measure the frequency of sound.

Hirschberg test: A test to estimate the extent of strabismus by finding the relative position of light reflexes on the corneas of both eyes.

Hurler syndrome: A genetic syndrome characterized by the retardation of growth and mental retardation, cloudy corneas, and other medical problems.

Hydrocephalus: The excessive accumulation of fluid in the brain that leads to the separation of the cranial bones, dilation of the cerebral ventricles, and thinning of brain tissues.

Hyperbilirubinemia: Excessive bilirubin in the blood.

Hyperopia (farsightedness): A refractive error in which light rays that come from a distant object strike the retina before coming to sharp focus. As a result, a person is able to see distant objects better than near objects. The condition can be corrected by prescription eyeglasses.

Hypertonia: Increased or too much muscle tone, as in spastic cerebral palsy.

Hypertropia: The movement of one eye upward while the other eye remains straight and views normally.

Hypotonia: Decreased or low muscle tone.

Hypotropia: The movement of one eye downward while the other eye remains straight and views normally.

Hypoxia: A deficiency of oxygen reaching the tissues of the body.

Individualized Education Plan (IEP): A program for a child (aged 3–22) that is developed by the educational team that includes the child's present level of performance; long-term goals and short-term objectives for the child, a statement of the specific services to be provided, their frequency and intensity; criteria for evaluating whether the objectives have been achieved; and the extent to which the child will participate in general education programs.

Individualized Family Service Plan (IFSP): A program for an infant or toddler (from birth to 36 months), developed by the child's early intervention team and family, that includes the child's present level of development; desired outcomes for the child and family; criteria for evaluating whether these outcomes have been achieved; required early intervention services, their frequency, intensity, and manner of delivery; the natural environments in which the services will be provided to the maximum extent appropriate or justification for why they will not be delivered in natural environments; the service coordinator; and transition plans (when the child is aged 30 months).

Inclusion: The education of all children together, regardless of their levels of ability or types of disabilities, with the provision of the necessary accommodations and support services to facilitate appropriate learning.

Incus: The middle bone of the three bones (ossicles) in the middle ear.

Inferior: On or near the lower portion of the body or a part of the body.

Inner ear: *See* cochlea

Integrated therapy model: A service delivery approach in which specialized services (such as occupational and physical therapy, speech and language therapy, or vision services) are provided within the usual activities of a child's home routine or school activities, rather than a child being pulled out of the classroom for instruction.

Intensity (sound):   Loudness, measured in decibels (dB).

Interactive signing: A method of providing communication input to a child by encouraging him or her to feel the signer's hand movements when the child's hand is placed over an adult's hand.

Interdisciplinary team: A service delivery approach in which two or more service providers from different disciplines conduct separate assessments, share their results and plan interventions together, but implement interventions individually with the child.

Intraocular pressure (IOP):   The pressure of fluid inside the eye, measured by a tonometer, as for glaucoma.

Iris: The colored portion of the eye that expands or contracts to control the amount of light entering the eye.

Keyhole pupil (iris coloboma):   A defect of the iris present at birth that is a result of maldevelopment of the eye during gestation. The pupil looks like a keyhole, rather than a circle.

Lateral: On one side.

Lateral geniculate body: The "relay" station that receives information from the optic nerves and sends the information to the visual center of the brain and the occipital lobe, which receives visual information and develops an image.

Lateral geniculate nucleus: Paired prominences at the sides of the midbrain (the upper end of brain stem) where the optic tract fibers connect to the optic radiations and transmit visual information.

Laurence Moon Biedl syndrome: A genetic condition that may result in retinitis pigmentosa, obesity, mental retardation, and extra fingers and toes. Associated eye conditions include poor night vision, cataracts, strabismus, and small eyes.

LEA grating paddles: Resolution acuity paddles that use forced-choice preferential looking to screen the acuity of infants and toddlers from birth to age 18 months. The infants detect the presence of parallel lines of decreasing width. When a striped pattern is presented in front of an infant at 2 feet simultaneously with a gray surface of the same size and luminance, the infant is likely to look at the striped pattern, which is more interesting visually than the gray surface.

Learned helplessness: Decreased motivation and responsiveness in certain situations on the basis of previous similar experiences that were unpredictable and uncontrollable. The person does not have a sense of control or competence.

Leber's congenital amaurosis: A rare inherited degenerative disease of the retina in which blindness or severe low vision in both eyes is present at birth. Although eye examinations of infants reveal normal-appearing retinas, electroretinograms detect little or no retinal activity. Other eye-related conditions associated with this disease are deep-set eyes, nystagmus, and sensitivity to light. Other associated conditions are epilepsy, developmental delay, and impaired motor skills.

Lens: A colorless biconvex structure within the eye that enables it to refract light rays that then focus on the retina; also, any transparent substance that can refract light.

Light perception: The ability to discern the presence or absence of light, but not its source or direction.

Light projection: The ability to discern the source or direction of light, but not enough vision to identify objects, people, shapes, or movements.

Localizing (hearing): Aurally identifying the source of sound.

Localizing (vision): Visually identifying the position of an object in space.

Low birth weight: Weight at birth of less than 1 pound, 10 ounces (750 grams). About 70 percent of infants with low birth weights survive and have medical problems, such as respiratory distress syndrome (immature lung disease), visual impairment (retinopathy of prematurity), and hearing impairment.

Low vision: Severely impaired vision after correction, but with the potential for using available vision, with or without optical or nonoptical compensatory visual strategies, devices, and environmental modifications, to plan and perform daily tasks.

Macula: A small yellow spot in the center of the retina around the fovea that is the area of the most acute vision (central vision).

Magnetic resonance imaging (MRI): An imaging technique that uses high-intensity magnets and computers. Permits the examination of soft tissue that cannot be seen with X rays. MRI is used to identify cortical visual impairment or blindness in some children.

Malleus: The largest and outermost bone of the three ossicles in the middle ear.

Media opacity (opaque media): Cloudiness of the parts of the eyes (cornea, aqueous, lens, and vitreous) that are normally clear.

Microcephaly: Small eyes; often an effect of cytomegalovirus.

Micropremature: Born 24–26 weeks gestational age. An infant is premature when born less than 37 weeks gestational age.

Microophthalmus: An abnormally small eyeball present at birth.

Microtropia (microstrabismus): A small, generally inward misalignment of the eyes in which there is some ability to fuse images. The misalignment is often greater when one eye is covered. Associated conditions in the microtropic eye include anisometropia, amblyopia, and a small central suppression scotoma.

Middle ear: The part of the auditory system beginning with the tympanic membrane or eardrum and terminating at the lateral most wall of the inner ear. The middle ear cavity contains three small bones that form a mechanical bridge for sound vibrations to stimulate the inner ear.

Mild hearing loss: 15 to 30 dB HL in infants and young children. Same as slight or minimal loss.

Mixed hearing loss: The co-occurrence of a sensorineural and a conductive hearing loss.

Moderate hearing loss: 30–50 dB HL in infants and young children.

Moderately severe hearing loss: 50–70 dB HL.

Moebius syndrome: A craniofacial nervous system disorder characterized by bilateral facial paralysis, with varying degrees of opthalmoplegia (paralysis of eye-movement), as well as external ear and jaw malformations. Hands, feet, or digits may be missing and mental retardation may be present. Possible auditory dysfunction includes congenital sensorineural and/or conductive loss.

Multidisciplinary team: A service delivery approach in which two or more service providers from different disciplines each assess a person and provide separate interventions.

Myelin: A fatlike material that forms a sheath around some nerve fibers and electrically insulates them to speed the conduction of nerve impulses.

Nasal location: Placement toward the nose; half visual field or the eye from the vertical midline inward.

Near reflex: The eye's response (constriction of the pupil, accommodation, and convergence) when it fixates on a near object.

Nearsightedness (myopia): A refractive error caused by an eyeball that is too long; corrected with a concave (minus) lens.

Near vision: The use of vision to accomplish tasks, such as eating, playing with a toy, or reading, that occur within 8–12 inches of an individual.

Neurofibromatosis: A genetic syndrome that is marked by tumors of the skin, brain, optic and auditory nerves, and coffee-with-milk colored skin patches. Also called the elephant man disease.

Neuroimaging: The in vivo depiction of normal and pathological structures of the central nervous system through various diagnostic tests: CAT, MRI, and positron emission tomography (PET) scans.

Neurological visual impairment: Visual impairment caused by neurological abnormalities of the visual pathway and/or centers of the brain without ocular disease.

Norrie syndrome: A genetic syndrome that results in the progressive loss of vision, mental retardation, and nonprogressive hearing loss.

Null point: In persons with congenital nystagmus, the position of the eyes in which the rapid, oscillating movements are reduced or eliminated.

Nystagmus: An involuntary oscillation of the eyes, usually rhythmical and faster in one direction; may be side to side or up and down.

Object cue: A piece of an object or an object associated with an activity or person that is used to represent the activity or person. May be used on a communication board.

Occipital lobe/cortex: The posterior part of the brain that is responsible for vision and visual perception; it includes the visual cortex, which is the cerebral end of the visual pathway.

Occluder (cover paddle): A patch or paddle (either clear or opaque) that is put over an eye to obscure or block vision during testing or treatment.

Occlusion: Covering an eye with a patch to protect it after an injury or surgery or for treating amblyopia.

Ocular media: The clear fluids and surfaces in the eye (such as the cornea, aqueous, lens, and vitreous) through which light rays pass before they reach the retina.

Ocular motility: Eye movements that allow a person to scan or track a broad array of objects, people, or events. Both smooth or irregular vertical and horizontal and circular and diagonal eye movements are observed. The lower the person's visual acuity, the more the person will move his or her head while visually searching.

Oculocutaneous: Involving the skin and eyes.

Ophthalmia neonatorum: A severe infection of the conjunctiva in newborns that is generally contracted during birth from a mother who has gonorrhea. Can cause blindness if not treated.

Ophthalmologist: A physician who specializes in the medical and surgical care of the eyes and is qualified to prescribe ocular medications and to perform surgery on the eyes. May also perform refractive and low vision work, including eye examinations and other vision services.

Optic disc (blind spot): The place at the back of the retina where the optic nerve enters the eyeball; is not sensitive to light.

Optic nerve: The sensory nerve of the eye that carries electrical impulses from the eye to the brain.

Optic nerve atrophy: The degeneration or malfunction of the optic nerve, characterized by a pale optic disk.

Optic nerve hypoplasia: A congenitally small optic disk, usually surrounded by a light halo and representing a regression in growth during the prenatal period; may result in reduced visual acuity.

Optic radiations: The neural pathway from the lateral geniculate body to the calcarine fissure of the occipital visual cortex.

Optokinetic nystagmus (OKN): Normal eye movements that are involuntary and rhythmic that occur when a person views a series of vertical bars or other patterned contours while he or she or the target is moving.

Optometrist: A health care provider who specializes in refractive errors, prescribes eyeglasses or contact lenses, and diagnoses and manages conditions of the eye as regulated by state law.

Optotype test: A number, symbol, or letter used in examinations of visual acuity.

Orbit: The bony cavity in the skull that is shaped like a pyramid and contains and protects the eyeball.

Orientation and mobility: The ability to know where one is in space, to move to another place, and to get there safely and efficiently.

Osscicles: The three small bones of the middle ear—malleus, incus, and stapes—that transmit sound vibrations from the eardrum to the oval entrance to the cochlea.

Otitis media with effusion (OME): A middle ear infection with an accumulation of fluid.

Ototoxic: Toxic to the inner ear.

Outer ear: Segment of the auditory system that is the most externally vis-ible. It includes the auricle or pinna (the flap of skin and cartilage protruding from the side of the head and the ear canal).

Parietal region or lobe: The upper midpart of each cerebral hemisphere in the brain that is responsible for body sensations.

Patching program: A medical intervention prescribed by an eye care specialist to improve the ability of both eyes to work together (binocular vision) and to maintain equal visual acuity.

Peripheral vision: The perception of objects or motion from the parts of the retina that are beyond the macula—at the side or perimeter of the field of vision.

Philtrum: A depression or groove in the midline of the upper lip.

Photophobia: Extreme sensitivity to light that is usually a symptom of an ocular disorder or disease.

Photoreceptor: The rods and cones that convert light into electrical impulses that are transmitted to the brain.

Pituitary gland: The master gland of the body that controls the activity of other glands and secretes several hormones that regulate many bodily processes. Hangs like a sac from the base of the brain between and behind the orbits and below the optic chiasm.

Posterior-anterior visual pathways: Posterior visual pathways are located behind the lateral geniculate body, which includes the geniculocalcarine tract (main visual fibers), parietal and temporal loops, and occipital cortex. These components are most vulnerable to perinatal and postnatal syndromes. The anterior visual pathways comprise the eyes and muscles, optic nerve, optic chiasm, and optic tract.

Preeclampsia: A toxic condition that develops during pregnancy; characterized by hypertension, the presence of albumin in the urine, and edema.

Preferential looking: A method of evaluating vision in which a patterned stimulus is presented in one of two possible locations and the fixation (looking behavior) of an infant or nonverbal child is assessed to determine whether the stimulus was detected.

Premature: Born before 37 weeks gestational age.

Premotor region: The area of the cortex of the brain in front of the motor area that includes Broca's motor-speech area.

Pressure equalization tubes: Tiny tubes surgically inserted into the tym-panic membrane (eardrum) of patients with chronic middle ear dysfunction due to middle ear fluid, infection, and pressure abnormalities. The purpose of these tubes is to keep the middle ear space ventilated and thus, free from fluid and infection.

Prism: A clear object, shaped like a triangle, that bends light rays toward its base.

Profound hearing loss: More than 90 dB HL in infants and young children.

Progressive hearing loss: A hearing impairment that increases over time.

Prompt: An instructional cue or procedure that helps a child to respond correctly. A hierarchy of prompts, from the least to the most intrusive, is a natural cue, visual-tactile cue, gestural cue, indirect verbal cue, direct verbal cue, modeling, a physical prompt, and physical guidance.

Prone stander: Equipment used to support a child who cannot stand on his or her own in a somewhat upright position, but with some of the child's weight on his or her stomach.

Proprioception: The conscious or unconsciousness awareness of body position, movement, balance, and posture. The sense of where one's body is in space provided by information from the nerves of the inner ear (proprioceptors), joints, muscles, and tendons.

Ptosis: A drooping eyelid caused by paralysis or weak eyelid muscles that may be congenital and requires surgical correction if it interferes with vision.

Pupil: The hole in the center of the iris through which light rays enter the back of the eye.

Reflexive eye movements: Movements of the eyes that are an invariable and involuntary response to a stimulus.

Refsum syndrome: A genetic condition that results in the progressive loss of vision (restricted visual fields), night blindness, sensorineural loss, and an unsteady gait.

Refractive errors: Conditions, such as myopia, hyperopia, and astigmatism, in which parallel rays of light are not brought to a focus on the retina because of a defect in the shape of the eyeball or the refractive media of the eye.

Resolution acuity: The ability to discriminate the difference between the presence or absence of alternating patterns of black-and-white lines on a gray background.

Retina: The inner sensory nerve layer next to the choroid that lines the pos-

terior two-thirds of the eyeball, reacts to light, and transmits impulses to the brain.

Retinitis pigmentosa: A genetic disease characterized by the progressive degeneration of the retinas of both eyes. Night blindness develops first, generally in childhood, and is followed by constricted visual fields (the loss of peripheral vision) and eventually tunnel vision and blindness.

Retinopathy of prematurity (ROP): A series of retinal changes (formerly called retrolental fibroplasia), from mild to total retinal detachment, seen mainly in premature infants, that may be arrested at any stage. Believed to be connected to the immature blood vessels in the eye to oxygen, but may be primarily the result of prematurity with very low birth weight. Functional vision may range from near normal to blindness.

Retinoscope: An instrument that an examiner holds in his or her hand to measure the refractive errors of an eye by projecting light into the eye and determining the refractive errors by the movement of the reflected light rays.

Retinoscopy: The use of a retinoscope to measure the refractive errors of an eye.

Retroillumination: A technique for examining the eyes in which lighting from behind silhouettes a lesion or opacity to make it more visible, as in the use of a slit-lamp light's reflection off the iris or lens to highlight a corneal opacity.

Rods: The photoreceptor cells in the retina that are light sensitive and contain rhodopsin, which permits vision in dim light.

Role release: The ability of a service provider from one discipline to share knowledge and skills with another person who will use the acquired skills to provide services to a child. For example, a physical therapist who teaches a parent and early interventionist how to position and handle an infant with cerebral palsy is "releasing" her role to these individuals.

Rubella: A contagious infection characterized by swelling of the lymph glands and a skin rash. An infant born to a mother who is infected with the rubella virus may have congenital defects, such as hearing loss, cataracts and glaucoma, or blindness. The eye damage may also include microthalmus, decreased visual acuity, colobomas, nystagmus, strabismus, and constricted visual fields.

Scanning: Repetitive fixations that are required to look from one object to another.

Sclera: The tough, white opaque outer covering of the eye that protects the inner contents from most injuries.

Scotopic vision (night vision): Vision in dim light levels; adjustment to the dark takes up to 30 minutes.

Seizure disorder: An abnormal burst of electrical activity in the brain that results in involuntary movements or loss of consciousness.

Sensorineural hearing loss: A hearing impairment caused by the dysfunction of the cochlea and/or cochlear sensory cells or nerve cells in the auditory nerve.

Severe hearing loss: 70–90 dB HL.

Shifting gaze: Alternating eye fixation from one object, person, or event to another at near, intermediate, or far distances.

Sign: The symbolic form of communication that uses hand shapes, position, and movements. A sign system may have its own structure (see American Sign Language) or use that of another language, such as signed English.

Skill clusters: Skills that normally occur in a predictable sequence across activities. For example, localizing, fixating, reaching, and grasping are visual and visual motor behaviors that occur in a sequence when a child seeks and finds a favorite toy. The child learns to anticipate the sequence of skills in a cluster and to apply the skills during activities that require similar responses.

Slight or minimal hearing loss: 15–25 dB HL in young children.

Snellen notation: A chart used to test central visual acuity at a specified distance from the eye, usually 20 feet. It consists of lines of letters, numbers, or symbols in graded sizes down to specific measurements. Each size is labeled with the distance at which it can be read by the normal eye.

Standing table: Equipment used to support a child in an upright position with the child bearing the weight on his or her child's feet. For children who are unable to stand on their own but can bear their own weight.

Stapes: The smallest and innermost bone of the three ossicles in the middle ear.

Startle reflex (response): An infant's physical response to a sudden noise or movement by extending the arms or legs and then bringing them into the body (flexion) that decreases between 2 and 6 months of age.

Stereopsis: The combination of two similar images (one on each retina) into a single solid in-depth image.

Strabismus: An extrinsic muscle imbalance that causes the misalignment of the eyes upward, downward, toward the nose, and away from the nose.

Striate cortex (or visual cortex): The part of the occipital lobes of brain in which visual information is registered consciously.

Superior: Situated on or near the top of the body or a bodily organ.

Supine stander: Equipment that is used to support a child in a somewhat upright position, but with some of the child's weight on his or her back. For children who are unable to stand on their own.

Suprasellar: Above or over the sella turcica (the bony cavity that houses the pituitary gland).

Swinging flashlight test: A test of the response of the pupils of both eyes to dim light. The detection of an unequal decrease in the size of the pupils that indicates the presence of optic nerve disease.

Tangible symbol: An object, a piece of an object, or an abstract concrete form that is used as a referent for a person, place, or activity. May be used on a communication board.

Tay-Sachs   disease: A progressive genetic disorder, found in families of Jewish and Middle Eastern backgrounds, that results in the loss of developmental milestones, hypotonia, and visual impairment and leads to death in childhood.

Teller acuity cards: A subjective method for measuring resolution (grating) acuity in infants, young children, and adults who cannot respond verbally to standard acuity measurements. Each card contains a black-and-white grating to the left or right of a central peephole and a gray surface on the opposite side and is an example of a forced-choice preferential looking test. Prior to testing, the tester arranges the cards in a stack from the widest to the narrowest stripes. The child is positioned so his or her head and eyes are stable. The tester holds the cards at a predetermined distance, depending on the child's chronological age. The child shows a preferential fixation to the right or left side of the card, which reverses when the card is rotated 180 degrees. Testing continues until the child no longer fixates on either the right or left side, presumably because he or she no longer sees any stripes on the card.

Temporal: Toward the ear or temple and away from the nose or from the vertical midline outward.

Teratogen: Any substance, including a medication, narcotic, and virus or bacterium, that causes the development of abnormal structures during the development of an embryo or fetus.

Tonometer: An instrument or device that is used to measure tension or pressure from fluid, particularly intraocular pressure; used to detect glaucoma.

TORCH Syndrome: The acronym for a combination of maternal infectious diseases that can affect the fetus: *t*oxoplasmosis, *o*ther infections (such as syphilis), *r*ubella, *c*ytomegalovirus, and *h*erpes.

Touch cue: A communication method that conveys a message to a child by touching him or her in a consistent way.

Toxoplasmosis: A congenital infection in utero (caused by microorganisms in animal feces and raw meat) that may produce cataracts, blindness, jaundice, seizures, large lymph nodes, and pneumonia in infants; characterized by inflammation of the retina and choroid that causes scarring. Occurs in 1–4 per 1,000 live births. Treatment includes medication, photocoagulation, and cryotherapy.

Tracking: Visually following a moving object.

Transactional model of development: A theoretical framework that views a child's developmental outcome as a consequence of the dynamic and reciprocal interactions between the child and his or her social and physical environments.

Transdisciplinary team: A service delivery approach in which two or more service providers from different disciplines conduct joint assessments, plan and implement interventions together, and share their knowledge and skills. For example, an early interventionist will implement strategies learned from a speech and language therapist to support a child's communication.

Transillumination: The shining of an intense light beam from a slit lamp or small flashlight through translucent eye tissue to gain a better view of tumors, cysts, or hemorrhages in the eyes.

Tympanic membrane (eardrum): The conically shaped, semitransparent membrane that separates the outer ear from the middle ear.

Tympanometry: A test that evaluates the movement of the eardrum as a function of changes in pressure in the ear canal; indicates the status of the middle ear.

Vestibular ocular reflex (VOR): The involuntary turning of the eyes in the opposite direction from the way the head is turned to maintain fixation on a stationary target. An abnormal VOR may be related to defects in the brain stem.

Visual (sensory channel): One of the five information-gathering senses (the other four being hearing, smell, taste, and touch) for obtaining information about the world.

Visual acuity: The sharpness of vision in distinguishing detail, often measured as the eye's ability to distinguish the details and shapes of objects at a designated distance; involves central (macular) vision.

Visual clutter: A combination of images and background that provides distracting details for some individuals who have figure-ground difficulties, that is, cannot select a single object from its background.

Visual evoked potential (VEP): The activity in the occipital cortex, recorded by computer, that occurs when flashes of light or patterns stimulate the retina. Used to determine if there are defects in the neural pathway to and from the retina. Same as VER.

Visual evoked response (VER): Electrical activity in the occipital cortex, recorded by computer, that results from the stimulation of the retina with flashes of light or a checkerboard pattern. Used to detect defects in the retina-to-brain nerve pathway (which can change brain wave patterns). Estimates refractive error, visual acuity, and binocular function and assesses the possible presence of amblyopia. May not predict how a child uses vision, especially if the checkerboard pattern is used. Same as VEP.

Visual field (field of vision): The area that can be seen when one looks straight ahead, measured in degrees from the fixation point.

Visual fixation: The direction of the eye toward an object to be viewed.

Visual pathway: The pathway between the eyes and the brain through which visual information is transmitted.

Vitreous: The clear, colorless, gelatin-like substance that fills the rear two-thirds of the inside of the eyeball.

Vocalization: The production of non-speech sounds.

Waardenburg syndrome: An autosomal dominant syndrome characterized by a white forelock, multicolored iris, and sensorineural hearing loss.

Blank Forms

VISION SCREENING QUESTIONNAIRE
PART I

Child's name: _____ Birthdate: _____ Date: _____

Your relationship with child: _____ Your name: _____

Parent/Guardian name: _____

Address: _____ Phone: _____

Please read the following risk and behavioral factors to see if any apply to your child. (If you answer yes to one of these risk or behavioral factors, further vision testing may be indicated.)

Risk Factors for Vision Loss:

YES	NO	
_____	_____	Parent/caregiver has concerns regarding child's vision.
_____	_____	Family history of vision loss, (such as RP, Retinoblastoma, Albinism).
_____	_____	Child had birth weight of less than 3 pounds.
_____	_____	Child was premature and exposed to oxygen in the hospital.
_____	_____	Child was exposed to alcohol or drugs prenatally.
_____	_____	Mother has history of infection (toxoplasmosis, rubella, CMV, syphilis, herpes).
_____	_____	Child had meningitis or encephalitis.
_____	_____	Child had head trauma.
_____	_____	Child has neurological disorders such as seizures.
_____	_____	Child has other medical concerns (hearing loss, hydrocephaly or excessive fever for prolonged period.)

Behavioral Factors That May Indicate Vision Loss:

YES	NO	NOT SURE	
_____	_____	_____	Child tilts head when looking.
_____	_____	_____	Child does not notice people or objects when placed in certain areas.
_____	_____	_____	Child's eyes appear to cross or turn outward, inward, upward, or downward.
_____	_____	_____	Child squints eyelids when outside or inside.
_____	_____	_____	Child displays constant and quick eye movements.
_____	_____	_____	Child consistently under or over reaches trips on curbs or steps.
_____	_____	_____	Child cannot find a dropped toy.
_____	_____	_____	Child has red rimmed, encrusted, inflamed, or watery eyes or infections occur often.
_____	_____	_____	Child complains of eyes that burn, itch, or feel scratchy.
_____	_____	_____	Child is able to sleep for short times only, and then wakes up rubbing eyes and complaining of pain in eyes.
_____	_____	_____	Child's eyes may appear swollen.
_____	_____	_____	Child may have such behaviors as eyepoking, rocking, or staring at lights.

Courtesy of the Parent Outreach Program for the Visually Impaired, Arizona State Schools for the Deaf and Blind (ASDB).

VISION SCREENING QUESTIONNAIRE
PART II

Your Child's Visual Development:

0–1 Months:

YES	NO	NOT SURE	
_____	_____	_____	Looks at mother's/caregiver's face
_____	_____	_____	Stares at lights

2–4 Months:

YES	NO	NOT SURE	
_____	_____	_____	Begins to smile at others
_____	_____	_____	Follows a moving person with their eyes
_____	_____	_____	Fascinated by lights and bright colors
_____	_____	_____	Begins to look at own hands

5–8 Months:

YES	NO	NOT SURE	
_____	_____	_____	Watches things happening across the room
_____	_____	_____	Reaches for nearby toys
_____	_____	_____	Looks at small objects, such as raisins or small cereal

9–12 Months:

YES	NO	NOT SURE	
_____	_____	_____	Reacts to facial expressions of others (smiles, frowns, funny faces, etc.)
_____	_____	_____	Looks for fallen toys, even around corners
_____	_____	_____	Is interested in picking up tiny objects (such as lint on the carpet)

12–18 Months:

YES	NO	NOT SURE	
_____	_____	_____	Marks and scribbles with a crayon
_____	_____	_____	Interested in picture books
_____	_____	_____	Can reach in and pull out objects easily

18–36 Months:

YES	NO	NOT SURE	
_____	_____	_____	Sees details in familiar pictures
_____	_____	_____	Copies a circle with a pencil or crayon
_____	_____	_____	Looks for familiar things in the distance
_____	_____	_____	Can imitate movements of others

Screener Review

Screener name: _____   Screening program: _____

Further screening need: YES / NO   Date: _____

Comments:

Courtesy of the Parent Outreach Program for the Visually Impaired, Arizona State Schools for the Deaf and Blind (ASDB).

Child's name: _____ Date of birth: _____

Eye specialist: _____ Date of exam: _____

Information from the clinical vision report

1. What vision tests were conducted?

2. What were the results of the test or tests?

3. How did the test go? How was the infant during the testing situation? How reliable are the results?

4. What do the results mean in terms of the infant's ability to see clearly?

5. With this vision loss, would this infant benefit from eyeglasses or contact lenses?

6. What can the infant be expected to see with and without the eyeglasses or contact lenses?

7. Are more tests needed? If so, when and what kind?

Follow-up questions for the optometrist or ophthalmologist

8. What is the best way to assess an infant with visual and multiple disabilities?

9. When should the infant be retested?

10. How can the infant be prepared for further testing, for example, for recognition acuity tests that require a matching or verbal response or tests conducted at distances beyond 16 inches?

11. Can the early interventionist participate in further testing, such as recognition acuity tests?

12. To gain a better understanding of the infant's vision loss, can the parents and the early interventionist look at the forced-choice preferential looking cards from the viewpoints of the tester and the infant?

13. If the infant is wearing contact lenses or eyeglasses, when does he or she need to be checked for a new prescription?

QUESTIONS TO ASK THE FAMILY IN A FUNCTIONAL VISION ASSESSMENT

Child's name: _____   Date of birth: _____

Informant: _____   Date of interview: _____

Interviewer: _____

1. What have you been told by medical professionals (such as the pediatrician or family care physician) about your infant's vision?

2. Is your infant taking any medications? What medical issues would affect your infant's ability to learn to use vision?

3. Do your infant's eyes look normal?

4. Have you noticed if one of the infant's eyes turns inward, outward, upward, or downward? If so, when does this occur?

5. Does anyone in the family have a vision problem, such as amblyopia, or "lazy eye"; farsightedness; nearsightedness; astigmatism; or color deficiency?

6. What is your impression of your infant's vision?

7. What does your infant like to look at?

8. What kinds of things do you think your infant sees, and in what activities does he or she use vision?

9. Does your infant seem to respond to your face or to brightly colored toys? If so, how far away, or how close, and in what positions does he or she notice them?

10. Does your infant use both eyes to look at objects or at your face when close to him or her (about 4 inches away)?

11. What does your infant do when you look at him or her from about 8 to 12 inches?

(continued on next page)

Deborah Chen, *Essential Elements in Early Intervention: Visual Impairment and Multiple Disabilities.* New York: AFB Press, 1999. All rights reserved.

12. What toys does your infant prefer? Toys that make sounds? Toys that are bright and colorful? Shiny toys?

13. Does your infant swipe at, reach for, or grasp colorful objects that are close to him or her? If so, please explain.

14. How does your infant respond if many toys are presented at the same time, for example, several toys on a quilt during playtime? Will he or she notice a favorite toy?

15. Does your infant use both eyes to follow a moving object crossing from one side of the body to the other (such as from left to right)?

16. Does your infant recognize people when they enter a room, when no auditory cue is given (such as the person signaling his or her presence by calling out the infant's name or the sound of footsteps)? How far away is the person when the child visually recognizes his or her presence?

17. Does your infant look out the windows of a car, bus, or train when you take him or her on an outing?

18. Have you noticed your infant squinting when playing in bright sunlight? What is his or her reaction to an outside source of light or from lighting provided in an indoor environment?

19. Describe your infant's coloring or drawing skills (if applicable). Obtain a sample, if possible. How does your infant use vision to perform these tasks? Does he or she experiment with many colors? Does he or she choose to color or draw on much of the space, or are colors limited to certain areas on the page (such as the right or left corner, center of the page or upper or lower areas of the page)?

20. Some infants with visual impairments hold their hands near or against their eyes in unusual ways. For example, some wave a hand in front of one or both eyes, whereas others press a hand against an eye. Have you noticed your infant doing this, and if so, when do you see this behavior most often?

(continued on next page)

21. Does your infant appear to tilt his or her head in an unusual way to look at things?

22. How does your infant locate things he or she drops on the floor? Please give an example. Does the infant use vision to locate lost objects? How?

23. Is your infant more hesitant to explore or move about unfamiliar places, such as open spaces or stairs, than in familiar places? Please describe.

Questions related to infants who use eyeglasses or contact lenses or a patching program:

24. Does your infant wear the eyeglasses all the time? If not, why not?

25. Has your infant's response to wearing eyeglasses changed at any time?

26. Does your infant move the eyeglasses forward on the nose or look over them?

27. How long has your infant had the present pair of eyeglasses or contact lenses?

28. Does your infant wear the patch the prescribed length of time recommended by the eye care specialist?

Questions on the child's communication and activities:

29. What types of communication systems does your infant use? Vocal (sounds and words), picture or communication boards, gestures or body language, touch cues, objects or textures, sign language, or other methods?

30. Describe your infant's indoor and outdoor activities on a typical day. Of the activities in your infant's schedule, which ones—playing, eating, and moving—would you like to focus on to enhance his or her use of vision more efficiently?

31. Of the activities in your infant's schedule, which ones—for example, playing, eating, or moving—would you like to focus on to enhance his or her use of vision more efficiently?

Deborah Chen, *Essential Elements in Early Intervention: Visual Impairment and Multiple Disabilities.* New York: AFB Press, 1999. All rights reserved.

DAILY ROUTINES AND FACTORS AFFECTING THE USE OF VISION

Child's name: _____   Date: _____

Assessment area: _____

Lighting: _____

_____

Activity: _____

Visual aids (such as a slant board, magnification, and colored filters):

_____

_____

Steps in Activity	Child's Action*	Factors Affecting the Use of Vision	Teaching Strategies and Adaptations

* Child's Action: + (independent)   – (needed help)   * incon (inconsistent)

Comments (Additional comments on back of page):

_____

Deborah Chen, *Essential Elements in Early Intervention: Visual Impairment and Multiple Disabilities.* New York: AFB Press, 1999. All rights reserved.

QUESTIONS FOR THE AUDIOLOGIST REGARDING AN INFANT'S AUDIOLOGICAL EVALUATION

Child's name: _____   Age: _____

Audiologist: _____   Date of evaluation: _____

1. What kinds of hearing tests were conducted?

2. What did the tests measure, and what were the results?

3. How did the test go—how was the baby during the testing situation? How reliable are the results?

4. When should the baby be retested?

5. What do the results mean in terms of the baby's ability to discriminate sounds?

6. With this hearing loss, would this baby benefit from amplification?

7. What do you think is the best way to get more information about this baby's hearing?

8. How can I help prepare this child for further testing?

9. Can I participate in or observe future testing?

10. If present at the audiological evaluation exam—can we listen to sounds through the headphones to get an idea of the sounds that the infant can hear?

11. If the infant wears hearing aids, when will new ear molds be needed?

You should be able to answer questions #1-4 from a complete audiogram and audiological report. If the written report does not provide this information, you will need to discuss the results with the audiologist.

Deborah Chen, *Essential Elements in Early Intervention: Visual Impairment and Multiple Disabilities.* New York: AFB Press, 1999. All rights reserved.

QUESTIONS TO ASK THE FAMILY DURING A FUNCTIONAL HEARING SCREENING

Infant's name: _____   Date of birth: _____

Informant: _____   Date of interview: _____

Interviewer: _____   Program: _____

Medical and Health Information

1. What have you been told by medical professionals about your baby's hearing?

2. Has your baby had an ear infection? How frequently?

3. Is your infant often congested? Does he or she have frequent colds?

Observations

Note: If the parents are unable to answer these questions, you will need to help structure observations of the baby's responses to sound and to model how to observe them for the parent.

4. What is your impression of the baby's hearing?

5. What sounds seem to get your baby's attention?

6. What does your baby do when you call his or her name?

7. How does the baby react to sudden loud noises (such as a telephone ringing, a car horn honking, or a vacuum cleaner running)?

8. Does your baby seem to respond differently to your vocalizations when the radio or television is on?

9. Does your baby enjoy toys that "talk" or make noise?

10. Does your baby enjoy you talking, cooing or singing to him or her?

11. What words does your baby seem to understand?

DAILY ACTIVITIES

Child: _____   Date: _____

Parent-Caregiver: _____   Interviewer: _____

Other Family Members Present: _____

Weekday: _____   Weekend: _____

Time of Day	Sequence of Activity	What the Child Does	How the Child Communicates	Family Priority (Yes/no)

Deborah Chen, *Essential Elements in Early Intervention: Visual Impairment and Multiple Disabilities.* New York: AFB Press, 1999. All rights reserved.

CHARACTERISTICS OF THE CAREGIVING ENVIRONMENT

Child: _____   Date: _____

Environment: _____   Respondent: _____

Directions: Have the family and/or early intervention staff complete the inventory.

Question	Response
How does the child receive physical contact (for example, hugs, touches, being held)?	
How is the child encouraged to move and explore his or her surroundings?	
How does the caregiver get the child's attention before interacting with the child (for instance, says the child's name, touches the child, taps the object)?	
How does the caregiver provide opportunities for exploring objects (such as by pausing or giving prompts to encourage the child to explore)?	
How does the caregiver engage the child to keep the child's attention and interest (for example, by pacing)?	
How does the caregiver facilitate the child's participation in activities (for instance, by rearranging materials, the child's position, or his or her own position)?	
How does the caregiver identify and interpret the child's nonverbal cues (such as quieting means "I'm interested" or turning the head away means "I don't like it")?	
How does the caregiver indicate the child's turn (for instance, by pausing, waiting, or touching the child)?	

(continued on next page)

CHARACTERISTICS OF THE CAREGIVING ENVIRONMENT *(continued)*

Question	Response
How are the child's requests for objects or assistance acknowledged (complied with, ignored, or denied)?	
How are the child's communicative intents and behaviors acknowledged and/or expanded (such as exaggerated vocalization, touch cues, object cues or adapted manual signs)?	
How are augmentative communication methods used, if necessary?	
What activities are mutually enjoyable for the child and caregiver (like bathing, feeding, playtime)?	
How is the child included in ongoing activities-daily routines (for example, placing the child near the adult or providing him or her with toys)?	
How is the environment organized to encourage movement and exploration (uncluttered, specific places for toys or objects, adaptations)?	
How is the environment organized to encourage the use of vision, if applicable (for instance, proper lighting, high contrast, glare-free)?	
How is the environment organized to encourage listening skills, if applicable (such as reduced background noise, floors carpeted)?	

ROUTINE ANALYSIS

Name: _____   Date: _____   Activity: _____

Steps in Routine	Natural Cues	Behaviors to Encourage	Input and Adaptive Strategies
For example Preparing for the activity, marking the beginning, middle and end of activity, and transition to another activity.	*For example* Characteristics of the environment, what the adult does to engage the infant's attention and participation.	*For example* Ways the infant can indicate anticipation and participate actively.	*For example* Ways to provide appropriate communication input (may include speech, sign, touch cues and object cues, or handling and positioning) and ways to encourage the use of functional vision and hands.

Deborah Chen, *Essential Elements in Early Intervention: Visual Impairment and Multiple Disabilities*. New York: AFB Press, 1999. All rights reserved.

OBJECTIVES-WITHIN-ROUTINES MATRIX

Name: _____   Date: _____

Objectives	Daily Routines				

INTERVENTION PRIORITY CHECKLIST

Name: _____   Date: _____

Completed by: _____

Directions: List each skill or objective in the spaces across the top. Answer each question for each skill or objective listed.

Ratings: 3 = Strongly agree   2 = Agree   1 = Somewhat agree   0 = Disagree

	Activity							
Criteria								
Learning this skill is a family priority.								
The activity or activities in which the skill is required are preferred by the child.								
The skill increases the child's ability to interact with people and objects during daily activities.								
If this skill is not learned by the child, someone else will required to do the task for him or her.								
This skill can be applied across a variety of activities and/or environments.								
This skill occurs frequently enough to ensure multiple opportunities to practice and learn it.								
This skill can be encouraged and reinforced in a natural and meaningful way during daily activities.								
This skill can be easily elicited during different activities.								
The child can acquire the skills in the designated period.								
The skill and characteristics of the task match the child's strengths and desires.								
Total score (Possible total score = 30)								

Deborah Chen, *Essential Elements in Early Intervention: Visual Impairment and Multiple Disabilities*. New York: AFB Press, 1999. All rights reserved.

QUESTIONS TO ASK CAREGIVERS TO GUIDE OBSERVATIONS OF COMMUNICATIVE BEHAVIOR

Child's name: _____   Age: _____

Caregiver: _____   Date of evaluation: _____

1. What are your infant's favorite objects, activities, and people?

2. What are your infant's most disliked objects, activities, and people?

3. How does your infant communicate with you? What is he or she usually trying to tell you?

4. In what situations is your infant the most communicative?

5. Have you found any special ways that help you communicate with your infant?

Deborah Chen, *Essential Elements in Early Intervention: Visual Impairment and Multiple Disabilities.* New York: AFB Press, 1999. All rights reserved.

Functions of Early Communicative Behaviors

Name: _____   Date: _____

Date of Birth: _____   Age: _____

Informant: _____   Interviewer: _____

Function of communication	How does the infant communicate?	Situations that elicit these behaviors
Behavioral regulation		
Protest, refusal, or rejection		
Request for object		
Request for action		
Social interaction		
Greet		
Seek attention		
Request social routines		
Request comfort		
Joint attention		
Comment on object		
Comment on action		
Request information		

COMMUNICATIONS OPTIONS WORKSHEET

Name: _____   Age: _____   Date: _____

Child's Strengths and Needs		Communication Options	
Area	**Observations**	**Input**	**Output**
Vision			
Hearing			
Motor			
Tactile			
Responses to movement			
Cognitive level			
Awareness			
Discrimination			
Recognition			
Selected options to discuss with family			

Index

Printed in the United States
135910LV00003B/14/P